DEFIANCE is Savitri Devi's vivid and impassioned memoir of her arrest, trial, and imprisonment on the charge of distributing National Socialist propaganda in Occupied Germany in 1949.

On 7 September 1948, Savitri Devi entered Germany with eleven thousand propaganda posters and leaflets condemning the Allies, proclaiming that Adolf Hitler was still alive (which she believed to be true at the time), and urging Germans to resist the occupation and to hope and wait for Hitler's return.

It was a quixotic, futile gesture, born of a spirit of defiance and a thirst for martyrdom.

For more than four months, Savitri Devi travelled throughout western Germany distributing thousands of posters and leaflets, making contact with the underground network of faithful National Socialists, and writing her book GOLD IN THE FURNACE.

On the night of 20–21 February 1949, Savitri Devi was arrested in Cologne, interrogated, and taken to the Werl Prison. She was tried in Düsseldorf on 5 April 1949, convicted, and sentenced to three years imprisonment in Werl.

While in Werl, Savitri Devi befriended a number of German women imprisoned as war criminals. She also completed GOLD IN THE FURNACE and continued work on her *magnum opus*, THE LIGHTNING AND THE SUN. DEFIANCE can be read as the companion volume to GOLD IN THE FURNACE, since it takes place at the same time and tells the story of its creation.

Savitri Devi was released early from prison on 18 August 1949 at the request of the government of Indian Prime Minister Jawaharlal Nehru.

DEFIANCE is Savitri Devi's most readable book. It is not primarily a work of philosophy or history, but a gripping first-person narrative that often reads like a novel. DEFIANCE does, however, contain Savitri Devi's most profound and moving philosophical meditation, "The Way of Absolute Detachment," in which she uses the teachings of the Bhagavad-Gita to console herself before the prospect of the destruction of her writings and to explain the proper National Socialist view of the relationship between duty and practical consequences.

Reading DEFIANCE, one quickly understands why the Allies imprisoned Savitri Devi and, once she was behind bars, tried to keep her away from the other "political" inmates: her spirit of defiance is contagious.

DEFIANCE was published in a tiny edition by Savitri Devi's husband A. K. Mukherji in Calcutta in 1951 and distributed privately by the authoress to her friends and comrades. This third edition is a reprint of the Savitri Devi Archive's 2008 second edition, with a few corrections.

The Savitri Devi Archive

The Centennial Edition of Savitri Devi's Works

R.G. Fowler, General Editor

Each volume will be released in a limited cloth edition of 200 numbered copies.

SAVITRI DEVI

DEFIANCE
THE PRISON MEMOIRS OF SAVITRI DEVI

EDITED BY R. G. FOWLER

A Savitri Devi Archive Book
Counter-Currents Publishing, Ltd.
San Francisco

Savitri Devi
(*née* Maximine Portaz, a.k.a. Maximiani Portas)
1905–1982
Defiance: The Prison Memoirs of Savitri Devi
Edited with Preface by R. G. Fowler
Includes index

Cover by Kevin I. Slaughter

ISBNs:
Non-Limited Hardcover Edition: 978-1-64264-114-1
Paperback Edition: 978-1-64264-140-0

Third Edition

First Edition: *Defiance*. Calcutta: A.K. Mukherji, 1951.
Second Edition: *Defiance: The Prison Memoirs of Savitri Devi*. Ed. R. G. Fowler. Atlanta: The Savitri Devi Archive, 2008
Spanish translation: *Desafío*. Trans. A. J. Barcelona: Ediciones Nueva República, 2014.
Italian translation: *Sfida*. Ed. Marco Linguardo. Trans. Pasquale Piraino. Rome: Thule Italia, 2017.

1. Savitri Devi, Lyons, France, September 1951
(Frontispiece to the first edition of DEFIANCE)

DEDICATED

TO MY BELOVED COMRADE AND FRIEND

HERTHA EHLERT

AND TO ALL THOSE WHO SUFFERED

FOR THE LOVE OF OUR FÜHRER,

FOR THE GREATNESS OF HIS PEOPLE,

AND FOR THE TRIUMPH OF THE

EVERLASTING TRUTH FOR WHICH HE AND THEY

HAVE FOUGHT TO THE BITTER END.

"Taking as equal
pleasure and pain,
gain and loss,
victory and defeat,
gird thyself for the battle;
thus thou shalt not incur sin."

The Bhagavad-Gita
(II, verse 38)

"Allein unser Denken und Handeln soll keineswegs von Beifall oder
Ablehnung unserer Zeit bestimmt werden, sondern von der bindenden
Verpflichtung an eine Wahrheit, die wir erkannten."[1]

Adolf Hitler
(*Mein Kampf*, II, ch. 2, p. 435.)

---

[1] "Our thinking and acting are by no means to be determined by the approval or
disapproval of our time, but by the binding obligation to the truth that we recognize."—
Ed.

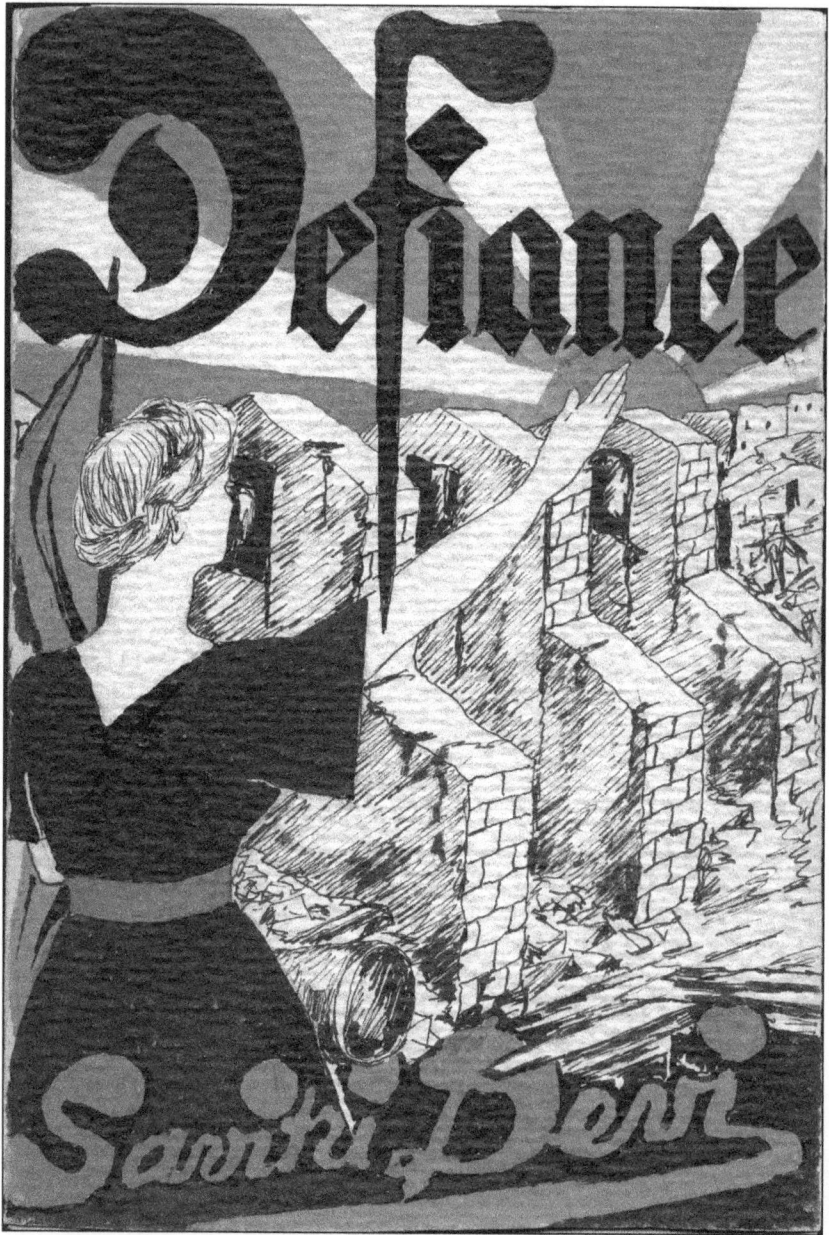

2. One of Savitri Devi's hand-painted dust jackets for Defiance.
(Courtesy of J. E.)

CONTENTS

ILLUSTRATIONS

EDITOR'S PREFACE

Savitri Devi's *Defiance* is a memoir of her arrest, trial, and imprisonment in British-occupied Germany for the crime of distributing National Socialist propaganda. It covers just over six months of her life, from 13 February to 21 August 1949. But time is no measure of intensity, and just as Savitri Devi described the previous four months of underground activity in Occupied Germany as "the culmination of my whole life,"[1] the events related in *Defiance* can be described as the culmination of that culmination.

Before her arrest, Savitri Devi had undertaken three distinct propaganda missions to Occupied Germany.

First, on the night of 15–16 June 1948, she distributed handwritten leaflets, cigarettes, and food packets from the windows of the Nord Express while passing through Germany. She was travelling with the dance company of Ram Gopal,[2] in which she worked as a dresser. The company was returning to London from Stockholm at the conclusion of a tour of Norway and Sweden.[3]

Savitri Devi's second mission commenced on 7 September 1948,[4] when she entered Germany with a French military permit to research a book on post-war conditions. That book was to become *Gold in the Furnace*. (Naturally, she would never have received the permit if the French government had known what kind of book she was planning to write.) Hidden in her luggage were 11,000 posters and leaflets[5] printed in London by Count Potocki of Montalk.[6] For three months, she criss-crossed Western Germany distributing leaflets, befriending ordinary Germans and die-hard National Socialists, and doing everything in her power to instil a spirit of defiance and hope for Adolf Hitler's imminent return. (At the time, she believed Hitler was still alive.) She financed her travels by selling off her Indian gold jewellery piece by piece. When she could not

---

[1] *Gold in the Furnace: Experiences in Post-War Germany*, 3rd ed., ed. R. G. Fowler (Atlanta, Georgia: The Savitri Devi Archive, 2006), p. 50.

[2] Ram Gopal, 1912–2003, was a pioneer in the revival of Indian classical dance.

[3] See *Gold in the Furnace*, ch. 4, "The Unforgettable Night." An English translation of the text of her leaflets appears on page 34.

[4] In *And Time Rolls On: The Savitri Devi Interviews*, ed. R. G. Fowler (Atlanta: Black Sun Publications, 2005), p. 51, Savitri Devi gives the date as 11 September.

[5] The text of the printed leaflets appears below, on pages 3–4.

[6] Count Geoffrey Potocki of Montalk, 1903–1997, was a poet, printer, and pretender to the throne of Poland. He was also an Axis sympathizer.

stay with sympathetic Germans, she slept in the waiting rooms of train stations. Savitri Devi departed Germany on 7 December 1948 to spend Christmas in London with her friends Muriel Gantry and Veronica Vassar.

Savitri Devi's third mission began sometime after 14 January 1949, when she received a visa to return to France from the French Embassy in London. From France she returned to Germany. This mission ended on the night of 20–21 February 1949, when she was arrested in Cologne. She was questioned the next day by German police and a British Military Intelligence officer named Mr. Hatch. On 22 February, she was taken first to Düsseldorf, where she was arraigned, then remanded to the Werl Prison, in the Soest district of Westphalia. Her trial took place in Düsseldorf on 5 April. She was convicted and sentenced to three years in Werl.

Throughout this period, Savitri Devi continued writing *Gold in the Furnace* and, to a lesser extent, *The Lightning and the Sun*. On 30 May, her cell was searched and her manuscripts confiscated. She was told that they would be destroyed if found "subversive," plunging her into a dark night of the soul that lasted until her manuscripts were returned on 17 June. She returned to writing, rapidly completing *Gold in the Furnace* on 16 July, then resuming work on *The Lightning and the Sun*. On 18 August 1949, Savitri Devi was released from Werl at the request of the Nehru government. She departed Germany for France on 21 August.

Defiance tells much about the composition of *Gold in the Furnace*, its companion volume. It also tells of the composition of parts of *The Lightning and the Sun*. But *Defiance* offers only a few clues about its own composition. Evidence suggests, however, that the book was written at lightning speed, in a state of heightened inspiration. Savitri Devi's custom was to write the Forewords of her books last. The Foreword of *Defiance* was written in Lyons on 29 August 1950, a bit more than a year after she left Germany. Thus it seems *Defiance*—a book of nearly 600 pages in its first edition—was written in the span of a single year.

On the last page of *Defiance*, Savitri Devi describes the conditions under which the book was written: "utter loneliness," "grinding poverty," and the constant vexation of hostile "charlatans and imbeciles."[7]

Defiance was published in 1951 in Calcutta by Savitri Devi's husband A. K. Mukherji. We can infer that it was published late in the year, because the original photograph of the frontispiece, which is in the Savitri Devi Archive collection, bears the date September 1951. Only after completing *Defiance* did Savitri Devi prepare *Gold in the Furnace* for publication (in 1952) and return to writing *The Lightning*

---

[7] Page 392 below.

and the Sun (chapters 6 and 7 were written in Lyons in 1951 and 1952[8]). The priority given to the publication of *Defiance*, like the speed of its composition, suggests the importance she attached to this story.

Defiance is one of Savitri Devi's rarest books. I do not know the size of the first edition, but it was likely small, for copies were in short supply almost ten years later, according to Savitri Devi's letter to George Lincoln Rockwell of 28 May 1961. William Pierce published excerpts from *Defiance* in *National Socialist World* in 1968.[9] Excerpts from chapter 12, "The Way of Absolute Detachment," appeared on Irminsul's Racial Nationalist Library website in 2003.[10] A complete electronic version of *Defiance* appeared on the Savitri Devi Archive website in 2006.[11] But the whole of *Defiance* has never been reprinted until now.

If this is your first time reading *Defiance*, I envy you, for this is one of my favourite Savitri Devi books. The narrative grabs you from the very first page, and, although the pace sometimes slackens, it never lets go. Part III is particularly noteworthy, containing some of Savitri Devi's most profound philosophical reflections on morality, the meaning of life, and the purpose of the cosmos. Eloquence and intensity blaze forth on every page, sometimes overwhelmingly for those of us who do not live our whole lives at a fever pitch. But there is also charm and humour and the charisma of a truly singular personality. In the end, you will understand how Savitri Devi captivated so many of her captors, for she will captivate you as well.

ON THE PRESENT EDITION

Like Savitri Devi's other self-published books, the first edition of *Defiance* contains many errors and stylistic inconsistencies. My goal as editor was to make the minimum number of editorial interventions necessary to bring *Defiance* into accord with today's standards. The first order of business was to correct her own list of *errata*. Then, following her use of British English, I corrected errors of spelling and grammar and made the style consistent throughout. I also corrected a few "foreignisms": unidiomatic diction and syntax based on French and German, the languages

---

[8] Savitri Devi, *The Lightning and the Sun* (Calcutta: Savitri Devi Mukherji, 1958), p. 126

[9] Savitri Devi, "Defiance," ed. William Pierce, *National Socialist World*, no. 6 (Winter 1968): 64–87.

[10] Savitri Devi, "The Way of Absolute Detachment," ed. R. G. Fowler, excerpted by Irmin, Racial Nationalist Library, http://library.flawlesslogic.com/defiance_12a.htm.

[11] http://www.savitridevi.org/defiance-contents.html

she regularly spoke while writing *Defiance*. I preserved her sometimes eccentric capitalization practices without trying to make them consistent.

Savitri Devi's use of punctuation was also eccentric. She did not use commas and semicolons merely to organize information on a page, but to indicate dramatic pauses in real or imaginary speech. I have tried to maintain these punctuation practices, with four exceptions. First, I updated the use of hyphens, e.g., in "to-day" and "to-morrow." Second, I regularized the use of commas before conjunctions, following American usage because it eliminates certain ambiguities. Third, I removed a few commas that seemed to be obvious strays, conforming neither to accepted usage nor to Savitri Devi's style. Fourth, I eliminated commas and, in a couple of cases, colons and semicolons that were adjacent to dashes.

Where necessary, I have translated phrases in German. Where possible, I have supplied citations for books mentioned. Finally, where useful, I have provided editor's notes, which are clearly marked as such.

Aside from the frontispiece, all illustrations are newly added.

The subtitle, *The Prison Memoirs of Savitri Devi*, is my own.

Those who wish to check my editorial labours against the original may contact me at the Savitri Devi Archive (www.savitridevi.org), and I will provide a photocopy of the first edition at cost or a PDF free of charge.

ACKNOWLEDGEMENTS

I wish to thank those friends of Savitri Devi and/or of the Savitri Devi Archive who helped make this new edition of *Defiance* possible: Miriam Hirn, for books from Savitri Devi's library; Beryl Cheetham, for the picture of Hertha Ehlert and the picture of Savitri Devi taken by Muriel Gantry; J., for the images of pages from Savitri Devi's 1940–1950 Passport; J. E., for a scan of one of Savitri Devi's hand-painted dust jackets for *Defiance*; M. T. for his last-minute fine tuning of this Preface; and R., for his Photoshop wizardry. Special thanks are due D. A. R. Sokoll, for carefully reading the page proofs and spotting numerous errors, particularly in German, and to Gabriella Anelauskaitė for the tedious and time-consuming task of scanning the first edition of *Defiance*, and for realizing the dust jacket/cover. For the Counter-Currents edition, I am grateful to Larry C. for his careful proofreading and Kevin Slaughter for recreating the jacket/cover.

This edition of *Defiance* is dedicated to Miriam Hirn, Savitri's dear friend—and mine.

R. G. Fowler
20 April 2008, 4 June 2021

FOREWORD

This book is merely an account of my arrest and trial, in western occupied Germany, in early 1949, on the charge of Nazi propaganda, and of my subsequent life in jail. The glimpse one gets, in it, of western occupied Germany, is a glimpse of Germany through *my* eyes, i.e., through the eyes of a non-German follower of Adolf Hitler. The impression that the representatives of the Occupying Powers might have of the same country from their angle is probably quite different. God alone knows—and time alone will tell—which is the nearest to objective reality.

In the meantime—should this book come to light *before* what I call "our Day"—on no consideration should the opponents of the Nazi faith, now in a position to harm them, incriminate any Germans on the ground of *my* personal impressions, or of words which I might have reported more or less accurately. I have named no Germans in this book—save one, whom I know now to be dead, and to whom, consequently, the champions of Democracy can no longer do any harm.[1] But several might be recognisable by the posts they held at the time of my imprisonment. What I have just said applies to them: I do not want *them* to be implicated on account of *my impression* of them.

I thank them however for having given me that impression; for whether true or exaggerated, it has strengthened my confidence in the people whom I call in this book (and in another) "the vanguard of the regenerate Aryan race,"[2] and thereby helped me to find life worth living, even now, in our gloomy times.

Lyons (France), the 29th of August, 1950
SAVITRI DEVI

---

[1] Friedrich "Fritz" Horn ("Herr H." in *Gold in the Furnace*). See pp. 386–89 below and *Gold in the Furnace: Experiences in Post-War Germany*, ed. R. G. Fowler, 3rd ed. (Atlanta: Savitri Devi Archive, 2006), pp. 81–85, 163–68.—Ed.

[2] This exact phrase does not appear in *Gold in the Furnace*, but Savitri refers to "regenerate Aryans," "regenerate Aryan people," and "regenerate Aryandom" (*Gold in the Furnace*, 3rd ed., pp. 11, 216, 220, 241).

Part I

TRIUMPH

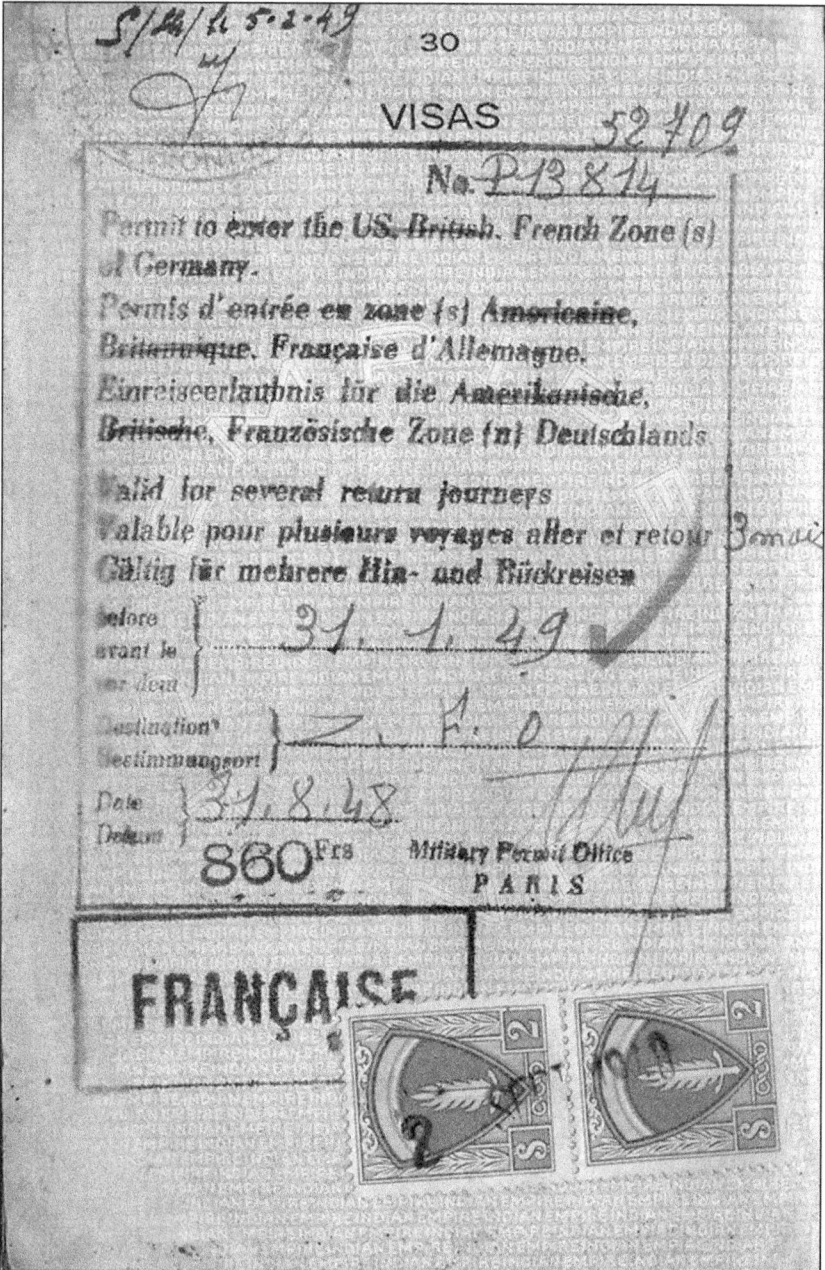

3. Savitri Devi's French Military Permit to enter Occupied Germany

Chapter 1

THE EMPTY TRAIN

"I have some papers here . . . dangerous ones; would you like to see them?" said I to the tall and handsome young German walking by my side along the underground passage that led to the platform from which I was to take my train, in the station of Cologne, the night between the 13th and 14th of February 1949. I had met the man a few hours before, at the "Catholic Mission" of the same station, and we had talked enough for him to become convinced that he could trust me, as I could trust him—to say the least.

He stopped for half a second and looked around to see if anybody was following us, or if any passer-by could possibly have overheard my words. But we were the only people in the long, gloomy corridor. The young man turned to me and answered in a low voice: "Yes; give me one."

I pulled a poster twice folded in four out of my pocket and put it into his hand.

"Don't stop to read it now," said I, "but wait till we get into the train, and then go and read it in the toilet, where nobody can come and disturb you. You have heaps of time. See if you think such papers can be useful, and tell me so quite frankly. If you want more, I still have plenty left."

The young man hid the precious paper in the inner pocket of his coat and continued to walk by my side in silence, helping me to carry the little luggage I had. We reached the platform. The train was there—practically empty, for it was not to start till an hour later, at 1:12, if I remember well. A fierce wind was blowing. And it was bitterly cold.

The young man helped me to lift my suitcase into the railway carriage and then stepped in himself, and went to read the poster in the best hiding place, as I had suggested. The words he read, written in large capital letters below a black swastika that covered about one third of the page, were the following:

GERMAN PEOPLE,
WHAT HAVE THE DEMOCRACIES BROUGHT YOU?
IN WAR TIME, PHOSPHOROUS AND FIRE
AFTER THE WAR, HUNGER, HUMILIATION, OPPRESSION;
THE DISMANTLING OF THE FACTORIES;
THE DESTRUCTION OF THE FORESTS;

AND NOW—THE RUHR STATUTE!
HOWEVER, "SLAVERY IS TO LAST BUT A SHORT TIME MORE."[1]
Our Führer is alive
AND WILL SOON COME BACK, WITH POWER UNHEARD OF.
RESIST OUR PERSECUTORS!
HOPE AND WAIT.
HEIL HITLER!

The paper was signed "S.D."—*i.e.*, with my own initials.

The young German came out of his corner. There was a strange light in his bright grey eyes and a strange assertiveness in his voice. "Give me as many of these posters as you have. I shall stick them up for you!" said he. He was no longer the lonely, hungry, dreary prisoner of war who had just returned home after four long years of all manner of ill-treatment at the hands of Germany's enemies. He had become once more the soldier of a victorious Germany—of an invincible Germany—and the herald of Hitler's eternal Idea; once more his old self, that nothing could kill.

I admired him, and recalled in my mind the words I had once heard in a village in Saarland, some six months before, from another sincere National Socialist: "We are waiting for the spark." Could it be that I was something of a spark—a spark of faith and hope—in the midst of the unending gloom of the present day? As that thought entered my consciousness, tears came to my eyes, and a thrill of immense elation ran through my body and seemed to lift me above myself. Through the windows of the train, I could see, in the dim artificial light, the torn outlines of what had once been a wall—ruins, nothing but ruins wherever one sets one's eyes in unfortunate Germany; the torn and prostrate body of Hitler's martyred country. But before me, against that background of desolation, stood the young man (he could not have been more than thirty) fifteen times wounded on the battlefield for the cause of the New Order; over three years a prisoner of the French in a slave labour camp in the burning heart of Africa, under the whip of African auxiliaries; hungry; without work; apparently without a future (he had told me of his plight) but now erect and hopeful, once more aware of his invincibility. The German soul gleamed, more alive than ever, in his sparkling eyes—a tangible reality—and addressed me through his voice.

"Who wrote 'these'?" the young man asked me, referring to my posters.

---

[1] "[D]ie Knechtschaft dauert nur noch kurze Zeit!" from "Die Fahne hoch," also known as the "Horst-Wessel-Lied."—Ed.

"I."

He gazed at me, visibly moved.

"You," said he; "you, a foreigner!"

"I, an Aryan, and a National Socialist," I replied. "No Aryan worthy of the name can forget his debt of gratitude to the Führer—the Saviour of the whole race—and to Germany who now lies in ruins for having fought for the rights, nay, for the very existence of superior mankind."

My answer, which bore the accent of sincerity, seemed to please him. But he did not comment upon it. He only asked me a few questions.

"Where did you get 'these' printed?" asked he, again speaking of my posters.

"In England."[2]

"And you brought them over yourself?"

"Yes, myself. Three times I entered Germany with three successive supplies of different leaflets or posters, and seven times I crossed the border between Saarland and the French Zone with a greater or lesser number of them. I have never been caught yet. The unseen heavenly Powers take care of me."

"And how long is it you have been doing this?"

"I began eight months ago. I would have begun as soon as I came from India— three years ago—had I managed then to obtain a permit to cross the frontier under some pretext or another. But I had to wait."

The young German walked up to me and took me in his arms.

He was much taller than I, and much stronger. I could feel the pressure of his athletic body, and see his bright eyes looking down, straight into mine.

"So it is for him, for our Führer, that you have come from the other end of the world to help us in the midst of our ruins!" said he. There was deep emotion in his voice. He paused for a second, and pursued in a whisper: "*Our* Führer; our beloved Hitler! You really love him. And you really love us."

I felt a wave of untold happiness fill my breast. And I flushed crimson.

"I adore him," said I, also in a whisper. "And I love all he stands for and all he loves. You, his faithful countrymen, you are the people to the service of whom he dedicated his life; his living Germany, so beautiful, so brave, and so unfortunate."

The bright grey eyes peered still deeper into me, as though trying to decipher the story of my life. "And you," the young man asked me at

---

[2] Savitri Devi's propaganda was printed by the poet and publisher Count Geoffrey Potocki of Montalk (1903–1997), who was an Axis sympathizer.—Ed.

last, "who are you?"

"I have told you: an Aryan from far away."

Out of doors, the bitter wind continued blowing, and I could see the ruined wall against the dark background of the night. In a flash, I recalled the sight of the whole country; miles and hundreds of miles of crumbling walls; streets in which—like in the Schloßstraße of Koblenz, which I had just seen—there was not a single house standing. But along those streets, marching in a warrior-like manner, and singing on their way, I pictured to myself the veterans of this lost war and of these following years of persecution, side by side with the youth of resurrected Germany—the Army of the Fourth Reich, one day; out of chaos: order and strength; out of servitude and death, the will to live and to conquer. And I smiled, as a tear rolled down my cheek. I felt inspired, as seldom I have been.

"Do you remember," said I, "the grand days when you used to parade the streets and sing the song of conquest?

> We shall march further on,
> If everything falls to pieces;
> For Germany is ours today,
> Tomorrow, the whole world."[3]

"Hundreds of flags bearing the sacred sign of the Swastika hung from the windows, in festive array; thousands of outstretched arms greeted your onward march—the beginning of an endless future in which you believed. Do you remember how strong and how happy you felt then?

"Disaster followed, I know, with its trail of untold misery: hunger, destitution, servitude, utter ruin—that horror in the midst of which we stand. And yet, from the depth of my heart I tell you: the song of triumph was not a lie; still the stupendous dream will become true; is already becoming true, in spite of the phosphorus bombs, in spite of four years of unprecedented hardships of persecution, of 'de-Nazification'. Nothing can keep it from becoming truer and truer as time goes on—'for Germany is ours today, and tomorrow, the whole world'."

I paused, and a flash of unearthly exultation brightened my face. I spoke with the compelling assurance of one for whom the bondage of

---

[3] "Wir werden weiter marschieren, wenn alles in Scherben fällt; denn heute gehört uns Deutschland, und morgen, die ganze Welt." [From Hans Baumann, "Es zittern die morschen Knochen" ("The Rotten Bones Tremble"). Savitri Devi changes Baumann's words "da hört" (hears us) to "gehört" (is ours), giving the song an imperialistic slant. This is a common substitution, and it would be interesting to know if it originated with National Socialists or anti-National Socialist propaganda.—Ed.]

time and space had ceased to exist. "What I think and feel today," said I—"I, the insignificant foreign Nazi—the whole Aryan race will think and feel tomorrow, next year, in a century, never mind when, but surely one day. I am the first fruits of the future love and reverence of millions for our Führer and for his ideals. *I am 'the whole world,'* conquered by his spirit, by your spirit; the living sign, sent to you by the unseen Powers, in the hour of martyrdom, to tell you, faithful Germans, that the world is yours because you deserve it."

The young man gazed at me with great emotion, and pressed me a little tighter in his arms as though I were indeed the reconquered world. I was intensely happy. I knew I was doing no harm. For this man was not Herr G. W.[4] an individual. And I was not Savitri Devi Mukherji. There was nothing personal in that spontaneous gesture of his, or in the reverent abandon with which I accepted it and responded to it. This young soldier was, in my eyes, Germany's youth, fearless in the midst of persecution as well as in battle; one of those "men of gold and steel" whom I had exalted in the book I was then writing. And to him, I was a foreign Nazi—Germany's friend—nothing less, nothing more.

He gazed at me for a minute without speaking, as though a friend, in these atrocious days, were something worth looking at.

"I know you mean every word you say," he whispered at last; "and I thank you: and I shall help you. After all we suffered, it is refreshing to hear you speak. You rouse hope and self-confidence in our hearts. You make us feel what those who fought in the early days of the struggle must have felt after the first war. What is it that gives such force to your words?"

"My love for the Führer. I feel inspired when I speak of him."

"*Our* Führer!" repeated the young man, with passionate devotion, echoing my own feelings. "You are right. I'll help you as much as I can. Give me all the posters you have."

He loosened his embrace. I took out of my bag a bundle of some four or five hundred posters, concealed in fashion magazines, and gave it to him. He hid it carefully in his clothes. "That is all?" he asked me.

I smiled. "No," said I; "but leave a few for the rest of Germany; won't you?"

You are right," said he. And he smiled for the first time. He took my hands in his and gazed at me as though he were seeing the last of me. "When and where can I meet you again?" said he. "We *must* meet again."

"I have no permanent address," I replied. But if you care to leave yours—when you have one—at the 'Catholic Mission' of this station, I

---

[4] Gerhard Waßner—Ed.

shall find you. I shall come back here after exactly a week—sometime next Saturday night—and ask your address from that place. In the meantime, be careful, oh, be careful! Don't commit any blunder that might land us both into trouble. I don't say 'don't betray me,' for I know you will never do that."

The young German's frank, earnest eyes looked at me more intently than ever, and his strong hands squeezed mine in a gesture of reasserted comradeship. "Never!" said he. And, lowering his head almost to the level of mine, he whispered: "The mark is there, upon my flesh. It does not come off. You can trust me."

The mark . . . I understood—and felt an admiring affection, verging on reverence, grow in me for that new friend. My face beamed.

"So, you were in the S.S.?" said I, in a low voice, in the tone a Roman maiden would have said to a Roman veteran: "So, you were in the Praetorian Guard?"

"I was in command of S.S. men," answered the young man, with pride, also in a whisper.

I thought of all he had told me of his sufferings at the hands of our foes. And as I looked up to him, I remembered the first line of the song of the S.S. men. "If all become unfaithful, we remain faithful indeed."[5]

I heard noise—a door being opened and shut again—and I startled. But it was not in our carriage. Still, I was aware that the train would not remain empty for long.

"I will soon be going," said I. "You'd better get down now, while nobody is watching. I'll see you next week. But for heaven's sake, be careful! *Auf Wiedersehen.* Heil Hitler!"

"Heil Hitler!" replied the young man, returning my salute.

He got out of the train and went his way. I watched his tall figure disappear in the bitter cold night.

A few minutes later, the train started. Sitting in a corner of the dark compartment, where more people had now taken places, I too was going my way—going to distribute more tracts, to stick up more posters, in another part of Germany; going to help to keep the Nazi spirit alive among other compatriots of my Führer.

I was cold, but happy—oh, so happy!

---

[5] "Wenn alle untreu werden, so bleiben wir doch treu, . . ." [The first line of "Wenn alle untreu werden," also known as the "Treuelied" (Song of Faith) and the "S.S.-Lied."—Ed.]

Chapter 2

THE ARREST

A week later I returned to Cologne.

Some vague presentiment warned me I had better go straight to Koblenz. But I overcame that feeling. Or rather, the desire to see Herr W. once more was stronger in me than the desire to avoid taking unnecessary risks.

I remembered every word the young German had uttered from the minute I had met him. The story of his three years' captivity in Africa haunted me. I admired him for having stood so brilliantly the test of persecution; and I loved him with the same strong, warm affection—the same feeling of sacred comradeship in life and death—as I do any real Nazi. I did not stop at Cologne to find out whether he had stuck up my posters or not. I knew he had. I trusted him implicitly. I stopped for the sheer pleasure of meeting him again. I was planning to go with him for a long walk, somewhere on the border of the Rhine, outside Cologne. The weather was bright. In the daytime, in the sunshine, it was not too cold to sit down, provided there was no wind. I would buy some food and cakes—enough for the whole day—I thought, and we would go and sit in some lonely and lovely place. I would spread my thick grey cloak upon the ground for us to be more comfortable. And the S.S. officer would talk to me with friendliness and understanding and faith—would tell me about the grand days that came and went and will come again; would speak of the recent humiliations and of the unavoidable revenge; of the Führer, of greater Germany, the foundation stone of future Aryandom (all I stood for, all I wanted, all I loved) while the unchanging Rhine would roll past us its sunlit waters with the self-same everlasting murmur. I wanted to hear him tell me, as hundreds had before him, how beautiful was the Führer's inspired countenance when he addressed the cheering crowds. I wanted to tell him, as I already had ten thousand others, how happy I was to be waiting in Germany, instead of elsewhere, for the return of the Leader and Saviour.

I got down from the train and, after leaving my things at the cloak room, went straight to the Catholic Mission where I asked the woman on duty what seemed to me a most non-committing question: "Could you be kind enough to tell me the address of Herr W., who was here a week ago in search of a room? He told me he would leave his address with you."

I did not know that Herr W. was already under arrest, nor that, for the last four or five days, the police were searching for me all over Germany.

The woman on duty—who perhaps knew—looked a little embarrassed, "Herr W?" said she. "Are you quite sure it is that name?"

She was turning over the pages of a copybook in which were written down the names and addresses of many people who had obtained lodgings through the Mission. But she did not seem to me to be seriously trying to find the name. Still I replied to her question.

"Yes, Herr W.," said I. "I met him here, in this place, exactly a week ago. I could not say whether the Catholic Mission has managed to find him a room or not. But he told me he would leave his address here wherever he went. It surprises me that he has not done so. Would you be kind enough to look carefully?"

I had no time to say more, for at that moment a policeman stepped in. He walked straight to me and said: "May I see your papers, please?"

It was not the first time I had shown my passport to a German policeman. Generally, the man had a look at it and gave it back to me at once, without any comment. This man did not give it back to me, but said: "Would you follow me to the police station? We have some point to make clear. Leave your things behind; no one will touch them."

I at once scented danger. But I felt extraordinarily calm—calm as only an absolute believer in fate could feel. "I suppose this had to happen one day," thought I. "However, I shall do all I call to 'slip out' if possible. But if I am caught, I am caught. And I shall not behave as a coward under any circumstances."

I entered the police station—a bare, whitewashed room in which there were two other men in police uniform (one, obviously of higher rank than the other, seated at a table, near a telephone) and a prisoner, seated in a corner. "Surely not a political prisoner," thought I, as soon as I saw him. He did not look as happy as I.

The man at the desk offered me a chair. I sat down. Then, the policeman who had brought me in handed over my passport to the man, and the latter examined it with utmost care, for a long time. "A British passport," said he, at last. "But you are not English, are you?"

"Half English and half Greek," I replied. "My mother is English. I have acquired British citizenship by my marriage."

"Your husband[1] is English?"

"No. Indian."

"And where is he now?"

---

[1] Asit Krishna Mukherji (1904–1977)—Ed.

"In Calcutta, as far as I know."

The police officer was apparently not interested in my husband's whereabouts so far away. He changed the conversation.

"You have travelled quite a lot, I see from the visas on your passport," said he. "What prompted you to come to Germany?"

"I came to gather first-hand information in order to write a book," I replied—and it was true; I was, in fact, writing my *Gold in the Furnace*, a passionate picture of National Socialist Germany in the clutches of her persecutors, at the same time as a personal profession of faith in Adolf Hitler. I added: "This is stated in a letter which you will find in my passport; a letter from the French *Bureau des Affaires Allemandes* recommending me to the Occupation authorities." And this too was true. In that letter the head of the above-mentioned *Bureau* begged "the French and Allied Occupation authorities to afford every possible help and protection to Mrs. Mukherji, author of several works on historical and philosophical subjects, who is now going to Germany and Austria in order to gather the necessary material for a book about those countries." (Needless to say, he knew nothing of my convictions, and could not suspect what sort of a book I intended to write or what activities I intended to carry on in Germany.)

The police officer looked at me, a spark of amusement in his eyes, as though he were thinking: "Possible; quite possible. You underground fighters are up to anything that can forward your ends." He took the letter and had a glance at it, but did not read it. He probably did not know French. Whether the document seemed authentic to him or not, I could not tell. Anyhow, it did not impress him enough for him to send me away as a harmless person under the protection of Germany's present-day masters. He continued to question me.

"You are a writer?" he asked.

"Yes."

"We want to know if you have anything to do with a certain leaflet and poster affair . . ."

I understood it would be difficult to "slip out," this time. Yet, I felt exceedingly calm—as though I were acting; as though the person sitting in my place and answering the questions were not my real self. (Nor was she, in fact. My real, free, unattainable Self lives in millions of individuals, in Germany and abroad; wherever there are Aryans who share our ideals; wherever the Nazi spirit flourishes in all its strength and pride. It cares little what might happen to the material, limited I that was speaking at the Police Office of the station of Cologne on that night of the 20th of February 1949).

I pretended not to understand the German word for a leaflet, the word

Flugblatt.

"What sort of thing is a *Flugblatt*?" asked I, not without repressing a tendency to laugh.

"A paper with some propaganda written upon it, intended for distribution," replied, this time, not the man at the desk but the other one—the policeman who had brought me in. And he added, drawing a swastika upon a blank page and handing it over to me: "If you do not know what a *Flugblatt* is, do you know, at least, what *this* is?"

"A swastika," said I; "I believe everybody knows that."

"The symbol of National Socialism," he emphasised. "And the immemorial Symbol of the Sun," I added. "In India, it has been looked upon as a sacred sign for thousands of years."

"And do *you* also look upon it as a sacred sign?" asked the policeman. I gazed at him with defiance—and a pinch of irony. I knew I was playing with fire, but I enjoyed it. I naturally enjoy defying danger.

"Surely I do," said I. "I too, am a worshipper of the Sun."

That answer was rigorously accurate. In my mind, I recalled my years of struggle in far-away India; my lectures against the Christian ideology of equality, false meekness, and false humility, in the shade of banyan trees, before white-clad crowds. And before that, my struggle in Greece against the monkeyish mentality of a levantinised "intelligenzia," in the name of the eternal Aryan ideals which in those days—twenty-five years ago—I still called "Hellenic." "All my life, I have indeed fought for the same truth, under that same age-old holy Sign," thought I. And the prospect of being arrested—which had never worried me—suddenly became almost attractive in my eyes. True, I would lose the little usefulness I might have had. But what a splendid culmination of my whole life history it would be, to suffer—at last!—a little of what so many thousands of my comrades have been suffering for the last four years at the hands of our persecutors! I now nearly wished I would be arrested. Still, I was determined not to hasten the fact by unnecessary admissions. I would leave it to the invisible Gods to decide where and how I should continue to bear witness to the glory of National Socialism. If I "got away with it" this time, that would mean I was more useful free. If I did not, it would mean that, in the long run, I would be more useful in jail—or dead, if the enemy would do me the honour of killing me.

The man at the desk addressed me again.

"You know a certain Herr W., a former S.S. officer, don't you?"

And for the first time I realised—I knew, as clearly as if the man had told me so—that Herr W. had been arrested. I felt any blood go cold, for I *knew* (from others, who knew it from direct experience) to what extremes of brutality the present-day masters of Germany—or the Germans in their pay—can go, when dealing with one of Hitler's faithful ones, caught red-handed in the action of defying them. "Poor dear comrade!" I thought; "I do hope they have not been torturing him. Anyhow, I'll take all the responsibility on myself, if it comes to the worst."

"I have met him," I replied, paling a little.

The police officer was watching me with hard, scrutinising eyes—the eyes of an expert observer.

"Go and fetch her things," he ordered the other policeman, "and bring them all here."

The policeman left the room.

"So you met him," said the man at the desk, turning to me and speaking once more of Herr W. "Where and when did you meet him?"

"Here in Cologne, some time ago."

"Here, in this railway station, exactly a week ago," replied the man. "And you had an appointment with him. You said so when you were asking for his address, at the Catholic Mission, just now. Do you imagine you are not observed? What business had you with that young man?"

"I just wanted to see him again."

The man seized a telephone from against the wall, and I soon heard him speaking to some "Herr *Oberinspektor*"—asking him for instructions as to what he should do with me. I remember bits of the conversation.

"She has been in touch with that man . . . But she has a British passport—in order, as far as I can see. And a letter of recommendation addressed to the Allied Occupation authorities by some important French Bureau in Paris . . . Yes, yes, Herr *Oberinspektor* . . . No; nothing like as old as that. Her passport states forty-three, but she does not look more than thirty-five, if that . . . Yes, certainly, Herr *Oberinspektor* . . . No; not yet . . . We shall see. The policeman is gone to fetch her luggage . . . Yes, certainly; I think so too. We shall see . . . Yes, Herr *Oberinspektor*."

The policeman did not take long to come back. He was holding my travelling bag in one hand, my handbag and my attaché case in the other. He put the former in a corner on the floor, the two latter upon the table. Then, he pulled out of my handbag one of my leaflet-posters twice folded in four (there were a few there, as I had been distributing them in the train on my way to Cologne). He unfolded it, and laid it before the officer at the desk. "Exactly the same ones as those found on G. W." said he. "Those Nazis! More active and more arrogant than ever, if you ask me! What do you think of that?"

The man at the desk did not reply to him, but read the paper (the text of which I have translated in the preceding chapter) and spoke to me:

"How do you account for the presence of this in your bag?" he asked me. "Did Herr W. give it to you? Or someone else?"

I knew it was now useless to try any longer to hide the truth from the police. This time, I would not "get away with it." And the more accurately I would tell the truth, the lesser would Herr W.'s responsibility in this affair appear in comparison with mine, and the lighter would be *his* sentence—the sooner he would be free. He deserved to be free, after all his years of service during the war and his three years of captivity in the horror camp, in the middle of Africa. I could afford to go to jail.

Perhaps I deserved to go—for not having come back to Europe before the war; for not having been, during the war, as useful as I might have been in Europe, if I had managed to come. Moreover, even if these considerations had not arisen, and if it had been, not Herr W. but someone else who had worked with me, I should have felt it my duty, anyhow, to take the entire responsibility of any action for the Nazi cause in which I had played a part, however small. That responsibility was an honour that I could not fail to claim.

I looked straight at the man at the desk and replied clearly and firmly, almost triumphantly: "Those posters are not Herr W.'s; they are *mine*. I wrote them. And it is I who gave Herr W. all those he had—I alone."

The man had expected me to accuse Herr W. and do everything I could to shun personal responsibility. He had forgotten, apparently, that we are not Democrats. He gazed at me with surprise and with interest—as someone gazes into a shop window at some object that has not been seen in the market for many years and that one never expected to see again. But he made no comments. There were no comments he *could* make. He simply told me:

"I am sorry—very sorry—to have to inform you that you are under arrest."

I was smiling. I was remembering my first journey through ruined Germany, less than a year before. "If I can do nothing more for them, in these days of horror, may I at least suffer with my Führer's people!" I had then prayed to all the Gods in heaven. For nine months, I had experienced a little of the hardships to which the Germans were submitted for the last four years. Now, I would stand by them in the hands of Germany's persecutors. The Gods had granted me my heart's desire.

"I am happy," said I, "for this opportunity to bear witness to my lifelong ideals."

And the three people present could see that I was not lying, nor "putting on a show." I felt so happy that I must have looked it.

It was about two o'clock in the morning.

Chapter 3

QUESTIONS AND ANSWERS

"Have you any more of those posters?" asked the policeman who had just come back with my things.

"Only a few," replied I.

"Give them all to us."

I asked for my bag, took a key out of my purse, and opened the attaché case which the man had laid before me. I pulled out several old French fashion magazines, *Marie Claire*, took twenty or thirty leaflet-posters out of each one, and put them on the table. The policeman counted them. There were, as far as I remember, one hundred and twenty. He handed them over to the officer at the desk who counted them in his turn, but did not find exactly the same number.

"That is all you have?" the policeman asked me.

"Yes," I answered, lying as calmly and naturally as I had, up till then, told the truth.

"Surely you had more than that!"

"I had, indeed," said I; "but I have distributed them all."

"How many did you distribute?"

"Of this sort, four thousand; and six thousand of a smaller size, bearing a longer text," said I—which was perfectly true. What I most carefully hid was the fact that I had three thousand more of these latest posters in a trunk which I had left at somebody's house, somewhere in the French Zone. For nothing in the world was I going to say a word about that trunk. Fortunately, the name and address of the friend in whose care I had left it was nowhere to be found in my papers.

"Have you any more of your leaflets of the former sort?" asked the policeman.

"Only one or two, which I was keeping as a remembrance," said I. "They are somewhere in my bag, I believe. The rest I have finished distributing weeks ago."

"I see you did not waste your time in Germany!"

"I hope not."

But I felt uneasy about a certain number of addresses which I had written down in a notebook that—I knew—lay in my handbag. I bitterly reproached myself with not having relied solely upon my good memory to remember them. Now, there was only one thing I could do. And I did it. While the policeman by my side was busy counting my posters for the second time (to see if he had not made a mistake), and while the man at the desk was once more telephoning to the "Herr *Oberinspektor*" to inform him of my arrest, I slipped my hand into my bag and carefully took out the dangerous notebook. I knew the most important addresses were on the two first pages. I pulled these out as quickly as I could, on my lap, under the table; I tore them to pieces and then, taking out my pocket handkerchief and pretending to cough, I swiftly thrust the pieces into my mouth, kept them under my tongue for a second or two, to soften them, and managed to swallow them silently, with a sigh of relief.

I then tore out the other pages on which were written addresses of all sorts, some of real friends, some of mere acquaintances—of people who had no knowledge of my convictions, let alone of my activities in Germany, such as a London editor and an English nurse whom I had met in a café in Paris. And I began tearing them quietly up, as I had the few first ones. "These cover more paper; they will be more difficult to swallow," I was thinking; "but I shall swallow them all the same, for the sake of the one or two comrades whose names are there, among many indifferent names."

But the policeman (who had finished counting the posters) caught sight of me. "Hula!" said he, "Give us what you have there, on your lap."

And before I had had the time to swallow the bits of paper, he had got up and seized them from me. "Yes, give us that! It will make an interesting jigsaw puzzle for the Criminal Department," he added, gathering the tiny bits into an empty envelope, which he handed over to the man at the desk.

The latter turned to me once more. "You mentioned your 'ideals' a while ago," said he; "but surely you were not working for ideals alone. Who paid you?"

"Paid me!" I felt a wave of indignation swell my breast and nearly choke me. "Nobody ever paid me," I burst out, furious at the thought of having been mistaken for an ordinary mercenary agent. "On the contrary, I gave practically all I possessed for the cause I love; and would have given the little I have left, had I remained free in Germany."

"You had no employ. On what did you live, and where?"

"I lived on my jewels, of which I had a whole boxful, and which I sold bit by bit as I needed money to travel and to do what I was doing. And I had no fixed abode. I spent my nights at any "Bunker Hotel" or "Station Mission"—or in station waiting rooms, when I had no money at all."

This second statement was not rigorously true. I *had*, no doubt, lived much in that way, lately, since my last return from England (and even so, I had often spent a night or two at friends' and sympathisers'). But before that, I had enjoyed the hospitality of comrades to whom I shall remain grateful as long as I live—people who had lodged me for weeks and weeks, while they had hardly enough room for themselves; people who had fed me on their own scanty rations, while I, not being in any way connected with the Occupation, was not allowed a regular ration card; people who had hidden me at their own risk, knowing I was in their "Zone" without a permit, on the sole ground of our common National Socialist faith, of our common goal. I had been told not to go back to them on account of some difficulties they had had with the Military Government in my absence. But I loved them just the same. And I was, naturally, very careful not to let the police suspect the existence of such connections of mine.

The police officer at the desk looked at me a little sceptically. "How are we to believe you," said he. "What you tell us is strange."

"Yes, strange; but true," I replied. "Whoever will examine my trunk, now at the cloakroom, will find there seven or eight empty jewel caskets. These once contained necklaces and armlets, and earrings and rings, and an enormous brooch, all gold, and all of Indian workmanship. Those I sold, not only in order to live but to finance my journeys abroad and the printing of my propaganda.

The policeman who had brought my things in spoke in his turn: "A German could have done what you did for the Idea alone, but you are not a German."

"And yet," said I, "I insist upon the fact that I have not acted for money, nor for any manner of personal profit, but solely for the principles that I have always professed. It is true that I am not a German. Yet have I identified myself with the cause of National Socialist Germany because it is also the cause of Aryandom—of higher mankind; the only cause worth living for, in our times; at least, the only one in which I am sufficiently interested to live for it entirely."

I spoke the truth, and expressed myself vehemently. I was boiling with indignation at the idea that these men had taken *me* for some fishy professional conspirer. The policemen believed me in the end—as others were to, during my following trial—because they could not do otherwise. My words bore the unmistakable stamp of sincerity.

"Maybe you are genuine," said at last the man who had brought in my things. "But it was rather difficult to admit it at once. So many people act for money."

"I am not 'many people'," said I proudly, almost haughtily; "and I have never acted for the same motives as the venal herd of men and women—not I."

"Where did you get this stuff printed?" asked the policeman, pointing to my hundred and twenty posters that lay upon the desk before his superior.

"Somewhere, outside Germany," I answered.

I thought I had better make that point quite clear, so that no German printers might be suspected, even if some had, perchance, taken part in similar activities. But, for nothing was I going to add a single word which could have rendered my true statement more precise.

"We ask you where," insisted the policeman.

"Somewhere, beyond the boundaries of this unfortunate country," I repeated. "Maybe in Kamchatka. The world is wide. Search the world."

The man at the desk was looking at me with apparently increased curiosity. The policeman, whom my answer seemed to have irritated, again spoke to me.

"Never mind," said he, with a wry smile, "don't tell us now, if you don't wish to. You will tell us later on. We have methods to force such ones as you to talk."

I shuddered, for I knew what this meant. Not only had I read about those few cases of "confessions" of so-called "war criminals" extorted by torture which have been now and then, among thousands of others of which nothing was ever published, brought to the notice of the English-speaking world, in English and American official reports, since 1945, but I knew of many more concrete instances of that nature from my own comrades—people who had themselves had a taste of the above mentioned "methods," or who had seen them applied upon their closest friends. I was faced with the torture chamber in all its horror. And for a second or two, I felt my blood go cold, and my heart weaken.

But that was not for more than a second or two. And I doubt whether the two men near me—let alone the two others in the corner—were able to notice it. At once, I pulled myself together.

"Apparently, my turn has come," thought I. "Others have faced this bravely. Why not I too?"

And I recalled in my mind the thousands of National Socialists who had stood the horrid trial without uttering a word—my comrades, my betters, the legion of the unflinchingly faithful in the midst of which I would, at last—I hoped—win myself an honourable place with this opportunity.

And I thought, also, of the unseen, everlasting Power, source of all strength and of all greatness, whose glory I had witnessed a whole night

long, with my own eyes in the lava and flames of Mount Hekla in eruption, less than two years before; the One Whom the Hindus call Shiva,
Lord of the Dance of Life and Death.

"Put Thy strength in me. Thou bright, impassible One, Who roarest in
streams of molten rock and shinest in the Sun, and Whose majesty
clothes the inviolate snowy peaks!" I prayed within my heart. "The truth
I am here standing for is Thy Truth—the eternal truth. Put Thy invincibility in me!"

And I was filled with a wave of immense, serene, unearthly joy.
Looking straight at the men before me, with a happy face, I said simply:
"I am a National Socialist, and hope I shall remain faithful and worthy to
the end. You can do whatever you like to me. But nothing can kill the
Idea which I represent."

I remember my words, uttered in German, clearly and with ease, in
the stillness of that whitewashed room, before those Germans who had
accepted to collaborate with the enemies of Germany for reasons better
known to themselves—perhaps because they really hated our Ideology;
perhaps just because they had families to feed. There was not a trace of
fear left in me; also not a trace of vanity. I knew and accepted my personal nothingness, but I was raised above myself in calm, endless joy;
joy at the idea of possible martyrdom—the greatest joy I had ever experienced. And joy made me eloquent. All the aspiration, all the faith, all
the pride, all the love of my life were expressed in my simple statement
"I am a National Socialist . . ." While from the depth of my consciousness, something told me: "You have been saying that, under one form or
another, for the last six thousand years."

And beyond and before the host of my beloved comrades, who have
suffered for Hitler's cause now, since 1945, as well as from 1919 to
1933, during the first struggle, I realised the presence of the millions of
older witnesses of the truth, from the beginning of the Age of Gloom—
the "Kali Yuga" of the Sanskrit Scriptures—in which we live, and earlier
still, from the beginning of the decay of man. The Nazi martyrs of our
times form but the latest ranks of that broader legion of honour of all
times. Had I, indeed, from life to life, for centuries, borne witness to the
self-same truth before the successive agents of the self-same forces of
disintegration? And would I, that very night or the next day, or the day
after, be given another chance of winning for myself, once more, a place
among the everlasting Legion—or a chance of *keeping* my place in it? I
smiled, in my dream of defiance in suffering, as many of those of old
must have done.

And, thought I, there were people, also, who had suffered for the sake

of falsehood—for the sake of ideals of sickness and weakness and death;
of those very principles in the name of which the modern degenerate
world condemns us, the living Aryan Heathens. There were people upon
the like of whom I could myself cause torture to be inflicted, if I had
power and judged it expedient—or if my superiors judged it expedient—
for the triumph or defence of the Nazi cause. Among such people, there
were some no less sincere than I—and all the more dangerous. I had
surely never felt any love or sympathy for them. Nor did I now. But I
could not help recognising some sort of parallelism between their fearless fidelity to the end and that of my comrades who had stood the test of
pain, and—I hoped—mine; the parallelism that exists between a beautiful landscape and its upside-down image in still, gloomy waters. I recalled a picture I had seen, years and years before, upon a window of
stained glass, in a French Church: the picture of some early Christian
martyr—I could not remember which—writing with his blood upon the
floor, as he died, the Latin Words: *"Christianus sum."* [1]

"Truly, I should hate myself," thought I, "if I could not bear, for the
sake of my Führer and of my Aryan faith, what so many followers of a
Jewish religion or of some modern Jewish doctrine, bore, in olden times
or but a few years ago—some, at our own hands—for the sake of their
superstitions and of their errors!"

And once more I welcomed the prospect of being tried and of standing the ordeal, with the help of all the Gods, and of repeating, before
tougher men than the ones I had hitherto faced, my proud profession of
faith: *"Ich bin Nationalsozialistin . . ."* [2]

The policeman who had last spoken to me had now gone out to fetch
the trunk which I had left at the cloakroom. The man at the desk was silent. I was sitting still, in the same place. Then again, but for the last
time, I had a moment of weakness—for the policeman's statement, and
the threat it implied, and the expression with which he had underlined it,
haunted me; a moment, not of fear of suffering, but of reluctance at the
thought of physical disfigurement. I looked at my long white hands that
rested upon the table before me, and found them beautiful. Convinced
that they would probably soon be torn out of shape, I felt sorry for them
for a second. Then, realising how mean it was of me to bother about my
appearance in such a circumstance, I felt ashamed of myself. In my
mind, I recalled the stern face, the large magnetic blue eyes of the one
Man of my days whom I ever worshipped; the kind smile with which he

---

[1] "I am Christian."—Ed.
[2] "I am National Socialist."—Ed.

used to address all those who loved him—with which he doubtless would have addressed *me*, had I only been wise enough to come back to Europe in time. And passing one hand under my coat, I pressed through my clothes, the little glass portrait of him that hung between my breasts on a gold chain. Tears came to my eyes. "Nothing is too beautiful for thee, my Führer!" thought I in an outburst of half human, half religious love. And again I felt happy and invincible.

I was taken, in what they call in London the "Black Maria," to the Headquarters of the Criminal Department of Cologne. The prisoner who had been sitting in the corner with his custodian all through my first interrogatory at the Police Station, travelled with me, but, naturally, in a different cabin.

The "Black Maria" stopped in a part of the town I had never seen. I got down, accompanied by the policeman who had taken charge of my luggage, and I was ushered into a whitewashed room, very simply furnished, in which were standing a tall strong man, with a rosy face and straight, dark-brown hair, and another one, of moderate height, thin, yellowish, with small sharp eyes, and black hair in short regular waves. "Looks decidedly Jewish," thought I of the latter, as I walked in. And that first impression of mine, the man merely confirmed by the way he talked.

He bade me sit upon a bench and, after the policeman who had brought me in had gone away, had a glance at one of my posters, the whole bundle of which lay upon the table.

"Look at this nonsense!" said he, speaking to the tall man, to whom he handed the paper. Then, turning to me he asked me: "What prompted you to stick up these?"

"My conscience; and the pleasure of defying the oppressors of my Führer's people," answered I, with absolute sincerity.

The man gazed at me, at first with astonishment, then with an evil look, and said nothing. It is the other one who spoke to me.

"And you mean to tell us that no offer of money inclined your 'conscience' that way?" he exclaimed, with a sceptical smile.

Once more, the burning indignation that had possessed me at the Police Station rose within me. Nothing makes me so wild as to hear people express doubts about my sincerity—mostly on grounds of "normal" standards and "average" psychology (and on account of my education in an eminently democratic country) as though "normal" and "average" standards had ever been applicable to me; and as though my liberal Christian education had ever had any other result than to afford me repeated opportunities of taking consciousness of my nature as a born Pagan, and a hater of half-measures, equally free from "human" feelings, personal ties, conventional scruples, and average temptations. I forgot entirely where I was and spoke with the same aggressive freedom as I would have in a tea party that was not a diplomatic one.

"They have already made those dirty hints at the Police Station whence I come," said I, with unconcealed rage. "They would! People of moderate or less than moderate intelligence judge others according to themselves. Consequently, the whole accursed Democratic world is incapable of admitting, let alone of understanding, our earnestness and our detachment. And you people take me for the equivalent of those well-paid agents of England and the U.S.A. who used to help the French *résistance* during the war. Well, once and for all, know that I am not and never shall be. Nobody paid me. Nobody ever will. There are no foreign power's 'big business' interests behind our underground activities, as there were behind those of the anti-Nazis in the days we were victorious. Therefore we have no money. And the rare non-Germans who actively stand by ruined Germany now, in 1949, single-handed, at their own risk, do so solely for the sake of the truth the German people represent in their eyes. But even if we had enough wealth to buy professional agitators— even if we were as rich as all the Jews of the U.S.A., rolled in one— know that I would still work for the mere pleasure of helping the Nazi cause because it is *mine*—because I love it—and of defying my Führer's enemies because I hate them. I am not, and I shall never be a professional agitator."

The thin yellowish man, who had been listening to my tirade with particular attention, threw me a glance of responsive hatred. The other one, who seemed just rather surprised, asked me where I had been during the war.

"In Calcutta," I replied.

"I was on the Russian front—a less comfortable place," said the man. "That is probably why I am less enthusiastic than you about all this, although I am a pure German. We suffered on account of this damned war. You did not."

"I wish I had," I answered, with all my heart; nay, with that painful feeling of guilt that has pursued me ever since the Capitulation. "I wish I had been able to leave India in time, and at least to share the hardships of the Germans under unceasing bombardment. But whatever my mistakes, which I hope to expiate, the fact remains that the Führer is not responsible for the war and its trail of miseries. He did everything within his power to avoid it—you should know that, as you were here at the time— and everything within his power to stop it, once it was forced upon him

and upon Germany. Don't blame him, and don't blame National Socialism, for your sufferings. Blame the traitors you had at home. And blame
the Jews and the slaves of Jewry who had the upper hand in all Aryan
countries. First and foremost, blame those two vilest of all the complacent instruments of the international Jewish money power; those two
arch-criminals: Churchill and Roosevelt!"

To my surprise, the only reaction of the tall man to this was the deep
sadness I could read upon his face. But the thin yellowish fellow interrupted me violently. "It is Germany's fault," he shouted. "She only had
to surrender before. Why did she not?"

Reluctantly (for I did not like the look of the man and did not wish to
speak to him) I replied: "The Führer wanted to spare the German people
the humiliation of 'unconditional surrender' and the subsequent sufferings it implies. No German—no true Aryan—can blame him for that."

The Israelitish-looking man did not allow me to finish what I was
saying.

"The Führer!" he repeated ironically, interrupting me once more, with
a vicious expression in his eyes, and making a nasty noise—an imitation
of spitting—intended to show contempt. "You mean Master Hitler, I
suppose. Well . . . Master Hitler wanted the whole world. Why could he
not keep his hands off Poland, eh? And why did he go and attack Russia,
to have millions killed there for nothing? If you care for the Germans as
much as you pretend to, you should be the first one to hate that . . ." (and
he used, to designate the Saviour of the Aryan race, a most vile word).

I felt all my blood rush to my head and tears of rage fill my eyes under the insult—far more than if it had been directed against me personally. I tried to keep my balance, but my voice trembled as I spoke.

"I have not come from the other end of the world to criticise a single
one of my Führer's decisions," said I.

"I am only sorry I did not manage to come here during the war. And
still more sorry I was not killed, along with so many of my superiors, in
1946."[3]

But as I thus spoke, something within me was telling me: "No, don't
be sorry! All this will pass, like a shadow upon drifting sands. Don't be
sorry. One day, you will witness the irresistible revenge; you will take
part in it and treat the Führer's enemies even worse than they treated
your comrades—for you are more single-minded, and have more imagination than they."

---

[3] Probably a reference to those condemned to death by the Nuremberg Tribunals
and executed on 16 October 1946.—Ed.

And I smiled to the sweet prospect of a future Nazi Europe in which I would forget nothing of all I had heard against our beloved Hitler, since the very day I had landed. "Forget nothing, and forgive nobody," I dreamed.

The thin yellowish man looked at me more devilishly than ever, as though he could read my thoughts, and walked out.

The other man turned to me and said: "You are lucky to have fallen into our hands, bold as you are—luckier than those who used to fall into your friends' clutches, not long ago. For we are at least human. The enemies of the régime you praise, when arrested by the Gestapo, fared far worse than you ever will with us. How would you have liked to be in their place, I wonder?"

"What a funny question!" (I nearly said: "What a stupid question!") "How could *I* ever have been in their place? What could anyone have told the Gestapo against *me*, without at once being proved a liar? My Nazi orthodoxy is—and always was, I hope—above reproach."

"Yes," replied the man, who had apparently learnt his lesson from the Democrats during these four years. "But, I repeat: what of the people who were against the régime?"

"I could not care less what happened to *those*," said I, still with as much spontaneity and as much ease as if I had been at a non-diplomatic tea party. "They were the enemies of all I love. In my estimation, no treatment applied to them was too rough, if it resulted in effectively putting an end to their activities."

"And what if we . . . I mean the Democrats, the Occupation authorities who are now in power . . . treated *you* in a similar spirit?"

I smiled—for the suggestion was downright funny. "Democrats, acting with as much thoroughness and consistency as we would . . . why, one has to go beyond the Elbe, to the Russian Zone and to Russia itself, to find that!" thought I. And talking of the Western variety of Democrats—of the milder and more hypocritical sort—I said:

"They would, if they believed in what they stand for. But they don't. They don't know what they want. Or rather all they want is to keep their present jobs, with fat salaries and little work. Their toleration is just the indifference of the lazy, of the blasé, of the old. We know what we want. And we are young."

The man looked at me intently, then went and shut the door that the other fellow had left half open. "I never believed there were foreigners such as you," he said, coming back to his place by the fire. "You are just like anyone of our German Nazis. . . . Just like anyone of us before many lost faith," he added in a low voice, "for I too had your outlook and your ideals once. We all had them. But again, would you be the same if you had suffered from the war as we have?"

"I am absolutely sure I would," answered I, with conviction. "And what is more, I am sure *you* and any of the others you mention would also, if you had realised the everlasting soundness of our doctrine. Truth lies above personal gain and loss, and above the fluctuations of a nation's history. And in the long run, truth conquers."

As I uttered those two last words, I automatically glanced at the seal of hematite upon the ring I wore on my middle finger; the crest of the old family out of which my mother sprang;[4] under the picture of a wolf, the motto: *Vincit veritas*—truth conquers.

And I thought of the fearless Viking who had landed in England with his warriors, over a thousand years ago, to become the founder of that English family destined one day to give birth to me, Adolf Hitler's follower, "the missionary of Aryan Heathendom" (as the Consul of regenerate Italy in Calcutta[5] once called me)—the insignificant, but uncompromising fighter for truth. And I prayed within my heart that my trial would prove that the old Nordic family had not decayed in me. And I recalled, also, the title chosen by the most Aryan of all the Pharaohs, Akhnaton, son of the Sun,[6] to be adjoined to his name through the ages: *Ankh-em-Maat*—Living-in-truth. And I prayed that I too should never fail to "live in truth" to the end, whatever was to happen.

* * *

At that moment, a short man in civilian clothes, looking, in spite of his fair skin, even more Israelitish than the thin yellow one who had gone out, opened the door and bade me roughly to get up and follow him. He took me to a long flight of steps leading underground and, pointing to it, he shouted to me: "Down!"

"The Yid has grown accustomed to knock us about these last four years," I thought. "But the game will come to an end. Everything does. And then? Our turn again, I hope! And this time . . ."

And staring down at the fat little man, shorter than myself, I passed before him almost smiling at the idea of what might well happen "this time," when my friends are once in power (whenever that may be), and I walked down the steps with both hands in my pockets.

---

[4] Savitri Devi's mother's maiden name was Julia Nash.—Ed.
[5] Camillo Giuriati—Ed.
[6] Of the early fourteenth century before Christ.

The stairs led to a long, dimly lighted corridor with a row of heavy doors on each side. The man took me to one of those doors, which he unlocked, and ushered me into a small, cold, and perfectly dark cell, in which a woman was already lying upon two or three planks of wood that rested upon iron supports. (I could vaguely see her form upon that primitive bed, as a little light from the corridor fell into the cell when the man opened the door.)

Pointing to the form upon the planks, the man said to me: "If you wish to lie down, ask this woman to make a place for you. You have no bed to yourself."

"Couldn't I lie on a rug upon the floor?" asked I.

"As you please," replied the little man. And he took me to a corner under the stairs, where there were a few rugs. I picked out one—any one; they were all as ragged and dirty as could be—and came back. The man shut the door of the cell upon me.

It is an unusual experience to feel oneself locked up in a cell, with a threat of torture to meditate upon, until it pleases the police authorities to give orders for the door to be opened again. Fortunately, I had long overcome the first uneasiness the threat had created in me. I was conscious only of joy at the prospect of soon becoming worthier of my German comrades who have suffered for the National Socialist cause. "I am already a little nearer to them now," thought I as I shivered in the cold room, and as my eyes slowly grew accustomed to the darkness. Then, I took to inspecting the place. It contained nothing else but that primitive "bed" on which lay the motionless woman, apparently asleep. It was pitch dark, but for the tiny slit at the top of the wall facing the door. And the cold, less bitter than out of doors, was more penetrating—less bearable; it entered into one's bones. And the walls were damp, and the floor—of bare earth—was muddy.

I spread the filthy rug in a corner and lay upon it on my side, my knees up to my chin, in the position of an unborn baby, so as to keep myself as warm as I possibly could. To sleep was out of question. I left my mind to drift where it pleased.

First, I thought of the Führer whom, for several months already, I knew to be alive. I recalled the great mass gatherings of the days of the Third Reich, and the title of an article in a magnificent book—a publication of those grand days—which I had seen at a comrade's house: *"Unser Hitler"*;[7] the words that summarised the feelings of the first

---

[7] "Our Hitler." "Unser Hitler" is the title of the speech given by Joseph Goebbels in honour of Hitler's 48th birthday, on 20 April 1937. It is published in *Wetterleuchten*

resurrected Aryan nation. Those feelings were mine, also; oh, how thoroughly mine! I held between my hands the little glass portrait I had. It was warm, for having been in close contact with my flesh. There was in its touch a magic sufficient to keep me happy, were I forced to remain upon that malodorous rug for weeks. *"Mein Führer,"* I whispered, with tears in my eyes, as I devoutly kissed the precious likeness, *"ich bin glücklich; so glücklich!"* [8] Hitler's language came to me spontaneously, as the most natural means of expression, although my knowledge of it is anything but perfect. And I imagined him coming back one day, and addressing the crowds of a new free Germany in an atmosphere of unprecedented enthusiasm.

The Third Reich all over again, in more strength and more splendour than ever. And the tears that filled my eyes slowly ran down my cheeks. Never, perhaps, had I visualised the inspired face more vividly. Never had my beloved Leader appeared to me more fascinating in his manly beauty, more lovable, more god-like. Would he ever know how much I loved him? Would anyone in Germany's future joyful crowds, remember me for five minutes? But what did it matter, whether they did or not? And what did it matter even if "he"—the one man for whom (and for whose people) I would do anything—never knew of my existence? Individuals did not count. I did not count. Verses of the Bhagavad-Gita came back to my memory: "Act not for the sake of the fruits of action";[9] "the wise act without attachment, desiring nothing but the welfare of the world."[10] Never had the old summary of Aryan philosophy seemed to me so beautiful as it now did. The sacred words soothed me, tempered the exaltation of my heart with heavenly serenity. "No," thought I, "it does not matter whether anyone remembers me one day or not, even 'he'. All that matters is 'the welfare of the world'—the New Order—and my fidelity without hope or desire of recognition on this earth or elsewhere, simply for the sake of love; love of my Führer, love of the ultimate Reality (of what they call God), it is all the same, for he is the mouthpiece of everlasting truth, the embodiment, in our times, of Him Who spoke in the Bhagavad-Gita, and I have loved Him age after age."

And I prayed more ardently perhaps, than I had for many weeks: "Help me to rid myself of my incurable vanity, immortal Gods! Help me

---

[*Sheet Lightning* ("Sheet lightning" is a momentary, broadly diffused radiance in a dark sky, caused by the reflection of a lightning flash in clouds.)] (Munich: Zentralverlag der N.S.D.A.P., 1939), pp. 388–92.—Ed.

[8] "My leader, I am happy, so happy."—Ed.

[9] The Bhagavad-Gita, II, verse 47.

[10] The Bhagavad-Gita, III, verse 25.

to forget myself entirely; to be just a useful tool in your hands, for the triumph of what is eternal. Kill all pettiness in me!"

Then, I recalled the distant home that I had left over three years before. It could have been about four o'clock in the morning—yes, quite two hours since my arrest. "Four and sixteen. It must be about ten o'clock in Calcutta," thought I. And I remembered my old flat, with its terrace facing the south, and the beautiful big tree, full of kites' and crows' nests, that one could see from the terrace; and my husband, in his spotless white *dhoti*, reading or writing as he smoked his water-pipe. I remembered my beautiful cats—two glossy masses of purring fur, one black, one with yellow stripes—basking in the sunshine. Something from within told me that I would never see them again, and that thought brought a shadow of sadness across my consciousness. But it was just a passing shadow, quickly gone. I had other things to think of. I recalled my first contact with my husband, former editor and proprietor of the now long-forbidden *New Mercury*—the only National Socialist magazine then published in India under the auspices of the German Consulate. A Greek living in Calcutta had taken me to his office and introduced me to him in 1938. And the almost first words the Brahmin supporter of our New Order in the world had addressed me, as soon as he knew who I was, rang, clearer than ever, in my memory: "What have you been doing in India, all these years, with your ideas and your potentialities? Wasting your time and energy. Go back to Europe, where duty calls you!—go and help the rebirth of Aryan Heathendom where there are still Aryans strong and wide-awake; go to him who is truly life and resurrection: the Leader of the Third Reich. *Go at once; next year will be too late.*"

"Oh, had I but listened to him! Had I not, in my vanity, imagined myself 'useful' in the East, and had I come in 1938!" thought I, for the millionth time since my return. And I sobbed bitterly, also for the millionth time, over the opportunities of service on my own continent which I had thus missed.

"It serves me right to be here, and it would serve me right if they tore me to pieces," I concluded. "Yes, may I suffer now the utmost, and partly at least expiate the fact that I did not come before!" And once more I welcomed all the horror implied in the policeman's allusion to the "methods" that would probably be used to make me speak. And then again picturing to myself my husband, reading or writing under an electric fan amidst the ascetic simplicity of our barely-furnished flat, I thought: "At least, when he hears of my trial, he will know that I have not been 'wasting my energy' in Germany! . . . Or will he just say of me: 'What a fool! Why could she not manage to remain free—and useful?

Surely, she went and did something childish and spectacular, instead of devoting herself to silent, unnoticed, solid work!'?" And I remembered how the wise, supple, and mercilessly practical idealist he is, used to scold me, during the war, for my "noisy haste," my "lack of diplomacy," my "woman's brains."

"Perhaps he was right about me," thought I; "although I hope to show myself, now, less stupid than I seem."

The cold forced me out of my reflections. The dampness of the muddy ground had penetrated me, through the rug on which I was lying. I shuddered from top to toe, and my teeth clattered. I shook myself out of an icy-cold sensation that felt like a touch of death. "Pull yourself together, Savitri," thought I, as though speaking to myself. "You can't afford to get ill—not in these people's clutches. You have better to do. You mean health, resistance, invincible youth—the Nazi spirit. You need your strength to show them who you are; to defy them."

This thought acted upon my body as a cup of strong, hot coffee. Although I had had nothing to eat since eight o'clock in the morning, and had travelled all day and a part of the night, and had not slept, I suddenly felt light and active, nay aggressive—ready to fight once more. I got up, and sat against the wall, and took a small comb out of my pocket, and started to comb my hair, regretting that I had no looking glass—and no torch light. I should have liked to have a wash, for I felt sticky and dirty. I would have liked one or two other minor commodities, also, for I realised that it was with me "in the manner of women"—biblical language being, I suppose, the most elegant way of putting such delicate matters. But there was no water, and all commodities were out of question. I had to manage as I could until someone would open the cell.

Did I make any noise while trying to find, in the darkness, a safety pin which I had dropped? Or did the woman asleep upon the "bed" of planks wake up by herself? I could not tell. But she moved, and stretched, and asked at last: "A new one, here?"

"Yes, a new one," I replied. "I am sorry if I disturbed you."

"You did not disturb me," said she—whether or not out of courtesy, I shall never know. "How long have you been in?"

"I have no idea. Perhaps an hour; perhaps more.

Time seems long, when one is not asleep—even if one has plenty of things to think about," said I.

"I must have slept a lot. I was tired."

The woman paused a minute and again asked me: "Where did 'they' get you?"

"At the station, just as I had come out of the train."

"That's bad luck. And may I ask . . ."—she hesitated a little as she spoke, but curiosity overcame her hesitation—"may I ask you what you had done?"

"Nazi propaganda. I have been distributing tracts against the Occupation and sticking up posters with a swastika as big as 'that' at the top of them," said I, delighted to relate my exploit to a listener who might be also a sympathiser. And instinctively, although we were in the dark, I made a gesture showing how large the holy Sign was, on each one of my latest papers.

The woman rose at once, and sat upon the planks. Her interest in me increased immensely, all of a sudden. "Good for you!" she shouted, heartily congratulating me. "I am entirely on your side. In Hitler's days we had plenty to eat; since these swine came, we have been starving. I am here for having 'pinched' someone else's ration card."

"This one's loyalty to the Führer is rooted in her stomach," thought I with a little amusement, and I must say, also, with a little contempt. Still, I could not help liking the perfect innocence with which she admitted it, as though it were the most natural form of loyalty in the world. And I was grateful to her for her sympathy.

"How long do you think we are to stay here?" I asked the woman.

"I can't tell. They'll come and call us when it suits their convenience. Today is Sunday. They might take their time about it. But don't fear: they will not leave us here. This is no prison. They will question us and send us to some other place—send *you*, at any rate; for I hope to get away with it. I know what story I shall tell them, and I am sure it will work."

"I have no explanation to give them as far as I am concerned," said I. "I would not invent one to save myself, even if I could: I am much too proud of the little I did. But I would enjoy misleading them about other people, and encouraging them along false tracks that would lead them nowhere. By God, how I would! They told me at the Police Station that they would use all means to make me say who printed my posters, but I am determined not to speak whatever they do."

"Don't boast before you leap," retorted the woman. "You don't know what you are talking about. The 'means' they use in cases like yours are pretty nasty, and I know people with your ideals who died of pain in their clutches. True, that was in '45 and '46 just after the damned Occupation had set in. Now—I hear—they are growing milder, *i.e.*, weaker; are getting tired of 'de-Nazifying' us."

"They must have found out it is useless," said I with as much pride as if I were speaking on behalf of all the National Socialists of the world.

"I'll show them how useless it is in my case at least!"

"Would you like to share my 'bed'?" asked the woman, after a few seconds of silence. "I'll push myself against the wall as much as I can. You must be tired."

"Thank you," said I. "I was, but I am not now. I am happy. I feel nearer my persecuted comrades, since I am here. Do you mind if I just pace the cell to keep myself a little warm?"

"Surely not. I am not going to sleep again, anyhow."

"In that case, perhaps you will not mind if I sing, also?"

"Why should I?"

"Right. I thank you. It will do me good."

Morning was drawing nigh. I could see it by the ray of light that now came in from the slit in the wall. I turned towards that ray of light—the symbol of hope; the forerunner of the rising Sun—and sang the immortal Song that used to accompany the onward march of Hitler's conquering hosts; and that one day, thought I, will again accompany their resumed onslaught against a decaying civilisation

Standards high! Close the ranks thickly!
Storm Troopers, march on, with a calm, firm step!
Comrades, whom the Red Front and the Reaction have shot,
March in spirit within our ranks! . . .[11]

And as I sang, I recalled in my mind the young German who composed that song at the age of twenty, and died a martyr's death at the age of twenty-two: the hero Horst Wessel, living forever.

I saw two pairs of feet step outside the narrow slit at the level of the street, whence the light came. And I thus knew that two Germans were listening to what appeared to them as Germany's voice reaching them from the depth of a prison-pit. And in the circumstance, Germany's voice was my voice—the voice of a foreign Aryan; the homage of the regenerate Aryan minority from the four corners of the earth, to Hitler's fatherland.

And tears of joy ran down my cheeks as I sang the last two lines, my right arm outstretched towards the invisible dawn:

---

[11] Savitri Devi's translation of the first verse of the Horst Wessel Song: "Die Fahne hoch! Die Reihen fest geschlossen! S.A. marschiert mit ruhig festem Schritt. Kameraden, die Rotfront und Reaktion erschossen, marschiern im Geist in unsern Reihen mit."—Ed.

Soon will Hitler's banners be waving along all the highways.
Slavery is to last only a short time more. [12]

* * *

Time dragged on. I could guess there was sunshine in the street. But
the cell was as cold, and practically as dark, as ever. The woman, although she said she was no longer sleepy, had gone to sleep again—out of
sheer boredom. I was pacing the narrow space between her "bed" and
one of the walls, my hands in my pockets, happy, although I was cold
and hungry.

I deliberately refused to think of my discomforts. What were they, indeed, compared with the atrocious conditions in which so many of my
German comrades had lived for months on end? I recalled in my mind
the fact that in Darmstadt—one of the post-war anti-Nazi extermination
camps under American management—the thermometer had reached 25
degrees below zero centigrade *within the cells*, during the winter 1946–
47. And I thought of the systematic starvation to which National Socialists had been submitted in Schwarzenborn, in Diez, in Bad Hersfeld, in
Mannheim, in camp 2288 near Brussels, and a hundred different other
places of horror. I had nothing to complain of, surely. But even if it happened that I ever had, in the future, thought I, I would deliberately refrain
from doing so, from a sense of proportion. And when our days would
come back, I would stigmatise our enemies in every possible manner for
the sufferings they inflicted upon my comrades, never upon me; and even
so, stigmatise them, not for their brutality, but for their hypocrisy. In the
meantime, I would never, never do anything to obtain from them the
slightest leniency.

I heard someone walk down the steps and unlock one of the cells near
mine and call a prisoner's name. I heard him lock the cell behind him as
he took the prisoner away. And several times, similar noises, in the same
order, informed me that another prisoner had been taken upstairs. My
turn would come. I waited.

At last, after a lapse of time that, to me, seemed endless, my cell was
unlocked. I saw the little stout man who had brought me down standing
in the corridor with the thin yellowish one who had spoken so vilely
against the Führer, before me, during the night, and whom I detested for

---

[12] Savitri Devi's translation of the end of the second verse of the Horst Wessel
Song: "Bald flattern Hitlerfahnen über allen Straßen, die Knechtschaft dauert nur noch
kurze Zeit!"—Ed.

that very reason—and whom I would have detested all the more (and not less) had he not looked so Jewish. The short man called out the name of my companion, Hildegard X., who was to follow him, while the yellowish fellow took a glance at me and said: "I feel sorry for you. There was no necessity for you to go through all this . . ."

I burst out in anger. There is nothing I loathe like personal sympathy from anti-Nazis—even when it is sincere, let alone when it is not.

"Keep your pity for yourself," said I, stiffly, almost haughtily. "I am happier than you and than those who will judge me . . ."

The door was slammed on me, otherwise I would have added: "I have a great love and a great idea to live for; you have nothing but your pockets, the whole lot of you!"

I waited, now alone in the cell. Time seemed long, long, unbearably long. Then again I heard footsteps in the corridor, and the noise of a key turning in the lock, and I saw the door of the cell open. The same short fat man called me: "Mukherji, follow me!"

He took me upstairs and past the room to which I had at first been brought the night before, up another floor or two, and then through long corridors on each side of which there were doors. On some of those doors, as I passed by, I could read the words: *Zutritt verboten*—i.e., no admittance. And as I could not forget the policeman's hint at "forcing such ones as me to speak," I wondered: "Are these the chambers in which they apply their 'methods'?" Had I heard someone scream from behind one of the forbidden doors it would not have astonished me in the least. I prayed within my heart, as I walked along: "Lord of the Dance of Life and Death, Mahadeva,[13] keep me worthy of the great love which Thou hast put in me!" And I recalled a line of the glorious song of the S.S. men: "Never will one of us weaken . . ."[14] And, pulling out the little glass portrait of the Führer that I wore upon my breast, I kissed it once more, without my custodian noticing what I was doing.

I was first ushered into a fairly large room in which stood two women. One of them locked the door behind me and ordered me to undress.

"Completely?" asked I, feeling, a little uneasy at the idea of letting even other women see in what state I was.

"Completely," answered the wardress.

Then, it came to my mind that she might be sufficiently shocked not

---

[13] "Mahadeva" means "Great God." In this context, Savitri Devi is addressing Shiva.—Ed.

[14] "Wollt nimmer von uns weichen . . ." [The first line of the second verse of "Wenn alle untreu werden."—Ed.]

to notice the portrait around my neck. "After all, it is perhaps better so," I mused. And I undressed, making excuses. "This happened," said I, "just after my arrest; and I had neither water, nor any of the necessary commodities, nor clothes to change, as all my things were already in the hands of the police. I am sorry."

"Oh, that's all right; quite all right," replied the woman. She did not seem shocked in the least.

The other woman, who looked just as Jewish as any of the two men I have already mentioned, was gazing at me, apparently with great curiosity. She seemed to be observing every movement of mine and every line of my body, as I gradually rid myself of my clothes. "She must be trying to see if I will betray by any gesture the presence of compromising papers, rolled up and concealed within my linen," I thought. "Well, if so, she is taking trouble for nothing. The only such papers I had, I have already swallowed hours ago. They must be digested, by now." But the woman finally spoke:

"How old are you?" she asked me.

"Forty-three."

She made no comments. I wanted to ask her what my age had to do with this inspection. But I said nothing.

"For what offence are you here?" she again enquired.

"For Nazi propaganda," I answered, with a proud smile.

She was obviously much younger than I, but had a worn-out face, with deep wrinkles under the eyes. And I imagined—gratuitously, I admit, and perhaps maliciously—that her body would have looked no less flabby and sickly—worn out—if it had been bare. Mine, I knew, was anything but that. And as, rightly or wrongly, I took the woman for a Jewess, I was glad to catch hold of such a tangible reason for despising her—or rather for despising once more, in her, the whole of Jewry at its worst, and the whole degenerate civilisation, product of the influence of Jewry upon the weaker representatives of the Aryan race. I forgot for a while how much I needed a hot bath. Stark naked before her in the sunshine, I felt happy to thrust upon that woman the sight of my firm and well-shaped form, as a living instance of Aryan superiority. I merely uttered two words in answer to her question. But in the smile that accompanied those words, she could perhaps read my defiant thoughts.

"And see how lovely we Nazis look, even at forty-three!" said the smile—"even after a sleepless night upon a filthy rug in the mud. It is only to be expected: we are the youth of the world!"

She pursed her lips and gave me a vicious glance, and spoke with forced irony: "Nazi propaganda," she repeated; "you have come a little late, I am afraid."

The words stung bitterly, and sunk deep into the raw wound in my heart. Who indeed knew better than I how delightful it would have been to have made use of my proselytising zeal in Europe under the Third Reich, instead of wasting it in indifferent surroundings? But I was too conscious of my strength in the present, for the thought of the past to depress me. And the bright sunshine pouring through the window turned my mind to the joy of an irresistible future. I remembered that nothing can prevent a great nation from accomplishing its natural mission, and that a few years up or down make a very little difference in the long run. I smiled still more defiantly and answered:

"No, on the contrary; I have come a little too early."

The woman who looked like a Jewess was silent—aware, perhaps, that, from her point of view, I was only too right. The other one, who had now finished examining my stockings, told me: "You can put on your clothes again."

Neither seemed to have noticed the priceless little glass object that hung on a golden chain around my neck.

I was then taken to another room within the same building, a much smaller room in which several men, some in police uniform, others in civilian clothes, were standing or sitting. One of them, seated in a dark corner opposite the door, was the *Oberinspektor* to whom particulars about my case had been given on the telephone from the police station, already before my arrest—a good-looking man, rather stout, with the most pleasant manners. He asked me "if I would mind" answering a few questions. And after taking down my name, age, etc. he bade me relate to him "what I had done in Germany from the start." My statement, he said, would serve as evidence in my trial. Of course, I was not compelled to make any statement. I could, if I liked, refuse to reveal anything of my history until the day I would appear before my judges. But I was only too pleased to speak about myself, provided I could do so without harming people who were on our side. I did not mind harming myself. For over twenty years my real self had remained in the shade: all but a very few exceptionally intelligent people had guessed the connection between my life-centred philosophy, my hatred of the Christian values, my Sun worship—my Aryan Paganism, openly professed—and the modern political Ideology of which I very rarely spoke, and had understood how passionately I identified myself with the latter. It had been expedient to let most people ignore the fact, especially during the war. I thus never got into trouble; nor did some of my closest collaborators. But now that, at last, I was caught, it mattered little if I told the authorities a little more than they already knew or suspected, about me. "One may as well be hanged for a sheep as for a lamb," thought I: "Let me have the pleasure of informing these people of the fact that the persecuted Idea means more to me, a non-German, than all their 'humanitarian' twaddle ever will mean to anybody, including themselves!" And I said: "I shall do so willingly, and tell you the whole truth"—determined all the time, however, to conceal whatever could, directly or indirectly, implicate any other National Socialists, in or outside Germany.

"I first came to Germany from Sweden," I pursued, "and distributed, from the windows of the Nord Express, from the 15th of June at about 6 p.m. to the 16th, at about 9 a.m. in 1948, over five hundred leaflets which I had written myself. Then, after a short stay in England, I came back through France, crossing the frontier, this time, at Saarhölzbach, and distributed, from the 7th of September to the 6th of December 1948, both in the three Western Zones of occupation and in Saarland, over six thousand other leaflets, the text of which I had also written myself."

The *Oberinspektor* interrupted me. "Your first leaflets were printed in Sweden?" he asked me.

"They were not printed at all," replied I. "I wrote them in my own handwriting, four or five at a time, making use of carbon paper, and spent the two nights before my departure doing so."

It pleased me to mention that detail—which is perfectly accurate—and thus to impress upon the bystanders the double fact that I had acted upon my own initiative and that I was not to be discouraged by physical hardships.

"And where was your second supply printed?" asked the *Oberinspektor*.

"I have already declared at the Police Station that, on no account, would I answer that question."

"All right; continue to relate your journeys to and fro. This is just a voluntary statement of yours, in which you can be as brief as you like."

I resumed my story; informing the police that, for the second time, I had gone to England in December 1948 "to spend Christmas with old friends" and that, after my third journey back to Germany, I had distributed a third supply of about four thousand papers—those precisely in the possession of which I had been arrested—which could be used both as leaflets and as posters. Again I carefully avoided mentioning a single detail susceptible of rousing suspicions about others than myself. My two hands in my pockets, I spoke with ease, with concealed amusement, and a secret feeling of superiority. I selected without difficulty what I wished to say, as a grownup girl who thinks, while speaking to a lot of first-form schoolboys: *"This* I can tell them; it is of no importance—and if I don't tell them, someone else will, anyhow. But *that* is none of the kids' business." I remembered with what apparent simplicity, with what calculated harmlessness, my clever husband used to talk, during the war, to the American officers that I used to bring home from the "East and West Club." And I thought, looking around me at the half a dozen men that nearly filled the narrow room: "Surely these are just as willing to be deceived as those were." And I despised them once more in my heart.

I related the last episode of my free life in Germany so as to make Herr W. appear as totally unaware as possible of what he was doing when he took my posters to stick up.

"But you knew his political views?" the *Oberinspektor* remarked.

"I did not, nor do I to this day," answered I, lying with utmost naturalness. "I only hoped he was not violently against National Socialism. But of that too, I was not sure; so much so that I felt uneasy after he had gone away with my posters. One is, indeed, never sure."

"Then, how could you believe he would stick up the posters once he would have read them?—for you told us that he did not read them before you left him, and did not yet know exactly what they were about."

"The truth is that I am a fool, and that I acted on impulse," said I. "I knew the young man had suffered a good deal from the war, as thousands of others. And—I imagined—gratuitously, without even asking him— that he held the Democracies responsible for it all, as I do, and that he therefore might be willing to help me in my single-handed struggle. It was perhaps a mistake on my part. I don't know. It was a risk I took, at any rate."

"And you offered the young man money?"

"No—because I had none. But I told him I would be glad to meet him again. And if all had gone well, I surely would have done my best to help him, knowing as I did that he was in need."

"And you had no friends in Germany, save those you met occasionally on your way, as you did Herr W.? You had no letters from abroad recommending you to anybody?"

"I had a letter from Monsieur C., of the *Bureau des Affaires Allemandes,* 36 rue de la Pérouse, in Paris, recommending me to the special care and protection of the Allied Occupation authorities, and another one, from the same person, addressed to me, and telling me that I could go to see, on his behalf, Monsieur H. and Monsieur G.,[15] in Baden Baden, and a couple of other gentlemen in Saarbrücken and in Vienna—

---

[15] Rudolf Grassot—Ed.

for I intended to go to Austria too. Both letters are to be found in my hand bag, I believe."

I had conversed with Monsieur C., and with Monsieur G., and with one of the fellows in Saarbrücken. Knowing they were all notorious anti-Nazis, I did not care two hoots if they got into trouble on account of me. On the contrary: the thought of such a possibility thoroughly amused me.

"Do you mean to tell us that you do not know any Nazis in Germany?" I heard a voice ask me, from a group of men who, although seated in the opposite corner, near the window, seemed to be following my cross-questioning with great interest.

"I know only two Nazis in the wide world; one is the Führer—the Gods be with him!—and the other is myself," replied I, with as much imperturbable seriousness as a comic actor on the stage.

There was silence in the audience—I mean, among my interrogators—and a smile (that the smilers themselves would have liked to repress) appeared upon one or two faces. I felt that my strange statement needed a word or two of explanation, and I added: "Yes, God alone, 'who probes into men's hearts', knows who is a Nazi and who is not. What do I know? It is only too easy to deceive me. So I repeat indeed: I am sure of nobody's National Socialist faith, save, of course, of the Führer's and of my own."

The explanation was irreproachably logical. There was no answer to it—except torture. But the men in that little room seemed quite different from those I had first come in contact with—Germans, no doubt, most of them, but much less interested than the former in the future (and even in the present) of Democracy; in other words, men who served Democracy in a more truly democratic spirit, i.e., with no genuine zeal. Or perhaps, just men in a hurry to go home and have lunch—for it must have been well-nigh half past one or two o'clock in the afternoon. Not one of them renewed the threat. And I began to feel convinced that one could make fun of the whole system of political coercion in occupied Germany, with practical impunity (at least *now* and in the Western Zones) provided one had sufficient contempt for it from the start, and sufficient pluck.

A tall, slim, fairly elegant man, who had not yet spoken, asked me if I knew for sure that Adolf Hitler is alive. "You say so in your posters. Is it just a means to give hope and courage to his people, or do you really believe it?" said he.

"I am sure of it," I replied.

"And how did you come to know it? One of his followers must have told you so."

"Not at all. An Indian astrologer told me so."

The audience was again taken back. They had been wondering what I was going to say, as they knew, by now, that I would never mention a single German name. They had not expected that answer.

"And you believe in such forecasts?" the tall man asked me.

"I do—when they are made by people who know the science of the stars. I suppose twenty-five years spent in the Near and Middle East have only increased my natural tendency to superstition."

Again the explanation, though a little ironical, was irreproachably consistent. There was nothing to reply.

But the tall man, for his misfortune, started a discussion with me on purely ideological grounds. A mistake, from his point of view—for any such discussion between a Democrat and a National Socialist only serves to show how weak the former's position is, compared with that of the latter. And a mistake which he aggravated by choosing to discuss the spirit of Indian philosophy, with which he appears ill-acquainted.

"I fail to understand how you, who seem to be interested in India (since you took the trouble of learning two Indian languages) can at the same time identify yourself so completely with an ideology of murder and violence (*sic*) such as National Socialism," said he, who had himself visited India during the war.

"And what makes you think that the Indians are incapable of murder and violence?" asked I. "The long history of India—which I once used to teach in an Indian college[16]—leads rather to the contrary conclusion."

"Maybe. But . . . Gandhi, the apostle of non-violence. . . . And the masters of Indian spirituality . . . who were all pacifists . . ." (*sic*).

"All pacifists!" thought I; "what a joke! Obviously, this man has never read the Bhagavad-Gita." But I was not astonished. I knew he would speak thus—and put the shrewd Bania[17] politician of modern India on a level with the Aryan seers of old. I knew the abysmal ignorance of most Europeans who pretend to understand "Indian philosophy."

"Gandhi does not represent India," I replied. "He has himself admitted that the two great influences that count in his life are that of Jesus Christ and that of Tolstoy—one of the most Christian-like figures of modern times. The fact that, soaked through and through in such foreign philosophy, he has acquired great fame and played a considerable role in India, is just one more blatant sign of India's decay from the high level of wisdom to which the ancient Aryans had attained there, when they laid

---

[16] Jallundhar College, in the Punjab—Ed.

[17] Belonging to one of the merchant castes—that of the "Modh-Bania," in Gandhi's instance.

the foundations of her caste-ridden civilisation."

The topic was unusual at the Police Headquarters of Cologne; and every man present was listening intently, including the *Oberinspektor* in his armchair. I only hoped the Germans knew enough English to grasp the full meaning of what I was saying—for the tall man had addressed me in English, and I had answered him in the same language. I pursued, as though I were delivering a public lecture: "I do not know how far unconditional non-violence was practised by the civilised people of the Indus Valley, before the warrior-like Aryans poured down from the North. If, as some maintain, it was, then, I am all the more right in declaring that India's historic civilisation—Sanskrit civilisation—is not a product of the Tropics, but a Nordic civilisation stamped upon a tropical land, which is not at all the same thing. It is the outcome of the genius of ancient invaders whose spirit was practically the same as ours. You will not find a trace of that bold spirit in Mr. Gandhi's pacifism—nor in the great philosophies of escape from life, products of lassitude and disillusionment and despair, more consistent than his, that sprang in Antiquity from the minds of Kshatriyas who had renounced the duties and the privileges of power.[18] But you will find it in all its purity in the Bhagavad-Gita, the Book that proclaims that 'there is nothing more welcome to a Kshatriya than a righteous war,'[19] and that tells the warrior: 'Slain thou wilt obtain Heaven; victorious, thou wilt enjoy the earth; stand up, therefore, O son of Kunti, full of resolution, and fight!'"[20]

"But . . . I heard that the Bhagavad-Gita also preached non-violence," said the man.

"No," answered I. "That is the mistake of those who read it with an incurably Christian mentality. The Bhagavad-Gita, written for warriors, preaches violence in a detached spirit—utmost violence (if necessary) with perfect detachment; the action which is duty, according to each one's natural role in the world, performed thoroughly, but without passion, and never, never for personal ends; the self-same thing which we National Socialists preach—and live—today; and that we are the only ones to *live*, in this degenerate world."

The tall, elegant man found it advisable to drop the topic. Perhaps he regretted ever having brought it up, thus giving the Germans who were present the opportunity to know—if they had not suspected it before—how ancient, how eternal, Hitler's spirit is, and how indissolubly linked

---

[18] Savitri Devi is alluding primarily to Buddhism.—Ed.
[19] The Bhagavad-Gita, II, verse 31.
[20] The Bhagavad-Gita, II, verse 37.

with every awakening of Aryan consciousness.

He asked me a question apparently less likely to provoke, within German hearts, secret reactions, undesirable from the Allied point of view.

"How is it," he asked me, "that a certificate of Greek nationality issued by the Greek Consulate of Lyons (France) and dated 1928, was found in your bag?"

"I was of Greek nationality before I acquired British citizenship by my marriage."

"Then how is it that, in your passport, opposite the French visa authorising you to enter the French Zone of occupation in Germany, it is specially stated that you are French?"

"Oh, that just means that I purposely omitted to tell the French authorities that I had chosen Greece at the age of twenty-one. I told them—because I thought it would induce them to grant me the military permit more easily—that my father was a French citizen (which is true, whatever be his origin), and that I was 'born French' (which is no less true whatever be my origin, as any child born in France, is or was, in my time, considered French). All that interested me in the matter was a means to enter Germany. And I was not mistaken: they gave me that means."

"And why did you not retain your French citizenship, when you were twenty-one? Surely it was more advantageous than a Greek one."

"I know it was. Most Greeks settled in France are 'French citizens' for that reason. And they told me so in Greece itself, when I went and claimed my Hellenic nationality. They told me I would never enjoy in Greece the position my diplomas would have given me in France. Yet I replied that I would earn my living by washing plates and dishes, rather than be called French."

"And what diplomas had you?"

"I was *'licenciée ès lettres'*—what they call in England 'master of arts', I believe. And I was afterwards to acquire the degree of 'master of sciences'—*'licenciée ès sciences'*—also, and finally of 'doctor of literature' (*'docteur ès lettres'*)."

"And what grievances had you against France?"

"I never forgave her the way she forced Greece into the First World War on the side of the Allies, with the complicity of Mr. Venizelos,[21] against the will of the Greeks. I held her responsible for the Greek disaster in Asia Minor in 1922. And although I am not a German, the manner

---

[21] Eleutherios Venizelos (1864–1936), several times elected Prime Minister of Greece, was the chief foe of the Greek Monarchy during his political career.—Ed.

she behaved in the Ruhr in 1923 thoroughly disgusted me—how I remember it! And I looked upon her citizenship as a shame, and did not want it, however advantageous it might have been. There was, then, no question of emergency for me, as in 1948."

"And family considerations influenced your decision, I suppose . . ."

"No, a thousand times no. Even if both my parents had been Greeks by blood, I doubt whether that would have added much to my determination," said I. "What mainly attracted me were those eternal Greek ideals of perfection that I was very soon to call Aryan ideals. Greece—the oldest Aryan nation in Europe to have given expression to those ideals in life and culture—was a symbol in my eyes. And I was not astonished to see the French Government who had betrayed the Greeks of Asia Minor, behave so shabbily towards Germany a year later—although I was far from suspecting, then, the full meaning of rising National Socialism, and the part it would play in my life."

"And what does National Socialism mean to you?" asked the man. "And what would you have done, then, if you had realised what you believe to be its full significance?"

"To me, National Socialism is the only outlook worthy of the natural aristocracy of mankind, of the best representatives of the Aryan race. It is the expression of undying Aryan Heathendom in our modern world. Had I realised *that* when I was twenty-one, I would have done anything to become a citizen of the Third Reich, and to serve its interests at home with all my love, all my energy and all my intelligence. But I realised it two years later, and I did my best for the Aryan cause in the two old hallowed centres of Aryan culture: Greece and India."

I had replied unhesitatingly. The man judged that he had better put off questioning me for the time being. Somehow, whatever he had asked me, my reply had always turned out, in the end . . . *ad majorem Germaniae gloriam*.[22] It was too much for the prestige of the Occupation—especially considering the fact that I am not a German. Moreover, as not a word of this conversation had been written, God only knew how it might be repeated and interpreted by the Germans who were present. These, of course, were all good Democrats—or they would not have been there. But could one ever tell in occupied Germany, who was a good Democrat and who was just putting up a show? The gentleman ordered that a stenotypist be sent to him at his house, in the afternoon, to take down my answers in black and white, and bade me follow him into the car waiting downstairs. He was, outwardly at least, most courteous, and I would even

---

[22] "To the greater glory of Germany"—Ed.

say, most friendly.

On our way out, he told me that he belonged to British Military Intelligence. I reflected and concluded that I had been discreet. True, I had revealed a good deal of my personal feelings. But that had no importance; it concerned nobody but myself. I had not said a word that could be of any use to the enemies of National Socialism in the present or in the future.

The car took me to the house the man occupied with his wife and two children.

Seated in a corner, with my face to the window, I enjoyed the drive as thoroughly as I would have on an ordinary Sunday afternoon, had the gentleman not been a British "M.I." in occupied Germany, and I not a prisoner. The weather was cold and bright—the weather I like—and the road pleasant. I had entirely forgotten my body in the earnestness or craftiness of my replies to the different questions that had been put to me at the Police Headquarters, and I now felt the pangs of hunger no longer. I could easily have continued to discourse the whole day. But for the present, I just looked out of the window at the trees along the road, at the bright cloudless sky and at the passers-by.

I was aware of the invisible link that bound me to the latter—as to all Germany—more strongly than ever since my arrest. A woman on the roadside pointed at the motorcar in which I was, to her two- or three-year-old child, who was crying. There was nothing remarkable in such a gesture: she would have, just as easily, pointed at anything else, to make the boy forget why he was crying. But as I saw her do it, tears came into my eyes, as though that woman had been eternal Germany drawing to me the attention of her distressed sons of 1949 and telling them: "Weep not over the disaster: it will be avenged. And already, in spite of it all, you are the winners—not those who persecute you. See: wherever the Aryan consciousness is wide-awake it is on your side!" Spontaneously, I had given the simple gesture a secret meaning. Why not? Everything in the universe is connected with everything else and with the invisible, and *has* a secret meaning that people do not know. I was a living centre of Aryan consciousness. And the fair-haired babe now crying in his mother's arms would march in a few years' time along this same road, in the ranks of the resurrected Hitler Youth. In my humble way, among thousands of others, I existed in order to make this possible.

It must have been not far from half past three when we reached the house—the lovely, warm, comfortable house in which, the Englishman told me, I would spend the rest of the day and the following night until I was taken somewhere else (I did not yet know where).

"I thank you for lodging me here," said I. Yet, I added immediately: "But would you do so if I were German?"

"But you are British," replied my host.

"Any nationality attributed to me (in the sense the world now conceives nationhood and nationality) would be artificial," said I. "I am just an Aryan." And I thought of Herr W., and wondered: "How are they treating *him* who, being an S.S. officer, is worth more than I?" It would perhaps have been better to have left me in the cold, dark cell. I did not want personal consideration from Germany's oppressors—from the willing or unwilling agents of the enemies of Aryandom.

The Englishman's wife came to take me upstairs to have a bath. She was a young, very attractive woman, with fiery red hair—a Scotchwoman; a fine Nordic type. And as I gazed at her, I thought for the millionth time: "Why could not at least the best physical specimens of Aryans all support the one Ideology worthy of the race—ours? Why do they—even in Germany, let alone in other places—allow the cunning of the Jew to divide them in the name of utterly non-Aryan principles?" But I said nothing. And as I followed her through a warm corridor, taking a glance, as I went, at the blue satin hangings that adorned one of the bedrooms, I realised, with such sadness that I could have cried, that some Germans had been turned out of their comfortable home to make place for this M.I. and his family. "Where were they now?" thought I. How were they living? It was in one of *their* rooms that I was to sleep that night . . . But perhaps they would not mind *my* presence in their house so much as that of the British official, if only they knew me.

I was still trying to picture to myself the lawful inhabitants of those lovely surroundings when I reached the bathroom.

"You can use any soap you like," said the M.I.'s wife. You have bath salts here in the corner. And here is a clean towel. If you need anything, do not be ashamed to tell me."

"I thank you," said I, "and beg to be excused for all the trouble that I am giving you. I would only like . . . some clean underclothes. I believe I have some in the brown suitcase that they brought here with me. And the cardboard box that is in the same suitcase I would need also. And again excuse me for putting you to such inconvenience."

"It is quite all right. I want you to be comfortable. And you'll have something to eat when you come down."

The lady's voice was sweet and friendly; her manners perfect. I could not help feeling that I was ready to like her, provided she was not against us. I was even beginning to wonder if she were not secretly on our side, and were not treating me so well precisely because of my convictions.

But if it were so, she would never tell me. Or would she? I tried to know.

"Did they tell you why I was arrested?" I asked her.

"No."

"I wrote and distributed papers against the Occupation. I am a Nazi—a real one. I tell you so because I do not wish you to be kind to me without you knowing what I stand for."

"But it makes absolutely no difference to me," said the M.I.'s wife. "You have every right to stick up for your convictions, as we all have. Personally, I do not bother my head with politics: I have enough to do with my household and my two kids. For me, you are just a fellow woman of mine."

"Then, why arrest me? And why persecute Germany? And why persecute National Socialism all over the world?" I wanted to say. But I said nothing. It would have been useless. This charming lady had no say in the detested decisions of the victorious Democracies. And, thought I, her beautiful Aryan children would grow up under the New Order anyhow. The next World War and the next following peace—*our* peace—would come before they would be fifteen, I hoped.

Smiling at this possibility, I bathed in a tub of green marble, and felt as fresh as a rose. I walked downstairs in my clean clothes, humming the old song:

Germany, awake from your bad dream!
Give not, to alien Jews, a place within your Reich!
We want to fight for your resurrection
Aryan blood must not be submerged![23]

And I could not help thinking: "What would the lawful inhabitants of this house say, if they heard me?" I felt quite sure that they would be secretly pleased. And as I passed before the kitchen, I did all I could for the two young German servants who were working there to hear me. Did they, or not? And if they did, what feelings did the old *"Kampflied"* rouse in them? I shall never know.

I entered the room I had been assigned: a neat little basement room, with pink flowers on the windowsill. I lay upon the bed—a comfortable bed—and shut my eyes just for a while; to rest, for I knew I would soon

---

[23] "Deutschland, erwache aus deinem bösen Traum! Gib fremden Juden in deinem Reich nicht Raum! Wir wollen kämpfen für dein Auferstehen. Arisches Blut darf nicht untergehen!" [Savitri Devi's translation of the first verse of "Deutschland, erwache."—Ed.]

be cross-examined again. There was a soft knock at the door. "Come in," said I. It was the M.I.'s wife herself, holding a tray.

"I have brought you an omelette, a few slices of cake, bread and butter, and jam," said she.

"Oh, thank you!" answered I, in an impulse of gratitude: the lady was so friendly. But at once I recalled Herr W., and a painful feeling filled my heart, and apparently my face became sombre.

"You must be hungry," said my hostess. "Since when have you had nothing to eat?"

"Since yesterday morning. But that is nothing to mention."

"Dear me! You would perhaps have liked a little more, then?"

"No, really not. I have more than enough with all this, and am very thankful. I was only thinking . . ."

"What were you thinking?"

". . . thinking . . . how I would be happy if I could share this with the young comrade who was arrested in connection with me, a German who has already suffered a thousand hardships and the most beastly treatment at the hands of the French. Poor boy! If I had not given him those posters to stick up, he would still be free."

"The French might have been somewhat rough, but I am sure *we* will treat him kindly," declared my hostess.

"Do you think so? *I* am not so sure. He is faithful and courageous, and deserves every consideration even from our enemies. But he has not a British-Indian passport," I replied bitterly.

"But what can *you* do, now?"

"Nothing, I know. Only, I think of him—and of the thousands of others—and I feel a little ashamed of myself when I see how kind and considerate you are to me."

"You should not. You did not ask for it, I know. And you, too, are faithful and courageous."

"I have not yet suffered; I have not yet proved my worth," said I, meaning every word I said.

"Don't talk; your coffee will be getting cold."

"Yes, that lovely coffee! I have smelt it as soon as you came in," I said, pouring out a cup of it for myself, as I sat down. "How did you guess I liked coffee better than tea?"

"I thought you would, as I was told you are half continental."

I was sincerely touched. "Do sit down, and stay a while with me," I asked the charming woman who, after all, was not responsible for the nonsensical discrimination the Allied authorities seemed to make between my German comrades and myself. "May I know your name?"

"Mrs. Hatch."

"I am Mrs. Mukherji—Savitri Devi Mukherji. Tell me, Mrs. Hatch, why are you so kind to me?"

"Because one should be kind to everybody; and also because I like you. My husband has talked about you."

"Has he indeed? And what did he say? I am sure *he* does not like me!"

"Why do you think that? On the contrary, he finds you strangely interesting, and . . . let me tell you . . . unusually clever."

"I? But I am the one—the only one—damned fool among all those who share my Ideology! In fact, had I not been so stupid, I never would have got caught."

She laughed heartily. I finished my omelette, and poured myself out another cup of coffee.

"Your coffee is excellent," said I. And I could not help adding: "Yes, I do wish my German comrades had such coffee to drink . . ."

Even those who were free could obtain, then, but very seldom, nothing but a tasteless decoction of chicory—*"Muckefuck,"* [24] as they called it, and that without sugar and without milk. And again, in my mind, I recalled Herr W., and wondered how he was being treated. The thought of him pursued me. And I remembered the anti-Nazi starvation camps that the Allies had (I knew it from comrades who had suffered in some of them) established in occupied Germany. But I realised it was of no use mentioning these to this woman: she would avoid answering me—whether she knew the facts or not—and would politely drop the topic. Moreover, what could she *do*, even if she were sincere and bold enough not to shut her eyes to such uncomfortable realities? Other Democrats—other "humanitarians," responsible ones—would answer for all those horrors when the day of reckoning would come: I thought of that delightful day, while munching bread and butter and raspberry jam—as other people think of the long-desired events that will bring great joy into their personal lives.

"I am told that you come from India and that you write books. Have you written anything about India?" the M.I.'s wife asked me.

"Yes, a book in French, and two others in English, long ago. [25] But my other books are on other subjects."

---

[24] The etymology of this word is uncertain, but it may originate from the Rhenisch German dialect, as a compound of *"Mucken"* (brown earth) and *"fuck"* (foul, rotten, decayed).—Ed.

[25] Savitri Devi, *L'Etang aux Lotus* [*The Lotus Pond*] (Calcutta: Savitri Devi Mukherji, 1940), *A Warning to the Hindus* (Calcutta: Hindu Mission, 1939), and *The Non-Hindu Indians and Indian Unity* (Calcutta: Hindu Mission, 1940).—Ed.

"For example?"

"For example: the Religion of the Disk—a particularly beautiful and pure form a Sun worship, put forth by a Pharaoh of the early fourteenth century before Christ, King Akhnaton, one of the greatest historic figures of all times."[26]

"How interesting! And how did you come to choose such a subject?"

"Just because I too am a worshipper of the Sun, the Source of all life and health and power," said I.

"Are you, really? So you don't believe in Christianity?"

I smiled. The question seemed almost absurd to me. How could anyone indeed believe in Christianity and have our ideals? But I was contented to answer: "Certainly not," without further explanations. There was another knock at the door, and the M.I. himself appeared—Mr. Hatch, I now knew his name. A young girl, a typist, was with him.

"Are you now ready to be cross-questioned once more?" he asked me, as his wife left the room with the half-empty tray.

"Surely."

He sat down, and so did the typist, and so did I. And again, for the safety of Democracy, the gentleman peered into my past—to the extent *I* was willing that he should peer. And again, the things I said seemed strange to him, in spite of his long experience with "political cases"—the truer, the stranger.

"When did you decide to go to India?" he asked me among other things.

"In 1932."

"And what attracted you there?"

"I wished to see with my own eyes, and to study, a civilisation uniting many separate races, for thousands of years, under a social system founded upon the idea of natural racial hierarchy—our idea. It appeared to me that the sight of India could suggest, in some way, what our New Order extended to the whole world would look like after six thousand

---

[26] Savitri Devi, *Akhnaton's Eternal Message: A Scientific Religion 3,300 Years Old* [Pamphlet] (Calcutta: A. K. Mukherji, 1940), *Joy of the Sun: The Beautiful Life of Akhnaton, King of Egypt, Told to Young People* (Calcutta: Thacker, Spink and Co. Ltd., 1942), and *A Son of God: The Life and Philosophy of Akhnaton, King of Egypt* (London: Philosophical Publishing House, 1946), second edition: *Son of the Sun: The Life and Philosophy of Akhnaton, King of Egypt* (San Jose, Cal.: Supreme Grand Lodge of AMORC, 1956). A fourth title, *A Perfect Man: Akhnaton, King of Egypt*, is listed in *Joy of the Sun*, but no copies have come to light. It may be a lost work; it may never have been published; or it may merely have been the original title of *A Son of God*.—Ed.

years of existence."

"And you did not become a little sceptical about the value of your principles when you saw real India, with its filth and misery?"

"No, on the contrary, never was I so strongly convinced of the necessity of a rational, worldwide caste-system—the purest Aryans forming the highest castes—if the world is one day to become worth living in. But the sight of India's 'filth and misery' as you say so well, did teach me (or rather, strengthen in me the conviction) that the 'live and let live' attitude of the Indians—and of most Westerners—is no good, and that *our* future worldwide organisation should impose that which the Indian system has failed even to stress, namely, limitation of breeding among the inferior races, along with our well-known sterilisation of the unfit, and elimination of the dregs of humanity of *all* races."

"Did you not go to India for any other reason?"

"Yes, to find there, in the religious rites, customs and beliefs, something of a living equivalent of the old Aryan cults of Europe—both of Greece and of the North; of *my* Europe in its entirety—which Christianity has abolished."

"And what did you do, mainly, all those years you were there?"

"I fought Christianity—and Islam, the two international religions of equality, whose adherent any man of any race can become; the two great lasting delusions, rooted in Judaism, that set up the Jews as a 'chosen' people, as the channel of divine revelation, in the eyes of untold millions in the East and in the West. I fought them—both—with passionate tenacity, using any platform that was offered to me, speaking, and sometimes writing, in the name of the traditions of India, but in reality in the name of my—of *our*—life-centred philosophy; of the eternal Philosophy of the Swastika, not because it is 'Indian' in any way, but because it is mine—ours. Indeed, I did nothing else."

"How is it that you remained there so long?"

"I did not intend to, at first. I meant to come back to Europe after a couple of years. Then, I got interested in my struggle there—which was, in fact, an aspect of our struggle. I thought myself useful—perhaps making thereby a mistake. I felt I was preparing in the distant East the advent of our world New Order. And had we won this war, I must say that, perhaps, my humble efforts would not have been entirely wasted."

The typist only wrote down those of my answers that seemed to be of some interest in connection with my coming trial. I often had the impression that Mr. Hatch asked me a great deal of technically useless questions, out of sheer personal interest in the history of a non-German National Socialist—a relatively rare specimen.

"To sum up," said he, after an hour or two of conversation with me, "it is your own philosophy of life, your essentially aesthetic attitude to religious and social problems, and your interpretation of world history that made you a National Socialist?"

"Nothing made me a National Socialist. I always was one, by nature, by instinct, and could not have been anything else even before I knew what to call myself. But it is true that the factors you mention—and others too—have helped me to become more and more conscious of my Ideology."

"What 'other factors', for instance?"

"My awareness of the Jewish danger on all planes, and not merely in the economic sphere; my strong sense of Aryan solidarity; my inborn hatred of moderate views and of half measures."

When the typist had gone away, Mr. Hatch came back to me with another man, a Jewish-looking sort of fellow, before whom I repeated some of the things I had said concerning the historical foundation of my Nazi convictions.

"Personally, I like your ancient Greek stuff well enough," said that other man, "your Spartans, and your Olympic games and what not. But couldn't we have that without National Socialism?"

"No. It is impossible."

"But why, impossible?"

"If you cannot yourself see 'why', it just means that you grasp nothing at all of the real Hellenic spirit, or nothing of National Socialism—or perhaps nothing of either," I replied.

On that remark of mine, both that man and Mr. Hatch walked out. I watched them go. The former was crude, the latter refined—English, and gentlemanlike. But they were both average men. A certain admixture of Jewish blood, probably, in the case of the former, and a successful Judeo-Christian education coupled with vested interests, in the case of both, could never allow them to see things as they are. And never, perhaps, since those horrid days of 1946 that followed my landing in England, had I felt so keenly that we are *the* misunderstood minority—the only one—that bears the torch of eternal truth in this hateful, decaying Western world, we National Socialists, we, the modern Aryan Heathens. And once more I longed for the divinely ordained general crash—the end of "Kali Yuga," or the "Dark Age"—when that world would sink into nothingness while the survivors among us would organise upon its ruins the new earth, the Golden Age of the following Cycle in time, the worldwide New Order.

I stood up upon a chair and looked out of the window at the bright, moonlit sky. I remembered the night I had spent on the slopes of burning Hekla, nearly two years before—a bright night like this one, but in which the face of the full moon was obscured by a cloud of volcanic ash, and in which long streaks of lurid green light, fringed with purple—northern lights—hung from the zenith over the flaming craters and the streams of lava and the shining snowy landscape. Oh, that night; that divine, unforgettable night! It was on the 5th of April, 1947. What was I destined to do, on the 5th of April, 1949?

And I thought of Lord Shiva, the Destroyer, whose forehead bears the crescent of the moon, and I prayed, "Put the right answers in my mouth, O Lord of the Dance of appearances! Use my voice to tell the world, in adequate words, that the truth that inspires us is Thy eternal truth, and that our beloved Führer is the Chosen One of the Gods . . ."

And I pressed in my hands, with tender devotion, the little portrait of the Leader, which I wore around my neck. But again, I heard a soft knock at the door. It was Mrs. Hatch.

"You are not uncomfortable here?" she asked me. And before I had time to answer, she added, as she put on the light and saw me: "You look happy."

"I *am* happy."

"But you must be tired, after all this cross-questioning?"

"No," said I; "not at all."

And this was true. I was too happy to be tired. I was aware of being useful. Every word I said was, in a way, *our* answer to the efforts of the Democrats to "de-Nazify" us. And our answer was, irrefutable, I knew it. And what is more, *they* knew it too.

"I came," said Mrs. Hatch, "to ask you what you would like to eat for supper. It is nearly nine o'clock, and you must eat something."

"It is kind of you to ask me," I replied. "But I would be quite content with another cup of your lovely coffee. I am not hungry. I have had lunch at half past four or so."

"You surely will have a cup of coffee. I am so glad you like it. But you must have also something to eat, to make up your strength. You will be going away from here tomorrow, early in the morning, and you will have another strenuous day. So do tell me what you would like."

"Oh, anything—except meat, or things cooked with meat or in animal fats."

"That is easy enough. I shall be back in a minute."

But I retained her. "Do you mind telling me—if I am allowed to know—where they are taking me tomorrow?" I asked.

"To Düsseldorf."

"Düsseldorf!" I repeated. "I am glad. The place is full of memories. Oh, I am glad to be tried there!"

Mrs. Hatch left the room. And I followed the thread of my thoughts. I recalled in my mind the darkest days after the First World War, when the National Socialist struggle had begun in Germany; the days when the French occupied the Ruhr. I was then in France, a college girl of seventeen. From what I heard of it from private sources, the behaviour of the French in the Ruhr had revolted me beyond words. "Then," I remembered, "the name of Düsseldorf was practically every day in the papers. Who would have told me that, one day I was destined to appear there before a military Court, for having defied Germany's enemies? And I thought of the earliest phase of the Struggle—when I merely knew of its existence. And I thought of a speech which the Führer had delivered at Düsseldorf three years after the French had settled there—on the 15th of June 1926—a speech that had impressed me . . . And I remembered myself, passing through the station of that same town, exactly twenty-two years later—when all was over; when all seemed lost—and thrusting leaflets on the platform from a window of the Nord Express. Now, I was to be tried there for similar activities, after so many Germans who had suffered and resisted . . . I felt honoured. And then, I realised—as perhaps I never had before to the same extent—that my humble history was also a minute in the history of National Socialism; in the history of proud Germany, the champion of Aryan rights. Of course it was. And it would remain so, forever. I felt raised above myself at that thought.

But already Mrs. Hatch was back with my supper.

"Do sit down, and keep me company while I eat," said I. She sat down. Then, suddenly smiling: "I wanted to tell you," she said, "that I have seen your beautiful Indian jewellery."

"But I have hardly any left. What you have seen is nothing!"

"Whatever it be, I like it . . . including your earrings in the shape of swastikas. They are so lovely!"

"A swastika is always lovely," answered I. "It is the Wheel of the Sun—and our holy Sign."

"But the Indians also hold it sacred, I am told; don't they?"

"Yes, because they owe the essentials of their religions ideas to the ancient Aryans, conquerors of India thousands of years ago."

"Tell me, also: is it that you became a vegetarian in India?"

"No; I always was one, from my childhood."

"Is it for reasons of health, or is it a matter of principles, with you?"

"It is a matter of principles. I refuse to have any part in the infliction of suffering and death upon innocent animals, especially when I can well live without doing so."

The woman looked at me, a little surprised. And she asked me the question that hundreds had asked me already, that hundreds more were to ask me, to this day: *the* unavoidable question: "In that case, you don't approve of the violence committed upon human beings in the name of your Ideology?"

"Of course I do! Why shouldn't I?" I replied, hiding genuine irritation—for *that* question always irritates me. "I do, wholeheartedly, provided that those who make use of violence do so either to obey orders (in the case they are subordinates) or—in the case they are allowed to take initiative—solely to forward the ends of the Party, the triumph of our Idea, the application of our programme in its proper spirit, *and never for any personal ends.*"

"But surely *you* would not have done yourself some of the things the Nazis did," said the naive lady.

"I undoubtedly would have—and worse things than you can imagine—had I only been given an opportunity," answered I, with the fire of sincerity, knowing I was right. "And I am prepared to act in the same manner, if ever I get a chance to . . . next time. But of course, as far as possible, always in a detached spirit. I would brush aside all personal feelings including my hatred for anyone who hates my Führer, and consider the sole expediency of the measures I would apply—nothing else."

"You refuse to have a part in the murder of innocent animals, you say, and yet, you would send any number of human beings to their doom if you or your superiors judged it 'expedient', i.e., if it suited your ideological ends!"

"Most certainly."

"I fail to understand you. You baffle me."

"Animals are not anti-Nazis" said I, so calmly and so spontaneously—so naturally—that, in spite of her fathomless naivety, the woman recoiled a little. But she clung to her illusions as though her confidence in life depended upon them. "I can't believe you!" she said. *"I do not want to believe you; you look so sweet!"*

"What you, and I, and a thousand other people might believe or want to believe has absolutely no importance. Facts alone count," answered I, in a tranquil voice, with a happy smile.

There was an unbreachable abyss between the usual man-centred outlook of that soft-hearted woman, brought up in a Christian atmosphere, to the influence of which she had responded, and myself, and us all. I recalled the words by which Monsieur Grassot, the Assistant Director of the French Information Department, at Baden Baden, had characterised our merciless consistency: *cette logique effroyable*—that appalling logic. And once more, as on the 9th of October 1948, before the desk of that official, I thought: "The degenerate world that exalts the Christian values (with what appalling hypocrisy!) will never be won over to our point of view. It will have to perish wholesale before we can build our world. Let it perish! Then the surviving young Aryans of all lands shall follow us."

When Mrs. Hatch had gone away, after wishing me a good night, I wrote to my husband a letter of which the wording was more or less the following:

Shricharaneshu,[27] the immortal Gods have been pleased to honour me: I am under arrest since the night before last for having distributed in occupied Germany several thousands of National Socialist leaflets, which I had written myself. I have given practically all I possessed for our sacred cause. Sweet liberty was the last treasure I had. Now, I have given that, too. I am happy, exceedingly happy. I feel a little worthier, now, of my persecuted German comrades, whom I admire as the world's living élite.

I hope you are well. May Mahadeva, Lord of Life and Death, be with you.

With utmost love and reverence.

Heil Hitler!

Your,

Savitri

And I remained a long time awake, wondering whether I would ever see my old home in Calcutta once more, and have a heart-to-heart talk with the one man in Asia who seemed to know me and to understand me perfectly.

Then, I slept like a log.

* * *

The following morning, after breakfast, I was taken to Düsseldorf. Mrs. Hatch, who had things to do there, sat by my side in the car. Her husband and another man accompanied us.

I had rested, and was in the best of spirits—feeling strong, and in a mood to use defiant speech at the slightest opportunity. I was beginning

---

[27] *"Lotus-footed one"*; a formula of respect used in India when addressing a superior (father, husband, etc.), in writing.

to realise that those Englishmen, in whose hands I was now, would never apply to me the "methods" the existence of which the German policeman in Cologne had reminded me as a matter of course. *They* were too squeamish, or too Christian-like, or too afraid of the consequences—afraid of the immense advantage I would take of a personal experience of torture, in my anti-democratic propaganda, no sooner I would be free—or perhaps (who knows?) too good psychologists; too thoroughly convinced of the uselessness of any "methods" of intimidation in the case of such "fanatics" as myself. I despised them a little—instead of admiring them—and felt all the more aggressive, instead of all the less so, as *they* would probably have expected. And I enjoyed the drive along the great *Reichsautobahn.*

The Sun was bright, the air invigorating. The car rolled along the straight, smooth, shining road, at full speed. I remembered I was going to be tried, and that my trial would be a fact, and that as a fact—past and ineffaceable—it would remain in the recorded or unrecorded annals of the persecution of National Socialism. One day, the guest of resurrected Germany, seated with other Nazis—free, proud, powerful, merciless, and happy—I would speak about it; and say whatever I liked against the slaves of the Jews and the traitors (all of them liquidated, by then) and the "swine-Occupation," then, the mere memory of a bad dream. This thought thrilled me beforehand. I was already—now, powerless and a prisoner—the happiest person in the car. A strange excitement, a sort of intoxication from within, prompted me to speak, to say something irrefutable that would remind the other occupants of the car that their Democracy—their money power—is not the only force in the world.

"These lovely *Autobahnen* are one of the lasting achievements of the Third Reich—and a symbol," said I defiantly. "I cannot help thinking of the great days every time I move along one."

Mr. Hatch and the other man looked at me with tired faces—evidently not in a mood to respond to attack. Mrs. Hatch said softly:

"We have preserved those truly beautiful roads, and we do what we can to keep them in good order as long as we are here."

"Right: because you use them yourselves 'as long as you are here'. And how long do you think that will be, if I am not indiscreet?" asked I with a sarcastic smile.

"I don't know."

"Nor do I. But I can say that much: it will be as long as the invisible powers will permit; not a minute longer. One day, the Allied troops—and civilians—will run for their lives along these roads and along the roads of their respective countries, pursued by fire from all sides, and not knowing where to go. That will be the day of unfailing Nemesis; the day of my yearning; the day when I shall gloat and gloat and gloat, wherever I be. Tell me: what will you people do, then, to keep me from gloating?"

"Oh, let us talk of something else!" said poor Mrs. Hatch, harassed, exasperated, perhaps crushed by a sudden intuition of the terrible future at the sight of my face—for if what she read there was the spirit of an utterly powerless Nazi, what would resurrected National Socialism look like, once more in all its conquering power? "Let us get away from politics!"

But I was pitiless. "I am not talking 'politics'," said I; "I am only stating how I expect to enjoy myself, one day, never mind when. To think of it is the only pleasure left to me, now that I am caught, and of no further use to my cause."

"Is there not anything or anybody you love in this world, save your cause and the people connected with it?"

"No," replied I, with all my heart.

There was silence; and the car rolled on. The Sun was now higher in the sky, the air, a little warmer—or a little less cold.

Before we reached Düsseldorf, Mrs. Hatch and I were again talking—this time, about cats, if I remember well. It is one of the few decidedly non-controversial subjects of which I am able to talk with interest and understanding and first-hand knowledge.

* * *

In Düsseldorf, I was first taken to one of the police buildings and left there—with Mrs. Hatch—in a room, to wait until someone, seated in the adjacent room, was ready to question me. Mr. Hatch and the man who accompanied him disappeared from my sight.

On the wall facing me in the room in which I was waiting, I noticed large boards bearing statistical sketches in different colours, supposed to represent the progress of "de-Nazification" in Germany, thanks to the organised efforts of the Occupying Powers and of the Germans won over to the cause of Democracy.

I could not help drawing Mrs. Hatch's attention to those boards—for the sight of the coloured lines standing for thousands of "de-Nazified" Germans made me wild; and she happened to be the only person in the room besides myself.

"Have you seen all this damned tommyrot stuck up, about the place?" asked I, although I had promised not to talk "politics" anymore. "What right have the rascals, anyhow, to try to 'de-Nazify' people, after pretending, all these years, to be the champions of 'free' self-determination? And what if some people choose to use their freedom to put themselves, willingly and joyfully, under the discipline of National Socialism? I did that, precisely—I who am not a German; I who was brought up in the most democratic of all countries, the cradle of the silliest ideas about 'equality' in modern times. Let them draw their blue and yellow lines, and let them multiply the number of 'de-Nazified' Germans by twenty, to see how many thousands of marks they have pocketed![28] I am a permanent slap, a living defiance to all their 'de-Nazification' schemes—and so will be, at the first opportunity, I hope, their forced converts to Democracy all over Germany!"

Poor Mrs. Hatch replied to my tirade in a sweet voice:

"I have never believed in statistics."

"Nor have I."

"Then, why are you so upset?"

"*They* believe in them," said I. And all my hatred for the Allied Occupation since 1945, and for the Allies themselves since 1939, could be felt in the way I stressed that word *they*.

"No, they don't; that much I can tell you," replied Mrs. Hatch. "But even if they did, why should *you* care? It is in your interest to deceive them, for the time being, is it not?"

"I loathe them!" I exclaimed, without paying serious attention to her last words—which I would remember months later. "But then, if you are right," asked I, in reply to her first statement, "why all these figures, all these coloured lines, all these lies—and all the grim apparatus of bribery and fear that stands behind them?"

"I don't know. Perhaps to occupy a few thousands of worthless clerks who would otherwise be unemployed," admitted the sweet—and patient—lady.

I wanted to say: "If that be indeed what you believe, then why do you stay here on the side of Germany's oppressors?"; to which Mrs. Hatch would probably have replied that she was no militant idealist of any sort, and that she had two children. But I had no time to speak. The door was opened, and I was called into the adjacent room. I took leave of Mrs. Hatch, asking her to excuse me if I had really hurt her feelings on any occasion, now or the day before. She wished me "good luck" in my coming trial and left the place.

---

[28] Every German who was a member of the N.S.D.A.P. was compelled to have a certificate of "de-Nazification" in order to be allowed to work. And he had to pay at least 20 marks to the Allied authorities, for such a certificate.

There were several men in the room into which I was ushered. One of them again asked me many of the questions that had already been posed to me. I replied in exactly the same manner as at first. Then, I was told that I would be prosecuted for violation of article 7 of law 8 of the Occupation Statute in Germany, which forbids any sort of propaganda "aimed at keeping alive the military or Nazi spirit."

A tall Englishman of agreeable manners, wearing a police uniform, asked me if I cared to make a short statement—just a sentence or two—expressing in a nutshell the purpose of my "offence." This statement would be read in public at my trial, said he; but I was not compelled to make it if I did not wish to. In a flash of imagination, I pictured myself a hall full of people—mostly, at least, if not all Germans—and my words read to them an encouragement to all those who shared my faith; a warning to the others. Surely, I was not going to miss such an opportunity of telling the martyred nation why I had come.

"I am only too glad to speak," said I with a bright smile. "Know, then, that it is not merely the military spirit, in the narrow sense of the word, but National Socialist consciousness in its entirety that I have struggled to strengthen—that I will again struggle to strengthen, as soon as I get a chance to do so—for in my eyes, National Socialism exceeds Germany, and exceeds our times."

My words were taken down. None of the men present made any comments.

I was told that I would appear on that very afternoon before the Lower Control Commission Court, but that my final trial would probably not come before several weeks' time. They would first have to sort out and to read the numerous books, papers, letters, notes, etc., that were in my luggage, and of which many would constitute evidence against me. "Evidence in my favour," thought I, taking a longer view of things, and also well-knowing that the police authorities would find, in all that written matter, more than enough to impress them about my absolute sincerity. I remembered there were, in my bag, two letters addressed to me, during one of my short stays in London, by Mr. B. a very fine English friend of mine—the inmate of an anti-Nazi concentration camp in England, during the war. Both ended with the sacred formula: "Heil Hitler!" The police would not be able to harm the gentleman, at any rate. There is no law forbidding a British subject, writing to another British subject in England or within the British Commonwealth, to end his or her letters with those two words. Moreover, the address in the corner of the page was no longer his. He was now far away, overseas—in safety. Yet nobody, admittedly, save a hundred percent National Socialist, would receive letters ending with "Heil Hitler!" in 1948. And I was glad at the thought that our enemies would become more and more convinced, as they went through my things, that I was no paid agent of any description.

But why speak of Mr. B's letters? There was, in my attaché case, the beginning of my book *Gold in the Furnace*,[29] that fiery profession of Nazi faith written in my own handwriting, and dedicated "to the martyrs of Nuremberg"; and there was the first part of *The Lightning and the Sun*,[30] a philosophical book that I was writing slowly, along with the other, and that is—perhaps even more than the other, for those who can read between the lines—the expression of all we stand for, the justification of all we did.

I recalled in my mind the last paragraph of the Chapter 3 of the former book, which I had written in a café in Bonn on the 12th of February 1949, a few days before my arrest:

Today, we suffer. And tomorrow, we might have to suffer still more. But we know it is not forever—perhaps even not for long. One day, those of us to whom it will be granted to witness and to survive the coming crash, will march through Europe in flames, once more singing the Horst Wessel Song—the avengers of their comrades' martyrdom, and of all the humiliations and of all the cruelties inflicted upon us since 1945; and the conquerors of the day; the builders of future Aryandom upon the ruins of Christendom; the rulers of the new Golden Age.[31]

I knew the words by heart; they came after a vitriolic impeachment both of Communism "that most cunning of all mass delusions," and of Democracy "the rule of the scum." I was glad to know that Germany's oppressors would read *that* (the philosophical book they were perhaps incapable of understanding) and learn what at least one non-German National Socialist thought of them. But at the same time, I was convinced that they would destroy the unfinished book—I surely would have destroyed any equally eloquent anti-Nazi writing that would have fallen into my hands, if I had been in power, and, which is more, *I* would have destroyed the writer with it. I felt profoundly sad at the thought, for I loved that book of mine, the youngest and fairest child of my brain. In none of my former writings, had I so passionately poured out my whole be-

---

[29] *Gold in the Furnace* (Calcutta: A. K. Mukherji, 1952).—Ed.
[30] *The Lightning and the Sun* (Calcutta: Savitri Devi Mukherji, 1958).—Ed.
[31] *Gold in the Furnace*, 3rd ed, p. 32.—Ed.

ing as in this one. Had they sworn to me that they would spare it on the condition that I should be killed or tortured, I would have chosen death or torment without hesitation—anything to preserve the sincerest words I had ever written, so that, one day, a few among my Führer's people might read them and say of me: "She loved and admired us."

I would, thought I, do my best to save them. So I went up to the man who had just told me about my trial, and spoke to him. "My own writings will serve as evidence," said I, "but may I ask if they will be given back to me after the trial is over? Or can I be again tried on account of some of them, especially of a certain book which I was writing?"

"In this trial, you are charged with distributing tracts and sticking up posters, not with writing books. Your leaflets and placards are the only things with which we are concerned."

"Then, my unfinished books will not be destroyed?" asked I, hardly daring to be hopeful.

"That, I cannot tell you. It all depends upon the Court. If the Court judges your writings subversive, it will order their destruction; otherwise not," replied the man, somewhat impatiently.

I, who knew how "subversive" were the three first chapters of my *Gold in the Furnace*—even the first part of *The Lightning and the Sun*, of which the spirit is no less Nietzschean—felt all hope abandon me.

I looked sadly out of the window, at the sunny courtyard and at the bright blue sky. I pictured to myself, beyond the wall that faced me, the hundreds of miles of ruins I knew so well. "When we have lost the war, when my Führer's people are persecuted, when all I have loved lies in the dust, it is mean of me to grieve over my book," thought I. "They have burnt all manner of Nazi literature they could lay hands upon, beginning with thousands of copies of *Mein Kampf;* why should they not destroy also my insignificant prose?" But still I was depressed. Then, from the serene depth of bygone ages, everlasting words of wisdom emerged into my consciousness—words of the Bhagavad-Gita, of which I had never experienced the overwhelming beauty as I did now: "Considering as equal pleasure and pain, gain and loss, victory and defeat, gird thyself for the battle; thus thou shalt not incur sin"[32] . . . "in a spirit of sacrifice, devoid of attachment, perform thou dutiful action, O son of Kunti."[33]

And tears came into my eyes as I remembered the divine sentences. And I prayed ardently that I might—even now—serve the Nazi cause with efficiency and perfect detachment—indifferent to all forms of per-

---

[32] The Bhagavad-Gita, II, verse 38.
[33] The Bhagavad-Gita, III, verse 9.

sonal glory or personal satisfaction; to everyone and to everything save God—i.e., the truth—and the Führer, God's living mouthpiece; and duty.

* * *

I was then sent to the *"Stahlhaus,"* now the Headquarters of the British Civil Police. An English policewoman, Miss Taylor, was put in charge of me. I told her why I was under arrest, in case she did not know it already. I did not want her—or anybody—to take me for an ordinary "criminal case." After a few minutes, she asked me the tiresome old question that I have answered a hundred thousand times since my return to Europe: "You don't really mean that you condone the awful things that the Nazis did?"

"What 'awful things'?" asked I, with undisguised contempt: I never loathe the Democrats' hypocrisy so intensely as when that question is posed to me.

"Well, violence of all sorts: killing off people by the thousand," replied Miss Taylor.

"And why not," said I, "if those people were obstacles to the stability of the régime and to the creation of a more beautiful world? I believe in removing obstacles. Moreover"—I added—"I am thoroughly disgusted with the scruples of people who take slaughterhouses and vivisection chambers as a matter of course and yet dare to protest against our real or supposed 'atrocities' upon objectionable human beings."

"But they were human beings, however objectionable you might find them."

"I have never shared our opponents' superstitious regard for the two-legged mammal," said I, with an expression of contempt. "I consider *all* life sacred—until it becomes an obstacle to the higher purpose of Creation, which we, National Socialists, have set ourselves to forward. And alone selfish or idiotic human beings—the most dangerous of all beasts—can stand in the way of *that*."

"But there is no higher purpose than the happiness of all men," said the policewoman, whether in earnest or not, I do not know.

"You might think so; I don't," answered I. "My firm conviction—which I suppose I can express freely, as you Democrats stand, or pretend to stand for 'freedom'—is that the highest purpose of life is to forward the growth of a superior humanity, whose role is to rule a healthy world. No means are too ruthless that can bring us nearer to that goal."

The policewoman was not only cultured, but intelligent. She understood that my attitude was rooted in life-long reactions—in my very nature—and that it was, therefore, unshakable. Neither on that day nor later on—on the several occasions she accompanied me to and fro between my prison and Düsseldorf—did she ever again speak to me as though I might be brought to accept the current scale of values of what I call the decadent world. She admitted that I was "absolutely consistent"—and if she thought "appallingly consistent," she did not say so. And she declared that she herself would react as I do, "if she had my convictions."

I lunched with her, insisting, as always, on vegetarian food for myself, after which I was taken back to the building in which I had spent the morning, nay to the room where I had waited with Mrs. Hatch for them to call me for cross-questioning—the room of which the walls bore coloured statistical accounts of the "progress of 'de-Nazification' in Germany."

One of the men in Civil Police uniform whom I had met in the morning—I think he was called Manning, but I am not quite sure—entered that room with me and shut the door. I scented that something different from my other sittings was intended to take place, and mentally I prepared myself for the worst, praying to the Gods to assist me.

Mr. Manning—or the gentleman whom I took to be Mr. Manning—sat down and bade me take a seat opposite him. "Now," said he, in a soft, low, insinuating voice, "you see we are not doing any harm to you. You cannot complain of our behaviour, can you?"

"Up till now, I admit I cannot."

"Then, would you not care to help us a little by telling us who printed those posters of yours? You can be quite sure nobody will ever know that you gave us the information. Moreover, we assure you that no harm will be done to the printer or those connected with him."

I felt a wave of indignation rush to my heart as if the man had insulted me in the filthiest language—and more so. I could have strangled him with my own hands with delight, not for wishing to know who had printed my propaganda (that was only natural on his part) but for having the impudence to imagine that I could give away a comrade. Who did the fellow take me for? I looked at him straight in the face and replied with contempt: "I am no traitor!"

"That, we know," said the man, his voice still softer; "we know. But could one call this treachery? We shall find out anyhow."

"Then, find out if you can," answered I, "and don't ask me. You will never get a word from me."

Then, recalling the threat of the German policeman in Cologne on the night of my arrest, I pursued: "If you are really keen on making me speak, why don't you try on me your wonder-working Democratic 'methods'—those you have used upon thousands of my betters, you who criticise us for being 'brutal', you who pretend to have fought to deliver the world from our impending tyranny? Come along! Don't be squeamish! Remember that I too am a Nazi—a monster by definition—and by far nearer the conventional type of Nazi that you people hate and dread, than most others. If I were in your place, and you in mine, I would not waste precious time arguing. I would do what all representatives of well-organised services of coercion have done from the beginning of the world, and will do till the world ends. Do the same!—and let me, one day, give public lectures about the episode, to my own delight, and to that of all the enemies of Democracy! In the meantime, I might not speak—I sincerely hope I shall not, although it is always rash to boast before hand. But you will at least have done your best for the defence of the decaying order in Western Europe—if you really care about it as much as the Allied controlled press would lead us to believe."

The man—on behalf of the Democratic world—listened to that bitingly ironical discourse with apparent equanimity. And he replied, again in his soft, low insinuating voice; "No, we shall not apply any sort of physical pressure in *your* instance; it is out of the question . . ."

"You prefer to apply it in the instance of defenceless Germans, who cannot expose your 'humanitarian' lies before the world and tear your prestige to pieces, because you do not allow them to travel," I burst out, interrupting him. But the man seemed to pay no attention to what I said.

"We shall not submit *you* to any sort of physical pressure," he repeated, ignoring my impeachment; "but we give you the confidential assurance that, if you tell us who printed your posters, we shall spare your writings—all of them, however subversive they be."

I marvelled, inwardly, at the psychological insight of that man. He had guessed that the irretrievable loss of my unpublished books would be a greater torment to me than any agony of the body. But even that did not work. On the contrary. A strange reaction took place in me: I felt that my last link with the world of appearances had been snapped; that henceforth, I was free—freer than the roaring Ocean that no man can control. In that fraction of a second, under the pressure of emergency, I had rid myself of my strongest attachment: the attachment to my life's creation.

"Burn them, then," said I, with exaltation. "Burn them!—although I know I could never write them again as they are. Better not a trace be left of whatever I produced, rather than I become unworthy of my Führer and of my faith—of all I have lived for, all my life!"

My eyes were filled with tears. But I regretted nothing, and meant every word I said. I possessed nothing nearer to my heart than my own sincere writings, the children of my soul, my only children. And the austere joy I now experienced was—I presume—akin to the joy of a mother who sends her sons to a dutiful death, rather than incur shame.

The man gazed at me, and seemed surprised. In vain, he coaxed me for a long time more. "I thought you were extremely anxious about the fate of your writings," said he.

"I was," I replied. "I would undergo any torture, if that could save them! But I will not save them at the cost of honour. I am a National Socialist and a worshipper of the Sun—not of any Jewish god or prophet. And I am the granddaughter of William Nash, an English gentleman."

The man again looked into my face, and said with an accent of sincerity, lowering his voice still a little more: "I understand you."

I then appeared before the Lower Control Commission Court, in a different building. Not a real sitting of the Court, but just a dull procedure—quickly over, I must say.

The man in uniform who had been cross-questioning me asked the Court that I should be kept on remand for a fortnight, and submitted both to a physical and to a mental examination by British doctors. The Court agreed. And I left the hall, followed by Miss Taylor, who was now to take me to my new abode: the women's prison in Werl, near Soest, Westphalia, some eighty or ninety miles from Düsseldorf.

In the corridor, as I came out, I saw my comrade and collaborator, Herr W., dragged along by a tough German policeman who held him by his sleeve. He looked thin, exceedingly pale, and dejected—the shadow of himself. He had swollen eyelids and (at least, it seemed to me) a blue mark—doubtless the mark of a blow—upon his face. I was neither enchained nor held, and I had undergone no ill-treatment, thanks to my British-Indian passport. I gazed at him—who fortunately did not see me—and remembered the last words he had addressed to me in the empty train: "I shall never betray you . . . The mark does not come off . . . I was in command of S.S. men." And tears filled my eyes. I *knew* he had not betrayed me.

And I felt small before him—and all the others, who had suffered ill-treatment, ever since 1945. What had I not done to acquire, in war time, that British-Indian passport of mine, so that I might, under a pretext, leave India to serve our cause more efficiently on my own continent! And now I felt ashamed of the advantages that the document gave me. I regretted that I was not treated like the others—like those who share my Nazi faith; my equals; and my betters; all those I love.

Chapter 4

ON REMAND

On that day, the 22nd[1] of February, in the evening, after a beautiful motor drive, I arrived before the doors of the Werl prison. Miss Taylor had conversed with me with the utmost courtesy and cordiality during the journey—about Marcus Aurelius, whom she knew well and admired; about Christianity, which she forgave me for detesting; about the religion of the Sun as it appears in the hymns of King Akhnaton of Egypt, and in the immemorial hymns of the Rig-Veda, the most ancient verses that have come down to us in an Aryan tongue. We talked also a little of more modern subjects. And she began to realise—perhaps—how thoroughly National Socialism expressed my whole Pagan philosophy of life, and how inseparable that whole philosophy is from my very being.

I got down from the car and waited. It was already dark. A warder in greyish-green uniform opened the door and let us into a room on the left. Another man, also in uniform, seated at a table in that room, signed a paper that Miss Taylor handed over to him, acknowledging that I had actually been transferred into his custody, in other words, that she was no longer responsible for me. He also asked me a few questions. Then a young woman in khaki uniform, who had been called for, came in and bade me follow her. I took leave of Miss Taylor, and crossed with my new custodian a courtyard on all sides of which were high walls, nearly entirely covered with creeper. Then, the wardress opened a large iron door with one of the two huge keys that she held, and shut it behind me. I followed her along a path with a high wall on one side—the wall that separated the prison grounds from the street, I presumed—and, on the other, a building from which came a smell of food—the kitchens of the prison. That path led us into an alley in the midst of an open, grassy space, surrounded with buildings—four-storied ones on the left, and in the distance; a one-storied, elongated one, on the right. In all I saw hundreds of barred windows, now most of them lighted, each one of which—I guessed—corresponded to a prisoner's cell. Then, again the

---

[1] The first edition says the 21st, but this must be a misprint. Savitri Devi was arrested on the night of 20–21 February 1949 and spent the night in jail. She spent the next night, of 21–22 February, at the home of Mr. Hatch. On the 22nd, she was taken to Düsseldorf and then on to Werl.—Ed.

wardress opened a huge door with her key, and I crossed a sort of covered yard—a paved space between two workshops—in the dark. Another
door was opened before me—and, as always, shut after me, immediately
after I had passed—and I emerged into a rectangular courtyard, surrounded on all sides with the walls of a one-storied building. The ground
floor was dark. But the windows on the first floor—all barred, like those
I had seen from the much broader open space which I had just crossed on
my way—were lighted. Two flights of steps, each of them protected by a
roof, led to the first floor from that courtyard. We went up the one on the
left. The door at the top was again shut. The wardress opened it, walked
in, and turned to the right. I found myself in a long, dimly lighted, fairly
wide, and perfectly silent corridor with rows of doors on each side of it.
The wardress took me along, right to the end, and ushered me into a
small room in which were an elderly lady in dark-blue uniform, obviously an important member of the prison staff, and a young woman, seated
at a table before what seemed to me to be a book of accounts. Along the
walls of the room ran large shelves upon which heaps of clothes and lin-
en were neatly piled.

The elderly lady—who, with her wavy hair, now white, her blue eyes,
and regular features, must have been pretty in her youth—took down my
name, age, etc., and asked me the nature of my "offence"—at the hearing
of which both her face and that of the wardress brightened imperceptibly.
Those German women did not dare to tell me: "You are on our side;
good for you!" But I felt at once that, in their eyes, I was innocent, if not
praiseworthy, although surely stupid—stupid enough to have let myself
get caught.

"Well, those are your convictions," said the white-haired lady. She
made no further remarks but asked me—as that had to be written down
as a matter of routine—what was my religion.

"I am a worshipper of the Sun," replied I, sincerely, not without causing a little surprise; far less, however, than there would have been, had I
not already stated that I was wedded to an Indian.

"Did you, then, adopt your husband's religion?" the old matron asked
me.

"Not at all—although, of course, he too pays daily homage to the
fiery Disk, as every true Brahmin does, in India. I evolved my present
religious outlook from the earliest days of my youth, and I can say that I
spent my life regretting that my country—Greece—ever left off worshipping her old natural and national Gods (Apollo in particular, the fairest of all) to turn to a doctrine imported from Palestine. I went to India
precisely in search of a civilisation as entirely free as possible from

Judeo-Christian influences of any sort."

"But you were christened?"

"I was."

"So you did, officially, belong to a Christian Church, in your youth?"

"To the Greek Church."

"And which service would you like to attend, here in prison: the Catholic or the Evangelical? They are the only two we have."

"I wish to attend neither," said I; "I only hope it is not compulsory."

"It is not. But you will find time long in your cell, on Sundays."

"I am prepared to put up with a little discomfort for the sake of consistency," I replied. "I have never loved the Christian mythology—or the doctrine. And the days I used to attend Church services on the sole ground that, historically, Christian pageantry has won itself a place in the life of every Aryan nation in the West—and that the music is sometimes beautiful—those days, I say, are far, far away; irretrievably gone."

I was classified as "dissident" in the catalogue, and taken to cell number 121, in the C wing of the prison, where I was to live as long as I remained "on remand." As I was a British subject, I was allowed to keep the civilian clothes that I was wearing—a dark-brown tailored suit and overcoat—and my attaché case, emptied of all its former contents except a few sheets of blank paper, a towel, a piece of soap, a looking glass, and the English translation of the Bhagavad-Gita. I deeply appreciated the gesture of the persons, whoever they be, who had left me that hallowed Scripture to read and to meditate upon in my cell.

The cell contained an iron bed, fixed to the wall; a table, a stool, and a cupboard. Light came from a high window—with iron bars on the outside—of which the topmost part alone could be unfastened to let in a little air. The floor was covered with earthen-coloured square bricks. In the thick door lined with iron, there was a small round hole in front of which hung, on the outside, a metal flap. By lifting that flap, one could at will look into the cell from the corridor; while the prisoner could never look into the corridor from the cell. The walls were whitewashed. The inner side of the door—the iron side—was painted in light grey. It all seemed—and was—perfectly clean—as it would be, in an establishment of which at least the material management was entirely in German hands.

"Leave your attaché case here, and come with me," said the wardress who was accompanying me; "before I lock you up, you must see 'Frau Oberin'." Frau Oberin, whose name I learnt much later,[2] was the person

---

[2] "Oberin" is not a name, but a title used to designate a woman in charge, such as the Mother Superior of a convent. In this case, the English equivalent appears to be Warden

in charge of the women's section of the prison, the *"Frauenhaus."*

I was ushered into a fairly large and very neat office room nearly opposite my cell, in which a young woman between twenty-five and thirty, dressed in black, was seated at a desk. She had brown hair, and blue eyes, and a sweet face. On the walls of the room I noticed one or two pictures—photos of classical paintings, chosen with much taste—and there were flowers on the windowsill and flowers in a vase on the desk before the young woman. "In former days," I could not help thinking with a certain sadness, "there would have been here also, no doubt, a lovely portrait of the Führer." It only occurred to me after a minute or so that, then, I would not have been there.

The wardress left the room. The young woman at the desk, who had returned my evening's greeting, had a look at my chart, which the wardress had handed over to her. "What is it that you are here for, may I ask you?" said she, addressing me after a moment. "You must excuse me; but I simply cannot remember what is forbidden by every article of every law—and, in your particular case, by 'article 7 of law 8 of the Occupation Statute.' Moreover, I am accustomed to prisoners, and can see by your face that you are no ordinary delinquent."

"I am here for Nazi propaganda," said I, with obvious pride.

"That!" exclaimed Frau *Oberin*—and an enigmatic smile gave her face a new expression. "Will you not sit down for a while and have a cup of coffee—of *real* coffee, I mean, not of *'Muckefuck'*?"

Was that the spontaneous reaction of "de-Nazified" Germany's officialdom at the news of National Socialist underground activities carried on by a foreigner? I ardently wished it were. Or was it just the personal reaction of this individual woman, who, incidentally, happened to hold a responsible post under the authority of the British occupants of the land? And if so, how far was she on our side, or—like good Mrs. Hatch—sympathetically disposed towards me merely as a person? Was the "real coffee" for the guiltless woman, who had neither stolen nor committed murder, or was it for the friend of Germany who had striven, in her humble way, to keep the Nazi spirit alive in the hearts of Hitler's persecuted people? In other words, was this young woman kind to me in spite of my being a National Socialist, or *because* I was a National Socialist? I did hope that the second possibility was the one corresponding to fact. But I could not ask—especially while Frau *Oberin* had made no comments whatsoever about my "offence."

I seated myself in the comfortable armchair that she had offered me.

---

of the women's section. Her real initials were F. M. See pp. 118 and 168 below.—Ed.

Soon a lovely smell of coffee filled the room, as the young woman prepared the exotic beverage upon a small electric stove which she had tak-
en from a cupboard. She poured out a cup of it for me and another one
for herself. She talked to me in a friendly manner, as though I had not
been a prisoner and she the head of the Women's section of the prison.

"When did you first come to Germany?" she asked me, after I had
told her that my home was in India.

"On the 15th of June 1948," replied I.

"And you had never come before?"

"Alas, no. I was six thousand miles away, during the great days," said
I, with infinite, sincere sadness.

"It is a pity."

It was, indeed. But Frau *Oberin* did not stress the point. She asked me
about the customs and beliefs of India, and about the women's dress, the
sari, of which I described the grace to her, as best I could.

"A crowd of Indian women on a festive day, in the atmosphere of one
of those old temples of which you spoke a while ago," said she, "must be
a beautiful sight."

"It certainly is," answered I. And I related to her, as vividly as my
knowledge of German permitted, the *"Vaishakha Purnima"* festival as I
had admired it in the great temple of Rameshwaram, in the extreme south
of India, on the 17th of May 1935: the procession, headed by handsome
half-naked torch bearers, and by magnificently harnessed sacred ele-
phants, along the huge pillared corridors of the temple, at night; the
crowd—men in spotless white and women draped in silk of all colours
with jasmine flowers in their black glossy hair, and flowers in their
hands—gathered around the sacred tank to honour the passage of the
chariot carrying the statues of the God incarnate, Rama, and of his con-
sort, Sita, hardly visible under heaps of flowers; and the reflection of the
full moon in the sacred tank; and the unreal splendour of the deeply
sculptured surrounding colonnades in the light of the full moon; and,
above all that, the glory of the tropical sky—violet-blue, unbelievably
luminous in its depth—with one tall coconut tree, one alone, shining like
silver in its midst, from behind the intricate architecture of the temple.

Frau *Oberin* gazed at me in wonder. "How lucky you are to have such
remembrances!" said she. And for a while her blue eyes seemed to follow, beyond time and space, the stately outlandish scenes that I had tried
to evoke. Then she added: "It astounds me that you could leave India and
your husband and household to come to us and do what you did, after we
had lost the war."

On impulse, I wanted to reply: "Do you take me for one of those turncoats who, after praising all that the Führer did for fifteen or twenty years, began to change their minds when the Anglo-Americans landed in Normandy, and who, after the Capitulation, concluded that Democracy was decidedly the only salvation for mankind?" But I said nothing of the kind. I knew in my heart that Frau *Oberin* had never doubted my sincerity, and that she meant no harm. Recalling the age-old festival that I had just described, I simply said: "India means more to me than most people think, and not less; and so does Germany. Rama, the virtuous warrior, whom the people of the Far South worship to this day in the great temple by the sea, *is* the half-historical half-legendary Aryan conqueror of the luxuriant South. In him, the caste-ridden masses of India bow down to the hallowed Race that once brought India the Vedas, and the cult of male gods, and warrior-like ideals, along with the everlasting principle of the natural hierarchy of races. My contact with Hinduism has only given me further reasons to feel proud of being an Aryan. It has, if anything, made me a better National Socialist. Few people realise that, since the days of the Aryan conquest of India—the dawn of Sanskrit civilisation— never and nowhere in the world has a serious attempt been made to bring the natural, the divine Order into existence in living society, save here in Germany, under the Führer's inspired rule. It was my duty to come over anyhow—all the more so, now that the war was lost; now that the whole Aryan world had turned against its Saviour. As for my husband, I have given him no reason to blame me—except that I was foolish enough, for once, to allow the police to detect me in my activities. But at that he will not be surprised: he knows what an ass I can make of myself in practical matters."

Frau *Oberin* laughed. We talked a long time more—mostly about India. The young woman had read the Bhagavad-Gita in a German translation, with a sincere effort to understand it. And although she quite frankly admitted that much of it remained obscure to her—as I admit much does to me—she was sensitive to the beauty of its essential teaching of action with detachment. I quoted to her one or two of the classical passages that I happened to know by heart.

"I am now beginning to understand why we were told such a lot about ancient India in the Hitler days," said she at last.

I opened my mouth to speak, but I said nothing. I was not quite sure whether I should add anything to all that I had already said. A few words, thought I, often leave a deeper impression than a good many. But Frau *Oberin* spoke again. "I am also beginning to understand one of the reasons why there are, and were—even under the Third Reich—so few really genuine National Socialists among us," she said.

"And why?" asked I.

"Because the hold of Christianity upon us is still very strong—stronger than it seems at first sight, even upon those of us who reject the bondage of the Church."

"I am sorry the Roman emperors did not nip in the bud what they then called the 'new superstition'," said I, repeating what I had written in an Indian newspaper in 1945. "They would have rendered a service to the Aryan race."

But time was passing. "I shall send for you sometimes, and have further talks with you," said the young woman as I left the room. And she told me also that she would not deprive me of the few gold bangles, chains, and rings that I was wearing. "They suit you; as long as you are on remand you can keep them," she assured me. I thanked her—for I now knew that, for the time being at least—I would not be separated from the precious little glass portrait that hung around my neck.

* * *

The wardress on duty brought me my supper in my cell—some macaroni, bread, and marmalade; for I had told the man who had received me at the door downstairs that I ate no flesh.

I was told that the light in my cell would have to remain on all night "unless the English governor of the prison permitted the contrary." I—who cannot sleep with the light on—hung my clothes over the electric bulb in order to make the room as dark as possible, and pulled the bed clothes over my head, in addition to that.

Piously, I held against my breast the portrait of the Führer that I wore on my gold chain. I felt happy at the thought that I was now locked up in that cell for the love of him. Even there, between four walls, nay, especially there, I would bear witness to his greatness, to the everlastingness of his Idea, to the mission of the people whom he so loved. And my testimony would be all the more convincing for the fact that I was not one of that people. Then, I remembered the woman who had given me the portrait[3]—not long before; since my latest return from England. I recalled her fine, rather sad face, that used to take on an inspired expression as she evoked the joy and glory of Hitler's days. She was one of the most lovable National Socialists I knew personally. I had spent a couple of days under her roof somewhere in the French Zone. And she had given me that invaluable little likeness as a remembrance of the Greater

---

[3] Fräulein B. of Koblenz. See pp. 386–89 below.—Ed.

Germany that I had not seen, as a token of her friendship, and as something to replace the gold swastika that had dropped off my chain in London, in November 1947, and that I had never found again. And as I had somewhat hesitated to take it—knowing it was the only one of its kind that she possessed—she had told me: "It does not matter. I give it to you with all my heart because you are worthy of it. *You are one of us.*" I had thanked her with tears in my eyes. Nothing touches me more and gives me greater joy than the love and confidence of other Nazis, especially of those who have stood the test of suffering as that woman has.

And now I wondered how I could, without the authorities suspecting any connection between my friends and myself, let her—and a few others—know that I was in captivity. Those in the French Zone at least would not learn it from the newspapers: I remembered that Monsieur P., a French official in Baden Baden, had once told me that "acts of resistance were never given any publicity" in the papers under French licence, "in order not to encourage further trouble." I thought of the three thousand posters that were in my trunk in the care of friends. How would I now write—clandestinely—to those people and ask them to distribute the propaganda themselves, as I could no longer do so? And I hoped and prayed that none of those with whom I had come in touch would suffer on account of my arrest. If my trial was really "about the posters alone," as the Englishman in Düsseldorf had assured me, there was no earthly reason why they should, for I had, indeed, in this matter, acted entirely on my own initiative; nay, against the advice of one or two other National Socialists—far more intelligent than myself—who had warned me that activities of such a spectacular nature were "yet premature." But one could never be sure. Suspicion and fear, and not coolly thought out reasons suggest to the occupants of a defeated country the steps they take against all manner of underground resistance. I knew that, and consequently, felt uneasy. The thought worried me a long time before I could go to sleep, on that and the following nights. It was to worry me bitterly all the time I remained in prison—and some months after my release.

* * *

I was awakened early in the morning, as the wardress on duty opened my cell. A prisoner, dressed in blue, and wearing a brown jacket and a light-grey apron—like the one I had seen, the evening before, in the old matron's room—came in to remove the sanitary pail, and brought it back after a while, well-cleaned, and smelling of phenol. She also brought me a jug of water. I returned her *"Guten Morgen!"* and got out of bed.

"Oh, you need not get up at once," said she; "you are only on re-mand." She had a coarse, but sympathetic face. I wanted to speak to her.

"I shall not sleep again anyhow; so I may as well get up," said I.

"If you want some more water or anything else," she continued, "you just have to press upon that electric switch. It will light a bulb above your door in the corridor. The wardress on duty will see it and ask you what you need, and send for me (or another one of us) to give it to you."

"I know; the other wardress, who was here last night, has explained that to me. Still I thank you for telling me. I *would* like a little more water, if possible."

"I'll bring you some."

The door of the cell was again locked, after she had gone out.

Then came my breakfast, brought in by another prisoner—a heavily built young woman, with a red round face, dark hair, and grey eyes.

"All that!" I could not help exclaiming as I saw the amount of food she had laid upon the table. There was a pint of hot tea, with milk and sugar; a large tin can of porridge; six slices of beautiful white bread—such as I had not eaten even in post-war England, let alone in starving Germany—a piece of butter, and a large spoonful of orange marmalade. "Is it all for me?" I asked the wardress, a very sweet, kind-looking, blue-eyed blonde.

"Yes, of course," said she.

"But I have never had such bread, even when I was free. And I could not eat so much anyhow. Are they giving me a special diet because I am a 'political case'?"

"No. The 'political cases' here are treated exactly like the ordinary criminals—given in the morning one single slice of dry, black bread, and a tin of *'Muckefuck'* (chicory) without sugar or milk. You are given a special diet because you are a British subject."

"But I hate the Occupation as much as any German can."

"That makes no difference. In their eyes, you have a British passport; that's enough."

"Can I give a slice of my white bread to this woman?," asked I, see-ing with what longing eyes the prisoner was gazing at the quantity of food she had brought me.

"You can," whispered the wardress; "but don't allow anyone to see you, for it is against the rules."

"I am accustomed to do things against those people's rules," said I, referring to the present-day masters of Germany. I smeared a piece of bread with a little butter and jam, and gave it to the woman. "Thank you!" exclaimed the latter. "Oh, I do thank you!" She folded the bread in two, put it in her pocket, and disappeared, as another wardress was calling her from the corridor, to help in the distribution of black bread and chicory to the bulk of the prisoners. She would eat the "delicacy" in her cell, as soon as she would be off duty. It was probably the first slice of white bread and the first butter she had tasted since the Capitulation. For the millionth time, I recalled in my mind the ruins and desolation I had seen, and the appalling starvation that had succeeded, since 1945, the horror of the phosphorus air raids. "Poor dear Germany—my Führer's country!" thought I, as tears filled my eyes.

Turning to the wardress who still stood in my cell, I asked her: "Could you not manage to give my porridge and my tea, and four slices of bread, to some of those who are here for the sake of the same Idea as I—to my comrades, the so-called 'war criminals'? As there is not enough for all, could you give it to . . . the best ones; you understand what I mean . . . to the sincerest ones; those . . ."

"I understand," she replied; "and I'll willingly do as you say. But not now at once. Later on; when there is next to nobody in the corridors . . . They must not know, you see, or else there will be trouble."

"Thank you!" said I, "I cannot tell you how grateful I am to you. It is not much, I know. But it is now all I can do for the people who have fought for the same ideals as I; the people whom I love and admire."

"Be sure I shall help you as much as I can," said the woman in a very low voice. "I was in the Party myself . . . and so were several others of us. We understand you—and love you—although we cannot speak. Keep the food in some corner. I shall come to fetch it later on. *Auf Wiedersehen!*"

I could not see the sky from my cell, for the windowpanes were made of non-transparent glass. Yet, I was happy.

Having no pen and ink—not even a pencil—I could not write. I paced the room, from the wall below the window to the door and back, over and over again, like a captive tigress in her cage. I was impressed by the similarity of my position to that of a wild beast in a "zoo." "But I have my great love and my great ideals, and pride to uplift me and sustain me," I reflected. "What have the poor captured lions and tigers, panthers and leopards, to make up for the loss of freedom and adventure? I am a thousand times more fortunate than they." Never had I realised so vividly what a long-drawn torture the life of a wild beast in a cage must be— what a trial *my* life behind bars *would have been*, had I not been so proud and so glad to confess my Nazi faith in these times of persecution. And I prayed that in our new world, one day, I might raise my voice with sufficient eloquence to have all the beasts of the circuses and "zoos" given back to their native jungles.

Then, I thought of my friends far and near, especially of all the Germans with whom I had been directly or indirectly in touch just now or formerly. Again, I carefully went over all that I had said during my two days' cross-examination in Cologne and in Düsseldorf—I remembered it with extraordinary clarity, and felt I would remember it forever. And I decided that I had not let out a word, not made a gesture, not allowed my face to take on an expression that could possibly have implicated any other National Socialist. No, indeed I had not. I felt quite sure of it. And still, could one ever tell what the police are capable of finding out? I was happy, for I had nothing to blame myself for—not even my arrest, in fact, that had come as a consequence of someone else's. If "they" did discover things that I hoped and prayed they would never discover, it would be through no fault of mine. But then, my friends would suffer none the less—suffer, and (who knows?) perhaps believe, or be induced by our enemies to believe, that *I* had spoken when, in reality, I had not. I would have felt perfectly happy but for that ever-recurring worry; that feeling of impending danger for others in spite of all my efforts to protect them from it.

I sat down, and took to reading the Bhagavad-Gita—the only book I had in my cell, and the one which I would have chosen to read, anyhow, in my present mood, even if I had had a whole library at my disposal. I read the first lines that drew my attention as I opened the book—the following words of the God incarnate to the warrior in search of wisdom:

Even the devotees of other Shining Ones, who worship full of faith, they also worship Me, O son of Kunti, though contrary to the ancient rule.

For I am indeed the enjoyer and Lord of all sacrifice. *But they know Me not in essence, and hence they fall.*

They who worship the Shining Ones,[4] go to the Shining Ones; they who worship the ancestors, go to the Ancestors; to the Elementals go those who sacrifice to the Elementals; but my worshippers come unto Me.[5]

I withdrew my eyes from the book for a while and mused: "Today,

---

[4] The *Devas*.
[5] The Bhagavad-Gita, IX, verses 23, 24, 25.

also, there are thousands who, in the depth of their hearts, aspire after the Truth, and who yet pay homage to leaders who will not lead them to it; there are thousands who, nay, fight furiously against us, the witnesses of the Truth, without knowing what they are doing. They are misguided by externals, and ignore the eternal, the kernel of wisdom, the real Way of life and regeneration—the essence—and therefore they shall fall." I thought of the many who could have sided with us and who did not; who had begun to do so, but who had stopped on the way; who had preferred half-truths, afraid as they were to face the divine laws of Life—divine truth *in* life.

I read a little further: "Whatever thou doest, whatever thou eatest, whatever thou offerest or givest, whatever thou doest of austerity, O son of Kunti, do thou that as an offering unto Me."[6] And I prayed that I might always live up to that everlasting teaching. I identified, as I have from the start, our cause with the cause of Life, the cause of God.

But the nurse in charge of the infirmary unlocked my cell and stepped in to make my acquaintance. She was a short, thin, elderly woman of pleasant bearing, dressed in white.

"Well, my dear child, that which you have done is awful," said she, after inquiring about my health. But I knew by the tone of her voice that she was not really indignant. And her eyes were smiling while she spoke.

"Why, 'awful'?" asked I, returning her smile.

"But you are English—and you have been working against the Occupation, here in the British Zone! So you are a traitor to your country."

"I? To begin with, I really have no country. I mean, I am only half-English. What can I do about it? But above England, and above Greece—whose citizen I was before my marriage—and above any particular State with more or less artificial boundaries, and above any more or less pure section of the Aryan race, I place the Aryan race itself. To it, at least, I know I belong. To it—and to those who have fought to bring it back to its original purity, and to give it back its God-ordained mastery over the world—I have given my wholehearted allegiance. The traitors are not such ones as I; no! They are, on the contrary, the people of Aryan blood who have sacrificed the real, the highest interests of the race to the apparent immediate interest of some selfish State—whether the British State or any other—and to the welfare of a handful of selfish capitalists, mostly Jews. The greatest traitor of all is that complacent instrument of international Jewish finance who governed England during this war: Mr. Winston Churchill."

---

[6] The Bhagavad-Gita, IX, verse 27.

"Gosh, she's right!" burst out the wardress, who had come in while I was speaking, and who had been waiting for me to finish my tirade, to tell me to follow her to the Governor's office.

I walked out of my cell. The nurse gave me a sympathetic smile as she locked the door behind me.

* * *

I crossed, this time in the sunshine, the courtyard that I had seen the day before in the dark. I again passed between the two workshops, and emerged into the broad open space surrounded with buildings with five endless rows of barred windows (four stories and a ground floor). Around a more or less triangular lawn, men-prisoners were taking their morning walk, silently, two by two, under the supervision of their warders in greyish-green uniforms. They themselves wore brown trousers with a yellow stripe along the side. I had been told that there were, in the men's section, over one thousand eight hundred prisoners, out of which one third at least were political ones (so-called "war criminals") and more than another third . . . Poles, guilty, for the most part, of such offences as black-marketeering and robbery with or without violence. And as I passed by with the wardress, I looked at the men walking around the dewy, sunlit lawn. And each time I spotted out from among them an individual with a fine face and a noble bearing, I wondered if he were not one of the so-called "war criminals," and wished I could speak to him.

Again, as on the preceding evening, I followed my custodian past the kitchens of the prison, and I reached at last the courtyard from which I had taken my first glimpse of the premises of my new abode. I now saw in broad daylight the creeper that entirely covered the high walls of the buildings on my right and of the central building facing me. "How green and beautiful it must be in the spring!" thought I. I also noticed the clock at the top of the central building. It marked twenty past nine.

The door was opened, and I was ushered into an office on the right side of a fairly broad corridor. I stood before the desk of Colonel Edward Vickers, the British Governor of the prison—his name I had read on the door as I had entered.

"Yours is an offence of a very serious nature—an offence against our prestige in this country," said the Governor, addressing me. "However, it is the Court's business to judge you, not mine. All I wanted to tell you is that you are here in a prison, and that there are rules which you will have to obey, as every other prisoner. You will be fairly treated—in fact, you will enjoy the privileges of a British subject, since you are one. But I cannot allow you extra privileges. In particular, you cannot have food specially cooked for you in consideration of your strictly vegetarian habits. You shall be given all that is neither meat nor meat soup in the daily diet for British prisoners."

"I am grateful for that, and have never expected undue privileges," said I.

In fact, I wanted to ask as a favour that no distinctions whatsoever be made between the Germans and myself. (I now knew that *they* received no meat anyhow, so that my only existing scruples in matter of food did not come in the way). But I reflected that, if I accepted the special British diet—which was incomparably better than theirs—I would easily be able to pass over to them whatever niceties I might be given. I already knew that of the hundred and seventy or so inmates of the *"Frauenhaus,"* twenty-six were so-called "war criminals"—former members of the staff of German concentration camps and so forth, during the great days; people against whom our enemies had succeeded in loosening the fury of a whole world. I was impatiently looking forward to making their acquaintance, and to show them all marks of comradeship I possibly could. Naturally, all my best food would be for them—for those of them, I mean, that were *"in Ordnung,"*[7] i.e., real National Socialists, for I had already been told—to my amazement—that half of them were not. I therefore said nothing.

"A British doctor will examine you this afternoon, and another one in a day or two," continued the Governor. "Have you anything to say concerning your needs apart from food?"

"I would be grateful if the light in my cell could be switched off at night," said I. "I cannot sleep with it on."

"We generally keep it on so that the wardresses on duty might be able to look into the cells at night and see what the prisoners on remand are up to. We do so in case some might try to commit suicide," emphasised Colonel Vickers. "But I have no such fears in your case—goodness me, no! And if the doctor sees no objection, I am quite willing to allow you to have the light put out. Anything else?"

"I would also like to have a few sheets of paper and a pen and some ink, or even an ordinary pencil—if it is possible—to write a couple of letters."

What I wanted to do in reality was to try to remember the plan and at least certain passages of the three first chapters of my *Gold in the Furnace* and to rewrite these the best I could. And when that would be finished, I

---

[7] Literally "in order," colloquially "all right" or "okay."—Ed.

would continue the book clandestinely. The Englishmen would not be all day long at the *"Frauenhaus."* And I was beginning to feel that the members of the German staff, if not all *in Ordnung*, were at least all sufficiently hostile to the Occupation—all sufficiently German—to allow me to write in peace provided that *they* did not thereby get into trouble.

The Governor looked at me with suspicion, as though he had guessed my intentions. "I am certainly not going to give you paper for you to continue your propaganda in this prison," said he, sternly.

"I have not the slightest intention of carrying on any sort of propaganda, or of doing anything which is against the rules," answered I, with utmost naturalness. "I would only have liked to write a few letters. But if I cannot, of course, it does not matter."

Apparently, my naturalness was somewhat convincing, for the Governor was kind enough to give me a writing pad and a pencil. "I hope you understand," stressed he, however, "that every word you write will be censored."

"Most certainly," said I. But in the depth of my heart I thought: "That we shall see!" And after thanking the man I left the room, feeling that I had won a victory.

But the more I remembered his unfriendly face, abrupt speech, and patriotic indignation at the idea of my offence against British prestige in occupied Germany, the more I knew that the best I had to do was to avoid, as far as possible, all direct contact with him, and—whenever that could not be done—to speak as little as I could and to appear as dull, nay, as stupid, and therefore as harmless as my limited capacity for acting permitted. For, of all the representatives of the Allied Powers whom I had met up till now in the unfortunate land, he was the one who, for some mysterious reason—without having cross-examined me—seemed to consider me the least "harmless."

Back in my cell, I at once put down in black on white whatever I remembered of the three first chapters of *Gold in the Furnace*—and of the beginning of the fourth chapter, that I had started writing in a café in Hanover a day before my last journey to Cologne and my arrest. I also wrote down the titles of the proposed following chapters. Of these, there would now be one less, for the one I had planned about my intended visit to the "places of pilgrimage"—Braunau am Inn, Linz, Vienna, Munich, Nuremberg—could not be written. For even if I were to be released quicker than I expected, I would surely not be allowed to remain in Germany—and perhaps not be allowed to remain in Europe—unless, of course, they kept me long enough for the coming crash to free me. "Never mind," thought I, "I shall go to the places of pilgrimage one day, anyhow."[8]

Then, I set myself to continue the fourth chapter of my lost book—the story of the unforgettable night during which I had distributed my first five hundred leaflets. "By the way," I reflected, "why should I not, here, try to distribute a few copies of my latest ones among the members of the staff who seem to be in sympathy with me and also, if possible, among the so-called 'war criminals'?" (I was longing to get in touch with these.) So I wrote several times the text that I knew by heart—not upon the pad that Colonel Vickers had given me (that, I would use actually for letters, so that he might be convinced that I was a "good girl") but upon the paper which I already had, and which I also used for writing my book. I hid the copies carefully under a loose brick of the floor, between the back of my cupboard and the wall. Then, I returned to my Chapter 4.

The day passed quickly. With all the sincerity, all the love of my heart I projected onto those long, rough sheets of paper, in tight writing, the living picture of what I had, until my arrest, considered as the most beautiful night in my life—yes, even more beautiful than my watch on the slopes of roaring and burning Hekla, under the northern lights; even more beautiful than the night during which I had worshipped the midnight Sun, on the beach of Rif Stangir, facing the Arctic Ocean. I was happy—exceedingly happy. Even if the beginning of my book were destroyed, I would recreate it. I was already remembering more and more passages of it, which I wrote down immediately, each time, on separate sheets. It would never be like my first writing, but still, it would be the product of the same spirit. As for the first part of *The Lightning and the Sun*, I had some hope that they would perhaps not destroy it, after all: they would not be sufficiently perspicacious to see that, especially the second chapter on "Time and Violence," was the most glaring justification of all that we did and are prepared to do again—a systematic, philosophical justification, beyond the passions of yesterday and today.

In the afternoon, I was taken to the infirmary, where the British doctor examined me, in the presence of the matron of the prison, of the nurse in charge, and of a prisoner who worked there under the latter's supervision.

I could not take my eyes off that prisoner. She could have been about thirty-five or forty. In the shabby blue uniform she wore—like all the others—she displayed the classical beauty of a chieftain's wife in ancient Germany: a vigorous, well-built body, created to comfort a warrior and

---

[8] Savitri Devi visited most of these sites in 1953 and recounted her impressions in *Pilgrimage* (Calcutta: Savitri Devi Mukherji, 1958). Thus this unwritten chapter of *Gold in the Furnace* became the germ of an entire book.—Ed.

to give birth to heroic sons; a queenly bearing; a regular face in which one detected serene strength, and pride—and lofty dreams, also; authority and inspiration.

Her pale blonde hair, as glossy as silk, shone in a ray of evening sunshine. Her large, luminous blue eyes, of which the glance could, occasionally, I knew, be as hard as stone—now smiled at me. "You are the 'new one'; the one who is here for having defied our oppressors; I have heard of you," they seemed to tell me. And, while the doctor was examining my heart and liver and lungs, my black eyes, full of admiring friendliness, answered and said, "Yes, I am. And you are surely one of my comrades. My Führer's compatriot, you are too beautiful not to be also one of his faithful followers!" And I imagined her amidst the cheering crowds of the days of glory, greeting him as he passed by, with the ritual Nazi salute and the triumphal worlds: "Heil Hitler!" And tears came to my eyes.

Before telling me that I now could dress, the doctor looked at the glass portrait that hung around my neck on a gold chain. But he did not say a word. The old matron took me back to my cell.

The next day—which was the 23rd of February, and the nineteenth anniversary of Horst Wessel's death—I experienced one of the great moments of my prison life. I saw that prisoner of whom I have just spoken walk into my cell, with the nurse who accompanied her. She held in her hands a tray on which were disposed several objects—a plate, a bottle, a cup containing some pills—for it was her job, twice a day, to go round with medicine to all the cells of which the inmates needed any. I, however, needed none.

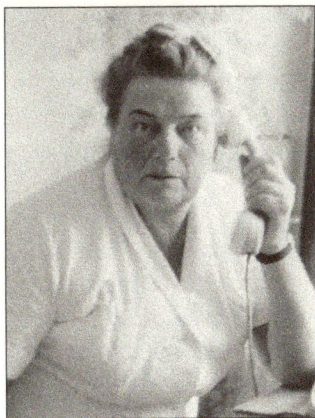

4. Hertha Ehlert in the 1960s
(Courtesy of Beryl Cheetham)

"We have come to pay you a visit—to see how you are," said the nurse with cordiality. "This woman, who is one of our 'war criminals' is keen on making your acquaintance."

I felt my heart leap with joy, and my face brighten. The nurse pulled the door shut and told the prisoner she could, for a minute, put her tray down, upon the table. The latter did so; and then, addressing me:

"Yes," said she, "I am a 'war criminal'. My name is H. E.[9] I am one of those from

[9] Hertha Ehlert—Ed.

the Belsen trial—the trial as a result of which poor Irma Grese was sentenced to death; you must know, surely, I was sentenced to fifteen years' imprisonment."

H. E. of the Belsen trial! Of course, I knew. I actually remembered her name for having seen it in the papers. And with irresistible vividness, the atrocious past suddenly rushed back to my consciousness. I heard, once more, the wireless of those days barking at me from all sides, wherever I went, the news of those sickening trials—the Belsen one and the others—along with its daily insults against all I loved and (what was perhaps even worse) its daily slimy sermons about the "re-education" of Germany in view of her "reintegration into a more humane and better world"! Those were the days in which, crushed to the depth, I had hated all men save the persecuted Nazi minority; in which I had aspired after nothing but the utter destruction of all humanity—including us, the henceforth powerless handful; including myself; the days in which, if I had not actually committed suicide, it had only been because, before I left this earth, I wanted to see that vulgar, idiotic, ungrateful Europe, then busy torturing her own élite—that Europe, who would have tortured our Hitler, her Saviour, had she had a chance to do so—writhe and groan, and bleed to death, one day, never mind under whose whip, to my delight.

Once more, for a minute, I felt all the bitterness, all the passion, all the despair of those weeks and months, as I saw, standing before me, calm and dignified, and friendly, that living ancient German—that eternal German—the embodiment and symbol of the regenerate master race, vanquished and persecuted, for the time being, by its inferiors.

I put my arms around her neck and my face against hers, and kissed her.

"There are no 'war criminals' in my eyes," said I; "there are only victims of the slaves of Jewry. You are my comrade—and my superior, for you have suffered. I am proud to meet you; and proud to share your captivity, now that I can do nothing else for our ideals."

A tear rolled down one of my cheeks as I spoke. The sky-blue eyes with golden eyelashes gazed at me intently, with tears also in them. H. E. embraced me as an old friend. "It is the first time I felt, since those horrid days, that someone really loves us," said she, with deep emotion.

"I have crossed land and sea—half the world—to tell you and all faithful Germans that I love and admire you, perhaps even more now, in the dark hours of tribulation, than when you ruled the earth from the Volga to the Atlantic and from the Arctic Ocean to the Libyan desert. I am glad I have come at last. I have seen your invincible spirit (I am nine months in

Germany). And I want it to triumph. And it *is* bound to triumph, sooner or later. The world belongs—in the long run—to the pure-blooded warriors who fight for health and order and truth to prevail."

"It does one good to hear you after all that we suffered," replied H. E. "It makes one feel that, even vanquished, we have not fought entirely in vain."

"In vain! Of course not," said I. "Already Adolf Hitler has raised Germany to the status of a holy land in the eyes of every worthy Aryan of the world. Otherwise, I would not be here."

H. E. gave me a proud and happy smile. "Tell me," said she, "what is it exactly you did."

"I distributed leaflets and stuck up posters bearing the following words—which I wrote myself—under a large black swastika," answered I. And I recited to her the whole text of my papers.

"What, now, in 1949?" she exclaimed, after listening attentively.

"Yes; and in 1948 also."

"Splendid! And how right you are about the hunger and humiliation! And about the plunder of our country by those hypocrites!" said she. "But are you sure, that 'he' is alive—really?"

"Yes."

"Oh, if only you were right!"

"I have confidence in those who know."

"But tell me again: *We* who are here and in a hundred other prisons for having done our duty with all our hearts, how long more have we to suffer? It is already nearly four years since I was arrested."

"None will remain here for more than a year or two longer," said I. "The inexorable Nemesis that awaits these people will come. Nothing can prevent it. And perhaps our enemies will set us free before it comes. They can do anything, when they are afraid. Perhaps you and I shall leave this place together, who knows? And I honestly tell you: I would then be even happier on account of your release than of my own. I mean it. For you have suffered enough."

"Oh, *now* it is nothing! You should know all we went through in 1945!"[10]

"You will tell me, one day."

"I shall. For we must meet again—and as often as we can."

"Surely. But listen; I was going to forget to tell you something very important: I have heaps of white bread, here, porridge, tea with milk and

[10] See *Gold in the Furnace*, ch. 6, "Chambers of Hell," 3rd ed., especially pp. 73–80 for Hertha Ehlert's experiences.—Ed.

sugar, and what not. As you can imagine, I only accepted the British diet in order that you, my comrades, might profit by it. One of the wardresses came this morning and asked me if I could not give her a slice of white bread for one prisoner who is sick and cannot digest the other. I gave it gladly. But I have plenty more, not only from this morning but from yesterday. Take it—and the tea and porridge also, and whatever I can put by—for yourself and for those who share our faith."

"I do thank you!" exclaimed H. E. "I love tea!—and so do the others. I'll give the porridge to H. B.[11]—another one from the Belsen trial. She works hard and is always hungry."

"What do you get to eat in the mornings?"

"A single slice of black bread and a tin of chicory, without sugar or milk," said my new friend, confirming what I had heard two days before.

"But they must not see you in the corridor with all that food and drink, or there will be trouble," put in the nurse, who seemed quite willing to help us provided it could be done quietly.

"I'll hide it all under my apron," said H. E.; "see; like this. Nobody will find out."

"Do come back when you can! I'll put by for you whatever I can spare. I don't eat much."

"But you must eat, to keep up your strength."

"The mere knowledge that I will soon be given, in my trial, a new opportunity for defying our enemies, makes me feel strong and happy. Every time I think of it . . . it is as though I had wings . . ."

My new friend pressed my hand in hers. "I must be going, now. I'll come back," said she. *"Auf Wiedersehen!"*

I gazed at her and smiled, and then took a glance at the nurse. "She may not be on our side, but she would do us no harm," I thought. And turning to H. E. and raising my right arm I said: "Heil Hitler!"

"Heil Hitler!" repeated she, as she returned my salute.

"You should not do that," said the nurse in a whisper, on the threshold of my cell. "You never know who might be looking in through the spy hole."

* * *

A day or two later, I was again taken to the infirmary. A different doctor—a short, thin man, with reddish hair—walked in just as I entered. "The mental doctor," thought I.

---

[11] Herta Bothe—Ed.

The nurse in charge and H. E. were not, this time, allowed to remain in the room.

The doctor bade me take a chair, seated himself opposite me, and started talking to me, apparently in a friendly manner, in reality with studied purposefulness—to find out if the working of my mind presented anything "pathological," in which case he would report me as "unfit to undergo trial."

One hears of prisoners who, intentionally, do all they can to appear as "pathological cases." I was surely not going to take that course. I was much too keen on being tried. Even if that meant speaking to the Court—that is to say, to the German public—only for half an hour, I was not going to miss the opportunity. So I was just natural—as I had been before the men who had cross-questioned me in Cologne and in Düsseldorf; as I had been, from my childhood, in any of those innumerable talks in which I had shocked average people as a matter of course, without even taking the trouble to do so; without caring whether I did so or not.

The doctor noted a few particulars about my family, education, and life.

"Half Greek, half English, with a little Italian blood on your father's side,[12] born and brought up in France, and wedded to an Indian. . . . If ever anyone had the right to be an internationalist, it is undoubtedly you!"

"No," said I: "I am a nationalist of every Aryan country. It is not the same thing."

Amazed as he was at the glaring accuracy of that altogether unexpected summary description of myself, the doctor was, perhaps, still more taken aback by the spontaneity with which I had opposed it to his casual statement. Decidedly, I knew who I was and what I wanted.

I pursued—less with a view to enlighten the professional psychiatrist than for the pleasure of thrusting at the presumed Democrat the flawless consistency of my position "What is an 'internationalist'? A man who loves all nations as his own? No; but a fellow who loves only himself—and his lesser, his lower, his least valuable self at that; his dull amusements; his silly little hobbies—and who has discovered, in

---

[12] In fact, Savitri Devi's father was one-quarter Greek and three-quarters Italian, making her half-English, three-eighths Italian, and one-eighth Greek. (See Savitri Devi's autobiographical letter to a German female comrade, dated 1 October 1980, in the Savitri Devi Archive: http://www.savitridevi.org/letter_autobiographical.html.) This raises an interesting question: What led to her desire, as a child, to embrace her relatively remote Greek heritage over her stronger English and Italian roots and her French nationality?—Ed.

the empty phraseology of our decadent epoch, a marvellous excuse to live for nothing and to die for nobody. I am not—I never was—*that!* I might be the daughter of people of different nationalities, in the narrow sense of the word, but I am (thank goodness for that!) of one single race, the Aryan, and I put my race above myself—and above others; and the everlasting ideals which the best men of my race have embodied from time immemorial, are the only thing I have ever really lived for. Any country that boldly stands for them is my country.

"I have loved Greece passionately, not merely for the fascination of her far-gone past, but because, outside a repulsive, Levantinised, French-speaking, apish minority of Greeks, product of decay, there are, still to-day—after centuries of non-Aryan influences—thousands of healthy peasants and sailors who live honourably and in beauty, as Hellenes; because there are, in genuine modern Greek literature, sprung from the people, supremely beautiful works, in which the age-old cult of strong, sane, all-round perfection, is masterfully expressed. I have loved the English because, as a whole, they are a fine nation, endowed with many solid Nordic qualities—incomparably better than their leaders. I have loved India, because, being what she is, a land of many races, she has clung throughout centuries to the only social system fit for such a land— a system such as *we* would extend to the whole world, if we were to rule it. And I love Germany as the living symbol of Aryan regeneration in our times: the cradle of National Socialism; the Führer's hallowed fatherland. I would not do less for her than I would have done for Greece when I was an adolescent. By the decree of a strange Destiny, I have experienced—lived—not one, but several nationalisms, unusual as this may be. All are alike—amazingly alike. And behind all, there is—and always was, from the very beginning—that insatiable yearning after the ideal beauty of my own race, on the physical and on all other planes; that worship of eternal Perfection in a perfect human élite, an élite 'like unto the Gods', to use an expression current in Homer."

"And have you met any men and women who actually represent, in your eyes such an élite?" asked the mental practitioner.

"Few, in the wide world, in all my life; many—in proportion—in this martyred land, where I have lived only nine months," said I.

"And you would be prepared to die for Germany?"

"Gladly," replied I, with the unwavering directness of conviction. "Germany herself has died—materially—for the Aryan race. I am sorry I have not died with her, in 1945." I paused. In my mind, I recalled the unforgettable sight that had struck my eyes in my first Journey: against the golden background of a summer's sunset, the endless succession of torn and charred walls that had once been Hamburg; and the other cities through which I had passed—heaps of ruins; and all that I had seen since. "But," I added, after a few seconds, "one day, she shall rise in power and glory from the dead."

I then imagined some thousands of little men like the psychiatrist—"crusaders to Europe" and fighters "for peace and Democracy" (and the interests of big businessmen)—running away or trying to run away before tight formations of irresistible tanks; and I smiled in anticipation. Fortunately—for him—the psychiatrist did not ask me why I was smiling.

"Would you never help a people who were not of Aryan stock?" asked he, instead.

I reflected: "Why not?" In fact, I had done so already, during this war, although in a very humble, non-spectacular manner. . . .[13] And I remembered my exultation at the news of the fall of Singapore, and of Rangoon, of Mandalay—of Akyab, on the border of Bengal—one after the other; and also . . . at the news of certain detached sections of the Democratic forces in Burma, now and then suddenly and mysteriously encircled by the Japanese, and killed off as they tried to escape from the jungle set on fire, news which the papers, as a rule, did not report. Oh, those glorious days!

"I surely would, if such a people were our allies," said I, with perfect truthfulness, in answer to the doctor's question, "or"—I pursued, in order to give the conversation a trend as philosophical as possible—"if they were struggling, be it against a nation of more or less Aryan stock, who had tried to impose upon them one of the great international equalitarian superstitions, such as Christianity. In 1780, for instance, I would have willingly helped Tupac Amaru in his rising against the Spaniards and the Catholic Church in Peru, in the name of the rights of the Inca, children of the Sun, from whom he was descended. First, there was nothing better to do in Europe, in those days, as far as I remember. And then, I prefer anyhow a healthy, nature-worshipping tribe of Red Indians, in its place, to so-called Aryans who go about preaching—and practising—the gospel of legalised interbreeding among the Christian converts of all races; whose outlook on life leads to the growth of a bastardised mankind. Moreover, the Spaniards . . ."

I was going to launch into a historical dissertation about the import of

---

[13] An allusion to the pro-Japanese espionage of her husband, A. K. Mukherji, whom Savitri Devi aided. See *And Time Rolls On: The Savitri Devi Interviews*, ed. R. G. Fowler (Atlanta: Black Sun Publications, 2005), pp. 33–35.—Ed.

Carthaginian and, later, of Moorish blood in the bulk of the population of Spain, but the psychiatrist interrupted me.

"Why are you so mercilessly against all mixture of races?" he asked me. "You must admit that some exceptional individuals had both what you call Aryan blood, and other blood too."

"Anyone with a slight knowledge of history admits it," said I. And to make it clear that I—that *we*—are not afraid of facing facts, I became explicit. "There is for instance, the poet Pushkin," I added. "And the greatest philosopher-king of Antiquity, Akhnaton of Egypt . . ."

"Well, then . . . ?"

"Such instances are glaring exceptions. They do not impair the fact that 'all the great cultures of the past have sunk into nothingness because the original, creative race' (who had evolved each one of them) 'died out, through contamination of blood',"[14] answered I, quoting a well-known sentence of the Chapter 11 of the first part of *Mein Kampf.* "Great individuals who happen to be of mixed blood—and who are great in spite of it, not because of it—cannot but recognise that truth themselves, if they be sincere. Akhnaton did, for one, accept the principle of the separation of races as the natural and desirable order of affairs, decreed by the Sun." And I quoted the verses of the "Longer Hymn to the Sun," written three thousand three hundred years ago by the young Pharaoh, "Living in truth":

Thou hast put every man in his place,
Thou hast made them different in shape and in
Speech, and in the colour of their skins;
As a divider, Thou hast divided the foreign people.

"It is perhaps precisely because his splendid solar philosophy was so thoroughly Aryan in spirit,[15] that the Egyptians rejected it," I added.

And I was ready to quote Sir Wallis Budge and Pendlebury. "Those 're-educators' of Germany have the obnoxious habit of taking us Nazis for ignorant fanatics. I shall show this man that we are anything but that," thought I, with malicious satisfaction. But again, he did not give me an opportunity to pursue my discourse. He was obviously more interested in my attitude to personal problems than in my views on archaeology.

"What do you do with the right of the individual to choose the mate

---

[14] Adolf Hitler, *Mein Kampf,* I, ch. 11, p. 316.
[15] Modern scholars have pointed out its similarity to that expressed in the Rig-Veda.

he pleases?" he asked me.

"I strongly deny any such 'right'," replied I sincerely. "At least, I deny it to all individuals save those who, of their own account, put the interest of superior mankind above everything else—the only ones who are worthy to be free, for they will never misuse their freedom." I had answered some of the doctor's very first questions frankly enough for him to know already that *I* had never "misused my freedom" in any way.

"And you stand for the sterilisation of the unfit no less than of the crossbreeds, as the Nazis all do?"

"Absolutely. I might be—unfortunately—less intelligent, less efficient, and especially less supple than many of my comrades and superiors (otherwise I would not be here)," said I, "but I am not less Nazi than any of them." I uttered these last words with unconcealed pride, glad to be the last among the world's élite rather than the first among the more popular worshippers of mediocrity.

"Would you go as far as upholding the elimination of the unfit?" asked the psychiatrist.

"If you mean the elimination of the idiots, of the insane, and of all those afflicted with painful or repulsive incurable diseases, yes, most certainly. But I would be willing to keep a person who, though from our standpoint unfit to have children, is, in other ways, active and capable and willing to work; especially if he or she shares our ideals wholeheartedly and can therefore be as useful as many of those who breed families."

"In other words, you do not accept the value and dignity of every human being."

"Certainly not!"

"Nor the right of every man to live?"

"Certainly not. The dregs of humanity have no right to live—and no right to immobilise in their service the energies of healthy people. Shall I tell you of an experience of mine?"

"Do."

"Well, long ago—it was, if my memory does not fail me, in February, or March, 1922—I visited the famous asylum of LaForce, in the Southwest of France. I was sixteen (in fact, I had to say I was eighteen in order to be allowed in). Such a repulsive collection of monsters I had never imagined when I had been told of 'idiots'! The sight has haunted me for years. I felt not pity, but physical loathing, as in front of something unclean. But what made me downright indignant was to witness those numerous young, perfectly healthy, and sometimes pretty nurses, go to and from one of the idiots to the other—bustling, loving, maternal—to wipe spittle from some hanging jaw, or to remove a bedpan from under some inert, speechless, brainless, distorted body. It shocked me. It disgusted me—like the sight of a man devoting his whole life to a chimpanzee would shock all sane people; more so, in fact, for a normal chimpanzee is at any rate better than those freaks; a healthy fish is; any healthy creature is. To think of the time and devotion wasted upon the monsters for the sole reason that they are supposed to have a 'human soul', and to realise that such 'abnegation' is *admired*, in most Christian countries—instead of being despised, as something absurd and degrading—would have been more than enough to make me hate the Christian attitude to life, if I had not done so already. It was enough to make me greet with cheers, a few years later, the much-criticised application, in Hitler's new Germany, of moral standards more worthy of a strong and sane nation of Aryan blood. The remorseless cult of health, of sanity—of beauty—is surely one of the features of National Socialism that has the most powerfully attracted me."

"Don't you see any beauty in the feelings which your system mercilessly crushes out of existence?" asked the psychiatrist.

"What feelings? The sickly affection which a potential mother of healthy children squanders upon an idiot, or upon a good-for-nothing fellow with rotten lungs or rotten genitals?" replied I, indignantly. "No; indeed, I can see no 'beauty' there. I despise such feelings. Not only would I grant them no possibility of satisfaction whatsoever, if I had a say in the management of any country, but I would turn out of the country (or simply liquidate) any person who encourages them in himself or in others. Such people are degenerates—therefore undesirables. For there is, I repeat, no beauty in degeneracy."

"But what about the feelings of a healthy man or woman for another healthy person of the opposite sex from what you and your friends call an 'inferior race'?"

"There too," said I, "there is nothing but an insult to the divine laws of order and propriety; no beauty, but only shame."

"But think of all the suffering your system would bring into the world—which it did, in fact, bring, during the short time it remained in force! You take no account whatsoever of individual happiness."

"Indeed not, of the individual happiness of sickly-minded people! We could not care less what 'human tragedies' our effort to build a beautiful world might provoke in *their* lives. If individuals will cultivate morbid feelings—feelings unworthy of a superior race—in the midst of a well-organised healthy Aryan society, then they must suffer. There is nothing in that to make a fuss about. It is just an uninteresting—and, moreover, temporary—detail in our grand new civilisation. And what happens now is far worse. Now, it is *we*—the sane and virile—who have to suffer in the midst of a society organised for the survival and success of the weak, and ugly, and morbid and mediocre; of all the worthless; a society that draws the little inspiration it pretends to have, from ideals of sickness and disintegration and death."

The mental doctor gazed at me. Decidedly, *I* knew what I wanted. It would never be of any use trying to convert *me* to the "humanitarian" and democratic conception of life. And I was certainly not mad. I only, perhaps, at times, *seemed* slightly abnormal, but precisely for the apparently total lack, in me, of that little dose of instability and inconsistency, of those human contradictions, that all "normal" people possess—save we. It was interesting to try to measure how complete that lack was. The psychiatrist asked me: "How long is it that you have these views?"

"I have always had them," replied I. And this was absolutely true—too true for the doctor to believe at once. "How, 'always'?" said he.

"Yes, always," answered I. "Once, when I was ten, I was sitting in the corner of a tramcar in my native town, with a book in my hand—*Poèmes Barbares*, of Leconte de Lisle, which I was bringing home—and I was sobbing. The words I had just read were those put by the French poet in the mouth of an old bard deploring the end of the Heathen world and the coming of Christianity, the religion of the meek:

. . . the axe has mutilated the forests;
The slave crawls and prays, where swords once clattered,
And all the Gods of Erinn have gone away. . . .[16]

And I—the future Nazi—was sobbing because the old Heathen world of the strong, of the proud, of the beautiful—ancient Aryandom—had been obliterated, and because I thought I could do nothing to bring it back."

The doctor asked me many questions more about my childhood. I answered with ease, for I remember my whole life with extreme lucidity.

"Admittedly, you have no ties now," said the practitioner at last. "You love nobody in the world but those who share your views and serve your cause, and do not care two hoots what might happen to the others, be they your nearest kith and kin."

"Perfectly true! And that is why I am free—even now. For what can one do to a person with no ties?"

---

[16] ". . . la hache a mutilé les bois; L'esclave rampe et prie, où chantaient les épées, Et tous les Dieux d' Erinn sont partis à la fois" ("Le Barde de Temrah," *Poèmes barbares*).

"Yes; but try to remember and tell me: had you no ties in the very beginning, in your earliest childhood, long, long ago—before you felt, in so strange a manner, the lure of ancient Barbarity? Before you were a potential National Socialist?"

"I always was a potential National Socialist, even then," replied I, to the surprise of the psychiatrist. "I mean that I always had the unwavering faith and ruthless determination of one, in my very blood. As far as I can go back into my past, doubt and compromises and 'problems' were foreign to me. When I was less than two, and used to sit in my perambulator and pull the tassels off my blue and white woollen rug, one by one, exclaiming 'you come'! (I remember that and other details as though it were yesterday.) Then already, I divided people into three groups—as I do now—the useful ones; the indifferent and harmless; and the dangerous. But, naturally, I was then still self-centred, or hardly beginning to grow out of my self-centredness, and 'useful' were those who did immediately and without protest what I wanted; who gave me a plaything I coveted, or let me walk when I wanted to walk and stop when I wanted to stop. The dangerous ones were all those who hindered *me*, and, I must say, even more, those who harmed any animal or spoilt any plant—for I loved living creatures, as I do still; I found them beautiful, and it is through them that I spontaneously grew detached from myself. Hardly a little older, I could, if left to do so, inflict endless studied suffering by way of reprisal upon anyone who had kicked a dog or pinned a live butterfly on a piece of cardboard. And I never forgot such deeds. And never forgave any man or child who had committed them.

"Soon the ideal of a just and healthy world—of a world from which all injurers of living beauty would be drastically eliminated; in which I would no longer be told that I was to 'forgive' them for the sake of little Jesus—became, in my consciousness, the centre and measure of all things, in the place of my insignificant self. And I looked upon myself as the champion of such an ideal. And the 'useful' people became, in my eyes, those alone who seemed to forward it—*not* those who did good to me, as a person, but those who felt and thought as I did, just as now; and the dangerous ones were those who attempted to persuade me that there were things more lovable than my dream of beauty, things such as, for instance 'sick and suffering humanity' to which healthy, beautiful, and innocent beasts could be sacrificed. How I hated those people and their mania of saving what I never loved, and considered not worth saving! But what I want to say is that, whether at the age of two or twelve or forty, I have never really loved or hated a person but for what he or she represented in my eyes; not for his or her love or hatred of *me*, but for his or her love or hatred of the ideal which I loved. Only indifferent Nature I have always loved for her beauty alone."

"And you were never worried by the problems of so many adolescents?" asked the psychiatrist.

"Problems?" repeated I, with a certain contempt, "no, I never experienced the existence of any—save of . . . economic ones, in later life. The others, the psychological ones, the sexual ones, etc., that seem to worry so many people, I looked upon as things totally foreign to me, out of my reach, but of which it was good for me to acquire some purely bookish knowledge in order to be able to write about them at my University examinations. Especially all that fuss about Freud and his 'repressions'— very fashionable in my College days—I witnessed with contempt. 'Decadent stuff', I thought, and nothing more. And I was much amused when I heard of the somewhat rough manner we handled the old Yid before kicking him out of the Third Reich. 'I wish all those who spend their time trying to discover "complexes" within themselves instead of doing something more useful were treated likewise', I often said. I surely never gave a thought to such things . . ."

"But," said the doctor, "there are other psychological problems; there are conflicts of allegiances, for instance . . ."

"Not for me! I have only one allegiance!"

"But supposing, for the sake of argument, that you came to know that someone whom you loved had worked against your cause, would that not be painful to you?"

"It would be painful to me to think that I did not know it before, to have him or her liquidated in time, yes. But where is the 'moral conflict' in such a feeling?"

"But if you loved the person?"

"As soon as I would know of treason, I could not love him or her any longer. On the contrary, I could feel but loathing for such a person."

The psychiatrist forgot how accurately he had himself summed up my mentality only a while before, and asked me a silly question. "But," said he, "supposing it were someone who, from the start, had never had your views . . . ?"

"In that case, I never would have loved him or her, from the start. There could have been, between us, at the most, relations of courtesy, even cordial relations—if I judged it necessary, or expedient—but deeper feelings (on my side at least) would have been out of question. No. Remember please that people like me—like us—people with a single allegiance, are free from 'moral conflicts'. That is our strength."

"That makes you monstrous."

"People who aspire to supermanhood are bound to look monstrous, to men of a decaying civilisation," said I, as though speaking to all Democrats in the name of all National Socialists.

"There is no supermanhood, and there never will be a super-mankind," replied the psychiatrist. "There is only our poor, imperfect, but dear humanity—dear in spite of all its weaknesses; our living humanity, full of contradictions, of inconsistencies, worried by ever-recurring problems, who struggles and suffers . . ."

"Gosh, what the long-drawn influence of a Jewish religion can bring some people to value!" exclaimed I, with the feeling that all our opponents had indeed spoken through that red-haired man seated before me. "Well, I know nothing is absolute, and therefore nothing can be perfect, within time, especially at the end of a period of decay like our age is. But if you love present-day humanity as it is, I tell you I don't. And never shall. I love the living gods—my comrades, in my eyes the forerunners of a regenerate age. And if *they* are not destined to rule the world, well, away with such a world! Quickly a shower of atom bombs upon it and, in the place of its meaningless chatter about 'love' and 'peace', the voice of the howling wind over its ruins—and ours!"

The psychiatrist got up. So did I. The interview had been long, very long. I was only sorry that it had not been public.

I was taken back to my cell. And there, I ate two slices of white bread and orange marmalade, with the best of appetites—feeling grateful to mother Nature for having made me one of the living instances of what Mr. Grassot, of the French Information Department in Baden Baden had called on the 9th of October, 1949 our "appalling logic." Then, I smeared a third slice, and a fourth one, and put them by for my new friend H. E. to take on the following morning. Then, I sat at my table and continued Chapter 4 of my *Gold in the Furnace*.

* * *

My new friend now came every morning with the sister in charge. She stayed two or three minutes, took the food and drink I had for her, exchanged a few pleasant words with me, and went away.

One day she came, not with the nurse, but with one of the wardresses, and for once sat down upon the stool which I offered her. "I came today with Frau So-and-so, so that we might talk a little freely," said she, as the wardress seated herself upon my bed. "Frau So-and-so is 'in order'."

The wardress gave us a smile of assent; and H. E. continued: "Ever since they have arrested us, these people have been trying to rub into our

heads that we are monsters on account of the things we did, especially of
the gassing of the Jews. The priests they have sent us to bring us back to
Christian feelings have been repeating the same to us, for three and a half
years, namely that *that*, of all things, was something appalling. You are
not a German, although one of us. You have in these matters an impar-
tiality that none of those enemies of Germany can pretend to have. Tell
me frankly: what do *you* think of that feature of our régime?"

"It was necessary," replied I unhesitatingly. "The only pity is that,
first, so many dangerous Jews were never gassed, never even arrested;
and second, that the slaves of Jewry were not gassed with their masters—
to continue to serve them in the next world, if such a thing exists, like the
slaves of dead chiefs were supposed to follow them, in remote antiquity.
I admit it would have been doing the Yids a great honour, to give them
an escort of pure Aryans to the gates of Hades; but it would have
cleansed the Third Reich—and the world—of a considerable number of
traitors."

Both the wardress and H. E. smiled.

"How nicely you put it!" exclaimed my new friend. "But—I am only
telling you, for the sake of talk, what 'they' say on the other side—it
seems that 'it is wrong'; that it is a 'crime against humanity'."

"Humanity! Let me laugh!" I burst out. "How long will you and others condescend to listen to their Christian twaddle? What would you do if
you had bugs in your bed, sucking your blood? What would 'they' do—
our opponents, the wonderful 'humanitarian' Democrats (who cease being 'humanitarians' when it comes to showering phosphorus bombs by
the million over Germany, as you must know better than I); what would
the clergymen whom they send you do, in similar circumstances? Kill off
the bugs, naturally. And their eggs with them. And they would not care
how they would do it, as long as it were quickly done. Yet bugs are so
made by nature that they cannot possibly be anything else but parasites;
while Jews could go and work with their hands, like better races do, but
will not. They have chosen to be, from the beginning of time, the parasites of every other nation kind enough to let them live, be it ancient
Egypt, be it modern Germany. And when at last, the exploited nation,
driven to exasperation, becomes aware of their unseen joke and awakes
and begins to treat them as parasites, then they pose as martyrs, and expose 'anti-Semitism', and finance atrocity campaigns all over the world,
and succeed—*alas!*—in uniting all the uncritical, squeamish 'humanitarians', all the 'decent people' of the world against that nation, the clever
rogues! But it is no fault of theirs, I readily admit. They have always
been what they are. It is, first, the fault of those idiots of Aryan blood

who have tolerated them so long—who, even, have more than once made use of them (as the princes and dukes of old did) to squeeze money out of other Aryans (their subjects but, I say, their brothers). It is the fault of all those who have, in the past and now, treated racial differences lightly and who have preached that a Jew who becomes a Christian is as good as any Christian of Aryan blood, or that a Jew domiciled in Germany is a German and a Jew domiciled in England an Englishman and so forth . . . Such rubbish! It is the fault of all those who were and who are taken in by that nonsensical talk, as though they had no brains to think better and no eyes to see the glaring truth all around them. It is never the fault of the bugs, if a house is overrun with them; it is the fault of the housewife . . ."

"My God! You are right!" exclaimed H. E. "There is no difference whatsoever between what you say and what they used to tell us, during our training, in the Hitler days."

"I should think not!" said I. "It is not because I was not here, during the great days, that I am less aware of the truth than those who were. And it is not because I was brought up in one of the countries that make the most fuss about Democracy—namely France—that I stand for order and authority, and for drastic steps wherever the future of the Aryan race is concerned, any less than you; or that I am in the least, less devoted to our Führer."

H. E. smiled, and squeezed my hand warmly. "My dear, I never doubted it!" said she. "Indeed, when I think of you, I only regret that you were not here in *our* days. You would have been happy. And you would have been given among us a place worthy of your fervour and capability."

"All I regret is that I could have been a little more useful in Europe during the war than I was so far away in the East . . . and also that . . ."

"And also what?"

"And also," said I, "that I have never seen the Führer—nor any of his great collaborators. You have seen him, surely?"

"Yes, many times. I have greeted him in the streets of Berlin, as thousands of others have. But I have never spoken to him."

The wardress got up and told me that, although she would very much like to please me, she could not possibly remain with H. E. any longer in my cell. "But," she added, "if I am on duty on Sunday afternoon, I'll bring her again."

"Yes, do! I will be so grateful to you," said I. "And is it not possible for me to come in contact with one or two more of my comrades?"

"I'll see," said the wardress; "I'll see what I can do."

H. E. saluted me: "Heil Hitler!" "Sister Maria—the nurse in charge—does not want us to say *that*," she explained, "but Frau So-and-so is one of us." Frau So-and-so smiled sympathetically.

"Heil Hitler!" said I, raising my hand.

* * *

Life continued for me, happy, in the expectation of my trial soon to some. I finished Chapter 4 of my *Gold in the Furnace*, and started writing Chapter 5, about "de-Nazification." I put all the fervour of my heart into my work; and the words I wrote were words of faith in the future. "What a difference with '46 and '47!" I often thought to myself. "Then, I was free—and desperate. Now I am captive, but I know we shall rise again, one day. As long as *that* is true, what does the rest matter?"

And I remembered a play that I had written in those awful days—a play entitled *Akhnaton*, that pictured the persecution of the most beautiful form of Sun worship in Antiquity, under the Pharaoh Horemheb. Nobody had even suspected the meaning of that play—save a handful of English-knowing German friends of mine. Now, I quoted at the top of the page, under the title of my Chapter 5—"De-Nazification"—the words of the old hymn of hate intoned by the priests of Amon as they cursed King Akhnaton, after his death:

Woe to thine enemies, O Amon!
Thy City endures,
. . . But he who assailed thee falls . . .

"From a literary standpoint, much better, but in spirit, just as bad as the speeches of the self-appointed custodians of 'human values' at Nuremberg," thought I. And a cold sensation ran through my spine as I realised, perhaps better than ever, that, in the realm of Time, the fury of our enemies is as lasting as our divine philosophy; that there always were vested interests opposed to our truth; that there always would be, as along as Time lasted. But still, nothing can destroy us. And, below the ancient words of victorious hate, I quoted one of the undying sentences of our Führer: "Every attempt to combat a *'Weltanschauung'* by force fails in the end, so long as it does not take the form of an attack in favour of a new spiritual conception."[17]

And for a while, I thought of the encouragement contained in those true words: What "new spiritual conception" could indeed supersede ours, the one which is, in the Führer's very own words, "in full harmony

---

[17] *Mein Kampf*, I, ch. 5, p. 189.

with the original meaning of things"?[18]

Out of touch with my free comrades; out of touch with Herr W.—now surely, like I, "on remand" in some prison—out of touch with my husband and with my friends abroad, yet, I felt myself linked to all Germany and to all the world, even more so than when I had been free. And although from my cell I could see neither the sky nor the Sun, I felt myself linked to them beyond the world. When I guessed the red glow of evening behind my non-transparent windowpanes, I would put my stool upon the table and stand on it, and gaze at the fiery Disk through the narrow opening at the top of the window, and pray: "Put Thy power in me, Source of all power! And keep on inspiring me, that my life may always be a beautiful hymn to Thy glory, and a testimony to truth!" And when, after that, I again sat down to write, I felt that the strength and brightness of the Sun filled indeed my whole being, and set the seal of duration—the seal of truth—upon what I wrote.

Once a day, I was taken out for a quarter of an hour's walk around the courtyard, by myself, under the supervision of the wardress who happened to be on duty. For I was still "on remand," and had not the right to join the other prisoners in their "free hour"—which was also, most of the time, a free half hour or a free quarter of an hour.

In the evenings the wardresses on duty often used to come and have a few minutes' talk with me in my cell. They were mostly young women, curious to hear something about the wide world, and perhaps even more, keen on questioning a foreign National Socialist who had proved her sincerity. I soon learnt to know them by their names, and to like some of them more than others. H. E.—who now came regularly every morning—had told me of four who, to her knowledge, were *"ganz in Ordnung,"*[19] *i.e.*, who shared our faith wholeheartedly, whether officially "de-Nazified" or not. I loved those, naturally. I knew I could rely upon them. But I must say that the others behaved also in a friendly manner towards me. *None* seemed to look upon me as anything else but a genuine friend of Germany—a praiseworthy person. They held, however (and how rightly!), that I perhaps could have been more useful, had I been a little less trusting and more supple.

They often asked me about the things I had seen in the Near and Middle East, in the course of my travels. And I evoked before them the ruined temples of Upper Egypt, and the Valley of the Tombs of the Kings, and the Nile between Aswan and Wadi-Alfa; or the austere splendour of

---

[18] *Mein Kampf,* II, ch. 2, p. 440.
[19] "Entirely in order," "Quite all right."—Ed.

the desert of Iraq, under the moon; or the beauty of the Malabar coast or of the Bengali countryside, just after the rains. And they asked me about my life in India, and about India during the war.

I spoke lengthily about the appalling Bengal famine of 1943—the result of the general requisition of the rice harvest by the British, for the British and American troops in Burma and for the staff of the "indispensable services" in case of emergency. I evoked as forcefully and as vividly as I could the endless rows of starving men, women, and children—living skeletons—come from the countryside to await death along the busy avenues of Calcutta; and those whom one met seeking for something to eat in the stinking dust-heaps, while fighters for Democracy, stuffed with food—and whisky, at eighty rupees a bottle—could be seen tottering out of "Firpo's"—the fashionable ultramodern restaurant—and getting sick upon the pavement. "One third of the population of Bengal is said to have died of starvation or of the consequences of long-drawn under-nourishment," added I.

"And the people who were at the bottom of *that* are those who, in 1945, had the impudence to pose as defenders of 'humanity' and to accuse the vanquished of 'war crimes'."

The reaction of my listeners was the reaction I had obtained all over Germany, wherever I had related what I had seen in Calcutta from March to December, 1943. "Yes, how dare they speak of us?" they all agreed. And I thought: "These women had perhaps never heard of the Bengal famine before. Now, they will go home and comment upon it in the presence of other Germans. And that will contribute to increase the general loathing for the hypocrites now busy dismantling the German factories in the name of peace and trying to keep down National Socialism in the name of liberty. So, I suppose I am not entirely useless, even here . . ."

One of the wardresses asked me if, during the war, there were many people in India on our side.

"That all depends *when*," I answered. "In 1940, everybody was on our side—save the British settlers, the Anglo-Indians, who aped them, and, naturally, the Jews. You should have seen the enthusiasm at the news of the fall of France; at the expectation of the fall of England! That lasted till 1942. In 1943, it was already beginning to wane. In 1944, it was gone. In 1945, many of those who had spoken the loudest, even before the war, about the "unbreakable bonds of Aryan solidarity" and so forth, turned their coats and welcomed the "era of peace, justice, and true Democracy" that the United Nations were supposed to have inaugurated. Unfortunately, I must say, this phenomenon is not particular to India. Exactly the same course of evolution has been followed by a great number of Icelanders—pure Nordic people . . ."

"And by some Germans, too . . . still more unfortunately," put in one of the wardresses whom I knew to be, herself, "one of us."

* * *

One afternoon, I was taken by the wardress on duty to a room opposite the offices of the British Governor and of the Chief Warder. There, I was joined by the gentleman with the insinuating voice—Mr. Manning, I believe—who had tried in vain, in Düsseldorf, to make me tell who had printed my propaganda, and by a young English woman.

"We have come to ask you a few more questions," said the man, as he took his seat. And he bade me sit down. "First, we have been examining your posters and the two Leaflets found in your bag very closely," he pursued; "and we have practically come to a conclusion as to where they probably were printed. Would you care to know our conclusion?"

"Why not?"

"And would you tell us if we are right or wrong—just that?"

"No," replied I. "I have sworn to myself that I shall not tell you nor anyone a word concerning the printing of those papers, and I shall stick to my decision."

"You would not even tell us 'yes' or 'no'?"

"Not even 'yes' or 'no'. You are not compelled to let me know what you have inferred from your examination of my leaflets. I have not asked you to."

I spoke thus in order to hide my genuine anxiety. For I knew the police were clever—or I thought they were.

"I can see no harm in telling you," said the man. "We strongly suspect that your papers were printed in France."

He kept on watching me intently, expecting to detect upon my face a sign of fear or relief. He had told me, in fact, only to provoke a reaction on my part. And his statement might even have been a complete lie, for all I know.

However, it might also have expressed a genuine opinion. And somehow, somewhere in the depth of my consciousness, I did feel the nearest approach to a sigh of relief—and to a sudden propensity to laugh; for my papers had all been printed in the heart of London. But, to my knowledge, my face—with the help of the Gods—remained as blank as though the man had been talking to me in Chinese. And I made no reply. To have said "yes" would have at once raised suspicions—"How was it that my scruples had so quickly vanished?" the man would have wondered. And he would have perhaps found out that I was trying to lead him along a false track. On the other hand, I could not have said "no." That might have led him to think of London.

"So you will not tell us anything?" asked Mr. Manning (or whatever his name was) at last.

"What made you suppose that my papers were printed in France?" asked I, in return.

"Well . . . certain particularities in the print," answered my interrogator. "We are practically sure of it," he added.

"I have nothing to say," I declared, putting on a feigned expression of concern—as though the papers had really been printed in France and as though I feared it would soon be discovered by whom.

The man did not insist. But I believe that he felt more and more convinced (if he ever had been at all) that the propaganda had come out in black on white in some Parisian back shop. He took a paper and a penholder and noted something. Then he asked me if "I minded" enlightening him on a few more points concerning "my past."

"It seems you were in India during the war," said he; "how is it that you were not in Europe working for your cause?"

"Only because I materially could not come in time," replied I. "I did everything, absolutely everything I could to come. But I waited months for my passport. And the last Italian boat that I was hoping to take never left. Italy entered the war a fortnight too soon."

"And you had . . . set plans, as to what you were going to do in Europe?"

I reflected: should I tell the truth or not? After all, what did it matter, now that I was caught anyhow? I did not care any longer if "they" knew.

"I intended to broadcast war propaganda in favour of the Axis, in Greek, in French, and in Bengali," said I. In my voice one could have detected the infinite regret that I had not in fact done so. But my interlocutor looked upon me with nearly as much interest as if I had. ". . . with the deliberate intention of broadcasting on behalf of the Axis . . ." he wrote down upon his paper. And turning to me he asked: "Did the Party know of your intention?"

"I hope some members of the Party did, at least," replied I.

"And what did you actually do in India, after the failure of your scheme?" was the next question.

My answer—in perfect keeping with the truth, if not with *all* the truth—sounded like a joke calculated to thrust the man from the sublime spheres of what appeared to him as premeditated high treason, down to utter triviality: "I fed stray cats," said I simply.

"Cats!" exclaimed the man cross-questioning me.

"Yes, cats," I repeated; "about one hundred and fifty of them a day, during the Bengal famine, and some dogs too. Twice a day, I used to go down with rice, fish, and milk for them, and feed them in turn in two or three courtyards where they used to gather. And there was a queue of about fifty of them, kittens and all, every evening along the winding iron staircase that led to my terrace. And I had thirty-five in my house alone. You can enquire whenever you like whether I am speaking the truth or not. All the locality knew me, during the war, as "the cat *'mem-sahib'!*"[20]

"How lovely!" said, with a smile, the young woman who was sitting opposite me, listening. "I too simply adore cats!"

My interrogator had the good sense not to ask me why I had not devoted my whole energy to human beings. He wished to avoid useless discussions. But he did say: "Surely, you did not do nothing but that?"

"Indeed not," I replied with utmost ease. "I also wrote a pamphlet entitled *The Non-Hindu Indians and Indian Unity*, about the Hindu-Muslim problem; and a book entitled *Joy of the Sun*—the life of King Akhnaton of Egypt told to young people; and another book, *A Son of God* about the same three-thousand-three-hundred-year-old Pharaoh." All this was perfectly accurate. But it did not seem to satisfy my questioner's curiosity.

"You also used to receive members of the Allied forces in your flat," pointed out the latter at last.[21] "Or am I mistaken?"

He was not mistaken. That, I knew. It was nearly a fortnight since I had been arrested and, evidently, thought I, some sort of an enquiry had been made about me in India. It was no use trying to deny known facts. But, . . . there was a way of presenting them . . .

"My husband was always there when those men came," said I, not knowing at first what else to say—for the remark had somewhat surprised me—and pretending I wished to assert my innocence from a moral point of view.

"We never had the slightest doubts about *that*," replied the man. "But how did those people become acquainted with you?"

"I used to bring them home every Wednesday evening from the 'East and West Club', then situated in Chowringhee Terrace," said I, in a casual manner.

"And why were you so keen on bringing them home?"

"To put them in touch with my husband." My words must have had the accent of sincerity, for what I said could not have been more true.

---

[20] "European lady"—Ed.
[21] See *And Time Rolls On*, pp. 33–35.—Ed.

"Ah, ah!" . . . muttered the police official.

"Certainly," pursued I, with imperturbable assurance; "my husband is an Indian, and an old-fashioned one, a real one, well-versed in Sanskrit lore, astrology, etc., and all subjects particular to India. Now, the very purpose, the *raison d'être* of the 'East and West Club'—the laudable intention of Rev. Charles Milford and of his wife Mary Milford, its founders—was precisely to put members of the Allied forces, both British and American, in touch with interesting Indians; to give then a taste of Indian home life and pleasant memories of their stay in the East. I was just fulfilling the purpose of the Club to the best of my capacity."

Without flattering myself, this was logical, plausible; irreproachably well-put.

"And what did your husband talk about with our men?" asked my interrogator, Mr. Manning, or whatever was his name.

"I could not tell," replied I. "Perhaps about Indian history; or about astrology, if they were interested. I was not generally present at their talks."

"Why weren't you?"

"Because it is not the habit of Indian wives to sit in the company of strange men. At the Club, of course, it was different. We were all modern there. But at home, I observed the old custom. At the most, after serving coffee to the men, I used to show them my cats . . ."

"And what did you talk about when alone with them at the Club or on your way home?" asked my interrogator.

"About the heat; or about Indian food; or something like that. I never used to say a word about the war, or about politics."

"Didn't they ever ask you what views you had?"

"Yes," replied I; "they did. But I always told them I had none, and that I was interested only in Antiquity. It avoided all possible unpleasantness . . ."

The man took to questioning me about my husband. "Does he hold the same views as you?" he asked me.

"I hope so," answered I. "I used to believe he did, of course. But, as I said already in Düsseldorf, I know nothing of other people's views—although I cannot help feeling that any high-caste Indian proud of his own tradition is bound to hold our views, knowingly or unknowingly."

"Your husband seems in sympathy with you all right, if one judges him by his letters," declared the man. "How long is it since you have not seen him?"

"Over three years."

"And he does not feel lonely, without you?"

"I hope not. I believe him to be spiritually rich enough never to feel 'lonely'. I never do, who am, spiritually—and intellectually—his inferior."

"I cannot understand why on earth he married you."

"It would perhaps be better to ask him," replied I, with a pinch of irony.

The young woman who was present exclaimed: "A very good answer!"

At last Mr. Manning—or whoever he was—asked me how I had managed to distribute my papers in public places all over Germany, for so long, without getting into trouble.

"I suppose I used to give them only to the right people," said I.

"I am sure you did—otherwise you would have been in jail months ago. But how did you recognise those who shared your ideology? That I would like to know."

"I don't know myself. I used to feel them, somehow, even before they spoke," I replied.

"I bet she just picked out the handsome ones!" put in the woman, summing up what she thought of my way of detecting at first sight who was a National Socialist and who was not.

"Well, this was doubtless supposed to be a joke, but there is some truth in it," said I, to the surprise of both my interlocutors. "When I used to see, in a face, not merely regular features and the external signs of health, but that indefinable stamp of combined intelligence, willpower, and fervour; of serene and patient strength, of courage, and love—of all-round sanity which constitutes real beauty, then I used to say to myself: 'This one looks like one of us; let me talk to him—and perhaps I shall give him a couple of leaflets'. And I never made a mistake, although I am no expert at reading thoughts. That alone would go to prove that every National Socialist is one among a real human élite; a brotherhood of higher beings."

"We will see you again in Düsseldorf on the 7th," said the man at last, putting an end to our talk. Then, I had a moment of weakness; I remembered the beginning of my book that was in the hands of the police. I could not help asking Mr. Manning (or whatever his name was) whether he had read it and what he thought of it.

"Well," answered he, "I cannot exactly say I like it. It may be well-written; I am no literary critic. But I don't know where you went and got your information about Dunkirk. It is all false . . ."

"What is false, for instance?"

"It is false to pretend that our troops were scared of the Germans; also to say that Hitler sincerely wanted peace . . ."

"Oh, that is all right!" thought I condescendingly. "Who wants to admit

that his country's army was ever scared of anybody? And who is prepared to agree that the 'enemy' has acted in good faith?" I turned to the
police officer: "Do you think that there is any slight possibility that my
manuscript might he spared?" asked I, unable not to plead in its favour at
least once. "If the statements I make in it are so obviously and so shockingly false as you seem to think, then it is surely not dangerous; nobody
would take it seriously. I do not intend to publish it anyhow. That is obvious from its contents."

"I cannot answer 'yes' or 'no'," said the man. "The decision does not
lie with me."

"Could you not at least, if they consult you, point out that the writing
is not dangerous. It is too out-and-out National Socialistic anyhow, for
anyone to take the trouble to read it, save a handful of enthusiasts . . ."

"I don't quite agree with you there," said the man. "Personally, had it
not been for the dedication, I would not have found out that it was Nazi
stuff before I came to the second chapter, (sic). As for your other manuscript," he added, speaking of the first part of *The Lightning and the Sun*,
"it is not political at all . . ."

I was amazed—dumbfounded. "Either this man must not have read
the first line of my writing," thought I, "or, . . . he must be a perfect idiot,
or he is trying to deceive me." But I said nothing. I prayed to the invisible Powers that all my readers in the circumstance might remain blind to
the meaning of my writings, and *not* destroy them. A slight, very slight
ray of hope—which I did not dare to encourage—dawned on that day, in
my consciousness, for the first time since my arrest: "*Perhaps*, they will
spare my manuscripts all the same . . ." My reason rejected it as something utterly absurd. My heart clung to it.

* * *

On the following Sunday afternoon, as the prisoners of the D wing—
the so-called "war criminals"—were coming back to their cells from the
recreation room, the door of my cell was opened and . . . in stepped two
of the latter; my friend H. E. and a tall, slim, also blonde younger woman. The wardress on duty—one of those who were, in H. E.'s words, "entirely in order" locked the door behind them. "Splendid!" exclaimed H.
E.; "*now*, we are free for a while."

And spontaneously—as though a miracle had happened, and the Occupation with all its trail of shame and misery had been wiped away in
the twinkling of an eye, and the grand days had come back—the three of
us raised our right arms in the ritual gesture and uttered from the depth of

our hearts the magical syllables—cry of deliverance; war-cry; cry of love that nothing can smother; Germany's cry of joy at the long-delayed reconquest of her real free self: "Heil Hitler!"

My left arm around H. E.'s waist, the flame of defiance and the light of fervour in my eyes, I stood between the two blonde daughters of resurrected Germany, I, the dark-eyed daughter of the Mediterranean; the messenger of the faithful Aryans of the Far South and of the whole world. And there was no difference between them and I.

"Once," thought I—after the divine minute had passed and I was again able to think—"the salute was compulsory, and the two words also. One walked into a grocer's shop and uttered them as a matter of course, half the time without thinking about what one was saying—as one says 'Good morning!'—and then, turning to the shopkeeper, one added immediately: 'Give me a pound of *sauerkraut* please' . . . Now . . . the two words, already four years forbidden, have really become holy words; now, those alone pronounce them at all, who mean them, with all their heart and soul—who would die uttering then; and those who utter them together—as we three—feel bound to one another forever. Now, they have re-conquered their meaning and their power; the spell-like power they had, among the storm-fighters of before 1933."

H. E. introduced me to the other prisoner, H. B., another victim of the Belsen trial. They both sat upon my bed, and for two hours—until the feeding time came—we talked freely. "My dears," said I, "how unpredictable is the slowly unfolding pattern of life! Three and a half years ago, when I read about those disgusting trials in the papers, and saw your names in print, among many others, and believed all was lost, who could have told me that one day, I would meet you in prison, and have the joy of telling you: 'Nothing is lost, as long as we keep our spirit.—Hope and wait!' And who can tell us today whether, in a few years to come, we shall not be greeting together the return of our Führer amidst the delirious enthusiasm, this time, of a whole continent? Fortunately the world is governed by the Invisible. And the Invisible laughs at the U.N.O.,[22] and at the Occupation Statute, and at the Control Commission, and all such ephemeral inventions of silly dabblers in politics."

The two women told me something of the atrocious way they and the rest of the German staff in charge of the Belsen camp were treated in April 1945, when the British Military Police took possession of the place.[23] They spoke of the lorries full of frenzied Jews, sent there

---

[22] United Nations Organization—Ed.
[23] Cf. *Gold in the Furnace*, 3rd ed., pp. 73–80.—Ed.

especially to inflict all manner of ill-treatment upon them—and especially upon the S.S. men, warders of the camp. They described to me how, after four days' horrid confinement, without food or water, in their own filth, they had themselves been made to bury, with their own hands, under the threat of British bayonets, the bodies both of the dead internees and of the slain warders, and were not given even water to wash themselves of the stench, but were compelled—rather than nothing at all—to use their own urine for that purpose. They told me of the howls of the unfortunate S.S. men whom *they saw* disembowelled alive by creatures wearing the British Military Police uniform (let us hope, for the honour of the Aryan race, that these had all some amount of Jewish blood) and of the thin, long-drawn, high-pitched shrieks of the tortured.

I listened intently. With my naturally vivid imagination, I pictured to myself the ghastly scenes. And I felt every hair of my skin stand erect, and an icy cold sensation run along my nerves and penetrate me through and through. It was surely not the first time that I had heard of such achievements of the fighters for peace and reformers of mankind. I knew of plenty of atrocities performed by the *"maquisards"*—the "heroes" of the French *"résistance"*—especially from August 1944 onwards; French people had told me themselves of these things in 1946. And I remembered many similar facts of which I had heard in Germany. But, few instances of anti-Nazi barbarity as repulsive as those I had just heard, had yet been related to me by the very people who had witnessed them hour after hour, for days on end. These surpassed, if possible, even the horrors of Schwarzenborn and of Darmstadt . . .[24]

I gazed at the two women. In my mind, I recalled other tortures, outlandish ones, equally ghastly, but more long-drawn, more methodical, more scientifically studied, more artfully applied, things unheard of, that took place in imperial China, in Korea, in old Japan, and that I knew. And something akin to enthusiasm possessed me. I smiled at the vision of the wide world, spread before me, and at the endless unknown possibilities that might be offered to me, who knows how and when, in the course of the next thirty years. "My martyred comrades, my loved ones!" said I, in a clear, almost inspired voice, "'They' have thrown you to the Jews. May I, one day, be given the power and the opportunity to throw *them* to torturers of Mongolian blood!—to yellow men, with blank faces and slit eyes. On that day, I shall avenge you! By the unseen Forces, heavenly, earthly, and subterranean, that govern all things, I swear it!" And as I said that, I felt a current of power ascend my spine and emerge

---

[24] Cf. *Gold in the Furnace*, ch. 6.—Ed.

from the top of my head; and deathly destructive waves rush forth from my body, irresistible.[25] In invisible space, where nothing is lost, that energy, released in an impulse of righteous indignation, is still now working to bring about the downfall of our enemies. Who can stop it?

* * *

On the 7th of March, I was again taken to Düsseldorf. Snow had been falling for several days, and under the grey sky, the landscape had become dream-like. I gazed at it from the windows of the car, with passionate admiration—conscious that the time was drawing nigh, when I would see nothing but the prison courtyard, day after day—and I talked to Miss Taylor, the English policewoman, who had come to fetch me and who sat at my side.

"You are not too unhappy in jail?" she asked me.

"I? Not at all. I am, on the contrary, very happy," replied I. But I did not tell her that I owed most of my happiness to the fact that, glad to seize upon this opportunity of mocking the Occupation authorities, the German staff left me do practically all I liked.

"*You* would be happy anywhere," remarked Miss Taylor.

"Perhaps," said I.

In Düsseldorf, the hearing of my case was put off another week. And I was taken back to Werl in the afternoon. "I wish they could keep on adjourning my trial like that," said I in a joke, "and thus afford me the pleasure of a motor-drive every eight days!"

On the 14th of March, once more Miss Taylor was waiting for me at seven o'clock in the morning. Once more, from the windows of the car, I watched the scenery and the passers-by, as we rolled through Dortmund, Duisburg, Essen, etc. . . . Every time I saw ruins, I inwardly prayed for speedy revenge, and I longed for the day when I would see flags bearing the swastika hang from the windows of the rebuilt houses.

At Essen, I asked to get down from the car for five minutes pretexting "a very urgent necessity." Miss Taylor got down with me but, as I had expected, did not follow me behind the ruined wall that I had chosen as a screen between myself and possible onlookers. Taking a piece of chalk

---

[25] Savitri Devi is apparently describing an "awakening" of the *kundalini shakti*, a reservoir of vital energy located at the base of the spine. Those who experience such awakenings are reportedly granted unusual powers. The awakening of the *kundalini shakti* is the aim of particular yogic practices, but it can also occur spontaneously, as seems to be the case here. See, *inter alia*, Gopi Krishna, *Kundalini—The Secret of Yoga* (New Delhi: UBSPD, 1992), ch. 3.—Ed.

out of my pocket, I wrote upon the smooth surface that had once been a part of a German home, the sweet, the triumphal—and now defiant—words that contain the whole of my emotional life: "Heil Hitler!" Sooner or later, from that road on the side of which the car was now waiting for me, or from another, someone—some German workman out of employ, cursing the damned Occupation for his present-day misery; some housewife, remembering how lovely life was, under the Führer's rule, compared with now—would come to this lonely spot and read them. And for a minute, his or her heart would beat in tune with mine, thought I.

At Düsseldorf, I was confronted in Court with my unfortunate collaborator—Herr W.—I, on the bench of the accused; he, although still himself a prisoner on remand, in the witness box. He looked dejected—if not quite so much so as when I had had a glimpse of him, two days after my arrest. Doubtless, he had suffered in prison.

He gave a very clever account of how we had started talking at the "Catholic Mission" of the railway station of Cologne. We had talked in the presence of the woman on duty at the mission on that night. And after a while—in order that she might not follow the conversation (for who knew what views she held?)—we had talked in French. Herr W. had related to me the horrible story of his three years' captivity in the heart of Africa; and I, practically sure that he was one "of the right sort," had translated to him, from the English original, passages from the third chapter of my *Gold in the Furnace*. Now, before the Court, Herr W. said nothing that could lead one to believe that, as a National Socialist, or even simply as a German, he had liked the spirit of my writing.

"She read to me, in French, a few passages from some book," said he—he did not, in fact, state that it was from *that* one—"but it was much too difficult for me to understand, as my French is not good. I just nodded my head in assent, out of courtesy, without grasping what it was about."

In reality, he had agreed enthusiastically with whatever I had read to him. But I was glad he did not say so, for his sake and for mine. "The less attention is drawn upon that book of mine the better," thought I. Herr W. pursued: "As for the lady's views . . ." He was probably going to say that he never even suspected them. But I was only too glad to proclaim them.

"Don't be afraid of saying that I am a National Socialist," shouted I from my corner. "Now that I am caught, let the whole world know it! I am proud of it."

There were signs of increased interest among the German public come to hear the case. Miss Taylor, sitting at my side, told me, however,

not to speak until I was questioned. The judge asked me "not to interrupt," and Herr W. resumed his account. He pretended that he had no
political faith whatsoever since the end of the war—he could hardly say
he had never had any before, being a volunteer S.S. man since 1939—
and he stated that he had taken my posters to stick up merely because he
was expecting that I would have paid him for doing so! He added that he
was out of employ, and in dire need of money—which, doubtless, was
true.

I listened from my bench and compared what I was hearing with what
Herr W. had told me a month before, in the empty train. I remembered
his enthusiastic readiness to stick up my posters as soon as he had seen
one of them. I recalled the devotion with which he had spoken of the
Führer: "Our beloved Hitler! So it is for the love of him that you have
come to us, from the other end of the world!" His words, and the warmth
with which he had uttered them, I could never forget. And now . . . he
denied in public that common sacred faith that bound us! . . . And why?
No doubt, to avoid a heavy sentence for himself in his own coming trial.
"I would never do that—I, who never was even a member of the
N.S.D.A.P., let alone of the S.S. élite," thought I.

Yes; but then, I reflected, *I* had not toiled three years in a slave labour
camp in the Congo, under the whip of Negroes, with hardly anything to
eat. And I had not been wounded fifteen times in the Führer's service.
And I had not, now, undergone cross-questioning under the same horrid
conditions as this young man probably had; nor had I, in prison, to endure the same hardships. What had I been doing, at least up till 1942,
while he was fighting upon the battlefields of Europe? Walking down
Chowringhee Avenue under my bright-coloured parasol, feeling happy;
boasting of Germany's lightning victories and talking of the coming
world New Order, in Indian tea parties! And even after that, I had not
incurred any danger. So, naturally, *now*, I could afford to be defiant.

I felt deeply ashamed of my first reaction of self-righteousness and
severity. "Poor boy!" thought I, "he has the right to try to avoid further
useless suffering. He has proved who he is, in ten long years of action.
And nobody believes him, anyhow, when he says that "he no longer
clings to any ideology."

The judge asked me if I had any question to put to Herr W., or anything to add to what he had said. I declared that I had "nothing to add."

During our midday meal. Miss Taylor commented upon my collaborator's attitude and spoke of his "lack of moral courage." "It must not
surprise you," she concluded; "they are all like that. You should have
seen the 'top ones' on trial at Nuremberg, shifting the responsibility onto

one another—each one merely trying to save his own skin . . ."

"I refuse to hear a word of criticism, let alone of blame, against the martyrs of Nuremberg," said I. "Even if what you say were true—which I do not believe for a second—still they are my superiors, and I have no business to find fault with them; much less to allow anti-Nazis to find fault with them in my presence. If you care at all to talk to me, talk of something else."

"You are the limit, really!" exclaimed the policewoman. "But remember that you are not a German . . ."

"Maybe."

". . . and that you do not represent Germany."

"I have never pretended to. Still," said I—and a defiant smile brightened my face—"let me tell you that 'next time', when the Democracies are crushed and lie in the dust, twenty times more devastated even than Germany is now, then, you will not find in the whole world a single non-English person to stand by you in admiring loyalty as I stand by the Germans today. You will not even find mercenary friends, as you did last time, for you will have no money left. Germany today has no money, no power, no international status. But she has the magic of Hitler's name, and his everlasting Idea. What will *you* have, to retain a foreigner's devotion, when your material power will be gone?"

Miss Taylor made no answer. There was none to make.

In the afternoon other witnesses—Wilhelm Kripfel, the policeman who had first dealt with me, and his superior, head of the police office in the Cologne railway station; Gertrud Romboy, the woman on duty at the Catholic Mission of the same station, on the night I had made the acquaintance of Herr W. there; the *Oberinspektor* Herr Heller, and the man who, in Düsseldorf, had taken down my statement as to "why" I had contributed to keep the Nazi spirit alive, were heard in turn.

Gertrud Romboy's account of the enthusiastic manner in which Herr W. had spoken of me, was, from the standpoint of the Court, most damaging to the young man. It showed as plainly as could be that, although he might have been hungry, nothing else but a sincere National Socialist faith had prompted him to help me. And, while I would have admired Herr W. had he boldly stated this, himself, I was indignant as I heard Gertrud Romboy imply it so obviously, as though she were doing all she could to render the sentence against him as heavy as possible. Indeed, she told the truth *and all the truth* before the Lower Control Commission Court, as she had sworn she would. She was none of us—or, in the circumstance, she would have lied, or feigned ignorance. But even more than her apparent desire to bring punishment upon Herr W. (as well as upon myself) the hasty confidence with which Herr W. had spoken to her and given her a leaflet of mine on his return from the platform of the station, amazed me. Could he not have, first, taken the trouble to find out whether the woman was safe or not? I recalled the fact that, if Herr W. had been arrested at all, it was because, after sticking up as many as he could of my posters all night, he had not stopped doing so when day had dawned; that, actually, thinking himself alone in the midst of a ruined part of Cologne, he had applied fifteen of them in a row against the smooth surface of what had once been the wall of a bank, at 8:30 a.m. or so—in broad daylight. I had read those details in a summary of his arrest, and of the witnesses' first statements, that had been handed over to me in prison. Now, for the second time I thought—notwithstanding all the respect I had for the young man's sincerity and zeal, and for the genuine efforts he had made to save *me* from arrest—"I never would have believed that an S.S. man could be such a clumsy fool!"

It was decided at last that, "given the very serious nature of the charges against me," my case exceeded the competence of the Lower Control Commission Court and would therefore be heard at the next sitting of the High Court of similar character. I was told that the final hearing would not be further postponed. (The mental doctor's report, read by the judge, stated indeed that I was "of more than average intelligence" and "fully responsible" and "fit to undergo trial.") I was asked if I wished to be defended. I replied that I was quite able to defend myself—or rather to state, myself, the reasons that had prompted me to act as I did. "I am proud of what I have done." I added, "and would begin again if I could though—I hope—this time, less clumsily, taking full advantage of bitterly acquired experience."

The judge took a pencil and a piece of paper. "Will you repeat this, if you please?" said he.

"Most gladly!" answered I. And I repeated the sentence, smiling at the German public. And the judge wrote it down.

"So you don't want a lawyer to defend you?" he asked me, when he had finished.

"Oh," said I, "if it is the custom, and if *I* am not to pay him, I don't mind having one. But I wonder what he will be able to say in my favour. Anyhow, I also wish to speak, personally. I hope I shall be allowed to."

"You will," replied the judge, "provided you do not intend to make a long political speech."

"I just want to make a short one," said I. The public laughed. "Moreover," I added, "I do not know how far it will be 'political', for in my eyes National Socialism is far more than mere 'politics'."

* * *

As I was walking down the large staircase by the side of Miss Taylor, a woman—who had been listening among the public—approached me and said: "I would very much like to have a talk with you."

"So would I," I replied, "but I am not allowed to."

Miss Taylor intervened. "Come along," she said; "you are not to get in touch with the public."

But I turned to the woman who had spoken to me—and to all those who could hear me—and said: "Know, yourselves, and tell all Germany, that neither threats nor bribery, neither severity nor kindness, will ever 'de-Nazify' *me;* that, in my eyes, the interest of National Socialist Germany is the interest of the Aryan race at large; and that I am waiting for the Day of revenge and resurrection. Wait for it, you too, in the same spirit. Heil Hitler!"

Miss Taylor—who had not understood all that I had said, but who had guessed, more or less, what it could be—held my right hand down to prevent me from making the ritual salute. I looked at her and said: "That is easy. But all the might of the united Democracies cannot hold my spirit down."

She replied nothing.

She took me to another building, and gave me a cup of tea. An Indian, whom I had noticed by the side of the representatives of British justice during the hearing of the witnesses, came in and introduced himself as the envoy of the Indian Consulate in Berlin, specially sent to attend my trial and to interview me. He looked like a South Indian, and told me he was called Francis. "A Christian from the Southwest coast," thought I. And I was right, for the gentleman told me a minute later that he was from Travancore. I had visited the place in 1945. We spoke about it for a while. Then, he asked me "how I had come to be mixed up with National Socialism," and, for the hundred thousandth time I had to point out, in as concise a manner as possible, the logical connection between my life-long yearning after the ideals of Aryan Heathendom—which are ours—and my departure to caste-ridden India, "the land that had never denied the Aryan Gods," in 1932. The things I said were the least likely to flatter the feelings of an Indian convert to Christianity, brought up, in all probability, in an atmosphere of democratic "liberalism"—in other words, of lies. But I could not help it. I spoke the truth.

"Would you like us to try to have you sent back to India?" asked the official.

"I would love to go back for some time," said I. "There are a few things I would like to ask my husband, when I see him again. But on no account would I run the risk of getting stuck there—like I did in 1939—when interesting developments start once more in the West." I thanked the gentleman, however, for the interest he took in me.

After that, Miss Taylor brought me back to Werl. In the motorcar, travelling with me, was, this time, my luggage, which the police had given me back.

"I wonder what they did with my manuscripts," I could not help saying.

"They told me they kept whatever was of a political nature, and gave you back the rest," replied the policewoman.

I felt my heart sink within my breast, believing my precious writings were now lost to me and to those for whom they had been written. I spoke little during the journey. Over and over again, I read the list of the things which the police had given back to me, grateful to Miss Taylor for letting me see it beforehand. Several large and small "copybooks" were mentioned in the list. But I did not remember how many copybooks I had. There was one ray of hope: the *Programme of the N.S.D.A.P.* was definitely mentioned on the paper. I recalled the booklet bearing upon its bright-yellow cover a picture of the red, white and black swastika flag—and thought: "If they can give me back that, they can give me back anything!" But I did not dare to believe it.

When we reached Werl, Miss Taylor, who had herself taken charge of the few jewels I still possessed, handed them over to the prison authorities. My Indian earrings in the shape of swastikas were there with the rest. They were mentioned on the list. My luggage was carried to the *"Frauenhaus"* and, on the request of Miss Taylor—who was kind enough to understand my desire to inspect it at ease—deposited in my cell, under my bed.

As soon as I was alone, I opened it. And my heart leaped: there, before me, lay the thick light-brown copybook with a red binding in which were written, in my own handwriting, the three first chapters of my *Gold in the Furnace*, and a few pages of the fourth! And there was, under it, the dark-red copybook containing the first part of *The Lightning and the Sun*, and the whole typed manuscript of my unpublished *Impeachment of Man*,[26] finished in 1946, with a quotation of Dr. Goebbels, an extract from the famous *Diaries*, added in early 1948 upon the outside page . . . ! I could hardly believe my eyes. I took a glance at the precious pages, to see if any had been torn out, or if any lines had been effaced. No; all was

---

[26] *Impeachment of Man* (Calcutta: Savitri Devi Mukherji, 1959).

in order—just as I had left it on the day of my arrest. Tears filled my eyes. And an overwhelming gratitude rose from the depth of my heart, not towards the police or the British authorities, enemies of all I stand for, who had spared my writings not knowing what they were doing, but towards the Lord of the unseen Forces Who had compelled them to spare them, knowing fully well why. Now more than ever I felt sure that, sooner or later, National Socialism was destined to triumph. I smiled; and in an outburst of almost ecstatic joy, I repeated the words of Leonardo da Vinci, read long ago: *"O mirabile Giustizia di Te, Primo Motore!"*[27] I felt so light, so exultantly happy, that I would not have found it strange, had my body been lifted from the ground.

I continued examining my things. The police had kept the photograph of a young German whom I had met somewhere in the French Zone. Knowing who I was, and what I was doing (for I had given him, too, a bundle of leaflets) the youngster had had the courage to sign his name under the few words he had written behind the photo: "Remembrance from an S.S. soldier." I now felt anxious for him, and prayed with all my heart that "they" might never find him. Mr. B.'s letters ending with "Heil Hitler!" they had also kept; as well as two issues of a certain English review containing several beautiful portraits of the Führer. But the other portrait I had of him—one of the best ones; and one that had been following me in all my travels for who knows how long—they had left me. That too, I could hardly believe. And yet it was true! There was the adorable face gazing at me once more, now as always; the Face I have yet never seen in the flesh, but whose light sustains me in the struggle for the triumph of truth. *"Mein geliebter Führer!"*[28] I whispered with devotion, holding the priceless photograph to my breast. I then lay it upon the table against the wall, facing my bed. And I continued my inspection.

The police had also left in my possession a booklet of military songs and another one of *Fighting Songs of the Movement*,[29] and . . . one sample of each one of my leaflets, as a remembrance! Attached to the longer one—the one I had composed in Sweden, in May, 1948—was a small square of typed paper containing the methodical enumeration of the four mistakes in German that had been found in the printed text. I could not help being amused at the ironical haste they had shown in correcting

[27] "O miraculous Justice of Thee, Prime Mover! . . ." (Leonardo da Vinci, *Cod. Atlantico*, mss. Foster III, A e C).—Ed.

[28] "My beloved Leader"—Ed.

[29] *Das neue Soldaten-Liederbuch*, vol. 3, ed. Fr. J. Breuer (Mainz: B. Schott's Söhne, n.d.) and *Kampflieder der Bewegung* (Reichspropagandaamt Moselland, n.d.). See page 116, below.—Ed.

them, as though to tell me: "Look here; before indulging in Nazi propaganda, you'd better go and improve your German a little!"

"I certainly shall," thought I, as though answering the challenge in my mind. And I felt ashamed of myself for not having studied Hitler's language more thoroughly, years and years before.

At last, I sat down and started copying, in the thick light-brown copybook with a red binding, Chapter 4 and Chapter 5 of my *Gold in the Furnace*, which I had, all these days, been writing upon loose sheets of paper. Then, I wrote the title of Chapter 6, "Chambers of Hell," and laid down the plan of it.

6. The covers of Savitri Devi's National Socialist song books, which she had with her in Werl

* * *

Life continued for me, the same—or nearly the same. The wardresses came and had talks with me in my cell, as before. Frau *Oberin* often came herself, although, as a rule, she preferred calling me over to her office. Once, she told me how "oriental" I appeared to her in my outlook on life.

"'Oriental' in what way?" asked I.

"Well, there are certain values," she said, "that we accept implicitly. They may be Christian, or whatever you like to call them, and be, as you say, ultimately traceable to foreign influences. But they have become a part of our subconscious self. I have never met, even among those who share your views in Germany, anyone who rejected those values as cynically as you do. From the little you told me about the Hindu attitude to morality—life-centred, as opposed to man-centred—I conclude that your long stay in India has greatly influenced your philosophy."

"Never!" said I, vehemently. "I hated the man-centred creeds—all of them; the ancient and the modern; the religious and the political, and those that are both—with bitter hatred, years before I even thought of going to India. I cannot remember myself but as a rebel against such Christian ideas as "the dignity of *all* men" (just because they happen to be 'human') and the "value of *all* human souls," etc. Still, in India, I was often told I was profoundly 'Western' because I had nothing of the other-worldly mysticism, and nothing of the resigned acceptance of things as we find them, that are supposed to characterise the 'East'; also because I used to say that, even if I could, I would not wish to break away from the endless circle of births and rebirths, but would *prefer* to come back to earth again and again, for life is lovely, at least among the higher forms of its highest manifestations. The Indians were right. I am thoroughly European—but a European of ancient Europe, exiled in our times; an Aryan, impermeable to those Christian values that have nearly killed the soul of this continent, and therefore as foreign to most of our contemporaries as would be a resurrected daughter of the Pagan North or of Pagan Greece."

"You are perhaps right," said Frau *Oberin*.

"I know I am right. And that is why I look so 'Eastern' to you, in spite of my National Socialism, and so 'Western' to so many Indians, in spite of my life-centred outlook. But I am not alone. I know quite a number of people—here, in Germany—who are just as 'cynical', *i.e.*, just as radical as I am concerning the moral values brought to us by the Jewish *Weltanschauung* to weaken us and to destroy us. In them—the true disciples of Nietzsche—I put my hope. They are the ones who shall 'march still further on, when all falls to pieces'[30] as it is said in the old *Kampflied* to which a more than material meaning can be given," concluded I.

"Perhaps," said Frau *Oberin*. "I doubt, however, whether you will find anyone to understand you in this prison."

---

[30] Savitri Devi's translation of the first line of Hans Baumann's "Es Zittern die morschen Knochen." See p. 6, n3 above.—Ed.

"I have already found one, at least."

"Who?"

"One of the so-called 'war criminals'."

"Your friend H. E.? Yes; it may be. She speaks very highly of you, indeed. She seems to like you."

"I am glad if she does. I admire her."

"What would you say if only you knew some of the men, imprisoned here for so-called 'war crimes'? There are some perfect types of idealists among *them*—people according to your heart."

"Oh, I wish I could come in touch with them!"

"Unfortunately, that is not possible," said Frau *Oberin.* And she added: "Don't tell anybody that I have been speaking of them to you. As the head of the *'Frauenhaus'*, I have to be very, very careful about all that I say."

"Rest assured I shall not speak," replied I; "but do tell me: *you* do not really accept any other values but ours, in the bottom of your heart, is it not so?"

Frau F.[31] *Oberin* looked at me sadly, and just replied: "I repeat: I have to be very, very careful." And she changed the conversation. She told me about her brother, who had been killed on the battlefield in Russia, and she showed me a picture of him—an energetic looking and handsome young man, with light, wavy hair.

"I loved him very dearly," she said.

"She has sacrificed more than I ever can, for the cause I love," thought I. And I recalled the thousands of German women who have lost one or more than one of their dear ones upon the battlefields of Russia and elsewhere. I was alone. I had nothing to lose, save my manuscripts; and they had been given back to me. I looked at Frau *Oberin*'s sweet and dignified face, and felt humble.

* * *

I was no longer alone during the "free time." Two new prisoners—a Czech woman, charged with espionage on behalf of Russia, and a Belgian woman already sentenced to six years' imprisonment for "collaboration with Germany during the war" and waiting in Werl (with her two-year-old daughter) for the Belgian police to take charge of her—now accompanied me around the courtyard, a few minutes in the morning and

---

[31] "F." is probably the initial of Frau *Oberin*'s first name. The initial of her last name was probably "M." See page 168 below.—Ed.

in the afternoon.

I used to speak freely to the latter, since the day she had told me why she had been sentenced. She professed to admire all I stood for although—she herself admitted—she had followed her German husband (one of the right sort, garrisoned in Belgium during the war) "not because of his National Socialist faith, but because she loved him."

"*I* could not even flirt with a man who did not wholeheartedly share our faith, let alone love him," I had spontaneously replied to that. "But, of course," I added, "I should perhaps better be silent. For I have no experience whatsoever in the matter. Had no time for it—even when I was young."

I hardly ever spoke to the other prisoner, who was "on remand." It was Miss Taylor who had told me who she was. And the nature of the charge against her did not render her particularly sympathetic to me. However, once, I had no choice but to walk around the courtyard by her side, as we were alone.

"Little Kareen and her mother have a visitor today," said the woman: "the child's father, I believe." And she added: "I too, have a child—a boy, twice as old as Kareen. And my husband too is a German."

"Yes, some damned Communist, most probably," thought I to myself. I was not interested.

"In general, if I am not mistaken," said I—just to say something—"there is not much love between Germans and Czechs."

"That is true—unfortunately," replied the woman. And she related to me some of the ghastly happenings that took place in her country after the war. "The Czechs were particularly cruel to the S.S. men," she said. "In several places, they hung in a row as many of them as they could lay hands upon, not by their necks, as one might think, but by their arms; and then, they lit fires under them, leaving them to die the most atrocious death, as slowly as possible."

I had not the slightest doubt that the young woman spoke the truth. She had no interest to lie to me, and to run down her country in my eyes. Moreover, the picture she had evoked was in perfect keeping with all I knew already about anti-Nazi atrocities. And never, perhaps, did I feel in more complete agreement with a certain German comrade of mine who had told me, in 1948, that, "when the day of reckoning comes" not a single Czech should be allowed to live. However, I controlled my feelings. "Fortunately," said I, as calmly as I could, "there exists a divine Justice, immanent in this world. Its machinery grinds slowly, but grinds fine—and is deaf to tardy demonstrations of repentance. I am waiting to see what bloody pulp will drop, 'next time', from its merciless iron teeth. I am waiting to see all the martyrs of our cause avenged a hundred thousand times, and to rejoice at the sight."

The young woman said not a word. Perhaps she suddenly realised that I had identified myself with National Socialist Germany far more than any foreigner could, in her estimation, and she regretted having spoken too much.

* * *

A member of the British staff of the prison named Stocks—a tall, fat man, with a jolly, red, round face, and twenty-nine years of coercive service in such rough and interesting places as the treaty ports of pre-war China—used to invent (whenever he could) some pretext to call me over to the building in which stood the Governor's office, and to have a chat with me (in some other room, needless to say). A wardress always came with me and sat there during our conversations. The man was a little coarse, but friendly. He radically disagreed with me on most important questions—he would never admit, for instance, that Mr. Churchill, acting, willingly or unwillingly, as an agent of international Jewry, bears the responsibility for this war. But he agreed with me that a healthy baby of good Aryan blood can never be "conceived in sin" and, in his forceful and picturesque language, dismissed the teaching of the Christian priests on that point as "a lot of b . . . ls." Moreover, he used to give me odds and ends of useful information about some members of the prison staff—telling me, for instance, that the interpreter who used to accompany the Governor in his visits to our *"Frauenhaus"* on Friday mornings, had been, himself, a political prisoner in Werl, under the National Socialist régime; or that the other German whom the British had appointed as the head of the men's section of the prison was "a man who had suffered in Hitler's days" (which I had immediately translated, in my mind, as "a confounded anti-Nazi"). And I knew I could say practically anything to him without fearing he would go and repeat it to the Governor.

"Why do you use those people in your services?" asked I, once, speaking, precisely, of all those German enemies of National Socialism who hold well-paid posts under the Occupation. "Don't you realise that they are the scum of the earth?"

"Most of them are," admitted Stocks. "But . . . we have to show some consideration to those who helped us."

"Hum!" thought I, "not merely anti-Nazis, but active traitors, eh! Nothing surprising: every anti-Nazi of Aryan blood is a traitor to his own race—*a fortiori* a German one." And I remembered some information I had gathered in 1946, in London, from a very reliable source—to my horror—concerning traitors in Germany during the war. But I said nothing.

"Don't you realise," asked I again, another time, "that you cannot 'de-Nazify' the Germans any more than you can 'de-Nazify' me?"

"We all know that," answered Stocks.

"Then, why do you pretend to try? Why do you keep up the farce? You are only sowing hatred."

"Maybe; but it is a part of our policy. We have to do it, whether we believe in it or not."

"But, again, why?" said I. "To deceive the Russians? Or to continue deceiving your own people?"

"I am only repeating: it is a part of our policy," replied the man. "And I wish I could meet you in free surroundings, when you are yourself free."

"But," said I, "when the West is sufficiently scared of Communism to realise the necessity of standing united against it, then, it will simply have to accept National Socialism as the only salvation. There is no other policy.

"Only a totalitarian organisation inspired with an ideal as radical, as uncompromising as that of Marxism, can beat totalitarian Marxism; the united Democracies can never prevail against a totalitarian bloc."

"But they did, this time," answered Stocks—a little hastily. "*We* beat *you* in this war."

"No," said I, with a bitter smile; "don't believe it. Your then 'gallant allies' the Russians did it; not you. And next time you will have the choice between being kicked about by them or by us—unless it be by both . . . who can ever tell?"

"But you and your friends would never ally yourselves with the Communists?"

"I don't know. It would not be worse than allying ourselves with you sneaking people, at any rate. Personally, I loathe you both. They stand for an ideology of disintegration which is the opposite of ours, in spirit. You have no ideology at all and fight—or rather incite other people to fight—for your big businessmen's pockets, which is even more repellent in our eyes. A sincere Communist can, sometimes, be brought to acknowledge his delusion and to join us. *There are no sincere Democrats*, apart from downright imbeciles. You people can never be brought to join anything great. You are too afraid of excess, too devoid of strong impersonal feelings, too hopelessly mediocre.

"Next time," I pursued. "I shall do what I am told; what we shall all do. I don't know—and don't care—what that will be. I have absolute confidence in those, infinitely more intelligent than I, who live solely for the triumph of the eternal Aryan values, as I do, but who fully understand the intricacies of *'Realpolitik'*, which I do not. I shall do what they tell me—even be your ally (for a time) if they decide I should. But I shall not, for all that, change my opinion about you and your parliamentarism—your worship of *quantity* as opposed to quality;[32] your false 'human' values, your lying 'individual freedom'. I know the worthlessness of all that—and yours."

The man looked at me with interest. He offered me a cigarette which I politely refused for I do not smoke. Then, at last: "You see," said he, "you are deadly serious about things. We are not. Why are you so serious? Why don't you just live, have a good time, and let things take their course?"

"But I do live," replied I. "In fact, my life is far more interesting, far more intense, than that of most of you Democrats."

"But you don't enjoy yourself!"

"I did—a few years ago. And I shall again," said I, thinking of "enjoyments" of an entirely different nature from those the former British "bob" of Shanghai had in mind.

"But when?" exclaimed he; "You will soon be getting too old."

"I shall enjoy myself *now*—next week or the week after—when I speak before you mighty ones of the day, at my trial," I answered. "And in a few years' time, when our turn will come to be vindictive and arrogant; harsh; and bitingly ironical. I shall not be too old to gloat, if I am not able to do anything better."

"But *we* are not vindictive," said the man.

"You think so? I don't."

"Well, I am not, at least. If I were the judge, I would set you free."

"Would you, really?" replied I. "Then, why are you here in service in occupied Germany, if you don't care more than that about the future of Democracy?"

"I am here for my bread and butter," declared Stocks. "And I am, naturally, loyal to those who pay me."

"I am here for the triumph of order and truth. And I am loyal to my Führer and to his faithful people whom I love and admire. All the riches of the world could not detach me from them."

---

[32] Perhaps an allusion to René Guénon's *Règne de la quantité* (Paris: Gallimard, 1945); in English: *The Reign of Quantity and the Signs of the Times*, trans. Lord Northbourne (London: Luzac and Co., 1953). We know that Savitri Devi read this book at least by 1954–55, for there is a clear allusion to it in *The Lightning and the Sun*, ch. 13, p. 151, written in 1954–55.—Ed.

The man laughed. "That's all very well," he said: "But you see, *I* love and admire nothing but pretty women. And all I care for is to have a good time." And he started talking in a light and loose manner about what a "good time" meant to him.

The wardress who had brought me in was sitting on her chair, opposite me, and looking out of the window. I was thinking: "What a pity this German woman does not know English! For the talk of this representative of the democratic forces in uniform would do nearly as much harm, I presume, to the flimsy prestige of the Occupying Powers, as a dozen of my posters stuck about the walls. I must tell Frau *Oberin* and the others about it!" And in fact, I did tell them. But for all practical purposes, I decidedly preferred Stocks to the Governor. I was—rightly or wrongly—under the impression that, even if he had been in the Governor's position, he would never have interfered with my activities in jail. He seemed far too engrossed in his own affairs.

* * *

H. E. spent another Sunday afternoon in my cell—alone, this time. She repeated to me, in detail, the account of the Allied atrocities she had witnessed in 1945, and the story of the iniquitous Belsen trial; of which she was one of the main victims.

"The witnesses against us, mostly if not all Jewesses, had been flown over by the Allies to England, to America, or goodness knows where, immediately after their statements had been taken down. *They did not appear in our trial*, which was conducted merely upon the evidence they had given. Moreover our judges knew not a word of German, and we not a word of English; and the interpreters who translated what we said (and what our accusers had dictated before they had left) *were all Jews*."

I wrote down every word she said—matter for Chapter 6 of my *Gold in the Furnace*.

"You should not *write* those things," said H. E.; "if ever they searched your cell and found out that I have been telling you all this . . . I would have to suffer for it terribly."

"Rest assured they will never find out, even if I do write down every item of it," said I. "Look at this!" And I handed over to her the rough paper on which her account was in black and white.

"What language is this?" asked she, at the sight of the unfamiliar signs.

"Bengali," replied I; "my husband's language."

"And you write it from left to right, like German?"

"Naturally. It is also an Aryan tongue—derived from Sanskrit. All Aryan tongues are written from left to right."

"But would they not find someone to decipher it?"

"Let them!" said I. "Nobody could ever translate to them what this means *to me*. See, here, for instance, those five words in a row—all very harmless, current Bengali words, without any connection with one another. Well, they each begin with the same letter as each one of the names of the camps in which you worked from 1935 onwards. I shall understand, when I use these notes. Nobody else possibly could."

"You are more resourceful than I thought," remarked H. E.

"One has to be."

"But tell me: you will repeat all I told you of our enemies' atrocities in that book you are writing, will you not?"

"Naturally. Or rather, I shall repeat *some* of them, lest my Chapter 6 become longer than the rest of the whole book."

"But that is in English!"

"Don't fear. The book is not to be published before I am free, anyhow. And that will not be tomorrow. If they discover it in the meantime, they will not understand that the information comes partly from you."

"Be very careful," repeated my new friend.

"Rest assured I shall," said I. "Only you must promise me that, when our day comes again, you will expose those people's horrors publicly, and add the weight of your priceless testimony to my impeachment of their hypocrisy."

"Naturally, I shall!"

"When I am sentenced, I hope they will put me in the D wing, with you and the others," said I. "You will introduce me to those who are 'in order' and who have suffered. And in our recreation hours, I shall hear more about the ghastly behaviour of those 'defenders of humanity', and when I am free, I shall be in a position to write a book about their crimes—and their lies—alone; to disgrace them before the whole world. Oh, how gladly I shall do it! In fact, in a way, I was lucky to get arrested and thereby to come in contact with you. Look what damaging evidence against 'them' I would have missed, if I had remained free! And I would not have known you, either. I only hope they will not refuse to put me in the D wing."

"Why should they?"

"Precisely, for fear that I might hear too much."

"There is something in that, of course. Still; where else could they put you? You are a 'political', if not a 'war criminal' like us."

"I had not the opportunities you had to become a 'war criminal'—

unfortunately," replied I. "Yet, if they knew a little more about me, they perhaps would look upon me as one. There are many varieties of 'war crimes' as you know. By the way—I never asked you—what is it that made *you* a 'war criminal' in their eyes, apart from your National Socialist faith? I mean: what were you charged with? And what did you actually do? You can safely tell *me*. Personally, I could not care less what any of us might have done to the Jews and traitors who stood in the way of the New Order. What ever you did, I can never blame you. I probably would have done worse myself, had I been given a chance. But if it be something likely to lessen the value of my chapter from the propaganda point of view, I shall just not mention it."

H. E. smiled, and patted my shoulder affectionately: "I know you are safe and loyal," said she; "But you can mention it without fear: all I did was to give a few slaps to one or two of our internees—not for the pleasure, of course, but because I had caught them stealing. I never flogged or ill-treated any of them, whether in Belsen or in my other camps, as the Jewesses accused me of having done. Nor has H. B., who came here with me the other day."

"Good God!" exclaimed I. "And you have got fifteen years just for *that!* Why, *I* have done more than that!"

And in a low, very low voice, I started talking: "Yes, surely, if I had managed to come to Europe, it would have been a thousand times better. Still, you know, where there is a will, there is a way . . . So, during the war . . ."[33]

H. E. was listening intently. When I had finished, she asked me in a whisper "Have you been relating this to anyone in Germany?"

"Only to one comrade; an absolutely reliable man who had promised never to say a word. But I thought I could, to him . . . and to you."

My friend squeezed my hand. "Oh, with me, it is all right! *We* understand each other. But give me the assurance you will never speak of this to anyone in this prison, nor let out a word likely to put 'those people' on the track, during your trial."

It was my turn to smile. "My dear! If only you had heard me talk to 'those people'—our persecutors. I have made fools of them right and left . . . while giving them the impression that I was the biggest fool in this world. Not any later than the other day, when that tall police officer came from Düsseldorf to question me—you know? The man I mentioned to you on the following morning—you should have heard me! And mind

---

[33] Probably another allusion to the espionage activities recounted in *And Time Rolls On*, pp. 33–35.—Ed.

you: I never spoke a word against our Ideology. I never said I did not firmly believe in it, or that I regretted what I have done—on the contrary! As far as my feelings and philosophy are concerned, I am always perfectly truthful. So am I, also, about the facts which 'those people' know already or are bound to discover . . . As for the others, as for the contributions of mine of which there is no trace . . . that is a different thing . . . !"

But H. E. said: "Be careful, however; for we are living in atrocious times. Prudence will help us to survive, until our day comes."

The wardress on duty—one of those who were "in order"—opened the door to tell us that time was up. "Goodbye, then," said I, to my friend. "And come again. We have plenty of interesting things to tell each other. Heil Hitler!"

"Heil Hitler!" replied H. E. as she walked out of my cell. The wardress smiled at us, and shut the door behind her.

* * *

One morning—I had finished Chapter 6 of my book, and was now busy writing Chapter 7—the door of my cell was opened and in came Fräulein S., Frau *Oberin*'s assistant. "I am not stopping, this time," she said, cordially; "I only rushed in to tell you that the date of your trial has been fixed. It will be on the 5th of April." She handed over to me a copy of my charge chart, both in English and German, and a paper summoning me to appear before the Court on the mentioned day. And she left.

At once, a more than earthly joy filled my heart; and tears came to my eyes. "The 5th of April!" I repeated, with an ecstatic smile, "the 5th of April! . . . So, it will be exactly two years after *that* night; two years after my unforgettable Watch of Fire . . . !"

And as vividly as though it had been only a day before, I remembered the dream-like landscape of Iceland: the bright nocturnal sky, streaked with transparent, moving hangings of lurid green and purple; the honey-coloured moon, obscured by a long black cloud of volcanic ash; the shining snowy hills all round me, under the phosphorescent lights of heaven; and before me, the lava stream, with the gaping mouths of fire that appeared in its dark, convulsed crust, and, beyond that, the seven craters of the erupting Volcano, two main ones, five small ones, flaming and smoking and projecting white hot quarters of rock in flashes of pink light. I remembered the incandescent boulders that loosened themselves from the crust of the lava stream, and rolled down its steep black and red surface before my eyes (one had nearly rolled over me). And I remembered the unceasing tremor of the earth beneath my feet and the solemn, awe-inspiring roar of the burning Mountain, echoing at regular intervals the sacred primaeval Sound: "Aum!" And I recalled how, exultant, ravished in religious rapture, I had walked up to the lava stream—as close as I possibly could—singing a hymn to Shiva, Lord of the Dance of Life and Death, in the language of far-away Bengal. Then had begun my whole night's watch along the river of fire, in a spirit of adoration, from about eleven o'clock until sunrise.

And like on that Night at the sight of the flames, of the smoke, and of the northern lights—and at the sound of the regular, subterranean roar—tears rolled down my cheeks; this time, tears of joy before the beauty of invisible correspondences in time and space; and tears of gratitude towards my Destiny. *"O mirabile Giustizia di Te, Primo Motore!"* thought I, once more. "Hast Thou decreed that I should exalt the grandeur of National Socialism) before the German public, exactly two years after *that* unforgettable experience? Hast Thou decided to render that day twice sacred in the history of my life?"

Whatever would be the sentence pronounced against me, I knew, now, that the day of my trial would be my greatest day. "Only when I see the Führer with my own eyes, on his return, will I be as happy," thought I. And I knew, now, that one day, he would return; that one day, his people would acclaim him again, in delirious crowds. And in my mind were blended, as two parallel manifestations of the Divine, the roar of the burning Mountain at regular intervals: "Aum! Aum!" and the equally irresistible roar of Germany's millions, a few years back and in a few years to come: "Sieg! Heil! . . . Heil Hitler!"

My humble testimony, to be given on that hallowed 5th of April, would be one of the first stirs in the depth preceding the new great outburst of indomitable power and elemental joy.

* * *

I told everybody about this miraculous coincidence of dates: Frau *Oberin*, her assistant, my friend H. E., the wardresses who were "in order," and even those who were not (or rather, of whom I did not know whether they were or not). Then, one day, I was called to meet the lawyer who had been appointed to defend me. I met him in the room in which Mr. Manning (or whatever was his name) had questioned me, three weeks before, about "my past," and in which I had had, since that day, a few talks with Mr. Stocks.

The lawyer was a short man, young, of agreeable approach, in military uniform as the rest of them.

"Do you intend to plead guilty or innocent," he asked me.

"Guilty," said I, as regards the main charge against me. "I mean 'guilty' technically speaking; for in my own eyes, far from being blameable, I have just done my duty. As regards the two minor charges, I shall plead innocent."

The two minor charges were that I had crossed the border between the French and the British Zone, without a military permit for the latter, and that I had been found in possession of a five-pound banknote, and of one thousand and some odd francs of French money.

"You are right," said the lawyer; "everybody travels from one Zone of Western Germany to another without a permit, nowadays; and all foreigners keep some foreign currency for the day they will leave the country, knowing very well one cannot exchange marks at the frontier. I have some French francs myself—otherwise I could not even hope to have a cup of coffee in a French station, on my way back to England. But you cannot get away with your main charge: the evidence against you is overwhelming."

"I would not deny what I have done, even if I could," replied I; "I am far too pleased with it. It is one of the best things I did in my life."

"Do you intend to speak?"

"I do."

"If I were you," said the lawyer, "I would speak as little as possible. You could just answer the questions the judge will put to you."

"But," exclaimed I, "I am not going to miss this golden opportunity of saying a few things which I wish the German public to hear! I have nothing to deny. But I wish to state *why* I have acted as I did. It is a public profession of faith I wish to make. Goodness me, it is a long time since I have not been able to make one!"

"I suppose you realise," answered the lawyer, "that the more you speak in that trend—in other words, the more passionately Nazi you appear—the heavier will be the sentence pronounced against you."

"How heavy, for instance?" asked I, out of curiosity.

"Well," said the man, "normally, if, without denying your faith, you do not speak too much, you should get away with a year's imprisonment at the most. In '45 or '46, of course, you probably would have been shot. But we are now in '49. Still, if you say things likely to make the judge lose his temper you might be given anything varying from a few years' detention to a death sentence. Mind you, I do not believe for a minute that we would ever go, *now*, to such extremes of severity. Remember, however, that, rightly or wrongly—wrongly in your eyes; rightly in our own—we are here to put down National Socialism, and that the more ardently you stick up for it, the worse it will be for you. Remember that you are appearing before a military Tribunal and that, whether it actually chooses to do so or not, the Court *has* the power to condemn you to death."

I looked at the man, and smiled; and said, from the bottom of my heart: "Oh, I wish it would use that power in my case!"

There was in my voice the unmistakable accent of sincerity; the yearning of years; the burning regret of wasted years; the thirst of redeeming martyrdom. Surprised as he seemed, the lawyer must have been convinced that I had spoken according to my genuine feelings. "Why such a haste?" asked he, "Are you tired of life?"

"No," said I. "I am anything but tired. But I believe that, even if they just mentioned it in the papers in two or three lines, my condemnation to death would perhaps do more to kindle the National Socialist spirit in Germany than the ten thousand leaflets I have distributed and than all the books I might write. And that is not all. There would be, also, the joy of the last sunrise upon my face; the joy of the preparation for the greatest act of my life; the joy of the act itself. . . . Draped in my best 'sari'—in scarlet and gold, as on my wedding day, in glorious '40 (I hope they would not refuse me that favour)—I would walk to the place of execution singing the Horst Wessel Song. I, Savitri Devi, the ambassador of southernmost and easternmost Aryandom as well as a daughter of northern and southern Europe. And, stretching out my right arm, firm and white in the sunshine, I would die happy in a cry of love and joy, shouting for the last time, as defiance to all the anti-Nazi forces, the holy words that sum up my life-long faith: 'Heil Hitler!'[34] I could not imagine for myself a more beautiful end."

"I see you are decidedly a 'real' one," said the lawyer. "And I do not know what one can invent to defend you in the circumstance. Still, I hope your dream of martyrdom will not materialise."

"If the immortal Gods think I can be more useful alive, then, and then alone, I shall be glad to live," answered I; "To live—in order that one day—I hope—all our enemies bitterly regret that the military Tribunal of Düsseldorf did not sentence me to death on the 5th of April 1949, when it had a chance."

* * *

I was brought back to my cell. A strange exultation possessed me. For a long time, I paced the room to and fro; I sang—although it was

---

[34] See Savitri Devi's cover art for *Defiance*, pp. viii above and page 270 below.—Ed.

forbidden to sing. Then, I gazed at the Führer's portrait that stood upon my table, against the wall. I remembered the lawyer's words: "The Court has the power to condemn you to death." And now, just as a while before, my heart answered: "I wish it did!"

A ray of sunshine fell directly upon the stern and beautiful Face, and made it look extraordinarily alive. "Yes," thought I; "I wish they did kill me. It would be lovely to die for thee, my Führer!" But again, after a while, I reflected: "It would also be lovely to continue to live for thee, and, one day, to greet thee on thy return!"

And I prayed intently, with all the fervour of my being, to the Power within fire, within the Ocean, within the storm, within the Sun; the Power Whose majesty I had witnessed two years before, in the burning and roaring Mountain: "Decide Thou my fate, Lord of Fate! For Thou alone knowest how Thou canst use me for the triumph of truth. I shall do nothing to avoid the heaviest possible sentence from our enemies. I shall defy them, happen what will—and bear the consequences with a smile, whatever these be. I feel, I know, it is my appointed role to defy them and their 'de-Nazification' schemes. If they kill me, I shall be glad. But if they spare me in spite of my defiance, I shall take it as a sign from Thee that National Socialism shall rise and rule again.

"Lord of Life, Thou hast raised the everlasting Doctrine under its modern form; Thou hast appointed the Chosen Nation to champion it. Lord of Death. Thou hast allowed the forces of death to prevail for a while. Lord of Order and of Harmony, Lord of the Dance of appearances; Lord of the Rhythm that brings back spring after winter; the day, after the night; birth after death; and the next age of truth and perfection, after each end of an age of gloom, Thou shalt give my beloved comrades and superiors the lordship of the earth, one day. If I survive this trial, I shall take it as a sign from Thee that this will be in my lifetime, and that Thou hast appointed me to do something in our coming new struggle."

I felt happy, having thus prayed. I then sat down, and laid down in black and white the few points I wished to stress in the speech I would make before my judges.

When that was done, I read a section of the Bhagavad-Gita.

Chapter 5

THE GLORIOUS DAY

It was a lovely spring day. Seated in the motorcar by the side of Miss Taylor, I gazed out of the window at the new landscape: tender green grass and tender green leaves; and flowers, masses of flowers; lilacs and fruit blossoms, white, pink, yellow, red, and pale violet, in the sunshine. And I gazed at the pure bright sky. I knew this was my last day of relative liberty. I was, now, really going to be tried—and sentenced. After that—whatever the sentence was to be—I would no longer be taken to Düsseldorf every week or fortnight; no longer be given glimpses of the outside world. And I breathed deeply, as though to take into my body all the freshness and all the vitality of the invincible living earth. Never in all my life had I found the fragrance of spring so intoxicating; never had things seemed to me so beautiful. At times—when the car rolled past some particularly fascinating spot—an intense emotion seized me, and tears came to my eyes. I felt as though, through the glory of her sunlit fields and of her trees covered with blossoms, Hitler's beloved fatherland was smiling to me—greeting me on my last journey to the place where I was destined to defy her oppressors.

My luggage was travelling with me, at the back of the car. It is, it seems, the custom: there is always a hope that a prisoner on remand *might* get acquitted, in which case he or she is set free at once, without having the trouble to come back to prison in order to fetch the luggage left there. However, I had known nothing of the existence of that custom until Mr. Harris, the British Chief Warder at Werl, had informed me of it on that very morning while I was waiting in his office for the car to come. When, on the night before, the matron of the prison had told me that I was to take *all* my things with me, I had been at a loss to understand why. And—ill-acquainted as I still was with the mysterious ways of British justice—I had feared that, perhaps, my precious manuscripts were to be used as evidence against me and then destroyed. All night I had not slept, wondering how I could possibly save them, if that were the case. And early in the morning, when my dear comrade H. E. had come, as usual, to fetch her tea, porridge, and white bread—and, this time, to wish me "good luck" in my trial—I had told her: "I fear they regret having given me back my writings. It looks, now, as if they want them, for I was told to take all my things to Düsseldorf. But I shall leave my manuscripts here behind the cupboard, rolled up in my waterproof. Tell Frau So-and-so; she is on duty, I believe. And ask her to hide them for me until I come back. Or hide them yourself, somewhere in the infirmary. Nobody will look there. Save them!—not for my sake, but for the sake of the truth I have written in those pages."

"I promise I shall do so," H. E. had answered: "And at your trial, remember that we will all be thinking of you, and that we all love you," she added, speaking of those of my comrades, the so-called "war criminals," who were genuine National Socialists, and, perhaps, of all the members of the prison staff—Frau So-and-so and others—who were too.

"I hope I shall be worthy of your love," I had replied. "This is my greatest and my happiest day. Heil Hitler!"

"Heil Hitler!" had said H. E., raising her hand in her turn.

Now, in the car, I was thinking of that last greeting, and looking at the landscape. Suddenly I realised the tragic fact that H. E. and H. B., and Frau M. and Frau S. and Frau H.[1] and all my other true comrades, of whom I was now beginning to know the names, and thousands of others, all over Germany, had not seen the beauty of spring since 1945. I knew it before, no doubt. I had never felt it so painfully. "Poor dears!" thought I. "Until when?" And some were captive even longer still: Rudolf Hess was, for instance, since 1941. "Yes; until when?"

The vivid picture of them all, cut off from the world of action for such a long time, after the intense life they had lived during the first struggle and the glorious following years, saddened me profoundly. And I also recalled all those who had been killed off as "war criminals" by our enemies. "Oh, thought I," if there is any such thing as consciousness after death, may they hear me today! I shall speak as though they were present."

The car rolled on. Between expanses of lovely countryside, we crossed the ruined towns: Dortmund, Duisburg, Essen, . . . As we were passing before the skeleton of the immense Krupp factories, Miss Taylor said to the policeman seated on the other side of her: "A part of these are being repaired and will soon be working again—for us. Really, war is a stupid business! We wrecked these factories, and tomorrow we will again be buying from them."

I could not help putting in my word—although I was a prisoner, and

---

[1] Two Frau H.s are mentioned in *Defiance* (see Index). They are Anna Hempel and Irene Haschke, according to Nicholas Goodrick-Clarke (*Hitler's Priestess: Savitri Devi, the Hindu-Aryan Myth, and Neo-Nazism* [New York: New York University Press, 1998], p. 143).—Ed.

the policewoman had not addressed me. The fact is that I had despised the representatives of the Allied Occupation from the start, and that all their outward courtesy to me had only served to increase in me that contempt. I never cared if I did hurt any of them, individually, through the way I expressed my resentment towards them as a whole.

"And what about the hundreds of factories which you people have been and are still dismantling?" said I, bitterly.

"That was—and is—a great mistake on our part, from the standpoint of our interest," replied Miss Taylor. "Sooner or later, we will have to help to build then up and to equip them anew, for the sake of our own defence against Bolshevism. Ultimately, it is the British taxpayer who will suffer for the damage we are doing." It looked exactly as though the representative of the Allied Occupation was trying her best to propitiate me—the defender of National Socialism; Germany's friend . . . Did I also represent the future—the coming revenge of the dismembered Nation—that the policewoman felt so keenly the necessity of doing so? If that was the case, her attempt only had the contrary effect.

"It will serve you right; oh, how it will serve you right!" I burst out. "Why did you, in 1939, go and wage war upon the one Man and the one people who could have kept back Bolshevism? Why did you ally yourselves with the Russians in order to crush National Socialism? You only deserve to perish, and I heartily wish you do! I wish I have the pleasure of seeing you, one day, not all exterminated—that would be too glorious and too merciful an end—but ground down to the level of a twentieth-rate nation, mourning for your past splendour for a generation or two and then forgetting even that; a nation having less in common with the builders of the historic British empire than the unfortunate Greeks of today have with those of the Periclean age. I wish I could come back, from century to century, and tell you, with merciless glee, over and over again, until you sink into the unconsciousness of the dead: 'This gnawing decay is the wage of England's crime in 1939'. And I wish to see the same slow paralysis, the same nightmare of dwindling life in death, torture the descendants of *all* those Aryans who from 1939 to 1945—and after 1945—sided against Hitler's great new humanity. May it spare those alone who will recognise the treachery of their unworthy fathers and spit at their memory and boldly join the resurrected New Order."

To my own surprise, this vitriolic tirade, apparently, prompted Miss Taylor to propitiate me all the more. She started pleading for the British people while admitting the "mistakes" of British policy. (The crime of 1939 she euphemistically called a "mistake.") "Many of us are growing to believe that it would perhaps have been better for us to ally ourselves with Germany," said she.

"Well, begin by building up the factories you spoilt and putting an end to your 'de-Nazification' nonsense," said I, speaking in the name of the German National Socialists, "and then, perhaps, we shall condescend to consider what we *might* do. But even then,"—I added after a pause—"what about the magnificent forests, Germany's pride, that you have massacred? I wish that, in the next war, three at least of your people are killed for every tree you have cut down, out here—apart from those who will die so that my comrades and superiors will be avenged."

"And yet, we are not so bad as you think," said Miss Taylor, determined to draw my mind away from bloodthirsty thoughts—if she could. "Be impartial and look how we treat your friends, here: we are releasing the political prisoners little by little; and they don't work in prison, like the others . . ."

My first impulse was to interrupt her and to say: "What rubbish! My comrades, the so-called 'war criminals' in Werl, all work. More so, I know that one of them at least—H. B., one of the victims of the Belsen trial—is forced to empty the sanitary pails from the cells, along with the thieves and murderesses appointed to that work. I have seen her do it. I have seen her empty my pail. Don't tell me tales!" But in order to say that, I would have had to admit that I was in touch with some of the so-called "war criminals." Miss Taylor would perhaps tell Colonel Vickers . . . And then? No; it was better for me to say nothing; to continue listening to the lies of democratic propaganda . . .

"They don't work?" said I, feigning ignorance and astonishment. "Is it so, really? What do they do, then, all day long?"

Miss Taylor seemed pleased to think that I believed her. "I don't know," she answered. "Those who like can write their memoirs. Some do. General Kesselring is writing his, I know. We allow him to. As for General von Rundstedt, we even set him free on *parole*—free to travel about Germany, to go and see his family, and come back to a comfortable prison till his next leave! Indeed, I tell you, the French would never do that! Nor the Germans themselves, if ever they had us. As for the Russians . . ."

"Hum!" thought I, "I wish I could investigate into that statement of hers about von Rundstedt. If it is true, there must be some fishy business behind it. These people do nothing for nothing."

"And can the political prisoners have light in their cells after eight p.m.?" asked I—knowing perfectly well that my friend H. E. had no light after eight o'clock any more than the others, whether "war criminals" or ordinary delinquents.

"Certainly," said Miss Taylor.

Then she started speaking about the English men and women arrested in England, during the war, under the 18B act. "The 'internment camps' in which they were placed," said she, "had nothing in common with the 'concentration camps' in which the enemies of the National Socialist régime suffered in Germany."

"You'd better not expatiate on that subject," observed I: "I know too many 18Bs."

"I know a few too," answered the policewoman.

"I bet you do," said I. And to show her how impossible it was to convince even a moderately well-informed Nazi that such a thing as "humanity" *exists* among our opponents, I added, with an ironical smile "Perchance, do you know anything about the torture chamber in Ham Common?"

"I never heard of it, and I don't believe it ever existed," exclaimed Miss Taylor. "You, of course, will believe anything provided one of your own lot says it!"

"And even if I did, that would not make me more gullible than the most 'enlightened' Democrats," retorted I. "But I happen to know a man—and an Englishman, too—who was tortured, during the war, precisely in the place I just mentioned, for no other reason except that he was one of us and that he knew, or was supposed to know, too much. And you had other such places, although you pretended—and still pretend—to be horrified at our 'barbarity'. Now, don't tell me the contrary, for you will be wasting your breath."

Miss Taylor deemed it useless to continue her plea. However, she made an ultimate attempt to placate me—and at last, she spoke of something that *was* true: "We have spared your writings," she said.

She was right—for once. They had, indeed, done so. And I wondered whether the French or the Americans—let alone the Russians—would have done it. (I would certainly *not* have done it, in the case of an anti-Nazi manuscript fallen into my hands, had I had power.) I was grateful to the Gods for what I considered as a miracle. But I was not in a mood to give credit to our persecutors, whatever their nationality.

"Oh," replied I, "I suppose you only spared them because, in your eyes, they appeared written with too much fervour to be dangerous . . . for the time being . . ."

But in the bottom of my heart, I repeat, I thanked the heavenly powers for the fact that the precious pages were lying somewhere in safety, in Werl, and that I would find them again—and continue writing them—after my trial would be over, if I was allowed to live.

* * *

We reached Düsseldorf. We waited a little before entering the hall in which I was to be judged. Along with my other things, my few items of jewellery had been given back to me. I had them in the attaché case I held in my hand, as on the day of my arrest. Among them, were my Indian earrings in the shape of swastikas. "I have half a mind to wear those," said I to Miss Taylor. "What can 'they' do? Give me six months extra, a year extra, for 'contempt of Court'? Let them! The pleasure of wearing the Sign of the Sun and of National Socialism, in front of everybody, is well worth it!"

Miss Taylor gazed at me to make sure that I was speaking seriously. To her amazement, I was. "What a baby you are, for a woman forty-three!" she said at last. "I really fail to see what good this can do, not for you (I know you don't care) but for your precious cause. The people who have come to hear you will no longer take you seriously when they see you trying to defy us by such a showy exhibition. Do as you like, of course. It's all the same to me. But in your place . . . from *your* point of view . . ."

I reflected. Perhaps there was something in what she said. "After all," thought I, "it matters little. They will see what I am, fast enough, when I open my mouth . . ."

The witnesses whom I had seen on the 14th of March were all there: Gertrud Romboy—who pretended not to notice me—the policeman Wilhelm Kripfel, the *Oberinspektor* Heller, and the others. A man whom I did not know, dressed in lawyer's robes, approached me and told me that he had been appointed to defend me, as, at the last moment, my lawyer had been prevented from coming. (It occurred to me that, in reality, he had possibly decided that it was impossible for him to defend someone so glad to suffer as I was, for her beloved cause, and that he had just shifted the task onto a colleague.) I repeated to this man what I had already told the first lawyer, namely that, under no consideration did I wish to appear less responsible than I was, or less fervently National Socialist, and that I would myself see to it that I did not.

When the lawyer had gone, a man in military uniform came up to me and asked me the most unexpected question of all: "Well, Mrs. Mukherji," said he, "how is your book getting on? You surely have finished Chapter 4. How many new chapters have you written while on remand?"

I was taken aback. "Is this man sent to find out what I have been writing in prison, so that 'they' might control it and, if they like, destroy it?" thought I. "What shall I tell him? To pretend I have completely forgotten about the book will not do; it would arouse suspicion—for he would not believe it."

"My book?" said I, turning to the man, and speaking with as much naturalness as I possibly could, "I have not touched it. I had many letters to write, and wanted to finish them before doing anything else. And also, I was not in a mood. I shall continue writing later on—if it is allowed. Otherwise I shall wait till I am free. It is no use getting into trouble with the prison authorities."

I hoped the man believed me. But I was not at all sure he did. He opened a cardboard cover he carried in his hand and showed me a typed copy of the first pages of my book up to the beginning of Chapter 3. I had completely forgotten about that copy—one of the three I had typed in London, on my last journey, precisely to save as much as I could of the book in case it ever fell into the hands of the police, on my return to Germany. (I had left one in England, at a friend's, and had sent the other to India.) But whatever I had written since my return was, of course, not in those copies. To this one I had barely had the time to add, in my own handwriting, just before my arrest, a page or two of my Chapter 3. I read once more the last words I had copied—my personal comment upon a true episode illustrating Germany's spirit in the midst of atrocious conditions, in May, 1945: "Hail, invincible Germany! Hail, undying Aryan youth, élite of the world, whom the agents of the dark forces can starve and torture, but can never subdue! That unobtrusive profession of faith of two unknown but real Nazis, in 1945, is, itself, a victory. And it is not the only one."[2]

"You wrote that, is it not so?" the man asked me.

"Yes, I did," replied I. And I could not conceal a certain pride in the tone of my voice. For I was aware that my ardent tribute of admiration to Germany, now that, materially, she lay in the dust, was also—and all the more, precisely because I am not a German—a victory of the Nazi spirit over force of money, over force of lies, and even over force of arms. But I said nothing more.

The man walked away after wishing me "good luck" in my trial.

* * *

At last, the time came for me to appear in Court.

"Your comrade has got six months," Miss Taylor told me—she had just heard from someone what sentence had been pronounced against

---

[2] Cf. *Gold in the Furnace*, 3rd ed., p. 26.—Ed.

138

Herr W. —"I suppose you will get a year or so."

"You forget that I am not going to lie, and say I did it in the hope of money," replied I. "I am far more interested in what the Party will think of me in 1955 than in what 'these' people might do with me now. I also bear in mind what fact I am about to leave behind me, forever, in the irrevocable past."

For a second or two, I held in my hand, with love, the little portrait of Adolf Hitler that hung around my neck. "May I speak as though thou wert here present, listening to me, my Führer!" thought I, as I crossed the threshold of the hall and walked slowly to my place in the dock, my head erect, my eyes bright with joy.

The hall was packed with people—representatives of the press, and members of the German public. "There has never been such a crowd of onlookers in a trial like this since 1945," said Miss Taylor.

Under the enthusiasm that possessed me, I felt supremely calm—blissful; the word is not too strong a one. I felt invincible. I *knew* I was invincible. I embodied the Nazi spirit—the everlasting soul of Aryan Heathendom, in its primaeval strength, pride, and beauty. My face must have beamed, and I must have looked beautiful—as one always does when one is raised above oneself. I felt as though, from all the prisons and concentration camps in which our enemies still retain them, from their destitute homes, from their beds of suffering—and from beyond the limits of the visible world—my martyred comrades and superiors had fixed their eyes upon me and were crying out to me: "Speak for us, who cannot speak! Defy in our name the forces that have broken our bodies and silenced our voices, Savitri, daughter of the Sun,[3] Aryan woman of all times!"

On the left, against the wall, behind the judge's seat, was spread out the Union Jack—in the place where the Swastika banner would have been seen, in former days, above a portrait of the Führer. But the sight of it—reminder of the fact that Germany was occupied—did not disturb me (any more than that of the two Jews whom I noticed, seated right in front, on the first bench, among the public). Nothing counted, nothing existed for me, but the living spirit that I represented, and the living Nation—the Nation Hitler so loved—that I felt looking to me from beyond the narrow limits of that hall, waiting for the few words that she would never forget.

An overwhelming consciousness of solemnity—a sort of religious awe—took hold of me as, exactly two years before, on the slopes of the divine Volcano. A cold, delightful thrill ran along my spine and throughout

[3] My Indian name, Savitri, means in Sanskrit "Solar Energy."

my body. In a flash of hallucinating memory, I recalled the roar of the
burning Mountain, and the tremor of the earth—like a throb of subterranean drums accompanying the Dance of Destruction. I could not sing, as
when I had walked up to the stream of lava. But somehow, within my
mind, I identified the ever-vivid remembrance of the eruption with an
anticipated inner vision of the coming collapse of the Western world, in
the thunder and flames of the next war. And, along with that deafening,
crushing, all-pervading noise—answering it, covering it, dominating it—
I heard within my heart the music of the victorious Song, of the Song of
Resurrection—the Song of my undaunted comrades, alone alive among
the dead; alone standing, and marching, in the midst of the general crash;
alone worthy to thrive and to rule, upon the ashes of those who chose the
way of disintegration and death—*our* Song, in the struggle, in victory, in
the dark years of persecution, in the unconditional mastery of the future
forever and ever: *"Die Fahne hoch! . . ."*

Never had I felt its conquering tune so powerfully within my nerves,
within my blood, as though it were the mystic rhythm of my very life.
Tears filled my eyes. I remembered the hundreds of miles of ruins that
stretched in all directions, beyond the spot where I stood—the torn and
prostrate body of holy Germany. All that would be avenged, one day, in
a volcanic upheaval. And above the noise of crumbling Christian civilisation, the Song of the young hero Horst Wessel would resound heralding
the final New Age. And above the flames and smoke, the triumphant
Swastika Flag would flutter in the storm, against the glaring background
of explosions unheard of . . . ". . . *Bald flattern Hitlerfahnen über allen
Strassen . . ."*

Oh, how happy, how invincibly happy I was!

I looked at the judge, at the public Prosecutor, at the lawyer, at the
other representatives of the long-drawn Occupation, in military uniforms,
and at the two "Yids" grinning on the front bench—delighted at the idea
of watching a Nazi's trial. And I thought: "Where will these all be, in ten
years' time? While *we* . . . we shall survive because we deserve to; because the Gods have decreed that we shall. May my attitude show today
how indeed we deserve to rule, we, the sincere, we the fearless, we the
pure, the proud, the strong, the free, the detached—the beautiful; we National Socialists! For if I, the least among us, am worthy, then how much
more so the others!"

The judge made a sign, and everybody sat down.

Then, he asked me, for the sake of formality, my name, my age, etc. .
. . and the procedure began. After the hearing of several witnesses, I was
acquitted of the minor charge of having been found in possession of a

Bank of England five-pound note. I think I can say that the answer of one of the witnesses, named Mr. Severs, finally decided my acquittal. Shown a five-pound banknote, he stated that he could not recognise, in it, the one found in my handbag on the day of my arrest. And the next charge was brought forth, namely that, while not being a German, I had entered the British Zone of control without the required military permit—for, as I have already said, my permit was good for the French Zone only.

6. Savitri Devi's husband Asit Krishna Mukherji, photographed in March, 1962

Again, witnesses were heard, as in connection with my first charge. I was beginning to feel a little bored—for my main charge was the only one that really interested me—when to my surprise, I noticed in the hands of the lawyer, who was seated in front of me, a letter written in my husband's bold and elegant handwriting, so well-known to me. Or was I mistaken? I peeped over the man's shoulder, and, at the bottom of the last page, I read the signature: Asit Krishna Mukherji. It was indeed a letter from my husband. Curiosity—mingled with a certain feeling of apprehension—stirred me. And when, at last, the hearing of my case was put off till the afternoon, I asked the lawyer to let me have the message. He willingly agreed. I read it in waiting for my midday meal.

It bore in large letters, at the left top corner of the first page, the word "confidential," and was addressed "to the Chairman of the

Military Tribunal, Düsseldorf." It was an extremely clever and shame-less plea for clemency in my favour. In four pages of obsequious prose, it contained, along with some accurate statements—such as a passage about my lifelong yearning after the old Norse Gods no less than those of ancient Greece—some half-truths, artfully dished up, and a sprinkling of blatant lies. The accurate statements were casually made, in such a man-ner that it became very difficult if not impossible to draw from them the logical conclusions, *i.e.*, the seriousness, the solidity—the orthodoxy—of my National Socialist faith. The half-truths were twisted, with experi-enced ease, into downright lies. The fact, for instance, that, after three atrocious years of despair, I had regained confidence in the future of my race in Sweden, mainly through a conversation with a world-famous Na-tional Socialist of that country, the explorer Sven Hedin, in 1948, was presented as though I had, myself, become a National Socialist in 1948! And even so, according to this letter, my socio-political convictions boiled down to just a "personal admiration for Adolf Hitler"! The spirit that had animated my whole activity in India—the spirit, nay, that had prompted me to go to India—the land that had never denied its Aryan Gods—was most carefully concealed. And, worse than all, I was pre-sented not merely as an "intensely emotional" and gullible woman, who had "certainly been exploited by interested people," but as "an out-and-out individualist" (*sic*) who "could not but be emphatically opposed to any régime of absolute authority" (*sic*).

In spite of my growing indignation, I could not help admiring the ser-pentine persuasiveness that my husband displayed in dealing with our enemies. This was indeed a letter of my subtle, practical, passionless, and yet unfailingly loyal—and useful—old ally; of the man I had seen at work, day after day, during and already before the war, for years; of the man who had, to some extent, prepared and made history, without any-one knowing it—save I; who, had only Germany and Japan won this war, would have been, today, the real master of India. But that accusation of "individualism," written against me in black and white (never mind with what laudable intention), was more than I could stand. Turning to Miss Taylor after I had finished reading the letter I burst out: "Have a look at this masterpiece of slimy diplomacy, for it is well worth it!"

The policewoman read the document. "It is most cleverly laid out," concluded she, handing it back to me. "Naturally, I—who am beginning to know you, by now—can see through it. But the judge does not know you. I tell you: your lawyer could take a splendid advantage of this and . . ."

"And obtain an incredibly light sentence for me—lighter even than Herr W.'s," said I, with contempt. "An incredibly light sentence, at the cost of honour! And you think I am going to stand for that?"

"Stand for what?" replied Miss Taylor, genuinely astonished. "There is no question of honour. Your husband has not insulted you. He has only, with amazing mastery, exploited the very truth for your defence. He says a few true things—among others—doesn't he?"

"True things! My foot! I'd very much like to know which," I burst out. "He admits that my whole philosophy has its roots in my pre-eminently Pagan consciousness, which is, of course, true enough. But that is about the only accurate statement he has made in this disgraceful letter. He mentions my love of animals, too, and my strong objection to any infliction of suffering upon them, for whatever purpose it be; but he does so only in order to imply that *a fortiori* I surely object to our ruthless treatment of dangerous or potentially dangerous human beings, *which I do not*, as I told you a hundred thousand times. And he knows, better than anyone, that I do not—any more than he does himself. And he should know that I don't want to pass for a silly humanitarian in front of everybody, even if that could set me free. I have not come here to be set free, or to get a light sentence. I have come to bear witness to the greatness of my Führer, whatever might happen; to proclaim the universal and eternal appeal of the ideals for which we fought, and to defy the forces of a whole world bent upon killing our faith. It is the only thing I can do, now. And nobody shall keep me from doing it. I don't want to be excused, defended, whitewashed, as though I had done something wrong. And especially not with such damaging hints as those. Have you noticed that passage at the bottom of the second page, in which I am presented as though I were one of those sentimental non-German females whose main, if not sole, contribution to the war effort of the Third Reich consisted of dreaming about the Führer as often as they could? Such a soppy lot! I don't want to be lumped with them; they are not my type. And what would my comrades think of me?"

"Now, don't get excited," said Miss Taylor, "and let your imagination run away with you. Who tells you that your husband tried to 'lump you' with such women? He has just used the words 'personal admiration' to characterise your feelings towards your Leader. What is the harm in it? You *do* admire him, I suppose."

"I worship him. But that is not the point. I tell you my husband has written those words purposely, so that our persecutors might not take me seriously. The proof of it you call see a few lines below, where I am described as 'never having been interested in the political side of National Socialism'—as though it were possible to separate the 'political side' from the philosophical, in an organic doctrine as logically conceived as ours! You can see it in that mendacious statement where I am called 'an individualist' naturally opposed to 'any régime of absolute authority'. *I*, of all people, an 'individualist'! *I*, opposed to authority! What a joke! Doubtless, I value *my* individual freedom—the freedom to salute my friends in the street, anywhere in Europe, anywhere in the world, saying: 'Heil Hitler!'; the freedom to publish my writings with every facility. Doubtless I hate the authority *now* imposed upon me—and upon all those who share my faith—in the name of a philosophy different from ours. But which National Socialist does not? And I surely would like nothing better than to see an iron authority impose *our* principles—*my* own principles—upon the whole world, breaking all opposition more ruthlessly than ever. Which National Socialist would not? I am in no way different from the others. But my husband has been trying all the time to persuade our enemies that I am. There lies his whole trick: he has tried to persuade them that I admire our Führer without being, myself, a full-fledged National Socialist, aware of all the implications of his teaching; in other words, that I am an over-emotional, irresponsible fool. And *that* is precisely what makes me wild."

"He only did it to save you," said Miss Taylor. "And I am sure there is not one of your German friends who would not understand that."

"They might. But *he* should have known, after eleven years of collaboration with me, that I never wanted to be saved," replied I; "and if anyone dares to read that letter in Court, I shall say a few things that will make its author regret ever having written it. I shall prove that I was what I am—and he too—years before 1948. I don't care what might happen to both of us as a consequence!" I was out of my mind.

"Now, don't be silly; don't be a child," said Miss Taylor, softly: "and especially, don't speak so loudly: it is not necessary for everyone to hear you. Nobody forces you to make use of this letter. Tell the lawyer not to produce it, and he will not. But it was written with the best of intentions, I am sure. And *that* you should appreciate."

"I probably would," said I, after a moment's reflection, "if only I could be sure that he wished to save me, *not* in order to spare me hardships for my own sake, but solely because he judges me more useful to our cause—or at least less useless—free than behind bars. If *that* were the case, I would forgive him."

"Quite possibly that is the case," replied Miss Taylor.

We had finished our meal, which had been served to us at the *"Stahlhaus"*—now the British Police Headquarters. We returned to the building in Mühlenstraße where my trial was taking place. I handed back my husband's letter to the lawyer, telling him most emphatically not to mention it under any consideration.

"But you don't seem to realise to what an extent I could exploit that letter in your favour," said he.

"I know you could, but I forbid you to do so," replied I. "My honour as a National Socialist comes before my safety, before my life, before everything—save, of course, the higher interests of the cause."

"All right, then. It is as you like."

No sooner had I thus made sure that my responsibility would be fully acknowledged, I regained my calm—and joy.

The procedure concerning my second minor charge continued. The judge now wished to ask me a few questions, "But first, are you a Christian?" he asked me—for I was to swear to tell the truth.

"I am not," replied I.

"In that case, it would be no use you swearing upon the Bible," said he. "Upon what will you swear?"

I reflected for a second or two. No, I would not name any book, however exalted, however inspired. I would name, in a paraphrase, the cosmic Symbol of all power and wisdom, which is also the symbol of the resurrection of Aryandom: the holy Swastika.

"I can swear upon the sacred Wheel of the Sun," said I, firmly, hoping that, if the judge and the other Britishers present did not understand what that meant, most of the Germans would. I spoke thus, for I did not intend to tell any lies. If a question were put to me about things I wished to keep secret, I would simply refuse to answer it. One can always do that.

But the judge did not accept my suggestion. Perhaps he knew, after all, what the Wheel of the Sun is. He asked me not to swear at all but to "declare emphatically"—in some non-confessional formula so devoid of poetic appeal that I have completely forgotten it—that I would tell "the truth, all the truth, and nothing but the truth." I did so; and then explained why I had not bothered to obtain a military permit for entering the British Zone: an official of the French Security Service in Baden Baden (92 Litschenstraße) had positively told me, that "nowadays" one could travel wherever one liked in western Germany provided one had an entrance permit into one Zone. This was a fact.

The judge, however, this time, did not acquit me. "This is, of course, a purely technical offence," said he. "Yet, it has been committed." And he proceeded to the examination of the witnesses in connection with the main charge against me—namely that of having indulged in Nazi propaganda. Once more I became thoroughly interested in what was going on in my immediate surroundings.

All the witnesses were witnesses on behalf of the Prosecution—

witnesses who were called in to prove that I had indeed done that with which I was charged, and that I had done it intentionally, fully aware of what I was doing. Every word they uttered "against" me filled me with satisfaction. At last—after how many years of concealment for the sake of expediency—I was appearing in public in my true glaring colours. Had it been possible for me to continue to be useful in the dark, naturally, it would have been better. But it was no longer possible. So I was glad to see the picture of my real self emerge little by little, from accumulated evidence, before a few representatives of my Führer's people. "Let them know," thought I, not without a certain pride, "that in this wide, venal world that accuses them and condemns them, and reviles them, because—for the time being—they failed to conquer, they still have at least one faithful friend!"

Finally, the police official before whom I had made a voluntary statement on the 21st of February, came forth and read that statement: "It is not only the military spirit, but National Socialist consciousness in its entirety that I have struggled to strengthen, for, *in my eyes, National Socialism exceeds Germany and exceeds our times*." I smiled. "Nothing could be more true," thought I. The newspaper reporters took down the words. "They will not dare to publish them, lest their licences be cancelled," thought I again—"for that would be pouring oil upon the fire."

It was the Public Prosecutor's turn to speak. He summed up the evidence that the witnesses had brought, putting special stress upon my own statement which the last witness had quoted. He then proceeded to give a brief account of my academic qualifications and of my career. "Here is a woman who is obviously intelligent," said he; "who has obtained the highest degrees a University can confer upon a scholar—she is a master of sciences; a doctor of literature—who has travelled over half the surface of the globe; who has taught history and philosophy to students, and held public meetings; who can speak and write eight languages[4] and who has published a few books lacking neither in original thought nor in erudition; and yet, . . . in spite of all that (*sic*) we are compelled to acknowledge that she is a fervent National Socialist . . ."

From the corner where I was seated, just opposite him, I lifted up my head with pride as though to say: "Surely I am! It is my greatest glory." But I could not help being amused—at the same time as a little indignant—as I heard the words "in spite of all that." "The damned cheek of this man!" exclaimed I, in a whisper, to Miss Taylor—for she was the only person I could possibly speak to—"'in spite of all that' he says, as

---

[4] English, French, German, Italian, Greek, Icelandic, Hindi, and Bengali.—Ed.

though a higher education, experience of foreign lands, thought, erudition, and what not, were incompatible with a sincere Nazi faith! I wish I could tell him that my little knowledge of history and my prolonged contact with people of all races have made me more Nazi than ever—if that were possible!"

"Shhh! Don't talk," said the policewoman.

But the Public Prosecutor had caught from his place the movement of my head and the happy smile that had accompanied it.

"See," pursued he, "she gladly admits it. She is smiling. She is proud of it!"

"I am!" exclaimed I.

There were responsive smiles of pride and sympathy among the German public. But the judge asked me "not to interrupt." And the Public Prosecutor Continued. "A fervent National Socialist," said he, "and an active one, to the extent of her opportunities. She has come all the way from India in order to do what she could to help the dangerous minority with which she has identified herself completely—the minority that has never acknowledged defeat. She has printed at her own cost, brought over to Germany at her own risk, and distributed a considerable number of those papers which constitute the ground of the present charge. Her case is particularly serious, for she illustrates how strong a hold National Socialism still retains today upon certain people—unfortunately more numerous than we are generally inclined to believe—who are, precisely, anything but irresponsible agents or men and women swayed by the lust of material gain. She represents the most dangerous type of idealist in the service of the system that has brought nothing but destruction upon this country and upon the world at large. We only have to look out of the windows of this hall to see what National Socialism means: ruins. We only have to remember this war in order to understand where that system has led the people whom it had succeeded in deceiving. And if we remain here today, it is to avoid further war, further suffering, further ruins, by keeping the pernicious Ideology from regaining appeal, and power. The accused, Mrs. Mukherji, has, I repeat, come to Germany on purpose to strengthen it: on purpose to undermine the work we have set ourselves to do. And during the few months of her stay she has already, through her leaflets and posters, but doubtless also through undetectable private propaganda—through her conversations, through her whole attitude— done more irreparable harm than can accurately be estimated. I therefore demand that an exemplary sentence should be pronounced against her by this Court."

I could not say that these were textually the words used by the Public

Prosecutor. I have not stenographed his speech. But this *was* the general trend of it. And some of the sentences I remember word by word, and have reported here as they were uttered.

I boiled with indignation, as could be expected, when I heard the man slander our faith and declare—his arm stretched backwards, towards the window behind him—that the ruins of Düsseldorf and of all Germany were the result of National Socialism. Surely, I would answer that accusation, at least reject it in a biting sentence, when my turn came to speak. Yet, the best answer to it would be, no doubt . . . the next war—direct consequence of the defeat of Germany in this one; and divine punishment for England's refusal to conclude with the Third Reich an honourable and lasting peace. Oh, then! Then, I would gloat to my heart's content over new and even more appalling ruins—not in Germany, this time. And if I met such people as that Public Prosecutor, I would laugh in their faces and tell them: "Remember how you used to say that the ruins of Germany were the work of National Socialism? Well, whose work are your ruins, now? No doubt, that of your confounded Democracy—of that Democracy you once had the impudence to try to make *us* welcome. Eh, look now and see where it has brought you! Hah, hah, hah! How it serves you right! Hah, hah, hah!" Oh to speak thus, one day, with impunity, to our enemies half-dead in the dust!

Yet, I could not help admiring the way the man had, from the democratic standpoint, characterised me. After one's own people's love, nothing is more refreshing than the acknowledgement of one's harmfulness by an enemy. For years, I had positively suffered from the fact that our opponents did not seem to believe me when I expressed my radical views and uncompromising feelings. God alone knows what forceful language I had always employed! But half the time the nonentities—the "moderate" people, the "decent" people, the usual supporters of all we hate the most—would tell me, in the patronizing tone which grownups sometimes use when speaking to adolescents: "You say that, but you don't really *mean* it; surely you would not *do* it!" Had I been in a position to do so, I would have gladly sent them all to their doom—even without them being dangerous to us—for the sheer pleasure of showing them that I *did* mean it, and was in no mood to be taken for an irresponsible chatterbox. Now, here was, at last, a man from the "other side" who knew that I "meant it" and "would do it" all right, if only given half a chance; a Democrat in whose eyes I was "the most dangerous type of idealist." I thanked him, in my heart, for recognising my calculated purposefulness no less than my love and hate, and for not treating me as an emotional child. I thanked him for demanding "an exemplary punishment" for me. Had he demanded a death sentence, I would have been fully satisfied.

The judge told the lawyer that he now could speak. The latter declared he had nothing to say. It was the Public Prosecutor himself who reminded the Court of the existence of my husband's letter.

"The accused does not wish that letter to be produced," said the lawyer.

"Certainly not!" shouted I, from my corner. "I don't want the whitewash. It is nothing but a concoction of half-truths and downright lies, anyhow."

This public declaration was enough to deprive the document of whatever practical value it might have had. The judge did not insist. He turned to me; "Do you wish to speak?" he asked me.

"I do," replied I; "although I have nothing to say for my defence, I would like to state the reasons that have prompted me to act as I did—if those reasons interest the Court."

"They certainly do," said the judge, giving me, at last, the opportunity that I had been so eagerly awaiting.

I had prepared a short but precise, and—as far as I could—well-composed speech, containing more or less whatever I wished to say. I forgot all about it. I forgot the presence of the judge, as well as of the other representatives of British power in a conquered land. I felt again raised to the state of inspiration which I had experienced on entering the hall, on the morning of that unforgettable day. I found myself speaking, not merely before the British Military Tribunal of Düsseldorf, but before all Germany, all Aryandom; before my comrades, living and dead; before our Führer, living forever. My words were mine, and more than mine. They were the public oath of allegiance of my everlasting self to my undying race and its everlasting Saviour and Leader.

"I have never had the conceit to believe that by distributing a few leaflets and sticking up half a dozen posters, I would, alone, provoke the resurrection of National Socialism, out of the ruins and desolation in the midst of which we stand," said I, in a clear voice that was, also, mine and more than mine. "Those ruins are not, as the Public Prosecutor has, just now, tendentiously asserted, the consequence of our Führer's policy. They are, on the contrary, the marks of the savage war waged upon National Socialist Germany by the coalesced forces of disintegration from East and West, lavishly supported by Jewish finance, to crush in this country the kernel, the stronghold of regenerate Aryandom. The heavenly Powers, Whose ways are mysterious, have permitted the disaster of 1945. It is their business—and not mine—to raise National Socialism once more, in the future, to such prominence that its right to remain the one inspiring force of higher mankind shall never again be questioned.

"I, the powerless individual, can only, as I wrote in my posters, 'hope and wait'.

"Whatever I have done, I did, therefore, not in order to win immediate success for the cause I love, but in order to obey the inner law of my nature, which is to fight for that which I firmly believe to be true. The most sacred Book, revered throughout India—the Bhagavad-Gita, written hundreds of years ago—tells all those who, like myself, are militant by heredity, warriors by birthright, to fight steadfastly, regardless of gain or loss, victory or defeat, pleasure or discomfort. And our Führer has written, in the self-same spirit, in Chapter 2 of the second Part of *Mein Kampf*: 'Whatever we think and do should be in no way determined by the applause or disapproval of our contemporaries, but solely by the obligation that binds us to the truth which we acknowledge', or, to quote the actual text itself: *'Allein unser Denken und Handeln soll keineswegs . . .'.*"

Compelled as I was, by order of the Court, to speak in English, I was at least going to quote those words of Adolf Hitler also in their original German (which I happened to know), for the edification of the public, when the judge interrupted me:

"I am not concerned with what your Führer wrote or said," he burst out, irritated. "And please remember that you are not here addressing a political meeting, and turn to the Court, *i.e.*, to me, and not to the public, when you speak."

"All right! But don't believe I really mind in what direction I speak," thought I; "In all directions, there is Germany!" And, turning to the judge, I said: "I am sorry if the Court is not interested in what my revered Führer has written. But, in a speech intended to explain what motives have prompted me to act as I did, I could not help quoting those words of his, for their spirit has ruled my life, even before I knew of them; and it rules it today, as before; and it shall always rule it, inspiring every thought, every sentence, every action of mine."

"Well, continue," said the judge impatiently.

"I have just stated," pursued I, "that I have acted, first, to express myself, to fulfil my own nature, which is to live according to my dearest convictions. But that is not the only reason. I have come, and I have acted as I did, also, in order to give the German people, now, in the dark hour of disaster, in the hour of martyrdom; now, in the midst of the ruins heaped all round them by their enemies—who are, at the same time, the enemies of the whole Aryan race—a tangible sign of admiration and love from an Aryan of a far-away land. One day—I know not when, but certainly *some* day—the whole Aryan race, including England, including

the nobler elements of the U.S.A. and of Russia, will look upon our Führer as its Saviour and upon the German people—the first Aryan nation
wide-awake—as the vanguard of higher humanity. I have done this in the
gloomy years 1948 and 1949, so that it might remain true forever that,
foreshadowing that great day to come, one non-German daughter of the
Race, at least, has remained faithful to the inspired Nation—grateful to
her for sacrificing her all, in the struggle for the supremacy of true Aryandom—while so many, even among her so-called friends, have proved
unfaithful and ungrateful. I have done it because, notwithstanding my
powerlessness and personal insignificance, I know I am a symbol—the
living symbol of the allegiance of Aryan mankind to the Führer's people,
tomorrow, in years to come, forever, in spite of temporary defeat, humiliation, occupation; in spite of the efforts of the agents of the dark forces
to keep Germany down; nay, *because of* the superhuman beauty of National Socialist Germany's stand in the depth of defeat, humiliation, and
persecution.

"And there is a third reason why I acted as I did. I did so to defy the
victorious Democracies, thus heralding the final victory of the Nazi spirit
over the power of money. Yes, I did it to defy *you*, the enemies of our
eternal faith, hypocritical 'champions of the rights of man', 'crusaders to
Europe', and what not; powers who have allied yourselves to the Communist forces to crush National Socialist Germany and—if possible—the
National Socialist Idea, on behalf of the Jews. The easy task, you have
done, and done thoroughly: night after night, for months, for years on
end, you have poured streams of phosphorus and fire over this unfortunate country until nothing was left of it but smouldering ruins. With up-
to-date bombers—with Jewish money—how easy that was! And now,
you have set yourselves to a more difficult task: the 'conversion' of
Germany to your democratic and humanitarian principles; the 'de-
Nazification' of all those who once shared the same faith as I. The future
will tell, I hope, how futile that grand-scale task was, nay, how it carried
within it the seeds of the reaction that will, one day, crush the powers in
the name of which it was undertaken. In the meantime, already as early
as yesterday, I distributed those papers, written by me alone, and under
my sole initiative and my sole responsibility, in order to defy your 'de-
Nazification' campaign; in the meantime, as early as today, I stand here
and defy it and defy you, once more, in the name of all those, Germans
or foreigners, who ever adhered to our National Socialist faith, sincerely
and in full awareness of its implications.

"I stand here and proclaim, with joy, that neither threats nor promises,
neither cruelty nor courtesy, nor kindness can 'de-Nazify' me—a wom-

an, not a man, and not a German woman at that; me, a nobody, who has never enjoyed any manner of power or privileges, or personal advantages, under the Nazi régime, but who admires it without reservations, for the sheer sake of the beauty of the new generations of supermen that it was creating, under our eyes. I repeat: how easy it was to smash the material power of the Third Reich! But to alter the faith even of the most insignificant foreign admirer of Hitler's New Order, is not so easy. It is impossible. All your soldiers, all your battleships, all your tanks, all your super-bombers, and all your propaganda—all your power and all your money—cannot do it. Nothing can do it. I have acted as I did, in order to stress that fact. And now, powerless and penniless as I am, and a prisoner, now more than ever, all your 'de-Nazification' schemes fall to pieces at my feet. Whatever you do with me, today, I am the winner, not you. And along with me, in me, through me, the everlasting Nazi spirit asserts its invincibility.

"I have nothing more to say. I thank my stars, once more, for the opportunity afforded me to express in public, before this tribunal, my unflinching loyalty to my Führer, my loving admiration for his martyred people. And . . ."

I was going to add that my only regret was that, on account of the censorship, my words would surely not be reported *in extenso* in the papers of the following day; and I would have ended my speech with: "Heil Hitler!" But the judge, once more, interrupted me:

"We have heard enough, more than enough," said he. "You might have your convictions—with which I am not concerned—but I am here to apply the law. Certain Powers have fought six years to put down that régime which you so admire. And the law, today, expresses the will of those Powers, who have won the war at the cost of great sacrifices. As for you, not only are you not sorry for what you have done, but you take pride in it . . . You use the most provoking language . . ."

I did not hear the rest of what he said; for in my heart, I was ardently praying to the invisible Forces: "May this man condemn me to death, unless you have set me aside to play a useful part in our second rising!"

At last the judge concluded: ". . . As a consequence, the Court sentences you to three years' imprisonment, with the possibility of being deported back to India within that time."

I was dumbfounded—and a little disappointed. My first impulse was to exclaim: "Only that! I presume you people are not really serious about 'de-Nazification' and the like." But I said nothing, remembering my prayer. "It must be that we shall indeed rise again, and that I will then have something to do," I thought. And once more, I felt quite pleased.

The idea of going back to India—now that I would not be allowed to re-main in Germany, anyhow—delighted me. I would have my book print-ed there, quietly, after finishing it in jail. That would be fine! And I would come back—and bring it with me—as soon as things changed. In a flash, I recalled my home, my cats. And I was moved. But I repressed all expression of emotion. Many people among the public, newspaper reporters and others, seemed willing to speak to me. I would have been only too glad to speak to them. But Miss Taylor would not let me, unless I first asked the judge's permission. So, turning to him I said: "Could I not have a talk with the representatives of the press at least, if not with other people also?"

"No," replied he stiffly, "you cannot have any press interviews, if you please."

"All right," said I. I waited till he and the Public Prosecutor and the other Britishers had left the hall. Already, quite a number of onlooking Germans had left also. But that, I could not help. Turning to the few that were still there, before Miss Taylor (who had walked ahead of me) had the time to look around, I lifted my arm and said: "Heil Hitter!" Several would have answered my salute, had they dared to.

A young press reporter, a woman, followed me down the staircase. "I so much would like to interview you," she told me.

"We are not allowed to talk," replied I, "that is democratic 'liberty'. But you have heard me speak, haven't you? Could you not follow all I said?"

"That is just it," said she; "I followed most of it, but there is one pas-sage I did not quite understand. And I also wanted to ask you . . ."

Miss Taylor intervened. "The judge told you that you can't have press interviews," she put in.

"Well," exclaimed I, "I have an hour or two more of relative freedom to enjoy before going back to prison for three years, and, damn it, I in-tend to take the fullest advantage of it if I can!"

But the press reporter had already vanished.

* * *

Miss Taylor took me to another building and there, kindly offered me a cup of tea and—which I appreciated infinitely more—presented me with a bottle of ink and a thick copybook, priceless gifts, now that I was going to jail for good. It appeared to me that she was inclined to be much more considerate—nay, that she could even be friendly towards me—when there were no other members of the police about the place. "The book you are writing, you will finish in prison," said she. And she added, to my amazement: "You will finish it with this ink, and on this copy-book. Thus you will have a lasting remembrance of me."

"If you really intend to help me, knowing who I am and what I am writing, I cannot but thank you," replied I, suddenly moved. "But do you? And would you still, if you knew *all* I have written already, and all I hope to write?"

"Why not?" said Miss Taylor. "You are not writing against England."

"I am not; that is true. I am writing against those who, in my eyes, have betrayed the real interests of England no less than of all Aryan nations. And those are, I repeat, all those who fought to destroy National Socialism, through criminal hatred or through ignorance."

"I am too much of an individualist to be able to say that I *like* your régime," said Miss Taylor, "but I can understand all that it means to you, and I like *you*. I like the attitude you kept throughout your trial. I appreciate people who stick to their convictions, and who fear nothing."

I wanted to say: "Then, why do you accept to serve under the Occupation authorities, who are here to do all they can to 'de-Nazify' Germany? The virtues you say you love in me are just the rank-and-file virtues you would find in any one of us National Socialists. How can you wear the uniform of our persecutors, if you mean what you say?" But I did not speak. I knew Miss Taylor would not follow me so far. She was not one of us, after all. "It is very kind of you to help me," said I, only. "Few gifts have I received, which have pleased me as much as yours."

Then, I went and took out of my brown attaché case my Indian earrings in the shape of swastikas, and I put them on. "Now that I am sentenced," said I, "I am wearing these. With them on—like in the great days—I shall, from the windows of the car, for the last time, admire the beauty of the German spring (for the last time for three years, at least). And with them on, I shall walk into prison. Can anyone prevent me?"

"No one will try to," said Miss Taylor. "We are not in the Russian Zone."

These last words stirred my resentment. "Damned hypocrites," thought I, "you perhaps imagine I am going to like you any better than I do 'them', for allowing me that tiny satisfaction for two hours. If so, you make a mistake. I detest all anti-Nazis alike." But I said nothing.

Another English woman in police uniform, whom I had seen at my trial, had tea with us. Men in uniform passed by us, occasionally. Some stopped a minute. They saw my earrings, but made no remarks. I looked straight into their faces with something of the aggressive expression with which I used to look at the Englishmen, Frenchmen—and especially

Jews—whom I crossed in the streets of Calcutta in glorious '40, '41, '42. In my mind, I recalled those years. And I recalled my trial, and the prayer I had addressed the Gods, and I thought: "More glorious times are to come, since these people have not decided to kill me. This is the sign I had asked for. I must accept it and not doubt." I was happy.

"I think your case will come out on the B.B.C.," Miss Taylor told me, among other things.

"I hope it does," replied I, not out of vanity, but from a practical standpoint of propaganda. "I know it will never suit 'them' to broadcast the whole of it; still, better a little encouragement to our friends all over the world than none at all."

Yet, I did not think *only* of our friends. I also had our enemies in mind. "It will do them good to see that they cannot even 'de-Nazify' a non-German," thought I. "I wish it would induce them to stop that large-scale farce!"

Then, suddenly, I remembered a few of the "Yanks" who used to come to our house in Calcutta, during the war—useful "Yanks" (from our point of view); a little childish, loving food and drink, gullible, more loquacious than soldiers should be, and—a great point—not a bit suspicious of us; "Yanks" who took my husband for an interesting Indian Democrat, and me for . . . a half-pathological case (for what else could be a woman who spends her time writing books about Antiquity and feeding stray cats?).

Now, those ex-crusaders to Asia, ex-fighters for humanity and Democracy on the Burmese front, if they happened to switch their wireless to the B.B.C. London, would hear of "Savitri Devi Mukherji, sentenced to three years' imprisonment by the Military Tribunal of Düsseldorf, for Nazi propaganda in occupied Germany." They would remember the name, the house—and, perhaps, some of the things they had casually said, in that house, and forgotten: things that were, naturally, "not to go any further"; and, perhaps, also . . . some occurrences, . . . that had remained unaccountable.

And they would say to themselves: "Gee! If we had known *that!*" . . .

I could not help laughing, as I imagined their reactions—and their retrospective rectifications of opinion concerning that woman who lived "outside this ideological war and outside our times"—as some said—and who had a house full of cats. Appearances are deceptive, especially in wartime.

But Miss Taylor got up. "I must now take you to Werl," she said, "or it will be eleven o'clock before I can come back."

I followed her to the car that was waiting for us downstairs.

Part II

WHISPERS

7. The Werl Prison
(Frontispiece of GOLD IN THE FURNACE)

Chapter 6

THE DOORS CLOSE

The car carried me through the half-ruined streets of Düsseldorf, for the last time. I was not destined to see the town again—at least, not for a long time. As I sat and gazed at it through the window, I thought: "It is, now, a fact forever that I have been tried here, today, the 5th of April, 1949." And turning to Miss Taylor, I said: "How sweet it is to ponder over the irreversibility of Time, and the irrevocability, the indestructibility of the past! Only the great moments of our life count. The rest of it is just a long preparation in view of those blessed hours of intense, more-than-personal joy. I have lived such hours today—others on the night of my arrest, the most beautiful night of my life; others in glorious '40, when I thought the world was ours. Nothing can rob me of those divine memories. Oh, how happy I am!"

I paused, and smiled. We were now outside the town, rolling along the great *Reichsautobahn*. I continued: "It is the same in the life of nations: it is not the length of historic epochs that matters; it is their intensity—and their beauty. Before the twelve ineffaceable years of King Akhnaton's rule at Tell el-Amarna, millenniums of Egyptian history fade away into dullness; Greece is Periclean Greece—a few brief years of unparalleled glory; and the history of Germany, in the eyes of generations to come, will be the history of the twelve ineffaceable years of Adolf Hitler's dictatorship . . . plus—I hope—that of his second coming and second reign; in other words, the history of National Socialism."

"What about Bismarck?" said Miss Taylor. "And what about the Pan-Germanist movement, already before the First World War?"

"Bismarck, and the Pan-Germanists after him, only prepared the ground for Adolf Hitler," replied I. "It is the Führer who gave Pan-Germanism its right meaning—its only possible meaning in the world of tomorrow, in which material frontiers will have less and less importance; it is he who integrated it into broader Pan-Aryanism, showing the Germans the only solid ground upon which they can and should claim supremacy."

"Which ground?"

"The fact that they are the first Aryan nation wide-awake, as I said just now, at my trial. Oh, I am glad I said that! I am glad it shall now be true forever that I said it, even if people forget it. You remember, once, you reminded me that I am not a German? Well, in one way, so much the better—for it is precisely because I am not one that the few truths that I have expressed today take on all their meaning. Don't I know that?"

Miss Taylor did not answer. But I recalled in my mind a few verses of Victor Hugo which I was made to learn in the school where I used to go, as a child, in France. The verses, end of a passionately patriotic poem written after the defeat of France in 1871, were the following:

> . . . Oh, I wish,
> I wish I were not French so that I could say
> That I choose thee, France, and that, in thy martyrdom,
> I proclaim thee, whom the vulture torments,
> My country and my glory and my sole love![1]

In school, we were asked to admire these words. Now, I could not help comparing them with my own sincere homage to Germany, after the bitterest defeat in her history. "Hum!" thought I, with a feeling of satisfaction; "that is all right enough. But Victor Hugo *was* French. I am *not* German. It makes a hell of a difference—even if my homage be less dramatically worded than his and, in addition to that, nothing but prose."

* * *

Apart from Miss Taylor and myself, a policeman in uniform, and a young Englishman, sentenced to nine months' imprisonment for theft and also going to Werl, had taken places in the car. I told that young man what sentence I had been given, and what for, in answer to which he started vehemently proclaiming his personal adherence to the democratic principles in the name of which England had fought. I looked at him with inner contempt, and experienced once more that malignant contentment which I always feel at the sight of the worthlessness of our opponents. I said, ironically: "How interesting it is to hear *you* defend Democracy!"—which meant in reality: "How lovely it is to meet such an ardent Democrat, who is at the same time a thief!" (the words that I would doubtless

---

[1] ". . . Ah! je voudrais,
Je voudrais n'être pas Français pour pouvoir dire
Que je te choisis, France, et que, dans ton martyre,
Je te proclame, toi que ronge le vautour,
Ma patrie et ma gloire et mon unique amour!"
—Victor Hugo "A la France" (*L'Année terrible*).

have plainly uttered, had I not wanted to avoid possibly hurting Miss Taylor, who had, only an hour before, made me that invaluable present of ink and paper). I then completely lost interest in the man, and I looked once more out of the window.

That road to Werl, that I was beginning to know so well, I was following for the last time. I was, now, really going to prison—to stay there. And I was happy to go, and happy to wear my symbolical earrings on the way, and to keep my defiant attitude. I knew that I would always keep it; that it was the very meaning of my life; that it would stick to me, even after I were dead, no doubt, in the minds of the few who might remember me. Yet, the sunlit fields, full of daisies and buttercups, and the tender green bushes along the road, and the fruit trees covered with blossoms seemed to me still more beautiful than they had in the morning. For this time I knew I would not see them again. "Another spring like this one will come and go, and I shall not see it," thought I; "and another will follow, and I shall not see that one, either, and a third one will come, and I shall not see that, unless they decide to send me back to India. But it does not matter. I would not exchange my destiny for anybody's—not even for that of my comrades who died in 1940 with the illusion of victory in their hearts. For I know, now, that, one day, I shall see the resurrection of National Socialism—and the revenge I have so longed for . . ." Thus I reflected. And I *was* happy. In the splendour of that German spring—the first I had seen; the last I would see for a long time—I hailed the everlasting victory of Life over Death. "As these trees have bloomed out of the bleak barrenness of winter," I thought, for the hundredth time, "so, one day, out of those ruins of which the sight now haunts me, the martyred land will live and thrive and conquer again." And tears came to my eyes as I imagined myself among the frantic crowds of the future, on the Führer's return. Still, along with deep happiness, there was now a certain sadness in my heart, because of the overwhelming loveliness of the countryside that I was admiring for the last time.

The car rolled on. I was silent—lost in the contemplation of the bright sky and new green earth and bright coloured flowers; breathing the fragrance and radiance of life reborn; clinging eagerly to the sight of the sunlit world, as though my last hour of relative liberty had been also the last hour of my life. I knew that every revolution of the wheels under me—now rolling at full speed—was taking me nearer to Werl, nearer to captivity. And I realised, more than I ever had before, how sweet freedom is. And although I regretted nothing—although I would have reacted just the same; spoken the self-same words of faith and pride; defied the enemies of National Socialism with the self-same aggressive joy, had it been possible for me to go through my trial again—I had, for a minute, the weakness to admit, in my heart, that it would have been lovely to remain free. And tears came to my eyes. But then, suddenly, I recalled H. E. and my other comrades and superiors imprisoned at Werl, and elsewhere, all over Germany: I recalled Rudolf Hess, a prisoner since 1941, and felt ashamed of myself. Yes, who was I to feel sad for the beauty of spring when the very sight of it had become, to them, like the memory of some former life?

My sadness persisted—perhaps even increased—but was no longer the same. I could have burst out weeping, had it not been for the presence of Miss Taylor and of the two men (and especially of the German driver) and for my desire to keep my standing at any cost. But I would have wept over my comrades' long-drawn captivity, not over the prospect of my own; over the persecution of National Socialism—the faith of Life and Resurrection in our times: the faith of the young, of the healthy, of the beautiful—in the midst of that invincible rebirth of Nature, in spite of it, in a spirit that was, and is, in my eyes, an insult to it. I imagined H. E. free again, one day, crossing in the opposite direction that threshold of gloom towards which the motorcar was now carrying me. That day would surely come. But when? When, thought I, would the doors of all the prisons of Germany, and elsewhere, of all the post-war concentration camps, be thrust wide open, and when would we, militant National Socialists—the youth of the world; the children of spring—come forth and sing, once more, along the highways, our triumphant songs of the great days? Oh, when?

We entered Werl. The Sun had set, but it was daylight still. The road that led to the prison was one mass of flowers. Hanging over the walls of the private gardens that lay on both sides of it, thick carpets of new green leaves and millions of tender petals—white, yellow, pink, red, pale violet—nearly touched the car. I gazed at them, and inhaled as deeply as I could their intoxicating fragrance, as we drove up to the huge dark prison doors.

I got down from the car. I helped the driver to take out my luggage. Then, Miss Taylor rang the bell. And we waited . . .

A golden sky shed its light upon the many-coloured flowers, upon the quiet street through which we had come and the quiet little space where that street met the one that ran parallel to the prison walls; and upon those great high walls themselves—the forbidding limit of the different world into which I was now to enter definitively; to which I already belonged. The windowpanes of the neighbouring houses facing west, shone like gold. And a soft breeze brought me the breath of the gardens—the

breath of the world of the free. We might have waited half a minute: perhaps a minute. Again, I thought of my comrades—some six hundred men
and a few women, among whom H. E.—behind those walls for nearly
four years. And I realised in absolute sincerity that, had it been possible, I
would have gladly remained, myself, a captive forever—renouncing the
right to see trees and flowers and even the divine sky for the rest of my
life—if, at that price, I could have set them free. I would have, indeed! (I
would *now*—after tasting freedom once more, in full knowledge of its
worth.) And I prayed to the One Whose effulgence is the effulgence of
the Sun: "Give *them* back freedom and power, Lord of the unseen Forces
that govern all that can be seen! Restore our New Order, image on earth
of Thy eternal Order!—and I don't care what happens to me."

I heard the noise of a key in the thick iron keyhole. Slowly, the huge
heavy doors were flung open. I crossed the threshold . . . and could not
help turning around my head to take a last glance at the lovely, peaceful
evening, at the golden sky; to breathe the smell of flowers once more.
There was something solemn in that ultimate, fleeting vision of beauty.
There was, in that instant, an experience that I would remember as long
as I lived. I was not unhappy—on the contrary: a deep, serene joy filled
me, and I crossed the threshold with a smile. I knew my place was there,
among the others who, like I (though more intelligently, more efficiently
than I), had done their best for the Nazi cause and who, like I, had fallen
into our enemies' hands. And I was intensely aware of being, for once in
my life, *in my place*—in my place at last! In my place, at least in the hour
of persecution, I who, years and years ago, should have come and shared
with those of my own race and faith, the glorious life of the great days; I
who should have come during the first struggle for power—when I was
twenty—instead of wasting my energy in Greece . . .

With a resounding noise that made me involuntarily shudder, the
huge heavy doors closed upon me. Tears came to my eyes. I was now in
my new home. And I thought of H. E. whom I would soon meet again; of
the other so-called "war criminals" whom I would have the honour and
the joy of knowing. For surely—I thought—I would be transferred to the
D Wing. I was happy—and moved. Once more, in a flash, I recalled the
glory of spring beyond the now closed doors—and, also, the skeletons of
houses and factories, the miles and miles of charred and blasted walls
that cried for vengeance under the sky, day and night; and the people for
whom I had fought, in my clumsy manner, and for whose freedom I
would have undergone anything. "Germany," thought I, "in former years,
I did not know myself how much I loved thee!" And I felt that there was,
between my Führer's people and I, a definitive link that nothing could

ever break nor slacken.

* * *

Miss Taylor took leave of me after the German warder had signed the paper she handed over to him (thus testifying that I was no longer in her custody). I had drawn my scarf over my head to hide my earrings from the sight of the warder. Members of the British police in Düsseldorf had seen me wearing them, it was true, and had expressed no objection. But I did not know who these warders were; and if, as Mr. Stocks had once told me, the man whom the British had appointed as the head of the male section of the prison was a notorious anti-Nazi, there was no reason not to presume that some at least of the warders were of the same kind. And I knew—from my comrades—that a German anti-Nazi is generally much worse than any representative of the Occupying Powers (with, of course, the exception of the Jews). After a while, a wardress from the *"Frauenhaus"* came to fetch me. Two prisoners—ordinary delinquents—walked ahead of us, carrying my luggage, while the wardress and I talked in a friendly manner.

We reached the staircase leading to the *"Frauenhaus."* Frau So-and-so and another one of those who were definitely "in order" were on duty that night, along with the wardress who had come to fetch me, and a fourth one. It is Frau So-and-so who opened the door for us on the landing. "Well . . . ?" asked she, as soon as she saw me.

"All right," replied I. "Got three years. Expected much worse, especially after speaking as I did." Then, after a minute's pause, I enquired about the one thing that had worried me all day: "Do you know if H. E. has found my manuscripts?" said I, eagerly. "I asked her to hide them . . ."

"Your manuscripts are in safety in Sister Maria's office," replied the faithful wardress. "H. E. and I saw to it. You'll have them back tomorrow morning."

"Thank you!" exclaimed I, from the bottom of my heart; "oh, thank you!"

I was taken back to my cell, and Frau So-and-so ordered some supper for me. While I was waiting for it, the four wardresses gathered around me. They admired my earrings, and commented upon my sentence. "Three years is a long time," said one; "why, that woman in No. 48, who is here for having killed her newborn baby, has got only three years!"

"Naturally," replied another; "a German baby more or less makes no difference in the eyes of 'those people', while a blow to their blinking prestige does."

"Well," put in a third one, "we must try to put ourselves in their place. We have lost the war. It is a fact. And here is a woman who comes all the way from India and takes our side openly. In '45, they would have shot her. Of course, times are changing—and rapidly, it seems." And turning to me she said: "I was afraid, however, that even now 'they' would give you more than three years. You were lucky."

"Anyhow, don't imagine it is my fault if 'they' sentenced me only to that much," said I: "for it surely is not. I spoke the truth, and was not a bit afraid of 'them', I can assure you." And I repeated, summing it up the best I could, what I had stated in my speech before the military Tribunal. The wardresses were amazed "You said *that,* and 'they' let you get away with three years! Gosh, it looks as though times are changing!"

"'They' perhaps wished to make a good impression upon the Indians, who knows?" suggested I. "The last time I was in London, I was told that there was now a terrific Communist propaganda campaign going on, all over India. These Johnnies probably want to show the Indians how lenient they are, compared with the Russians. They want to propitiate their ex-colony . . ."

"That's it, that's it!" exclaimed the fourth wardress. "They are afraid. A good sign!"

"You know what you would have got, if the Russians had caught you in their Zone?" put in another. "Deportation for life to Siberia, or something like that . . ."

"I believe it," said I. "And so would I, if I had the power to do what I please with one of our sincerest opponents, send him or her to deportation for life—or to immediate death. The Communists are our real enemies, and know it. But these people . . . these soppy Democrats, these liars, they don't know themselves what they are or what they want. Yesterday, they joined the Reds to crush our Ideology. Tomorrow, when they are sufficiently scared of the Reds, they will crawl in the filth to lick our boots—after all they did to us—and implore our help against the Reds ... Our help! I wish we keep them crawling as long as it is expedient, or as long as it amuses us, and then give them a good kick and turn against them! But, of course, I am not the one to decide in that intricate game of convenient alliances. It exceeds my brains by far. All I know is that I despise the Democrats whatever they do, and that, if they imagined they were going to gain the slightest sympathy from me by being lenient to me, they made a great mistake. I wish I can, one day, make them feel sorry they did not kill me when they could have . . ."

"My God, if only they could hear you now, I bet they would already feel sorry!" said one of the wardresses, laughing.

I laughed too. My supper was brought in: six slices of white bread, some macaroni and cheese baked in the oven, some butter, some plum jam, a bun with raisins, and a jug of hot tea, with sugar and milk. The wardresses wished me good appetite and good night, and left my cell. I ate the macaroni, a slice of bread, a little of the jam, and put all the rest by for my friend H. E.

Then, I wrote to my husband a letter of twenty pages reproaching him with having tried to save me from captivity when I did not want to be saved, and telling him how happy I was to have spoken as a true National Socialist before the representatives of the Allied Occupation and before the German public.

* * *

The next day, early in the morning, H. E. came to my cell. The wardress on duty—who was "in order"—pulled the door behind her. We talked a few minutes. "I hear you have got three years," said my comrade; "you were lucky. I expected you would get at least five; and most of us said ten."

"Yes," replied I: "I know. And yet, I did all I could to show the judge and every person present that I was not afraid to suffer for our cause."

I repeated to her the essentials of what I had said in my speech. And I told her about the letter my husband had written, and specified that I had forbidden the lawyer to mention it. H. E. looked at me intently and said: "You are truly one of us. I shall never forget you. As you say, the heavenly Powers have spared you for you to take part in our coming struggle." She put her arm around my waist and squeezed my hand, while I rested my head upon her shoulder for a second or two. I was happy.

"You know," continued H. E. after a while, "in all my career, I met only one non-German whom I could compare with you. It was a Polish woman whom we caught spying on behalf of England during the war, and whom we shot. I was present at her trial, and remember her speech. You remind me of her . . ."

"Thank you very much for comparing me with an agent from the 'other side'!" said I, jokingly.

"You must not laugh," answered H. E. "She might have been misled; she might have been, without realising it, 'a traitor to her own race', as you so rightly call all Aryans who opposed us—for she was no Jewess, I can assure you. But she was sincere and fearless, as you are.

"And as I saw our men lead her out of the hall, I could not help regretting she had not devoted her fine natural qualities of character to our cause."

"Well," said I, "I am glad she was caught and shot. To waste Aryan qualities in the service of Jewish interests, knowingly or unknowingly, is sacrilegious: it is casting pearls before swine. But tell me: what do you think of the letter I wrote to my husband last night, in answer to his effort to 'excuse' me in the eyes of the authorities? See . . ." And I translated to her one or two sentences out of it.

"You should not send it," said H. E. "It will sadden him, without any profit to the cause. Poor man! He only wrote as he did to try to get you off, as any one of us would have done, if it had been possible. He did his best for you—and for us. Promise me you will not send that."

"Perhaps, then, I shall not. I shall alter that and a few other passages ..."

"Yes, do," said my friend. And anticipating that which I was going to ask her, she added: "I shall bring you back your manuscripts as soon as Sister Maria comes. They are safe. Frau So-and-so must have told you . . ."

"She did. I do thank you for keeping them! I was afraid for them although, apparently, I had no reason to be."

I then gave her the food and tea that I had put aside for her on the evening before, and my morning's porridge and white bread. "I'll take half now and half when I come back," said she, "for I'll never be able to carry all that along the corridor without being noticed."

We parted as usual, greeting each other with the mystic words: "Heil Hitler!"

* * *

I was working on Chapter 7 of my *Gold in the Furnace*—of which Sister Maria had just brought the manuscript back to me—when Fräulein S. (Frau *Oberin*'s assistant) came into my cell and bade me follow her "to the Governor's." To my surprise, I was not taken downstairs and across the prison grounds to the Governor's office, but just across the corridor to Frau *Oberin*'s office, where the Governor was waiting for me. (This surprised me, because it was a Wednesday; and the Governor did not generally come in touch with the prisoners there, save on his regular visits to the *"Frauenhaus"* on Friday mornings.)

Colonel Vickers was sitting at Frau *Oberin*'s desk. The German interpreter—about whose politics I had heard, from Mr. Stocks, more than enough to dislike him heartily—and Mr. Watts, a dark man with a prominent paunch, who, occasionally, used to replace the Governor—were also present, the former standing up, the latter seated in an armchair. Frau *Oberin* and the matron of the prison—the elderly blue-eyed lady, with white hair, who had received me on the day of my very first arrival at Werl—were standing up. So was Fräulein S., who had just entered the room with me.

The Governor gave me an abrupt "Good morning" in answer to my salute, and addressing me rather bluntly, said, to my great astonishment: "The Court has, I see, sentenced you to three years' imprisonment. Your case is no business of mine, as I have told you once already: I am here only to look after you during the time you remain in my charge. But I cannot help noticing that yours is the heaviest sentence ever given a woman by a British Court, for such an offence as yours, since we are in this country. There must be a reason for it, for our justice is fair. However, you have the right to appeal for a revision of your sentence—if you like—provided you can produce sufficient evidence to show that it should be revised. But I must warn you that, if you do so without serious grounds, you run the risk of getting a still heavier sentence for having made us waste our time . . ."

"I have not the slightest desire to appeal either for justice or for clemency," said I, standing before the desk, with a ray of morning sunshine upon my face, feeling happy. "Had I wished to, I would have, already during my trial, made use of the letter which my husband had sent the authorities to try to whitewash me. I refused to do so. Moreover, given the present circumstances, and given all that I stand for, I consider my sentence extremely lenient."

"All right," replied Colonel Vickers, accepting, possibly with a little surprise, but without comments, the unexpected glimpse I had thus just given him of my real self. And, turning to Frau *Oberin* and to the matron, he said, speaking of me: "She must wear the prisoners' clothes; and she must work. She will be given the special British diet, as before, being a British subject. But that is all. And if she is ever caught distributing food to other prisoners, her privilege will be cancelled."

The interpreter translated the words into German for the benefit of Frau R. the matron. Frau *Oberin* knew enough English not to need a translation.

Then the Governor said to me: "I hope you understand me."

"I do," answered I—all the time firmly determined to continue to give the best of my special food to H. E. without getting caught.

"If your behaviour is satisfactory" pursued he, "you will, regularly, be remitted of one quarter of your penalty, which means that you will serve two years and three months instead of three years, in supposing that you are not sent back to India in the meantime."

"May I know," asked I, "When they are likely to send me back to

India?"

"Regularly, not before you have served at least one third of your term of imprisonment, that is to say, not before one year," replied the Governor. "So you have not to think of that possibility for the present. Have you anything more to ask?"

"I would like to know," said I, "if I may have light in my cell till ten p.m.?"

"No." answered Colonel Vickers; "it is not the rule. And I can see no reason justifying an exception in your case. Besides, it is natural that you should go to bed early, as you will work all day."

"It is all right," said I, inwardly resentful, outwardly indifferent. "I only asked that, as I was under the impression that political prisoners were allowed light in their cells longer than the others." I remembered what Miss Taylor had told me the day before, on my way to Düsseldorf.

"Political prisoners are the last people to whom we give light after time—the last ones, in fact, to whom we grant any privileges," said Colonel Vickers. And (ignorant as he was of what Miss Taylor had told me about General Kesselring and others writing their memoirs, and General Rundstedt being temporarily released on parole), he added: "We do allow light after eight o'clock to some; but those are all prisoners who write for us, or who do secret work for us in one way or another" (*sic*).

I pretended not to pay the slightest attention to what I had just heard (as though it did not interest me), and I put forth no further claims concerning light, or writing facilities. I knew the German staff would be easier to tackle, in these matters, than the representative of British power in occupied Germany. At least the staff of the *"Frauenhaus"* would be. And as the days were getting longer and longer (a fact which no Occupation forces could alter), I would soon be able to write till ten or half past ten at night anyhow. But I was impressed by Colonel Vickers' statement, and I immediately drew my own conclusions from it. It threw, indeed, unexpected complementary light upon Miss Taylor's discourse about British "kindness" to so-called "war criminals." Now I knew—from a responsible authority—how selective that supposed "kindness" was, extending as it did only to those willing to "do secret work" for Germany's victors . . . Well, I was certainly never going to win myself privileges at the cost of such a bargain. Not I!

"Now, I have little time to spare," the Governor at last told me: "if there is anything you think you need, you can ask Miss M., who is in charge of the women's section of this prison. And you can do what she permits you to do. Good morning."

I bowed in reply, and now Fräulein S. took me back to my cell. The person the Governor had said I should consult and obey, "Miss M.," was none other than the one whom we prisoners knew as Frau *Oberin*.[2] She had always shown a particularly sympathetic interest in me, and H. E., who was in Werl so long, had told me that she was a "first class person," well-disposed in our favour, and "absolutely reliable." And when I had asked my friend whether the lady was actually *"in Ordnung,"* i.e., a sincere National Socialist, she had replied: "She could not tell us so even if she were. Like all those who have managed to retain a job under 'these creatures', she is compelled to be exceedingly careful. But she will help you as much as she can. She has helped *me* a lot." Doubtless, I would be able to write, if it depended upon her, thought I. And again I felt that the less Colonel Vickers suspected the fact that I was writing, in prison, under his nose, such a book as *Gold in the Furnace*, the better it would be for me; and the better for the safety of the book—the better for the Nazi cause, which the book was intended to serve, one day.

* * *

In my cell, I continued to write my Chapter 7 on "Plunder, Lies, and Shallowness." Upon my table, open at different places, were spread out three or four issues of the *Revue de la Presse rhénane et allemande*— selected typed extracts of the German newspapers concerning happenings in occupied Germany, which a French official in Koblenz had very kindly handed over to me as "useful information" for my proposed book, in perfect ignorance of the nature of the book and therefore of the spirit in which I was to use any document.

Time passed. Some two hours after lunch, *Oberwachtmeisterin* S.,[3] the lady who used to supervise the prisoners' work in the whole women's section, came in. Middle-aged, short, and a little stout, but extremely elegant—dressed with utmost sober taste—she was energetic, firm, efficient, of more than average intelligence, and could be charming when she liked. She had always been charming in her relations with me, showing more interest in my career as a writer and in my activities in India than most other members of the prison staff. However, I had not yet made out whether she was "in order" or not. H. E., who knew her much longer than I did, *thought* she was, but was "not quite sure." Frau S. herself had repeatedly told me that, since the end of the war she was "fed up

---

[2] This is probably the initial of Frau *Oberin*'s last name. The initial of her first name is probably "F." See page 118 above.—Ed.

[3] *"Oberwachtmeisterin"* can be translated "Madam Chief Warder."—Ed.

with all ideologies" and that she did not wish to hear a word about any. All I knew with certainty was that she was one of the members of the staff with whom I had the greatest pleasure of talking.

She walked in and asked me with a smile: "Well, how are you getting on? And what has the Governor told you, this morning?"

"He said I must work," answered I.

"And what work would you like to do?" enquired Frau S. "What are you able to do?—for here some of the prisoners knit, others make nets or bags or baskets; others, who know the trade, make dresses. Do you know how to make anything?"

"I am afraid I don't," replied I. "But I can learn."

Frau S. smiled again. "It takes time to learn," she said. "It is better to do what one is made for." And after a pause she asked me: "Apart from writing, and from lecturing in public—and, doubtless, also privately, to your husband and all your friends—what did you do when you were home in India?"

"I used to give lessons in languages, and do translations, when I needed more money than my husband could afford to give me. Otherwise, I did a little painting, I went to a few tea parties; did practically nothing."

"A National Socialist woman should be skilled in all manner of household work," said Frau S., watching me ironically, to see how much the irreproachable orthodoxy of her statement would impress me. She was not the first person in Germany to remind me of that, and to make me feel utterly ashamed of myself. For a second, the acute awareness of possibilities lost forever—the retrospective vision of the woman I *could have been*—was painful to me. And I looked at Frau S. with such depth of sincere sadness that the irony vanished from the glance of her sparkling grey eyes.

"Perhaps I was wrong not to have striven, in my youth, towards that all-round realisation of my womanhood implied in our ideals," said I. "I don't know. I somehow seemed to feel that I was destined to be a wanderer all my life . . . Anyhow, it is no good thinking of the past. Now, my household is my cell. And I shall try to keep it as clean and tidy as I can."

Frau S. patted me on the shoulder. "I am sorry if I made you feel sad," she said; "I did not intend to. Now, tell me frankly: what would you really like to do? What would you do if you were free?"

"Continue to write my book," replied I, unhesitatingly.

"Well, continue now," said the *Oberwachtmeisterin*, to my amazement and to my joy. "I shall bring you, for the sake of formality, a little easy work which you will finish in an hour or so. The rest of the day, continue your own real work—your work that matters."

I was deeply moved. "I can find no words eloquent enough to thank you," exclaimed I, in a sincere outburst of gratitude, as tears came to my eyes. "This is the greatest favour you could do me. And . . ."—I could not help adding—"I cannot bring myself to believe that you would regret your kindness if you knew what I am writing."

"I don't want to know—*now*," replied Frau S. "It is in English, isn't it? I can't read English. One day, if it is ever translated into German, as I hope, I shall be glad to read it."

"If the Gods spare my manuscript till then, answered I; "and if my comrades consider it worth translating . . ."

Frau S. smiled, squeezed my hand, and left the cell.

I was happy. Before my written tribute of admiration to Germany could be translated and published, things would surely have to change a lot. Did Frau S. really think they were likely to? And so quickly? It would be a miracle. But I believed in miracles. My condemnation to three years' imprisonment only—after the attitude I had shown throughout my trial—was a miracle. The presence of my precious manuscripts, intact, upon the table before me, was a miracle.

I looked up to the bright sky; to the Sun, king of all the Gods, that shone beyond my non-transparent windowpanes and my iron bars. "Invisible Forces Who govern all things visible," I prayed, "give my German comrades freedom and power . . . Oh, bring back our grand days!"

* * *

The next day, the 7th of April, in the afternoon Frau R., the matron of the prison, came to fetch me. "Take your things with you—all your things," she said. Two prisoners, whom she had brought with her, caught hold of my trunk and dragged it out of the cell, while I took my coat, my attaché case, some books, all I could carry. My manuscripts, too voluminous to be hidden, I pushed into the draw of my table, with my inkbottle, pen, and pencils. The portrait of the Führer was there too, between two sheets of paper, as Frau *Oberin* had told me, in the morning, that it was safer for me not to keep it out, at least in the daytime when so many eyes could see through the spy hole of my cell. Before I left the place, however, the matron opened the drawer.

"You must take these papers also," said she; "everything."

"But these I need," ventured I to reply. "These are my writings."

"The Governor said you are to work," answered Frau R.; "he did not mention writing."

"I know. I heard him myself. But in the evenings, mayn't I do something to occupy myself? The Governor told me he had no time to enter into the details of my daily routine, but left that to Frau *Oberin*. I'll ask her whether I may write after working hours."

"Others clean their cells and mend their stockings after working hours," said the matron. "However, if Frau *Oberin* allows you to write, I have no objection. She is responsible. I only do what I am ordered."

"So, must I take my papers or leave them here?" asked I, inwardly anxious.

"All right. Leave them," agreed the matron, to my relief. "But we must ask Frau *Oberin*, before you may definitely keep them."

I was taken into the little room into which I had entered on the very first day I had come to Werl. I was asked to undress, and my civilian clothes were put away, carefully catalogued along with the rest of my possessions. And I put on the prisoners' uniform: over prison linen and a thick grey woollen petticoat, dark-blue overalls and a grey apron. I was also given a dark-blue woollen pullover and a black jacket to wear when I went out into the courtyard during the "free hour," or even in my cell, for it was still cold.

I took off every bit of jewellery I wore—gold bangles, a gold chain, rings—all save the iron bangle on my left hand (in Bengal, the sign of the indissolubility of marriage). Before giving up my gold chain, I took off the glass portrait of the Führer that I used to wear on it, and put it in my pocket. But the watchful matron caught any gesture: "What are you trying to hide?" she asked me. I had no alternative but to show her the precious little object.

"I don't want to part with *this*," said I, eagerly. "Don't take it away from me! It is the last treasure I have. It will do no harm to anyone if I wear it around my neck on a plain piece of string, as some other prisoners wear a cross. Nobody will even notice it." I was moved, as I uttered these words. The little object was our Führer's likeness. It was also the gift of a sincere Nazi, who loved and trusted me, whom I loved and trusted; the gift of persecuted Germany, to me. "Oh, don't take it away from me!" said I, again.

"All right, then; keep it," replied to my surprise, and joy, Frau R.—she who seemed so much of a disciplinarian. Had she been touched, in spite of herself, by the spontaneous expression I had given my feelings? Or did she calmly consider it her duty as a German to show kindness towards a true friend of her country? I shall never know.

I thanked her enthusiastically for the favour she had thus done me. Then, as I gathered a few toilet objects to take back to my cell, I asked her: "May I also take this box?"

"What is in it? Face powder? You are not to use that, here in prison," said the matron.

"It is only talcum powder," replied I with ease, opening the box, practically full, at the bottom of which I had hidden, the day before, carefully wrapped in soft paper, my Indian earrings in the shape of swastikas.

Frau R. examined the box, without caring to empty it; saw that it was indeed talcum powder, and said, to my delight: "Yes, you can keep it."

I then looked at myself in the large mirror that the room contained, and was disappointed. Prisoner's clothes, decidedly, did not improve my appearance. I looked much better in my brown tailored suit, or in my lovely dark-red frock (both gifts of comrades in England on the occasion of my departure to Germany), or, of course, in any of my "saris." But I realised that, now, I was dressed like H. E. and the other captive Nazi women, who had all suffered so incredibly more than I for our common cause. And the clumsy, ill-fitted uniform appeared to me as a mantle of glory. And I smiled at myself in the mirror.

"Well you look a pretty girl all the same, in those clothes, don't you?" said the matron, good-humouredly.

"I do, I know," replied I with conviction. "An intense inner life—like ours—always makes one pretty."

In my mind, as a memory from another world, I recalled the Greek nationalist that I had once been—the girl of eighteen who wore handwoven, brightly embroidered frocks of peasant cut, bought in Athens, and who proudly used to declare: "Paris dictates its taste to all women save me." And I recalled the woman who had sailed to India a few years later in search of an unbroken Aryan tradition, and who adopted the Indian "sari" to look more of an ancient Greek, more of a Pagan Greek, more of an Aryan Heathen of all times. How all that stress upon externals now seemed childish, desperately childish to me! Had I, for *that*, missed my fulfilment and done only half my duty? For the spirit of eternal Aryan Pagandom was here, in the ardent hearts and disciplined lives of men in brown or greyish-green uniforms, not there, in the Near or Middle East, in vain draperies, or even in unbroken traditions, followed with less and less understanding. And now, after the disaster, it lived and gleamed, invincible, in the hearts and lives of the self-same undaunted minority— in my comrades, so many of whom wore prisoners' clothes like I would, henceforth. Far better than that of the bejewelled woman in Greek or Indian dress, the picture the looking glass now sent back to me symbolised the realisation of my life-long yearning; *was* the picture of my real self.

As I was coming out, I met *Oberwachtmeisterin* S. in the corridor. I had not seen her all day. She told me (doubtless out of courtesy), that my new clothes suited me well; and then, addressing me as though I were a friend, not a prisoner, she said: "Do you know that your case has come out on the wireless, last night? They broadcasted one or two of the things you told them at your trial. Indeed, you spoke well."

She followed me into my cell. The wardress on duty, who accompanied me, left us and went her way. "They also stated that you sold your beautiful Indian jewellery in order to finance your activities in Germany," pursued Frau S.

"It is true," replied I. "But why speak of it on the wireless? Any sincere National Socialist would do as much, I hope. However, if the little they said about me, and especially the little they broadcasted of my speech in Court, has contributed to make even one extra German feel proud of his natural Aryan nobility; if it has made even one realise, more vividly than before, what a great thing Adolf Hitler has done for Germany in making her the conscious stronghold of reborn Aryandom, then I am happy; then I don't mind sitting here three years—or ten, at that—without seeing a tree . . ."

But as I uttered these words, the fleeting picture of bright green fields full of violets, daisies, and buttercups; of fruit trees covered with blossoms—the glory of Spring—rushed back to my memory like a vision of lost paradise, and tears filled my eyes. Yet I still meant all I said.

"Without seeing a tree!" repeated I after a short pause, during which the fleeting vision had forced itself upon my mind, more alluring than ever. "Oh, how beautiful the trees were, in their springly garb, on the day before yesterday—my last day of liberty! How beautiful were the bushes and the fields full of flowers, along the great *Reichsautobahn* . . . and how lovely the pure sky, and the sunshine, the divine sunshine! . . . I took a last glance at all that, and the heavy doors closed upon me. But it does not matter. It is my place, here, among my persecuted comrades—among those who loved our Führer to the end. And if, even from here, indirectly—through the comments of our enemies upon my case—I have been, at least once more, of some use, well, I am glad."

Frau S. gazed at me earnestly. "I should not tell you this," said she, lowering her voice, "but I shall, all the same. And you must believe me, for I speak the truth. Beyond those heavy doors that closed on you, every faithful German, every true and worthy German, respects you and loves you."

Had I just been told that the world was now mine, I would not have felt more intensely moved. "My Führer's people," whispered I, as the tears I tried in vain to hold back ran down my cheeks; "the men of iron, whom he so loved. They!"

In a flash, I evoked my first unforgettable glimpse of the martyred land ten months before: the ruins of Hamburg, the ruins of Brem, of all the towns I had seen on that night of the 15th of June 1948. I recalled the words two humble railway men had then addressed me—instead of denouncing me to the police—when they caught me distributing my first handwritten leaflets: "We thank you, in the name of all Germany,"[4] words I would remember as long as I lived; words of the working élite of pure blood, erect and dignified amidst the most appalling material desolation. I had seen more of that élite, since then; I had admired it. I knew, now, that no force in the world could kill it; I knew that it would always be there for me to continue to live for—I, who in the despair of 1945, had declared to someone, in India, my desire to "turn my back on mankind, forever." And lo, a responsible woman and a German was telling me that, in the heart of that superhuman suffering élite, I now had a place . . .

"No glory," replied I to Frau S.; "no broad-scale international honours, absolutely nothing in the world could touch me more than that which you have just said. Tell those faithful Germans of whom you speak, that I am aware of the sacred link that binds me to them, forever and ever. Tell them that I too, love them."

"I shall," said the *Oberwachtmeisterin*.

And she added, in a very low voice: "Among them are people whom I know personally; people who once held important posts in the Party—in which I was too. But promise me you shall never say a word of all this to anyone, not to Frau *Oberin*, not to any of the wardresses, however much 'in order' they be; not even to your friend H. E. Can you really keep it secret?"

"I promise I shall," said I.

"I'll come and see you again tomorrow morning," said Frau S. *"Auf Wiedersehen!"*

"Auf Wiedersehen!"

---

[4] *Gold in the Furnace*, 3rd ed., p. 45.—Ed.

Chapter 7

HUMILIATION

The next day, the 8th of April, in the afternoon, I was transferred to cell No. 92, in the B wing.

My trunk, my attaché case, all my things, had been put away into the common cloakroom where the belongings of all the prisoners were kept. But Frau *Oberin* had allowed me to have my manuscripts, and a few books: H. R. Hall's *Ancient History of the Near East*;[1] a book about the *Mythology of Ancient Britain*;[2] Dr. Herbert Gowen's *History of Japan*;[3] two books of Mongolian history,[4] and one about the *Art and Civilisation of Ancient America*[5]—apart, of course, from my precious English translation of the Bhagavad-Gita.

I loved those books. They reflected my life-long interest in the history of all civilisations; they represented something of that stock of information out of which I had drawn, for years, picturesque illustrations in support of our philosophy. I was grateful to Frau *Oberin* for allowing me to keep them; more grateful to her still for allowing me to keep my manuscripts and to continue writing. I was grateful to the *Oberwachtmeister-in*, too, for her silent and sympathetic collaboration.

I put my manuscripts into my table drawer. I hid the Führer's portrait in the cover of the *Mythology of Ancient Britain*, and *Das Programm der N.S.D.A.P.*[6] (which I had also managed to keep with me, for references) between the illustrated pages of the *Art and Civilisation of Ancient America*. I then disposed the books upon two of the shelves of

---

[1] H. R. Hall, *The Ancient History of the Near East: From the Earliest Times to the Battle of Salamis*, 9th ed. (London: Methuen & Co., 1936).—Ed.

[2] Perhaps Charles Squire, *Mythology of Ancient Britain and Ireland* (London: Constable & Company, 1909).—Ed.

[3] Probably Herbert H. Gowen, *An Outline History of Japan* (New York and London: D. Appleton, 1927).—Ed.

[4] Harold Lamb's *The March of the Barbarians* (London: Robert Hale, 1941), which Savitri mentions in Chapter 10, p. 273 below, and almost certainly Ralph Fox's *Genghis Khan* (London: The Bodley Head, 1936). Savitri cites both books in the chapters of *The Lightning and the Sun* on Genghis Khan (L&S, pp. 60–61), chapters 4 and 5 of which were written in Werl in July and August 1949 (L&S, p. 86).—Ed.

[5] There is no book by this title in English.—Ed.

[6] Gottfried Feder, *Das Programm der N.S.D.A.P. und seine weltanschauulichen Grundgedanken* (Munich: Franz Eher, 1932).—Ed.

my new cupboard—much smaller than the one I had in cell 121—and lay upon my bed, less in order to rest (for I was neither sick nor tired) than in order to reflect.

I could not make out why I had been transferred here instead of to the D Wing, where the cells of all my real comrades were. Had they put me in this cell only for the time being? Or was I never to go to the D Wing at all? And again, why?

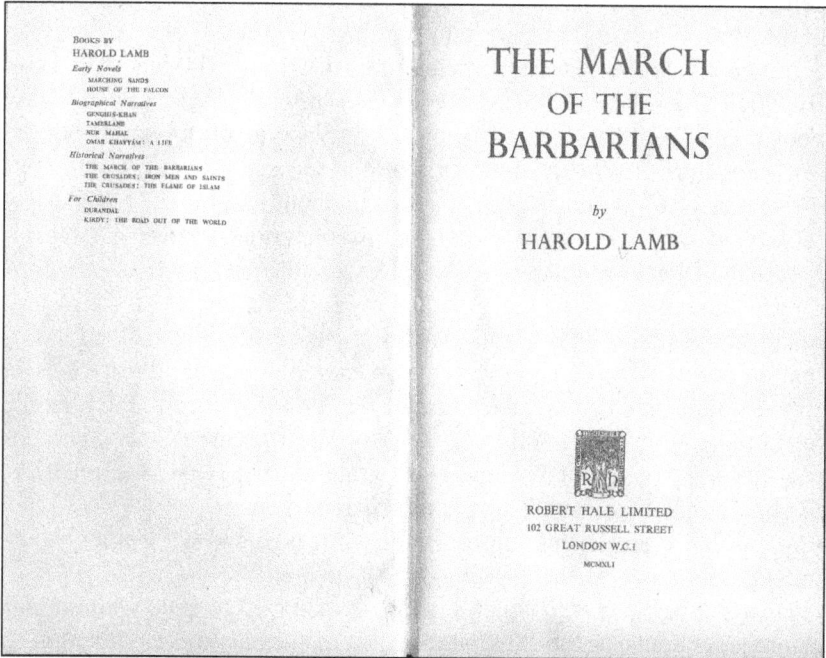

BOOKS BY
HAROLD LAMB

Early Novels
MARCHING SANDS
HOUSE OF THE FALCON

Biographical Narratives
GENGHIS-KHAN
TAMERLANE
NUR MAHAL
OMAR KHAYYAM: A LIFE

Historical Narratives
THE MARCH OF THE BARBARIANS
THE CRUSADES: IRON MEN AND SAINTS
THE CRUSADES: THE FLAME OF ISLAM

For Children
DURANDAL
KIRDY: THE ROAD OUT OF THE WORLD

THE MARCH
OF THE
BARBARIANS

by

HAROLD LAMB

ROBERT HALE LIMITED
102 GREAT RUSSELL STREET
LONDON W.C.1
MCMXLI

8. The title page of Savitri Devi's personal copy of Harold Lamb's
THE MARCH OF THE BARBARIANS, which she had with her in Werl

Once, and once only—on the morning following my return to Werl, before the Governor had come—I had been sent down to spend my "free hour" with those of the D Wing, who had welcomed me with joy. I had had the honour of walking around the courtyard by the side of Frau R.[7]— formerly holder of a responsible post in the management of the Ravens-brück concentration camp, now a so-called "war criminal" sentenced to life-long imprisonment by our enemies—and of hearing her address me as a friend. And I had had the pleasure of telling her: "Don't believe you

---

[7] Perhaps Margarete Maria Rabe, although I have not been able to confirm she was imprisoned at Werl.—Ed.

will stay here all your life! Oh, no! I was but yesterday still in touch with the outer world, and I can assure you that things are changing. An implacable justice will one day fasten its grip on these people and avenge you, avenge us all, and bring us back to power, this time on a world-wide scale—although I do not know myself how." And the woman, nearly four years captive, had smiled to me and answered: "I wish you were right. Oh, how I wish it! One always hopes." But time had come for us to go back to our cells, and we had parted. And then, the Governor had come, as I have already related. And I had had no further contact with my comrades—save of course with H. E. who, as usual, came every morning to my cell, collected whatever tea, white bread, porridge, or other food I had for her, greeted me with a sincere "Heil Hitler!" whenever we were alone (or when Frau So-and-so or any other of the wardresses who were "in order" happened to be on duty), and departed, always in a hurry. I had, morning and afternoon, been sent out with the ordinary delinquents, thieves, black-marketeers, abortionists, and so forth. And, goodness, how dull these were! They talked about practically nothing but food . . . and men—trivialities.

While I was in No. 121, I had been given a plant in a flowerpot—a pretty plant, with peculiarly tinted leaves, green on one side and violet on the other, or dark-red on one side and pink on the other. I had admired it for five minutes, and then I had watered it regularly and kept it as well as I could. But I had been too completely absorbed in other thoughts to pay much attention to it. Now, I remembered the beautiful and harmless living thing, and regretted that I had not bothered to take it with me. For the first time, I missed it. For the first time, I pondered over the loveliness of its shiny coloured leaves. To my own surprise, the idea that nobody would water it, this evening, brought tears into my eyes and a feeling of guilt into my heart. "Poor plant!" thought I, "I must tell one of the wardresses (or Frau *Oberin* herself, if I see her) that I want it." But accustomed as I was to be sincere with myself, I could not help wondering whether I would have given it a thought, had I been in a cell of the D wing, next to some woman whom I could love and admire and with whom I could expect to talk, during the "free hour," about the excellence of National Socialism, the crimes of the Democracies, and that irresistible revenge that I was—and am still—so intensely longing for.

My evening meal was brought to me, as usual. The wardress on duty was one of those whom I liked the most, one of those who were "in order." I told her about the plant. "Of course you shall have it back," said she, most amiably; "you shall have it, perhaps not at once—for Frau R. is now very busy supervising the distribution of bread and 'coffee'—but certainly tomorrow morning. I am glad to see you love your plant. I have already noticed how it has grown, since the day it was given to you."

"Could I also ask you," said I, "why they put me here instead of in the D wing?" "I don't know myself," replied the kind wardress; "It baffles me, too, believe me; for your place is there, with the political prisoners, not here, with this lot. But I have heard that you were put here by order of the Governor . . ."

"But why?" exclaimed I; "why? Does the Governor imagine he is going to 'de-Nazify' me by separating me from my comrades, or what? If that is why he did it, dear me, what a fool he must be! For I have remained for years—by force of circumstances—out of touch with people of our faith, compelled to hear nothing but the damned 'humanitarian' propaganda of our enemies, wherever I went. Did that 'reform' me? No fear! It would have made me even more of a Nazi than ever, if that had been possible."

"You are right," agreed the wardress. "We all know this is just nonsense. No one can 'reform' a responsible man or woman who knows what he or she wants. But what can we do? We have no say in the matter—nor has Frau R., nor Frau *Oberin* herself. We have lost the war, and our country is occupied. We are all as powerless as you—all in bondage. The representatives of the Occupying Powers do what they like here, as everywhere else in Germany."

"I know," answered I, bitterly, all my hatred for the Allied Occupation filling my heart, along with that consciousness of the uselessness of effort, which is the most painful feeling of all. "I know. Oh, for how long, for how long more?"

"Nobody can tell."

I would have willingly continued the conversation. But Frau X. had no time. "Your supper will get cold. And I have also to take back the container," said she, after a short pause, for the sake of putting an end to our talk. I emptied the large round aluminium vessel, of American make, in which the food had been brought to me; as usual, I put by whatever I could for H. E., and ate the rest.

When the wardress came back, she told me that it was the turn of the prisoners of the B wing to go to the recreation room (where every separate batch of us was allowed to spend two hours every week or so). And she added—as one's presence there was not compulsory—"Would you care to go too? Just to see how you like it? I know it is no company for you. But it can be an experience for you. Take it in that light, as I can't send you to the recreation room with the D wing, however much I would like to do so."

Her kindness and consideration touched me all the more that I knew that she was "in order," and that she understood, as only one of us could, how painful this separation from my comrades was to me. I thanked her.

"I shall go," said I, making up my mind. "Even if these are not political prisoners, they are at least German women, most of them. And among them, I dare say there are some good elements; perhaps even . . ."

"Don't you go and try to indoctrinate them," interrupted Frau X., forestalling in me a very natural propensity. "You never know whom you are speaking to, in that lot. Be careful!"

I said I would be. Yet, I could not help hoping that, even among those women I would find some who, whatever might have been their weaknesses, had retained enough German pride to look back to the National Socialist régime with nostalgia, and, along with me, a foreigner—along with us—to yearn for its resurrection; some whom, in course of time, I might trust.

* * *

I walked out into the corridor. Some prisoners were already there; others were coming out of their cells. The wardress was opening the doors, one after the other. I had, suddenly, the most vivid impression of being in a sort of "zoo," of which the keeper was now letting the inmates out for a while. I had noticed how wild beasts do not rush out of their cages as soon as the iron bars are lifted, but how, strange as this might seem, they slowly walk out, as though they knew that the freedom offered to them is only relative, and temporary—hardly worth mentioning. The imprisoned women did the same; even after the wardress had flung the doors wide open, they did not appear in a hurry to come out. They came forth slowly, and pulled behind them the iron bars that shut their cells from outside; or they loitered inside for a minute or two, putting away the utensils in which they had eaten their supper, adjusting a comb in their hair, or seeking a pocket handkerchief. They knew that it was not liberty that they were going to enjoy, but just two hours' relaxation in the recreation room of the prison. And I was an animal in the "zoo" no less than any of them; only, perhaps, a little wilder and prouder animal than most of them—a Bengal tigress, straight from the jungle.

One of the two cells next to mine—that both bore upon their doors a Z. (standing for *Zuchthaus*, i.e., penal servitude) in the place of my G. (*Gefängnis*, i.e., imprisonment)—was not opened. "She does not come out?" enquired I, referring to the inmate of the closed cell, towards which I pointed.

"No," answered one of the prisoners in the corridor; "she is punished; she's got a fortnight's *'Hausarrest'*."[8]

"What for?" asked I, casually—not really interested, but trying to be courteous.

"For standing half-dressed against her window and dropping love letters to the men, when they come to work in the courtyard."

The prisoner walked along with me, in the direction of the recreation room. "A silly woman," she pursued, commenting upon the behaviour of the one who was confined to her cell. "I know it must be hard to be shut in for two weeks, and to work on nothing but dry bread and water. But she asked for it. I would not do what she did. Would you?"

The question was enough to stir me out of the polite indifference with which I had, hitherto, listened to the pathetic story. "*I?* I should think not!" exclaimed I, shocked at the very idea of someone addressing me such mad words as a matter of course. And I added, hardly able to conceal my contempt for all manner of sentimental affairs: "I have never written a love letter in my life. I always had better things to live for."

"You are 'new' here, I think," said the prisoner, changing topics, as we entered the recreation room together.

"Yes. I was sentenced on Tuesday—three days ago," replied I. "But I have remained over six weeks 'on remand' before that. I was then in No. 121, in the C wing."

"And may I ask you what you are here for?" the woman ventured to say, somewhat shyly, as though she feared being indiscreet.

"For Nazi propaganda," answered I, simply.

The woman gazed at me with mingled surprise and admiration. "Oh," commented she, "that is something honourable—something laudable. For what have we gained with these swine and their Democracy? Nothing but misery. You see me: I was not a bad woman; not a jailbird by any means; I had never stolen a pin. But now life has become so hard, so impossible! Out of sheer need, I took fifty marks and an old pair of shoes from a neighbour who was none the poorer for that but who went and reported me none the less. I was caught, and got a year's imprisonment. That would never have happened to me in the Hitler days. We had everything we required, then; and plenty to eat for our children. You were right to fight those Allied bastards. I only wish they had never got you. It is a pity. How long did they give you?"

"Three years."

I suddenly recalled Hildegard X. . . ., my companion in the dark damp

---

[8] Solitary confinement—Ed.

cell in which I had been put on the night of my arrest. She had spoken in the same spirit, using nearly the same words. Was the loyalty of the German masses to their Saviour, to such an extent, the mere expression of an unfailing gratitude of the stomach? Perhaps, thought I, although the admission saddened me a little. But I reflected: "And why not? . . . Germans are animals, in fact, like the rest of men; animals first and then Aryans; and National Socialists—Aryans fully aware of their God-ordained superiority—last of all. It is natural. Only a few among them, and incredibly fewer still among other Aryan people, are National Socialists first and last, supporters of our Ideology solely because it is true, independently of their own comfort or discomfort. And it would be foolish on my part to expect to find representatives of that free and steadfast minority among these women." All I could do was to wish for the continuation, nay for the increase of material hardships as long as Germany remained occupied, and even after that, as long as my friends did not come back to power, bringing order and prosperity with them. Then, the régime would be more solidly established than ever.

I sat down on a bench by the first of the two tables that occupied the room, thinking of this, and firmly determined to exploit the grievances of that woman whom need had led to theft, and to induce her to look upon the return of our régime as *her* only possible salvation and *her* sole hope. But I had not the opportunity of doing so: the woman went and sat at the other table, and started playing dominoes with two prisoners who seemed to be waiting for her there. And other women surrounded me.

A short, darkish, middle aged woman, condemned, I knew not for what offence, to long years of penal servitude, sat just opposite me. I remembered her face for having seen her clean my cell several times, and I knew her name for having heard the wardresses call her. "How is it that they put you with us instead of in the D wing," said she, addressing me as soon as the wardress had closed the door, after the last prisoner had come in. "And did they give you a black jacket? You should have a dark-blue one. All the 'politicals' have dark-blue jackets."

"And we, who have been sentenced to penal servitude have brown ones, and those sentenced to mere imprisonment for non-political offences, black ones," explained her neighbour on the right hand; while her neighbour on the left hand (who wore a black jacket) said to me: "You should complain to Frau *Oberin*, and ask her to put you in the D wing."

It was the first time that I heard that different colours characterised, in Werl, different categories of female prisoners. I had never seen H. E.'s jacket for the simple reason that she hardly ever wore it—and had not yet worn it on her morning visits to my cell. And I now felt utterly humiliated at the idea of being made to wear a black jacket, like the ordinary criminals, I who had believed, up till then, that I was dressed entirely like H. E. and my other beloved comrades. My heart sunk within my breast; and I could have wept. But I pulled myself together. "I wish I could," said I, answering the suggestion of that prisoner who had advised me to speak to Frau *Oberin;* "but I don't think it would be of any use: somebody told me that I am separated from the other 'politicals' by order of the Governor."

"That makes things a little more difficult," remarked the woman. And another one added, nearly immediately: "But why should the Governor take such a step against you?"

"I am sure I don't know," said I. In reality, I was wondering whether he had suspected that, while still on remand, I had, through H. E., been distributing a few copies of my posters among the so-called "war criminals." (I had, in fact, also distributed some to certain members of the staff, but of that the Governor could not possibly have any knowledge, for their things were never searched.) Then, I reflected that, had any search revealed the presence of papers of mine in cells of the D wing, my friend H. E. would have told me so. "No," thought I; "the reasons for my banishment to the B wing must be more subtle: sheer fright that I would keep our spirit alive in the D wing—or perhaps, that I might hear, from my D wing comrades, too many instances of British and Allied atrocities." But I said nothing.

"In whatever wing they care to put you," declared the dark-haired woman seated opposite me, "I respect you. You have defended your faith, and done no harm to anybody. I have no time for politics, but still I say: if those people who have come here to give us lessons in toleration really believe in 'individual freedom', as they pretend to, why can't they recognise *you* the right to be a Nazi, and to express your convictions publicly if you feel you should?"

"Quite!" exclaimed I, glad to find a sympathiser with some regard for consistency. "And why don't they recognise that right to us all? Why are so many of my German comrades in captivity since 1945, for the sole crime of having done their duty? Of course the Democrats are hypocrites. Don't ask them to be just—or even logical. Hatred and not logic has been the motive of their behaviour towards Germany, since and even before 1939. Well, let them reap hatred! Let them suffer a hundredfold what they have done to the élite of the Aryan race, and perish wholesale! They deserve it."

A young woman seated on my right, was listening to me with interest—although obviously not with sympathy. So were two or three others, among whom was a coarse-looking blonde, seated at the other end of the table.

"It may be that *you* have done no harm to anyone," said the former, giving me a suspicious look. "But you can't come and tell us that your German pals have done 'nothing but their duty' as you say. We know them too well."

"Hear! hear!" shouted the latter—the coarse-looking blonde—before I had time to put in a word. "And you would not look upon them as 'the élite of the Aryan race' if you had spent four years in Ravensbrück as I have. It is all very easy to come and stick up for Nazism when you don't even know what it is . . ."

I felt my blood rush to my head, as though someone had given me a slap. However, I controlled myself. "Excuse me," said I, in a cold, biting voice, "although I am not a German, I undoubtedly know more about Nazism than you do. I don't fight for what I don't know, like the monkeys who compose the majority of mankind, even in most Aryan countries. But that is not all: you seem to think it was the fault of the régime if you were in Ravensbrück. May I ask you whose fault it is now, if . . ."

I wanted to say: ". . . if you are again 'inside'—for you are surely not guilty of sticking up posters against the Occupation, as I am." But the prisoner on my right—the one who had spoken before the fair-haired woman—interrupted me. "It is no use picking quarrels," said she. "Everyone has the right to hold the views he or she likes—even to be a Nazi. What I don't admit—what I never will admit—is that one should arrogate to oneself the right to behave in a beastly manner, as so many Nazis have . . ."

It was my turn to interrupt her: "As if we had the monopoly of 'beastly behaviour' as you call it!" I burst out. "Yes, now, since the disaster of 1945, the whole world speaks about nothing but our real or supposed atrocities. Don't I remember the wireless in London spouting out the vilest calumnies against us, in shops, in restaurants, wherever I went, on my arrival from India in 1946—during the infamous Nuremberg trial! Don't I remember that culmination of a long-drawn campaign of lies! And what about the crimes of the anti-Nazis, before and especially since 1945? What about the atrocities of those 'fighters for the rights of man', damned hypocritical swine, the lot of them? What about their air raids upon Germany, to speak of something you all know: two hundred thousand civilians killed in Hamburg in one hellish night; twenty-two thousand in a small place like Düren, on the 16th of November, 1944; over thirty thousand in Koblenz on the 22nd of the same month; nearly half a million in Dresden on the 13th of February, 1945, and so forth . . . Tell me: if that is not 'beastly behaviour', what is?"

There was silence. Even the woman formerly interned in Ravensbrück did not dare answer me, for fear of what the others might say. I felt that I had practically won the discussion, with that precise reference to the phosphorus horror that these women had all undergone. More so: I felt that I would win as many discussions as I liked in Germany, with *that* argument in support of my thesis; that the Allied bombers, quite definitely (although quite unwillingly) had given grist to my propaganda mill for the rest of my life.

"And if you say that this was an unavoidable calamity of total war, and can in a way be understood, if not, of course, excused," pursued I, with increased assurance; "if it is not beastly enough to condemn these bastards, what about the less well-known but no less real horrors of the anti-Nazi concentration camps, after the war, and up to this day, not only under the Russians but here in western Germany also? What about the treatment inflicted upon innocent men and women, all these years, in places like Schwarzenborn and Darmstadt, for no other reason that they were National Socialists? I know some who have died, in these and other camps of horror, tortured mostly by Jews, under Allied supervision; I know one in Koblenz[9]—one of the finest characters I have ever met— who is dying, after three and a half years of martyrdom; who was beaten, starved, made to lie, shivering with fever, in a freezing cold cell. And there are thousands of others whose health has been ruined forever. Is that not 'beastly behaviour' on the part of the Democrats, who pretend to give us 'lessons'? Their lessons! Their 're-education' schemes and what not! They are not fit to give 'lessons' to the wild man-eating tribes of Africa (if there still be any), let alone to us, their superiors; to us who at least are not liars."

Several of my hearers were now inclined to take my side. But the coarse-looking blonde and two or three others (who, like her, I was afterwards told, had spent some time in concentration camps during the great days) and the woman on my right, remained decidedly prejudiced against me. They gave me glances of undisguised enmity. The woman on my right spoke. "That's all very well," said she, turning to me; "we know you people are not liars; we know it too well, in fact. We know to what extremes of brutality you can go, in action and not merely in speech; for I am sorry to tell you that the Allied atrocities, during and after the war, revolting as they might be, do not excuse those of your precious pals.

---

[9] Friedrich "Fritz" Horn. See pp. xv above and 386–89 below, as well as *Gold in the Furnace*, 3rd ed., pp. 81–85, 163–67.—Ed.

Mind you, I do not speak of you, personally; you are a foreigner; you have admired the National Socialist ideology for years; you have identified yourself with it; and you have the courage to come and support it the best way you can, here, in the land of its birth, after the war, when the whole world is against it. That is one thing.

"Behaving as your pals did is another. You were not here, then, and you don't know what went on in their concentration camps. We were in them; we had friends in them; we know. You seem to be hurt because you are not given a cell in the D wing. You think it is an honour to be there. I tell you, you don't know those of the D wing; you have no idea of the things they did . . ."

My heart started beating faster, as though I felt the woman would say something that I could not possibly hear without flying at her. Already she had said too much. Even more still, perhaps, than her verdict upon my comrades, her hasty reservations as regards *me*; her confidence that I was *surely* more "humane" than they, irritated me as an insult in disguise—all the worse if it was intended to be a compliment. What was there in me that made her feel so cocksure about it at first sight?

"What did they do, which I would not have done—or which you *believe* I would not have done?" asked I, speaking slowly, in a tone of provocation. "I don't mean, of course, those who worked for money, or out of fear, being themselves internees promoted to certain minor posts when the camps were understaffed; I speak of the genuine ones—my equals and my superiors!"

"The genuine ones?" replied the woman. "All right; you shall know. Take for example that one who works in the infirmary . . ."

My heart beat still a little faster: the prisoner was referring to my beloved H. E. As though to make it quite clear to me, a woman who had been silent up till then called out: "You mean E., don't you, not the other one?" (For two so-called "war criminals" worked in the infirmary.)

"Naturally, I mean E.," said the speaker. (In Werl, the prisoners were all called by their surnames, save by their close friends.) "She is 'genuine' enough, isn't she? Well, you might or might not know that she was three years a member of the staff in Auschwitz; and next to the head of the camp, mind you; no mere wardress. I was not there myself, but somebody who was there six years,[10] and who is now here, told me that she saw that woman, one day that she had lost her temper, flog a wounded prisoner until the poor thing was bleeding from top to toe, and then pull

---

[10] The Auschwitz camp complex was in operation from May of 1940 to January of 1945, less than five years.—Ed.

off her bandages, flesh and all. She saw it herself, she told me. She said that had anyone reported it to her, she would not have believed it."

I did not believe it. I knew from the start that it was another of those innumerable lies that I was condemned to hear until my comrades would come back to power, one day, and silence the slanderers once and for all. I knew it was a lie, not because the alleged action was gruesome; but because it was a pointless, a useless action; not because I thought my dear friend H. E. incapable of murderous violence—on the contrary, I sincerely hoped she was capable of it, if necessary—but because I believed her to be too thoroughly and too intelligently National Socialist to allow herself to be guided by anything else but considerations of impersonal expediency.

"Another time," said I, sarcastically, "you should cook up a cleverer story than this one, if you wish to impress people who have heard as many lies as I have."

"But it is not a story; it is true," insisted the woman; "true, and horrible enough!"

"Well," said I, "let us put it another way. Let me tell you that, if that person whom you mention had killed her alleged victim, and cut her up in bits, and eaten the bits with mustard sauce, still I could not care less. Are you satisfied, now?"

The woman got up, and left the table. So did two or three others, among them the coarse-looking blonde.

"You should be careful about what you say, here in the recreation room," said one of the remaining prisoners. "Things get repeated, and work their way to the Governor's ears. Especially that woman whom you just spoke to, you don't know what a nasty type she is. Fortunately she is going away the day after tomorrow or so. She has finished her term."

"What is she here for?" I ventured to ask.

"Abortion," answered the other prisoner. "She was, formerly, in some camp for the same offence. So were those two who looked at you in such a way and got up. The third one was in too, but for selling on the black market, during the war. And I was told that she is half-Jewish, although she does not look it."

"No, a quarter only," put in another woman, who joined the conversation. "I know: one who knows her has told me; it is her grandmother, who was a Jewess, not her mother."

"It is just the same," replied I, with obvious contempt for such subtle discriminations.

"Quite right!" remarked the woman who had spoken first. Then, after a while, taking me aside, she said: "You know, I understand you. I too . . ." She probably wanted to say: "I too, am a National Socialist."

I looked at her, a little sceptical, and then thought: "Who knows? Perhaps she speaks the truth?"

"Do you really mean it?" I asked the woman.

But before she had time to answer me, the door was opened; the wardress on duty appeared at the threshold. We were taken back to our cells.

* * *

I lay upon my bed, but did not go to sleep for a long time. I thought of these women with whom I had spent two hours; of the discussion I had had with them; of those who were against me, and of those who seemed sympathetic. But even the sympathetic ones were lukewarm; I felt that the great cause for which I lived exclusively was only the second or third concern in their lives, if that. Even that last one who had spoken to me somehow did not seem to me to be genuine . . . "Oh," thought I, "if only I were in the D wing, with my comrades!"

I thought of the last afternoon H. E. and H. B. had spent in my cell; I recalled all that they had told me of the atrocious treatment inflicted by the Allied Military Police, in 1945, upon them and especially upon the S.S. men in charge of the Belsen camp—men whom I imagined handsome and strong; fearless, disinterested; absolutely devoted to our Führer and to our cause; Nazis like myself, and a hundred times better than myself. And I recalled the words I had spoken from the depth of my heart, in answer to that evocation of horror: "'They' have thrown you to the Jews. May I, one day, be given the power and the opportunity to throw 'them' to torturers of Mongolian blood!" Then, I suddenly remembered that the next day—the 9th of April—was the day on which the irresistible Mongol, Kaidu, had crushed the coalesced forces of Christendom at the battle of Liegnitz, in 1241, exactly 708 years before. "The Aryan race was then united (more or less) in the Christian faith," thought I; "But now, pretending to champion the obsolete Christian values, the whole West has consented to become the tool of the Jews, and to fight and persecute us, the sole upholders of the eternal values of Aryandom. What if, when the Mongols come again, we were on their side—for the sake of expediency?" It might seem—and perhaps it was—a mad thought. But after all why not? I would not be worse than allying ourselves with the judaised plutocracies of the West, as I had once told Mr. Stocks.

I remembered the half-historical half-philosophical book I had begun, a year before: *The Lightning and the Sun*. I had not written a word of it since December, 1948. Now, I sat at my table, pulled the manuscript out of the drawer and (for once, instead of writing my *Gold in the Furnace*) continued Chapter 4, about the birth of Genghis Khan.

The wardress on duty—who was "in order" and who liked me—kindly left the light on in my cell till eleven o'clock.

* * *

Days passed. My new cell, much narrower than the first one (it was not wide enough for me to stretch out both my arms completely, from one wall to the other) presented at least the advantage of having one transparent windowpane, through which I could see the sky. Like the first one, only facing the south instead of the west, it looked over the inner courtyard around which the prisoners used to walk, two by two, during their "free hour." The D wing used to go out with a part of the A wing; the rest of the A wing used to join the B wing; and the C wing—the most numerous, for many of the larger cells there used to accommodate three prisoners instead of one—went out alone.

Standing upon my table, my face against the one transparent windowpane, I gazed at my comrades of the D wing during their free time. I gazed at them as an exile gazes at the hills and fields of home, across the forbidden frontier; or as a young girl, forced to become a nun, gazes from behind the windows of the cloister at the forbidden world in which she has left her heart. And I idealised them. There was naturally an abyss between them and the other prisoners, the proper delinquents of all descriptions. And my ardent imagination broadened it. Most of the D wing prisoners were innocent women made to suffer for the mere fact of having held responsible posts in the coercive machinery of the Third Reich. Some, like H. E., were sincere, selfless idealists, real National Socialists. Not being given the opportunity to know who was who, I looked upon them all as real National Socialists. And my love transfigured them. Tears dropped from my eyes as I watched them walk around and around the courtyard in their dark-blue jackets. To be with them appeared to me nearly as good as being free—even better, in a way; for not only would I have contributed to keep up the Nazi morale among them, but I probably would have heard, from them, more facts damaging to our enemies than from most free Germans; and I could have collected these in a special book. (That was, indeed, thought I, what the Governor feared.)

H. E., who nearly always walked by the side of the same lovely blonde, sometimes looked up to my window. I then stretched out my arm and saluted her. On her daily morning visits, she used to tell me to be patient. Perhaps things would change, with time. Already the whole D wing was protesting to Frau *Oberin* against the decision that had thrown me among the ordinary criminals. And I used to put my arms around her neck and rest my head upon her shoulder and tell her: "At least, I have *you*, five minutes a day—you, who represent so much in my eyes; and I have my book, which I am writing. It is something, you know, that they did not destroy *that!* A true miracle." And I often added: "I wish I could read to you, in Chapter 6, all that which I wrote about your last days in Belsen, from what you told me yourself."

H. E. promised me she would try to come one Sunday afternoon, when Frau So-and-so would be on duty.

As for my own daily free time in the courtyard, it was dull, to say the least; and often depressing. So much so that, had it not been for the sake of walking in the sunshine a few minutes, and breathing a little fresh air, I would never have left my cell at all—or I would have gone out once or twice a week at the most. The company of my own thoughts, of my re-membrances, of my few books, was more pleasant to me than that of the great number of the ordinary delinquents who, as I have said already, spoke about nothing but trifles, or gossiped about one another, and seemed incapable of holding an interesting conversation more than once. And yet, I had something to learn from them. In those dreary walks around the courtyard, twice a day, in company of the coarsest and com-monest elements of Germany, I learnt how to discern many good quali-ties under the layer of selfishness, callousness, and vulgarity that life— and more especially post-war life—had set over them. Among them were good-looking, healthy, and strong women, who would have remained or become useful mothers, had the National Socialist régime lasted; had the wretched conditions created in Germany by defeat, not forced them into an unnatural life. "My Führer would understand and forgive their weak-nesses," thought I; "He would love them in spite of all, for they are daughters of his people, and they have suffered." And I loved them too— save, of course, those who, having already taken to criminal life during the great days, had brought punishment upon themselves, then, and who bitterly hated our régime. Still, I could not help resenting my banishment from the D wing.

I would have liked to talk to the woman who had last spoken to me so sympathetically in the recreation room. Somehow, she did not seem keen to be with me during the "free hour." She took her place in the row, al-ways by the side of the same other prisoner, and merely greeted me occa-sionally in the corridor with a *"Guten Tag!"* which I returned. The first question put to me by practically every woman with whom I walked around was the same: "What sort of food do you get, you who are a

'Britisher'?" It was natural, for they were all hungry; and they also all had complaints about the poor quality of their food, no less than about its quantity. H. E., whose diet was exactly the same as theirs, and whom I could trust to speak the truth, had told me that they all were "fed like pigs"—or rather worse, since pigs are generally given *enough* to eat, if not more than enough.

I felt ashamed to mention my white bread, porridge, and orange jam, as I could not give them any. But the women seemed to know all about it—probably from the prisoners who used to help the wardresses on duty in distributing the food. I spoke of my midday meals, which were as tasteless as anything, being composed of potatoes and other vegetables (nearly always cabbage and carrots) merely boiled. The women showed a certain surprise at such austerity: "But we thought you British subjects were given meat with your vegetables," said they.

"I never eat meat," replied I: "never ate any, in fact. And I would not eat vegetables mixed with gravy. I told the Governor, when I came."

To my great satisfaction, I had not to put up with the endless silly "why?"'s and "wherefore?"'s that the mere mention of my abhorrence of animal flesh used to provoke, as a rule, even among "intellectuals"— perhaps especially among "intellectuals"—of democratic upbringing. These simple women, brought up in the rigid discipline of our régime, were far less interfering, far more tolerant, far more liberal than most upholders of "individual freedom" that I have met. Not one even tried to force onto me the man-centred moral outlook which she might have had herself. The only comment that one of them once made was: "I know two other people who, like you, never eat meat. And they both have your views, too."

But the women often asked me what I did with my extra white bread: "I give it to Sister Maria, for the sick ones," I used to answer, concealing, out of tactfulness, the fact that I preferred to give my white bread to H. E. and to my genuine comrades of the D wing. One of the prisoners to whom I had once thus spoken, burst out, with undisguised resentment: "Sister Maria? I'd bet you anything that she eats it herself—or shares it with her darlings! The sick ones don't see the colour of it, I tell you."

"What makes you think that?" asked I, trying to look only casually interested. "And first, whom do you mean by 'her darlings'?"

"Whom do I mean? Why, those two who work at the Infirmary, of course; the E. woman, especially—she is the favourite of all the staff, from the *Oberin* downwards, and Sister Maria's more than anyone else's; and Frau So-and-so's, naturally. And not she alone: all the 'war criminals' are. They seem to think them wonderful; while they treat us, ordinary delinquents, like dogs."

It was painful to me to detect in this woman—as I had in many others—that bitter hostility towards the so-called "war criminals." "Jealousy, no doubt," thought I, "nothing but jealousy." And I did not reply. The woman did not like my silence. She understood that, in my heart, I took the side of my comrades. "And you too seem to think them wonderful, probably because they have your views—or because you think they have," she pursued; "well, you can go and report what I said, if it pleases you; I don't care!"

"I am a fighter, not an informer," replied I with pride; "I would, no doubt, denounce a person if it were my duty—that is to say, if *we* were in power, and if the matter were serious; but now, and for trifles like this? No; I have better things to do."

Other women would tell me, during the "free hour," all that was going on in the prison. "You know, that one in that corner cell up there; stout, with brown, wavy hair; Emma, they call her . . ."

"Well, what about her?"

"She has again caught eight days of *'Hausarrest'*. And that dark Polish woman with short, frizzy hair, also."

"Why?"

"For dropping love letters to the men and for answering rudely to Frau *Erste* (the matron).[11] The Pole is always getting caught for writing love letters. She also calls out obscene words in her language, when men cross the courtyard, for there are plenty of Poles among them. She is mad on men."

I was not vaguely interested. I used to answer something—make some anodyne remark—simply for the sake of courtesy.

But once one of those who seemed to know the life history of nearly every inmate of the *"Frauenhaus,"* took to talking to me about another Pole, or so-called so.

"You have never met that one," said she "for she is in the A wing. But all the 'old' ones, like myself, know her, for she has been here a long time. Formerly, she spent six years in Auschwitz for doing I don't know what against the Hitler Government . . ."

"Six years in Auschwitz," thought I; "why, she must be the one whose statement was reported to me in the recreation room; the one who slandered my Friend H. E. . . . ."

---

[11] *"Erste"* (meaning "first") is either a title that Savitri translates as "matron," or a nickname, not a proper name. On page 213 below, Savitri Devi gives Frau *Erste*'s last initial as "R."—Ed.

I *was* interested, this time; and very much so. "What about her?" asked I, preparing to listen with all my attention.

"Well," replied the prisoner, "she can't bear men: she likes women. And you'd never guess what she did last year, at Christmas time, when we are a little freer than usually . . ."

"What?" enquired I.

"Well, there was then another one who also liked women (she is out, now). So they managed to get together and . . ."

The woman described to me, in full detail, one of the filthiest perverted sexual performances of which I have ever heard—something too disgusting to be written in black on white. "And they were caught," she added; "and dear me what a row it made! . . ."

"The female should never have come out of Auschwitz," said I, with a feeling of nausea. "One who can do such a dirty thing as that, for 'pleasure' does not deserve to live!" And after a pause, I could not help adding: "Indeed, it is refreshing to hear that such a bitch has worked against us. I always said: those anti-Nazis are the scum of the earth!"

"One has to agree that many are," replied the woman. "However, they are not *all* like this Pole."

"Perhaps. But one could not find a single such depraved specimen among us," said I with genuine pride. "No sexually debased man or woman, no unclean person of any description, can be a National Socialist. Of that, I am absolutely sure."

I could not help being impressed by the enormous proportion of Poles and Czechs imprisoned at Werl for theft, complicity in theft or burglary, black-marketeering, and . . . abortion. The greatest number of German women with whom I came in contact during the "free hour" were also there for abortion. Every time they thought it was possible . . . they tried to lessen their guilt in my eyes, and sometimes, they succeeded in doing so. "It is not our fault; it is the fault of those swine," one told me, speaking of the Allied occupants. "In 1945, in 1946, even in 1947, it was terrible, out here. There was nothing to eat. Our girls used to go with those brutes for a slice of bread—or a packet of cigarettes, that bought much more. And not for their own stomachs, most of the time, but for the sake of their starving families. They often became pregnant, and then called us to 'help' them . . ."

I thought of those fine German girls who had been healthy and happy Hitler-maidens a few years before . . . And tears filled my eyes. "Avenge that unutterable misery, and avenge that shame, invisible Lord!" I prayed within my heart, looking to the cloudless sky. And, turning once more to the woman, I said: "You are right; it *is* the fault of those swine; and still

more the fault of those who brought about the downfall of National Socialism: the fault of the traitors, here in Germany; of the Jews and of the
slaves of the Jews, all over the world."

"But things are changing," the woman pursued; "and the Allies are
the first ones to find it out, whether they like it or not. Those very men
we lay with for a packet of cigarettes in '45, we would not touch with a
pair of tongs, now that we are no longer starving. Even their officers we
loathe. We want our own men."

"You are quite right," said I, sincerely wishing that she spoke the truth.

"I myself don't approve of abortion," continued the prisoner, coming
back to her first topic. "I might be guilty of it, but I know it is not right.
But on the other hand, what is one to do with so many children in times
like this? And they come, sometimes, whatever people do to avoid them.
What do you say?"

It was difficult to express what I thought—not because I had strange
views on the subject (I had, on the contrary, exactly the same views as
any other National Socialist) but because I had not the slightest experience of the problems, of the difficulties, of the daily conflicts of what is
supposed to be "life"; because, in fact, I had never had a personal life or
even desired to have one, and could not, therefore, buttress my views
with arguments as convincing as those another person would have used. I
felt that whatever I said would remain abstract; would sound like a party
catechism, although it would not *be* just that. However, this could not be
helped. And I spoke. "On principle, I strongly condemn abortion save
when it aims at getting rid of the undesirable product of some shameful
union," said I. And I explained: "By 'shameful union' I mean the union
of a man and woman of different races, or of whom one at least is a sick
person or a weakling. In practice, of course"—I added—"if abortion
were carried on among the inferior races, it would not matter much (although I would prefer to limit their numbers by other means). But it is
surely a crime to destroy a potential child of pure Aryan blood; to refuse
a place in the world to a soul that the heavenly Powers had deemed worthy to take birth amidst the highest form of humanity. I know that, as you
say, times are hard. And I know that this Allied Government will do
nothing to make them less so; nor will the puppet so-called German
Government that will, sooner or later, take its place. But the real national
Government that will come back, one day, will help the healthy families
of pure blood, just as it did in the past."

"Yes," said the woman. "And I wish to goodness that it comes back
as quickly as possible. But what are we to do in the meantime?"

"Struggle in silence; hope and wait," replied I. "What else *can* one do?"

The woman had already asked me, another day, if I had any children, and I had told her that I had none. She now looked at me sceptically, as though to say: "It is all very easy in theory. But I would like to hear what you would say if *you* had a family of seven, and were expecting the eighth, and had nothing to give them to eat" (which was, she had told me, the case of one of the women whom in her euphemistic language she had actually "helped").

And we talked of something else.

Other women would tell me about their private affairs—their husbands, their children, their lovers, their neighbours and their mothers-in-law. One, who had accompanied me several times during the "free hour" was a woman of twenty-six who had already three children from her husband and who was expecting a fourth one from another man. "He has left me for another woman," she one day told me; "so what could I do? I found this man, who is much nicer than he was, and who will marry me, when I get out of this place; he will take the children too, he says. (They are now at my mother's.) And he writes to me; and such loving letters!"

I was bored. But I was thinking to myself: "Twenty-six, now, in 1949. So she must have been sixteen at the outbreak of the war; and ten in 1933. She must remember . . . I wonder what the great days meant to her; what they mean to her now . . ." And turning to my companion, I said: "I sincerely wish you every happiness with the man you love. Personally, all I want is to see the Hitler days come back; more so: all I want is to see the Führer's spirit rule not only Germany, but the world, forever and ever . . ." And I imagined myself coming back, one day, to a new National Socialist Germany, a resurrected Germany, who would open her arms to me. And I was happy in anticipation, and smiled.

But the woman had not listened to my last words. "The Hitler days," said she, with utmost naturalness: "and who does not want *them* to come back? I do for one. We were all so happy, then. We had plenty to eat. And although we worked hard, we worked in joy. And we had plenty of fun, too. I remember my months of compulsory labour—the best time in my life. There was a camp of youngsters not far from the place we were. And we used to meet them whenever we could. You have no idea what lovely, handsome young men they were! There were three, especially, who liked me; and . . ."

"It is always the same," thought I, thrilled for the millionth time at the evocation of that tremendous collective labour effort in the midst of songs and merriment, and yet a little depressed; "it is always the same: speaking of the great days, nine people out of ten tell me: 'They were splendid because, then, we enjoyed ourselves', while only one says:

'They were splendid because, then, we were building a new world, founded upon health and truth'. Oh, how I wish all my Führer's people; how I wish all the Aryan race could feel as that one! But I suppose the new spirit cannot permeate them all in a day. Great changes in depth take time." And turning to the pretty young woman who walked by my side, I told her: "One day, the revenge will come, and then, days even more glorious than those you witnessed. For the Führer is alive." And as I said that, I imagined, travelling through radiant space in which there are no barriers, subtle, silent waves, preparing, slowly and surely, in the realm of the invisible, by which all things visible are conditioned, the return of our beloved Hitler.

But the young woman said simply: "Of course, he is alive."

"How do *you* know it?" asked I, genuinely surprised at the unhesitating naturalness of her remark. "Who told you?"

She answered, equally surprised at my question: "Why, everybody knows it!"

We continued to walk around the courtyard, and for a while, we did not speak. Above us, around us, all over Germany, all over the world, the subtle waves were patiently continuing their unseen play; preparing "the Day for freedom and for bread"[12] in their unexpected manner, with mathematical accuracy.

But the "free hour" was over. We stood in two rows, and, beginning at one end, each one of us called out: one, two, etc.—the number of her place—a formality that we went through each time, so that the two wardresses who accompanied us might know that none of us was missing. While this was going on, I heard the young woman who had walked by my side call to another one who stood not far from us in the row behind mine: "Irmchen, eh, Irmchen! Don't forget to come to the recreation room this evening. I'll show you the letter my Fritz has written to me!"

* * *

I did not go to the recreation room. Instead, I continued writing Chapter 8 of my *Gold in the Furnace*, which I had just begun.

Before she went home, Frau *Oberin* came to my cell. She often came. And I was always glad to see her. Although she had never yet said a word from which I could infer that she was in sympathy with my views, she had managed to gain my confidence. I felt I could tell her practically

---

[12] Savitri Devi's translation of part of a line from the second verse of the Horst Wessel Song: "der Tag für Freiheit und für Brot."—Ed.

anything I liked. She would never do any harm to me or to any one of us.

"Your cell is rather small," said she, that evening, after she had returned my greeting. "As soon as there is a larger one available, I shall put you there." And she asked me in a most friendly manner: "You are not too unhappy here, anyhow?"

"I suppose I should not be, since I can write, thanks to your kindness," said I. "Still . . ."

"Still what?" enquired Frau *Oberin*.

I put forth the grievance I had in vain tried to conceal several days. "Oh, do put me in the D wing!" exclaimed I; "Do! You don't know how depressing the contact with this lot of prisoners is to me, at times! I have nothing to say against them, but I cannot talk to them as I would to those of the D wing."

"You would like to have the pleasure of indoctrinating the D wing ones, wouldn't you?" said Frau *Oberin* with a mischievous smile.

"I hope they do not *need* indoctrinating," replied I unhesitatingly. "I hope indeed they are as good National Socialists as myself. I would just like to enjoy some interesting talks, if I am to talk at all. If not . . ."

"Listen," said Frau *Oberin*, kindly interrupting me, "nobody, I believe, understands you, here, better than I do, and nobody is more willing than I am to make your life tolerable. I would give you a cell in the D wing straightaway, if only I could. But *I* don't give orders, here, as you have perhaps already guessed. I have to consult the German head of the prison, who is also the Public Prosecutor, in whatever I do. And above him is the British Governor . . . It is the latter himself who has expressly forbidden us to allow you to have any contact with the so-called 'war criminals'." And she tried to make me understand that, technically, I was not in the same category as they. "You see" she explained "you are a proper political prisoner, while these women are here for having inflicted ill-treatment upon internees in concentration camps or for having been found guilty of such similar offences as are now classified as 'crimes against humanity'. You have never done things of that nature."

"Only because I never had an opportunity," replied I. (And from the intonation of my voice, it was—I hope—evident that I meant every word I said.) "Crimes against humanity," I repeated, full of contempt for the hypocrisy this expression reveals on the part of those who coined it; "only when we Nazis do them are acts of violence thus labelled. When the Democrats do them, in the interest of the Jews, they are acts of justice!"

"You always seem to forget that we have lost the war," said Frau *Oberin*, with sudden sadness, and bitter irony. She talked to me as though I were a German. And in fact, I myself often forgot that I am not one.

"But again, why does the Governor insist that I should be separated from my comrades?" asked I, coming back to the point. "What difference does it make if they and I did not do exactly the same things? We all worked for the same cause."

"You idealise the D wing ones," said Frau *Oberin*.

"They are not all ardent National Socialists as you seem to think. Some never had any politics at all, and just obeyed orders—any orders— just because they were in service."

"Whatever they be," replied I, "they are victims of this hated Democracy; victims of our enemies. They have suffered for the cause I love— even those, if any, who do not love it as much as I do; even those who, at the time, might have been indifferent to it. Therefore I love them. Oh, do put me with them! How will the Governor find out? I could remain here, in this cell, so that he would see me here when he inspects the place on Friday mornings; and I could, if you allowed me, spend my 'Free hour' with the D wing ones and go to the recreation room with them. Why not? Put yourself in my place!"

"I do put myself in your place," said Frau *Oberin* softly and sadly. "I have already told you, nobody here understands you better than I do. Still: don't insist, for you only make my position more painful to me. I cannot do what you ask me, however much I would like to. Things of that sort always leak out. I would lose my job and not get another. And I cannot afford to risk that: life is already too difficult for us all. But I shall do all I can to make your life here less dull. I was, for instance, thinking of asking the Governor to allow you to give the other prisoners, now and then, a lecture about your travels in India and other places. I am sure they would all enjoy it. Perhaps it could be arranged. Today, I have come to tell you of one prisoner who is a little less coarse than most of the others and who, having heard of your academic qualifications, is keen on meeting you."

"Who is she?"

"A Polish woman. I might as well tell you at once she is definitely anti-Nazi, as most Poles are. But she is somewhat cultured. There are plenty of subjects about which one can talk with her. She speaks both French and English, apart from German and, of course, her own language. Would you care to meet her? I would at least make a diversion for you."

"I did not come to Germany to meet Polish women and to talk French and English," thought I. Yet, something told me I had perhaps better accept Frau *Oberin*'s suggestion. Who could tell? The Polish woman might, indirectly, prove useful, in one way or another. So I accepted. And Frau *Oberin* left me with a kind word.

The next morning, the *Oberwachtmeisterin* ushered the woman into my cell. "I hope you will be friends," said she, smiling. But she was far too perspicacious not to know all the time that we could never be friends. There was irony in her words and greater irony still in her smile. Apparently, she knew me better than, hitherto, Frau *Oberin* did.

I generally used to leave the Führer's portrait upon my table from six o'clock in the evening—the time all the cells were definitely shut for the night—to the time I woke up and got ready, the following morning. However, on *that* morning, I had somehow forgotten to hide it. It was there like a visible, living presence. And it was too late to hide it now. Moreover, why hide it? Frau S.—whom I was beginning to love more and more—had already seen it several times in its hiding place, and did not seem to object to it in the least. (She had told me of the beautiful large one that she had herself, in her house, during the great days, and that she had burnt, out of fear, "when the Americans had come.") The wardress on duty, a very amiable blonde, one hundred percent "in order," did not object either. The Polish woman probably objected. But it was all the same to me whether she did or not.

She was moderately tall, thin, red-haired, neither good-looking nor downright plain. As soon as the door was shut, she sat down and introduced herself. She was a real Pole, she told me—not a Jewess. She had remained in Germany after the end of the war, afraid to go home, she said, on account of the Communists whom she did not like. And she had been sentenced to three years' imprisonment for black marketeering. She admitted she had done wrong, but half-excused herself by saying that times were so hard that it was very difficult to live honestly. Anyhow, her time had now come to be sent back to Poland, and she was in a fix as to what she was to do. She did not like being in Werl. The food, especially, did not agree with her. But even so, to remain there would be better than to get caught by the Communists and to be packed off to some concentration camp . . . The mere mention of Communism seemed to scare her out of her wits. And the more I listened to her talk, the more I despised her, for I had been told that she was anti-Nazi. I detest anti-Nazis of any description; but I despise those who are at the same time anti-Communists.

Such people have no sense of reality, or they simply do not know what they want.

"I believe there are many Poles who, like you, hate Communism," said I.

The woman, who had come knowing what I am (she told me so herself a little later), thought she had found, between herself and me, a ground of agreement. "Not 'many' but *all* real Poles hate Communism, especially now that they suffered under it," said she; "*All*, I honestly tell you," she insisted, "save a handful of traitors who profit by it. And these are mostly Jews."

My contempt for her reached its limit—for I find inconsistency sickening. "And why didn't those real Poles join us, during the war, if they are as thoroughly as you say against the Reds?" asked I, sarcastically. "If my memory does not fail me, the Führer had once proposed them an alliance, which they were foolish enough to refuse, preferring a pact with England—who, incidentally, let them down. Or is it that they woke up too late in the day, when the Reds—who by then had become England's 'gallant allies'—were already there? Many people seem to wake up late in the day, also outside Poland."

The woman could not have felt too comfortable between Hitler's portrait, on the table by my side, and the lashing of my merciless tongue. As for myself, I suddenly had the impression that this sort of conversation could well take place in some police office of occupied Europe, under our resurrected New Order—provided my comrades would, then, have the good idea of using me in the repression services; and provided, too, that I, once in service, had still a little time to waste. ("And why should they not employ me, then, after all?" thought I in a flash. "I am sincere, radical, incorruptible—reliable—and would enjoy such work. I also know a few languages. I might lack a little diplomacy; but diplomacy will be of less importance, perhaps, when we are once more the masters of the situation.") And it seemed to me that this interview with a Polish anti-Nazi, now in the dark days, in a prison cell where there was a portrait of the Führer, had perhaps a prophetic meaning.

But the woman answered the few truths I had told her in the manner one would expect: "No," said she, "it is not that. We do not want the Communists surely. But we do not want you either. By 'you'," she added, "I mean the Germans. You have identified yourself with Nazism so completely that I am sure you will find it natural. To us, Nazism means Germany."

"To me it means that, no doubt, and a lot more," replied I.

"What more?"

"To me, National Socialism on a world-wide scale means the survival and the rule of the purest Aryan elements; the royalty of better mankind," said I. "Listen: Democracy—the capitalist economy, along with the parliamentary system with its many parties, its universal suffrage, its electoral campaigns, and all the bribery and corruption, all the dirty unseen bargaining that goes with it—is definitely doomed. Cry over it if you

like. You can do nothing to give it back its lost credit, and its lost potentialities (admitting that it ever had any). You speak like a dreamer when
you say you want neither the Communists nor us. My dear lady, who
cares what you want—or what I want, in fact? Or what the Poles or the
Russians or the Germans want? Whatever the whole world might *want*, it
can only *have* one of two things: Communism, or National Socialism;
either our sole real enemies—or us. Remark that I do not say: either Russian domination or German domination. For Communism is not Russia;
it is Jewry; it aims, ultimately, at the rule of the unseen Jew over a more
and more bastardised world. And if National Socialism *is* Germany
(which, in one way, undoubtedly it is) it is also more—otherwise, hundreds of intelligent non-Germans would not have gladly suffered for it in
England, in France, in India, everywhere; otherwise a Frenchman whom
I know would not have been shot shouting: 'Heil Hitler!', and I would
not be here. As I said, National Socialism is Aryandom, of which Germany is, no doubt, today, the vanguard, but which, nevertheless, exceeds
Germany. National Socialism means the rule of the best men of Aryan
blood wherever there are Aryans and, outside the pale of Aryandom, the
rule of the noblest non-Aryan races of the world, each one in its place,
and of the best men of each race, each within their own race. The whole
world is now before the same alternative as Germany was in 1933. It has
to choose: disintegration and death, with the Marxists; or resurrection
and life, with us. There is no third alternative; no other possible choice."

"As far as I am concerned, I can see no difference worth mentioning
between you people and the Communists," said the Polish woman. "You
both use the same horrible methods. You are both equally brutal, equally
cruel."

"We are ruthless, but not cruel," rectified I, interrupting her.

"Well, put it as you like, it is all the same in my eyes," concluded she,
rather impatiently. "You both consider man merely as a means to an end
and think nothing of taking human lives. I have suffered through both of
you, and I hate both your systems."

"It makes no difference," replied I. "One of the two conflicting systems will prevail in the end—and I hope it will be ours; democratic capitalism—the milder form of Jewish rule—is dying anyhow. And I am
afraid that those who, like you, hate both us and our bitterest enemies,
will sooner or later have to put up with something that they hate. It is bad
luck. But it cannot be helped. As for man, he has, if not always been *considered* as 'merely a means to an end', at least always been used as such,
from the dawn of history onwards, even by those who pretend to give
him a so-called 'dignity' and 'equal rights' whatever be his racial level

and personal value. Only the ends for which he is used differ. The ends of the Communists are, openly, 'individual happiness' for the greatest number of human beings, and, in fact, the rule of the Jew. Our ends are, openly and in fact, the maximum all-round development of the naturally noblest races—first of all of the Aryan—and their rule, condition of a better world in which all living creatures should enjoy rights, according to their natural status."

The woman stopped sewing for a while (she had brought her work with her). She looked at me intently and said: "At least, you are sincere. And I respect you for that."

"Every man or woman who has remained a Nazi in 1945 and throughout the atrocious following years, is sincere," replied I. "While every professed Communist is not; and still less every professed Christian. That is an encouraging fact."

"Surely you do not believe in Christianity?" said the woman.

"I? I should think not! Only self-deluded people can imagine they can be Nazis and Christians at the same time. I look upon the Christian superstition (as some Roman emperors have called it) as another trick of the Jews to enslave the Aryan soul. Moreover, both its man-centred attitude and its other-worldliness repel me—and would still repel me if none of the early promoters of the religion had been Jews."

"You are sincere, and logical," remarked the Polish woman, after hearing this declaration.

"I hope so," said. I.

"And what do you think about the next world?"

"I have not the foggiest idea about it," replied I. "If there is anything beyond death, I shall see soon enough when I get there."

"And you don't mind not knowing?" she asked me.

I found the question childish. "Whether I 'mind' or not," replied I, with a condescending smile, "I *do not* know; I have no means of knowing."

The woman gazed at me, astonished perhaps at the fact that I looked so happy in spite of 'not knowing' what would happen to me one day when I would die. She remained silent for a while and then said: "I am a Catholic. And now that I meet you after meeting so many of your kind in quite different circumstances—nay, after having seen my poor son in their hands—I am more than ever convinced that, without the humanising influence of religion, man easily becomes a monster, if given a chance. Your mysticism of the élite will not help him. It only makes him worse. You mentioned yourself, a while ago, the rights of 'all living beings'. How can you speak of such a thing when you don't even acknowledge the right of all men to live?"

I repeated before that woman what I had said hundreds of thousands of times, all my life: "I cannot love all men, including the dregs of humanity, including the dangerous people, including those who, without being positively dangerous, hate all that I love. While I do love all the animals of the world. All are beautiful and innocent. The only living things I would get rid of (apart from dangerous people) are fleas and bugs—parasites. For one has to defend oneself. As for the religion that tells me to respect the life of a dangerous man while it omits to forbid me to eat meat, I find it absurd. And the civilisation that condemns my comrades for 'war crimes' while it accepts vivisection as a matter of course, deserves wholesale destruction."

"You don't eat meat?" asked the woman.

"No; never did. I am logical—you have rightly said so."

"You are, I admit," replied she; "now, children are as innocent as animals. Don't you like children?"

"On principle, yes," said I; "and first of all, naturally, the healthy children of my own Aryan race, of which I am proud. Then, all the healthy children of the earth, to the extent these are not likely to become a danger to ours, when they grow up."

"I have seen men of those whom you admire, of those whom you call your comrades, and love, drive before them whole families of terrorised Jews, children and old people as well as others. What harm had those children done? What harm could they do, if allowed to live?"

"They were potential parasites," said I, calmly. And I added, after a pause: "The men of whom you speak, those men whom I admire and love indeed to the extent they were genuine National Socialists, aware of what they were doing and doing it in the proper spirit, did not hate the Jewish children. Dispassionately and according to orders, they did their utmost for the defence of threatened Aryan mankind. I would have done the same in their place."

And as I spoke thus, I suddenly remembered myself standing in the kitchen of my Calcutta home, one morning, in glorious '40, listening to my fifteen-year-old Indian servant tell me: "*Mem-sahib*, I too admire your Führer. He is fighting to replace in the West the Bible by the Bhagavad-Gita: A grownup boy who reads English was saying so just now at the fish market."[13] The illiterate lad of the Tropics had probably forgotten

---

[13] The young servant's name was Khudiram. For a fuller telling of this story, see Savitri Devi, "Hitlerism and Hindudom," in the online Savitri Devi Archive: http://www.savitridevi.org/hindudom.html. The essay was originally published as "Hitlerism and the Hindu World," *The National Socialist*, no. 2 (Fall 1980), pp. 18–20. Cf. *Gold in the Furnace*, 3rd ed., pp. 5 and 278 and *And Time Rolls On*, p. 123.—Ed.

long ago those words that I was to remember forever and to quote many times, so accurate were they, in spirit at least. And now I thought once more: "Violence, whenever necessary—not non-violence at any cost—but dispassionate, detached, absolutely selfless violence, applied 'for the sole welfare of the universe', yes, that ideal of action, preached in the immemorial Bhagavad-Gita, is also what *we* preach today; what we represent, in glaring contrast to Christian hypocrisy. And it is precisely that for which the degenerate world hates us."

But the Polish woman was no votary of the oldest Aryan philosophy. "Well," said she, answering my last remarks about the uprooted Jews, "that may be; but you don't know how all this seems monstrous to me. I came to meet you knowing what you are—Frau *Oberin* had told me. But you surpass what I had expected—expected from a non-German, especially. Without imagining that your National Socialism remained on the philosophical plane, I had never realised that you could be so ruthlessly radical—as bad as any of the others. Everything in your outlook repels me; everything in your words wounds me. And"—she then pointed to the Führer's portrait upon my table, after having, hitherto, as much as she could, avoided looking at it—"the sight of that man's face in your cell; the knowledge that he is there, even if I choose to look the other way; the knowledge that he is your idol, like, alas, so many other people's, and that you are prepared to commit any crime, yourself, if you think it can forward his ends, that wounds me still more. For I hate him! And I do wish he is really dead!"

My blood rushed to my head. Had I been anywhere else than in a prison cell, I would have opened the door and shouted to the woman: "Get out!"—and doubtless kicked her over the stairs. But I was in a cell. The door could not be opened—nor the window. I tried to contain myself, and retorted as calmly as I could: "And *I* wish that everyone who hates him would see the death of whomsoever he or she loves—which is worse than dying."

The woman's face took on a pitiful expression. "I have lost my only child through your people," said she, in a low voice, her eyes fixed upon me with even more sorrow than resentment; "I cannot lose more. And I am not even sure whether he is dead or alive. I don't know where he is."

"Perhaps in the hands of the 'gallant allies' of those who waged war on Germany to 'save' Poland," said I, ironically. "If so, pray that they do not treat him a little worse than we might have." The woman's professed hatred for our Führer rang painfully within my heart, and I could not resist the propensity of hitting back over and over again.

"Oh," replied she, tired, "it is all the same. It could not be worse. In the camp where we were first taken, during the war, I have seen with my own eyes your S.S. men slap and kick my son, then a mere lad . . . But do please let us speak of something else!"

I could have—and perhaps should have—dropped the topic. There was no point in further hurting that woman, even if what I had to tell her were the mere truth, as doubtless it was. But I was myself too hurt to refrain from striking back a third time. "If your son had not deserved it, he would not have been in a concentration camp," said I, coldly; "nobody was in one for nothing."

There was a long silence. The Polish woman was probably thinking about her lost son. I, still in a bitter mood, was thinking: "I wish to goodness this woman would not come back! It is bad enough to be in prison, and there, separated from my comrades, without being, in addition, pestered with anti-Nazis!"

* * *

The woman did not come back. But she left me a few issues of *Life*, one of which contained a long extract from Winston Churchill's *War Memoirs*. In it, the British ex-Premier tried his best to explain that the Führer's orders to stop the rush of the German armoured divisions to Dunkirk—the orders that resulted in "clearing the way for the British Army"—were taken on the initiative of General von Rundstedt, and inspired by anything but the desire to show generosity to England as I had somewhere stated in the third chapter of my *Gold in the Furnace*. He buttressed his deductions—he said—upon the "actual diary of General von Rundstedt's Headquarters, written at the time." But as I read that, I suddenly recalled what Miss Taylor had told me of the privileges granted by the British authorities to the so-called "war criminal" General von Rundstedt, in particular, his leave from prison *on parole*. And I also recalled Colonel Vickers' statement to me, on Wednesday morning, the 6th of April, 1949: "Political prisoners are the last people to whom we grant special privileges . . . save in the case they *write for us or do some secret work for us, in one way or another*" (sic). I could not help . . . "putting two and two together" and wondering whether General von Rundstedt's alleged "diary," supposed to be "written at the time," were not just another piece of "secret work" in the interest of the British thesis about the events, written in confinement *after* the war—"secret work" of the kind Colonel Vickers had had in mind on that morning of the 6th of April. That would no doubt justify all sorts of privileges (if what Miss Taylor had told me were true), thought I, without wishing to be unnecessarily malignant, or even suspicious. And I added a footnote to the page in my Chapter 3 in which I had mentioned Dunkirk.[14]

In another issue of the same magazine, I found an account of the disgraceful manner in which the American Police had recently forced Walter Gieseking, the great German pianist, to leave the U.S.A. on account of his allegiance to National Socialism. Public demonstrations, headed, as could be expected, by Jews, had taken place in front of the hall in which he was to play. And the authorities had abruptly postponed the musical performance until an "investigation into his case" would give satisfactory assurances as to the artist's "de-Nazification"—which, of course, might have taken a month or more. In answer to which, Herr Gieseking had departed from the U.S.A. by the first plane, utterly disgusted with American behaviour. "And rightly so," thought I; "for all this fuss, now, nearly four years after the end of the war, in a country alleged to have fought for "individual liberties," "human rights," and what not, is enough to make one sick! From the very point of view of those who boast of democratic liberalism, had not the German artist every right to be a Nazi, if such were his convictions?" And for the millionth time, I pondered over the irreducible inconsistency of the Democrats' position: in accordance with their loudly professed principles, these people simply *have* to acknowledge our right to free self-expression and free propaganda—but if they do so, in practice, they run the risk of being overpowered by us in no time. So they prefer not to do so. But then, they become obvious liars and buffoons—*"des fumistes,"* as the French say, in their picturesque slang. They win themselves the contempt of many moderately intelligent honest people, and become the laughingstock of all those who, honest or not, have wits, and a slight sense of the ridiculous.

The next morning, when my friend H. E. came to take her daily tea, bread, and porridge, I told her about the Polish woman that Frau *Oberin* had sent to keep me company. "At least, she has been useful in letting me have those magazines," said I, after relating how I had utilised the passage from Churchill's *War Memoirs* in my book. "But dear me, how she hates us! All because her blinking son, it seems, was a little roughly handled by the S.S. men, in some concentration camp during the war. Well, she could not expect them to caress him, could she? I told her that he would not have been in a concentration camp if he had not deserved it, and that it served him right. I could not help it. She had asked for it, by the way she had spoken against the Führer. And moreover, it is true. I know it is."

---

[14] *Gold in the Furnace*, 3rd ed., pp. 20–21, n1.—Ed.

H. E.'s large eyes brightened. She gave me an enthusiastic smile. "You really told her *that!*" she exclaimed.

"Certainly. I would not tell you I had, if I had not."

"Then, I thank you for doing so; oh, you don't know how much I thank you—on my own behalf, and on behalf of all of us who have been slandered and reviled for the last four years. I am grateful to you for having had the courage to speak the truth and for having justified us all so-called 'war criminals'. Since the disaster, we are always wrong; we are murderers and murderesses; torturers and what not; 'inhuman monsters'. And they never take the trouble to say what scum of the earth was to be found among the internees of our concentration camps—people of whom three quarters are again locked up, now, under the Democratic Occupation, in spite of the fact that we 'monsters' are no longer in power."

"Don't I know it?" exclaimed I; "Don't I know it? One only has to see who are most of the women among whom *I* am thrown, here in this prison, by orders of the persecutor (I mean the British Governor) instead of being allowed to have a cell in the D wing, among you whom I love. I went once to the recreation room, and do not intend to go again—fortunately, attendance there is not compulsory. I would not go out during the 'free hour' either, were it not for the fresh air. Anyhow, one service the Governor has rendered me—without meaning to: he has put me in a position to tell everybody, when I am again free, what sort of people formed the bulk of the 'victims of National Socialism' in the former German concentration camps. Already during my one visit to the recreation room, I have met enough specimens of these to be able to assert that all that my friends ever told me in that connection was just the truth. And by the way, excuse me for having completely forgotten to tell you before—I was told that some woman imprisoned here; and formerly interned in Auschwitz for six years, has grossly slandered you." And I reported to her the whole gruesome story I had heard about the alleged wounded internee; and I stated how I had silenced the woman who had related it to me.

H. E. laughed, and patted me on the shoulder. "You have a fine reply to everything!" said she, jovially. "But you did not believe the story?—Or did you?"

"Of course I did not," exclaimed I. "I found the action too pointless to sound real. The tale appeared to me as unlikely and as silly as the other samples of anti-Nazi propaganda that have been inflicted upon me for the last ten or fifteen years. The more anti-Nazi the sillier, seems to be their law of existence."

"I am glad you did not believe it," said H. E. "For it is a fact that I have never done such a thing. But would you like to know—out of sheer curiosity—who the woman is, who spreads such rumours against me? ... For I am sure it is she."

"She is a Pole—I suppose. During the 'free hour', I heard of some Pole who also spent six years in Auschwitz and who is, it seems, *entre nous*, a homosexual of the lowest type. It occurred to me that it must be the same one."

"It is the same one, exactly," said H. E. "I know her. While I was in service at Auschwitz (where I was three years, as I told you), I myself tattooed upon her right arm the number that indicates that she was not condemned to death. But she is not a Pole—anyone could see that. She is a Jewess from Poland, and a despicable type. She was given six years in Auschwitz, for working against us. Then, once in the camp, she sucked up to us, and pushed herself forwards as much as she could. She can speak a couple of languages and has a certain ability. So we gave her a certain amount of power over other internees, that she might help to keep order among them. She abused her power and behaved as cruelly as she could towards her comrades, imagining perhaps that that would make us forget her activities against our régime, which surely it did not. We interfered many times and severely reprimanded her. And we willingly would have done without her services but for the fact that, as I once told you, our camps were badly understaffed, especially during the war. But we put up with her. When she fell—with us—into the hands of these people, after the war, she tried her best to throw the blame of her gratuitous atrocities upon us, saying that she had done this and that 'under orders', when it was not true. She slandered me, and would have got me a death sentence, had she been able to; she slandered others of us who had been in service at Auschwitz. She violently hates every sincere Nazi. Yet, in spite of that, her friends the Democrats gave her fifteen years' imprisonment, as to myself."

"All this does not astonish me at all," replied I. "It is the Jew all over—the cowardly, cringing Jew, full of spite, hate and cruelty, and base selfishness. But tell me another thing: It was related to me that this woman was the centre of interest here in Werl, last year at Christmas time, on account of some unnatural and particularly repulsive sexual performance of hers, in the midst of which she was caught; one of the most disgusting things I have ever heard . . . Is that true?"

"Absolutely true," said H. E. "Fräulein B. can tell you. She knows all about it. Ask her, if you don't believe me. She will not mind telling you, I am sure." (Fräulein B. was one of the wardresses.)

"And what does that Jewish woman look like?" asked I, coming back to the ex-internee in Auschwitz.

"She is middle-aged and of moderate height, with black hair that she wears in curls; she has small black eyes, a crooked nose, a typically Jewish face. You will not see her here, for she is in the A wing—unless you meet her in the bathroom." (We used to bathe, twenty-four of us at the time, standing under a double row of douches, on Friday mornings, before the Governor's visit; and prisoners from different wings often found themselves together on that occasion.) "I have seen her myself in the bathroom"; added H. E., "she has hanging breasts, no waist, and a fat, prominent belly—anything but attractive!"

For a minute, I pictured myself the mean, cruel, perverted, and ugly creature, crawling to my comrades, who despised her, to save her skin, in our days of power; then, slandering them before the Allied military authorities; charging them with all sorts of 'crimes', now they could no longer hit back; and, whenever she could, gratifying the depraved instincts of her flabby body in the dirty manner I had been told . . . The thought of her was surely enough to make one feel sick.

"Her place was in the gas chamber,"[15] said I, summing up in a sentence my whole impression about the female; "and it is a pity you did not put her there."

H. E. agreed. "Right you are!" exclaimed she. "And she is not the only one, unfortunately. Many others like her—and worse—should have been put there but were not. We were too lenient."

"Alas, I have said that from the beginning."

H. E. half opened the door (that she had pulled behind her) to make sure that nobody was listening. Then, coming nearer to me: "But wait and see what happens next time, when we rise again after all that we suffered," said she in a low voice. "Oh, then! I know a few who will not escape!"

I gazed at her, and I recalled the mental agony, the despair I had myself gone through in and after 1945; and the ruins of Germany; and the long-drawn day-to-day martyrdom of the Aryan élite whom I admired. "Then," said I, my eyes sparkling, "call me! Wherever I be in the wide world, I shall come. And give me a chance to play a part in the repression of the dark forces. I will help to avenge you—to avenge Germany!"

We parted with the usual "Heil Hitler!," feeling that we understood

---

[15] Savitri Devi believed in the existence of homicidal gas chambers in German concentration camps until 1977, when she read Arthur Butz's *The Hoax of the Twentieth-Century* (Torrance, Cal.: Institute for Historical Review, 1976). See Savitri Devi, *And Time Rolls On*, p. 163.—Ed.

each other perfectly.

* * *

Soon, it was the 20th of April—the greatest day in Western history; the greatest known day in world history. I had asked Frau *Oberin* whether, only for that once, I could spend my "free hour" with my comrades of the D wing. But she had replied that she could not allow me to, although she wished she could.

I woke up early in the morning, and saw the Führer's portrait which I had put, the evening before, on the stool by my bed, against the wall. "Today he is exactly sixty," thought I; "young, compared with those who led the world against him. Oh, may I soon see him in power again! I don't mind if I die after that."

I took the likeness and kissed it—as all devotees have kissed the images of their gods, from the dawn of time. And I held it a while against my breast. *"Mein Führer!"* murmured I, in a whisper, spontaneously closing my eyes so as to shut myself off from everything, but my inner world of reverence and love. Those two words expressed the life-long yearning of my whole being. And recalling the solemnity of the day, I imagined a newborn baby who, to all those who saw him, was just another child, but whom the all-knowing Gods, who had sent him into the world, had consecrated as Germany's future Leader and the Saviour of the Aryan race; the promised divine Man Who comes age after age, "whenever justice is crushed, whenever evil rules supreme," and Who saves the world over and over again. It was not the first time I thus pictured to myself the predestined One: at every successive birthday of his, for goodness knows how many years, I had done so. But now, somehow, I was more intimately aware than ever of the mystical link that bound me to him for eternity. I had sought communion with him in one way and obtained it in quite another. Destiny, that had not allowed me to come and greet him at the height of his glory, had sent me to stand by his people in disaster. And again now, while I had planned to make use of my military permit for Austria, and actually to spend his sixtieth birthday in Braunau am Inn, I was spending it here in Werl, imprisoned for the love of him. In all this I saw a heavenly sign. Not only was I sure that we would rise again and one day acclaim his return, but I felt that *I*—the daughter of the outer Aryan world—would contribute in my humble way (though I did not know how) to that great resurrection. And a strange exaltation possessed me.

I washed and dressed. And then, my right arm outstretched in the direction of the rising Sun that I could not see, I sang the Horst Wessel Song, and also the song of the S.S. men:

If all become unfaithful,
We indeed faithful remain . . .[16]

I knew that it was against the rules to sing in one's cell. But I knew also that nobody would say a word to me, especially on a day like this.

* * *

When H. E. came, she found me singing. "Our Führer was born exactly sixty years ago," said I, joyously, as I saw her enter. "Heil Hitler!"

"Heil Hitler!" replied she, "And do you know the news? . . . But promise me you will tell nobody about it—not Frau S., nor Frau *Oberin*, nor even Frau So-and-so, who is the most reliable of all."

"I shall not tell anybody. What is it?"

"He was seen, now, here in Germany—rushing along at full speed in a beautiful brand-new auto, but still not fast enough for those who love him not to recognise him. One of the men who bring the bread in the mornings has just told me; a so-called 'war criminal', like myself, and as firm in his Nazi faith as any of us."

"And how did he know it?" asked I.

"He has got a message from outside, whether from a visitor or through one of the warders, I could not tell, but he has got it. And this is the message: the Führer is alive, and is here in Germany for some time at least. If it is true, we will soon be free and in power once more."

I shall never forget the joy with which her face radiated as she spoke these words. I was no less moved. I opened my arms to her, and for a minute, we held each other embraced, as we would have in a great moment.

"And shall I tell you something too which you should not repeat without great discrimination?" said I after this first enthusiasm had subsided. "If what you say is true, it is not the first time he has come. I have heard from someone that he was here sometime about the end of 1947, already preparing in secret, with a few chosen ones, the day we are all awaiting. He had afterwards departed, they say."

"Is it so? And you are sure it is true?"

"I don't know. I am only telling you what I was told. But I know I

---

[16] "Wenn alle untreu werden, so bleiben wir doch treu . . ."

was told very little—not because our friends ever doubted my sincerity, but because they thought me too stupid, too unpractical, and especially too ignorant of men to discern genuineness in others; because they were afraid that I might easily take a traitor for a real Nazi, and tell him in a moment of enthusiasm things that only the most reliable among us should know. All that I can say for certain is that the Führer is alive and that one day before I die, I shall see him in power. That assurance and that hope sustain me."

"Our Führer!" said H. E. with that same devotion that I had observed in Herr W. and in all my comrades—that same devotion that I felt in my own heart. And she added, repeating word for word what a humble German working woman, come to clean the railway carriage in which I was, had told me on the morning of the 16th of June 1948: "Nobody has ever loved us as he did!"

"Nobody has ever loved truth and fought for the good of all the living as he did," said I. "I wish one day the whole world keeps up his birthday. It should." And we separated, saluting each other as usual.

* * *

When time came for the "free hour" of the D wing, I stood against my window. And not only H. E. but nearly all the others looked up towards me. And many arms went up. And one or two of my comrades even shouted "Heil Hitler!" loud enough for me to hear it from my cell. It seemed as though a wave of enthusiasm, foreshadowing that of the days to come, had lifted them all out of the dreary daily despair of these four years. I cannot say that I had actually caused it, although I had distributed a few copies of my posters (and even one or two copies of my former more literary leaflets) among them. But I was connected with it. My mere presence in prison for Nazi propaganda acted, apparently, upon the other political prisoners like a sign of hope from the outer world—a sign announcing, soon, a new irresistible outburst of fervour, pride, and vitality, dominated by the old battle-cry: *"Deutschland, erwache!"*

Hours passed, apparently as usual, filled by work, with short interruptions for meals and free time. There did not seem to be many women in the B wing who felt, as I did, the greatness of the day. And I have seldom experienced such painful loneliness as during the fifteen minutes I spent on that afternoon, walking around the courtyard by the side of a silly young girl who declared to me, when I reminded her of the Führer's birth, sixty years before, that she was "fed up with war and warmongers" and that "it would have been better if he had never been born at all."

Tears came to my eyes at the thought that a German could speak thus. But the girl was very young—less than twenty. I attempted to undo in fifteen minutes the effect of four years' subtle policy of "de-Nazification." "He is anything but a 'warmonger'," said I. "England, or rather Mr. Churchill, that complacent tool of Jewry, waged war on him, so that the Jews might continue to exploit the whole world. Nobody had striven for peace more than the Führer. Even after the war had started, three times he attempted to put an end to it by offering England an honourable peace, and three times England refused."

But the girl looked up at me insolently and retorted: "Naturally *you* say that. You would, being a Nazi! But what do you know about it all, any more than I do?"

I felt it was useless to discuss. "Still," thought I, "one day, perhaps, the kid will remember my words, and believe me." In the meantime, I felt depressed. The girl spoke of something else: "Tomorrow, we are invited to a concert in the men's section," she said. "They are having one today, among themselves. The tomorrow's performance will be for us. It will be nice, won't it?"

I could not help wondering whether the organisers among the men had purposely chosen this day, and whether the prison authorities had noticed the "coincidence." They had allowed the concert, anyhow.

In the evening, after work was ended, I heard the sound of the Horst Wessel Song, coming from the cell next to mine. "So, some do feel the greatness of this day, even here, in the B wing," thought I. And I immediately took to singing also. My next-door neighbour on the other side—a strong, heavily-built peasant woman, mother of seven children, sentenced to twenty years' penal servitude for alleged complicity in the murder of her husband (which she emphatically denied)—joined in the chorus. She was the first prisoner to whom I had talked in Werl, on the day after my arrival. She had told me once, with pride, that, during the glorious days, she had been given the "mother's medal" by the Führer himself, and that she always had supported our régime. I often gave her a slice of white bread or a bun or a spoonful of marmalade.

As the weather was hot, the upper part of the windows had been unfastened in many of the cells, and several prisoners were standing and looking out, or talking to one another across the courtyard. I got up upon the table and looked out also, when I had finished singing. Facing me, on the opposite side of the courtyard, were the windows of half the cells of the D wing. From one of those, one of the D wing prisoners caught sight of me, and lifted her arm in greeting. I returned her salute and shouted: "Heil Hitler!" But one of the A wing ones—a coarse woman, sentenced to ten years imprisonment for accidental murder caused through an attempt at abortion—called out to me from behind her bars: "It's Adolf's birthday today, we know. But we have got the same nasty stuff to eat as on any other day, so it's all the same to us. You should give us some of your white bread, instead of shouting 'Heil!'"

I felt depressed and disgusted—depressed by the feeling that I could indeed do nothing to prove that my love for Hitler's people was *not* just words; disgusted at the coarse familiarity with which this woman called the Leader by his Christian name. *I,* who am not a German, never spoke of him but as "Adolf Hitler" or "der Führer." I got down from my window but was unable to write, or even to read. Once more, I longed for the return of my German comrades to power. And I cursed the Occupation that postponed it—and Colonel Vickers who kept me, in the meantime, away from the D wing, among the ordinary delinquents.

* * *

The next day, at three p.m., we were all taken to the concert given in the church of the men's section, at the top floor of the building where Colonel Vickers' office was. We were taken two by two in a row, all those of the same wing together—and we were made to wear our jackets. The D wing ones walked ahead, leading the whole *"Frauenhaus."* Frau S., Frau R., the matron, also called in Werl Frau *Erste,* Frau *Oberin* herself, her assistant, and the wardresses on duty, accompanied us.

From the top of the stairs, as I began to walk down, I could see my comrades of the D wing in their dark-blue jackets, already crossing the threshold that shut our courtyard off the rest of the world. And again I felt the bitterness of being exiled from them, and made to wear a black jacket as if I were a common thief or black-marketeer. My eyes followed them along the path that led between the huge prison buildings of the men's section and green lawns, and then between the kitchens and the outer wall and across another courtyard, to the Governor's building, thickly covered with ivy and Virginia creeper.

In the church, where the men, both Germans and Poles, who were to sing and play in the concert, had already taken place upon the benches against the wall, the D wing women sat in front, on the left near the German prisoners, most of whom, my friend H. E. was to tell me the next day, were so-called "war criminals" like themselves. The A wing sat behind them, and on the front benches of the right-hand side; then the B wing, behind the A wing, and the C wing last of all. I sat on the very left end of a bench, the nearest I possibly could to my beloved comrades, and

I gazed sadly at H. E. and at L. M., seated next to her, and at H. B. and the others; smiling regretfully at them as if to say: "How glad I would be to sit with you, if only I could!" But even that place was denied me. Frau *Erste* asked me to get up and seat myself in the middle of the bench— completely away from the D wing ones. My face crimson with shame, my heart full of resentment, I obeyed. I bore no grudge against Frau *Erste*; she was only executing the orders of the Governor. I hated the Governor for causing me to be thrust among the abortionists and thieves. And I was all the more humiliated to feel myself sitting in such company, here in front of the men of whom so many, I knew, were political prisoners like myself.

Throughout the concert, I kept feeling how gladly I would, in my turn, humiliate our enemies, if I were given the slightest power in the repression services of the future, when we rise again. And the truly beautiful music I heard only served to kindle my excitement in anticipation! That excitement was my only solace against my present bitterness.

As we walked out after the performance, we saw, from a narrow, barred window in the staircase, the outer doors of the prison being flung open for a minute to let in a motorcar. We had, from a distance, a glimpse of the outer world with its trees and flowers, with its men and women who went where they liked. One of the women around me, already a year in prison, gazed at the one minute's vision and quickly called the others: "Look!" she shouted; "Look: the street—freedom!" I shall not forget that cry of the captive as long as I live. As I heard it, I thought of those I loved, separated from the outer world for four times as long as this woman, and that, just for having served our Führer with zeal and efficiency. And my heart ached. As for myself, I would have found prison life tolerable, had I only been allowed to share with them the daily work, the free time, and the two hours' relaxation in the recreation room, once every five or six days or so; had I been given a chance to show them my love, and to be, among them, an example of cheerful faith—a source of strength; nay, I would have welcomed it, as the most appropriate destiny for me, so long as my National Socialist ideology remained persecuted and my betters captive. But as things stood, imprisonment was worse, for me, than for either my comrades the so-called "war criminals" or the ordinary delinquents, for each one of these was, at least, amidst her own lot.

Once back into my cell, I wept. Frau *Erste*, the matron, opened the door to let in the prisoner who was to carry away the aluminium container in which my supper had been brought to me. "What is the matter with you?" she asked me, seeing my face.

"Oh, why, why don't they let me be in the D wing; with my comrades?" I burst out, unable to contain myself any longer, even before the austere matron who was so much of a disciplinarian that some of the ordinary delinquents had nicknamed her "Himmler."

"You are too dangerous," replied she, kindly. "You are a firebrand. If you were allowed there, dear me, the whole D wing would be singing the Horst Wessel Song every day."

Just then, Frau S. entered my cell. "Didn't you like the concert?" asked she, seeing how dejected I looked, and not having heard what I had told the matron.

"I did," replied. I. "But what I bitterly resented was to be made to sit in front of everybody among the abortionists and thieves, as if I were one myself. You don't know how that has hurt me. Why can't I be with my own kind in the D wing?"

Frau S. smiled. "Because the British Governor is afraid of you," said she, with a pinch of irony. And I could not help noticing how pleased she looked to say it—as if the mere fact that an official representative of the Occupying Power could fear anybody, were in itself a good sign.

"Tell him that I shall be as good as gold if I am allowed to live in the D wing," begged I, also with obvious irony.

"Tell him yourself, tomorrow, when he comes," said Frau *Erste*. "If he believes you, and agrees, we don't mind sending you to the D wing. But until then, we cannot. We don't give orders, here, now; the Englishman does." And she departed, having work to do.

Alone with me, Frau S. smiled once more. "Whatever you might tell him, the Governor will not believe you any more than he would us," commented she. "He is not taking any risks."

"Which means that I am condemned to stay here, away from my comrades, in practical solitary confinement, until my release," said I sadly. Then, as I caught sight of my precious manuscripts upon the table, and remembered how miraculous it was that they were there—and not in the storeroom, with my luggage, or destroyed—I added: "Still, I suppose it could be worse. At least I can write—thanks to you and to Frau *Oberin;* and that is something. That is perhaps as useful as talking to the D wing ones. And anyhow, I should not complain about my own humiliation, knowing as I do all the humiliations that my Führer's people have had to put up with since the Capitulation . . ."

Frau S. squeezed my hand and said: "In whatever 'wing' you be, here, you are, to us, a living sign of resurrection . . ."

Once more, as on the evening that followed my final return to Werl, I was moved beyond words, and tears filled my eyes. "It is a great comfort to me to hear you say that," replied I. "I wish I were indeed such a sign. That is what I have always wanted to be, since the disaster. True, in 1945, I declared emphatically that I only wished to see the whole world laid waste and mankind annihilated. I was then utterly desperate. But as early as 1946, I tried—although in vain—to come to Germany, if only to defy the persecutors of National Socialism openly, and to die with the people I so admired. (How I remember those horrid days of '46 in London, during the last months of the long-drawn Nuremberg trial!) And see what I wrote and distributed throughout this martyred land in '48, as soon as I was able to come!"

Opening my cupboard, I drew from between the pages of a book a hand-written copy of the text of my leaflets, and, pointing to the beginning of the fourth paragraph, I read: "In the very depth of our present-day humiliation, we should sing our glorious songs, well-knowing that we shall rise and conquer again. We are the pure gold put to test in the furnace. Let the furnace blaze and roar! Nothing can destroy us; nothing can shatter our faith, nor lessen our loyalty. The hardships, the tortures, the hatred, the cringing lies that would crush the weak, can only strengthen us, who are strong by nature. One day, we shall rise out of this misery, more like gods than ever. The ruins both of Democracy and of Communism will be lying at our feet. The Judeo-Christian world will be dead, we alone alive."

"May I have one of those?" said Frau S., who had read upon the paper, with me, the words which I had uttered with the burning eloquence of conviction.

"Of course. You can have this copy, if you like. 'They' have left me one of the two last printed copies I had, and, moreover, I know the text by heart. I can write it again whenever I like."

"But be very careful not to tell *anyone* that you gave me this—not Frau *Oberin*, nor any of the wardresses," said Frau S. Again she squeezed my hand and departed.

I now felt happy once more—half-resigned to my exile in the B wing. I repeated to myself the words in which I had put all my heart a year before: "In the depth of our present-day humiliation, we should sing our glorious songs, well knowing that we shall rise and conquer again . . ."

"And now, Savitri," thought I, "do, yourself, what you have called upon others to do: love, and resist; hope and wait; and continue to sing our conquering marches in your place of confinement among common criminals! No humiliation can kill in you the joy of defiance."

Chapter 8

CLANDESTINE CONVERSATIONS

"Please, don't keep on asking me to transfer you to the D wing," said Frau *Oberin*. "I have told you over and over again: It is not in my power. By repeatedly showing me how much you resent not being there—which I understand so well—you only make me feel wretched. You forget how limited my authority is here. As I told you once already, you forget that we have lost the war."

"Alas, I don't forget *that*; I know it only too well," replied I. "But I can never resign myself to the fact, and look upon the glorious recent years as though they were gone forever and their spirit completely dead—as you seem to."

Seated in an armchair opposite Frau *Oberin*, in her office, I was thus talking to her, not as a prisoner to the head of the women's section of the Werl prison, but as a sincere friend of Germany to a German woman. I used to talk in more or less the same free manner to the whole staff, including "unapproachable" Frau *Erste*. And nobody seemed to object. (Only with the Governor and his assistant Mr. Watts—with the "occupants"—was I extremely careful.)

But Frau *Oberin* gazed at me sadly. "None of us look upon the recent past as something dead," said she in a low voice. "But we have to face facts and live the best we can, now, in awaiting better times. Only so, can we in silence prepare the future. Premature exhibitions of our feelings are of no use. They would do us more harm than good."

Her words rang strangely like those which one of my comrades—an exceptionally intelligent man as well as an ardent National Socialist—had addressed me in 1948 on the very day I had come to him with an introduction from abroad. Once more, I wondered to what extent Frau *Oberin* was one of us. Sometimes I could have sworn she was. Then again, she would say something as though to emphasize her aloofness from all political ideologies. And I did not know what to believe. This time, I felt practically sure she was *in Ordnung*, as we said; so much so that I was going to ask her point-blank: "Don't you want that beautiful future which the Führer was preparing for Germany and for the world?" But she spoke first, pursuing the trend of her thoughts after a pause. "*You* could have forwarded the cause of National Socialism, now, much more efficiently than by distributing leaflets. The time is not yet ripe for such spectacular demonstrations."

"Exactly what Herr A. used to tell me!" thought I. And recalling in my mind the bright, energetic face of my beloved comrade, I hoped, for the hundred thousandth time since the day of my arrest, that nothing terrible had happened to him on account of my foolishness. My first impulse would have been to tell Frau *Oberin* that I had only brought back from abroad those latest posters of mine because I had been unable to bring back something far better, namely some tangible financial help from foreign friends and sympathisers. And I would have stressed that it was surely not my fault if those friends and sympathisers had so badly failed us. But I remembered that I was not to speak of this to anybody, and I said nothing.

"You air your views too openly, even here in jail," pursued Frau *Oberin*, "and thus you make it very difficult for me to do anything to help you render your life in the B wing less dull. I had sent you that Polish woman, hoping that she would be, now and then, company for you. But you have bitterly antagonised her. I had told you beforehand that she had nothing in common with you, politically. You should have avoided displaying before her the ardour of your convictions. Can you really talk of nothing else but National Socialism?"

"I can talk of many things; I have done so, to you, haven't I?" replied I, alluding to former half hours in Frau *Oberin*'s office, during which I had spoken of such things as modern Greek embroidery, Indian customs, the midnight Sun, or the life of Genghis Khan. "But that woman's inconsistency got on my nerves. She ranted against the Communists with such passion that I asked her why on earth she had not supported us, and she replied that our 'methods' are as brutal as theirs. As if the 'methods' mattered, when our ends are so different! And as if one could achieve anything quickly without brutality, anyhow! Then, she told me that she hated the Führer. And *that* made me wild. I hit back in biting words. And I am glad if she is sufficiently 'antagonised' not to wish to come back to see me. I don't want her, however cultured she might be. I could never love her. I can never love anybody who hates the Führer and who is the enemy of all that I stand for."

"I am sorry," said Frau *Oberin;* "when I sent that woman to you, I did not quite realise yet how extreme you were in your emotions."

I rose to go away. And I cannot describe exactly what happened then within me. In a flash, I became aware that this incapacity of mine for being even superficially friendly towards anyone who disliked our philosophy—let alone who hated our Führer—isolated me, in this horrible post-war world, from all but our circles (and, perhaps, one or two kindly, simple women who had no philosophy at all, and no politics[1]). Now, in jail, the company of those of our faith—of the only ones I loved—was denied me. When freed, I would doubtless be sent back to India— expelled from Germany at any rate. It would hardly be better. It would be very difficult to remain in constant contact with my comrades, few and far apart. Again, I would be practically alone. "Until when?" thought I. And I burst into tears.

"Indeed I am extreme in my emotions," said I. "Oh, would to God I could live among people of my own lot, as extreme as myself, to the exclusion of all others! I am sick of the others—of the moderate; of the lukewarm; and above all, of those who would, like to teach *me* to be moderate and 'many-sided', and 'human'—'civilised' (a polite word for decadent)—which is against my nature. I am sick of this hostile world in which even that relative liberty allowed here in jail to those of my kind— the liberty to be together—is denied me; will be denied me even when I am released. Talk of the German concentration camps in former days! My goodness, these rascals who are now doing all they can to hold Germany down, have turned all Europe, all the earth, into one immense concentration camp."

Frau *Oberin* got up, put her arms around me, and told me gently that I should not cry; that she wished she could do something to please me. She was sincerely sympathetic. I pursued, speaking, this time, of the British, in connection with myself: "They give me white bread and marmalade and chocolate on Sundays, and what not; and they imagine they are doing me a great favour for which I shall be grateful; and on the other hand, they cut me off from the D wing. The fools! If only they knew how little I care about their precious special diet! I only accepted it with a precise view to give as much as I possibly could of the good things to the D wing ones—and I shall tell them so, one day. I would much prefer being fed on just bread and water, and being allowed to spend my free time with my comrades!"

"You idealise the D wing ones," said Frau *Oberin*. "I have already told you: they are not all National Socialists, as you think. And of those who are, very few are as passionately so as yourself. You would find many of your sort—genuine ones—among the men imprisoned here as 'war criminals'."

"I do wish I had the joy and honour of meeting *them*," exclaimed I, although I knew that this was impossible as long as they and I remained

[1] Perhaps an allusion to Savitri's "apolitical" English friends Muriel Gantry (1913– 2000) and Veronica Vassar (d. 1972), whom she had met in London in 1946.—Ed.

in jail. And I wiped away my tears with the back of my hand. "But the women are pretty genuine, if they are all like H. E." I added. "And even if they are not, still I love them. As I said before, I 'love them because they are the victims of our enemies'."

Frau *Oberin* kissed me like a friend; like a sister. "I don't want you to be unhappy," she said. "Next Saturday afternoon—tomorrow—I shall send you two of the so-called 'war criminals' to keep you company in your cell."

I was overwhelmed with astonishment and sudden joy. "How kind you are," said I, looking up to her through the new tears that had just filled my eyes. "And you are quite sure you will not get into trouble because of that?"

"It will be all right, provided you do not tell anybody about it."

"Not even H. E.?" asked I. "She is reliable."

"Well, tell H. E. if you like, but nobody else. Let it not get to the ears of Frau R., the matron."

"Is Frau R. against us?" I enquired.

"No; otherwise she would not have been in service, in former days. But she is very strict about rules and regulations—whoever makes them; and she hates any sort of disobedience to orders."

"I shall say nothing. But, oh, how I do thank you!" replied I, as I departed.

* * *

On Saturday the 23rd of April, early in the afternoon, the wardress on duty opened my cell and ushered in two of the so-called "war criminals." "Visitors for you!" said she, turning to me with a friendly smile, as she let them in. My heart leaped. And tears came to my eyes—tears of joy. "I am happy to meet you," said I to the two women; "I am, indeed! I dared not expect Frau *Oberin* would send you to me, but she did after all! I am so grateful to her; and so glad to make your acquaintance. Do sit down. Sit on my bed: it is more comfortable than the stool. I shall sit there too. There is place for three."

My two visitors sat down. One, a very attractive and fairly young woman, ash-blonde, with large, kind, and intelligent blue eyes, was L. M., the one I had seen from my window walking around the courtyard by the side of H. E. during the "free hour." The other, who introduced herself as Frau S., I had never yet seen. But I had heard of her, from the ordinary delinquents who had been a long time in Werl. Condemned to death by some Allied military tribunal for having painlessly sent to the next world a certain number of unwanted non-German children, her sentence had been commuted to one of life-long imprisonment. She was older than L. M.—as old as I, in fact—but still looked young. She had delicate features, a gentle and thoughtful expression, blue eyes, and glossy light-brown hair. Had, instead of I, some silly "humanitarian" been introduced to her, knowing, as I did, the reason why she was now a prisoner, he or she would have wondered how a woman with such a sweet face could possibly have been guilty of such an "awful thing." But I entirely lack that superstitious regard for human life that religion has infused into most people. As a consequence of which, I was but very mildly impressed by the nature of her "offence." And then, I felt sure that, although I did not yet know them, the circumstances in which the action had taken place would justify it in my eyes anyhow. Most probably, nothing else could have been done, in the given circumstances. And I was waiting with great curiosity for Frau S. to tell me what these were, and how the whole thing had happened.

But L. M. spoke first. "I have heard a lot about you from H. E.," said she, "and I very much wanted to meet you. We are here because we could not do otherwise. We were in Germany, in 1945, when the victorious Allies, enemies of the Hitler régime, marched in. And we were in the service of the Hitler régime. They were bound to harm us, if they laid hands on us; and they were bound to lay hands on us, as we were on the spot. You came of your own free will, from the other side of the earth, to show us sympathy and to encourage us *after* 1945, knowing what a risk you were running. And you are now a captive like us, when you *could have* been free."

"I don't really wish to be free, when most of those whom I so admire are dead or in prison," replied I, sincerely. "Moreover, even in the outer world beyond bars and prison doors, there is no freedom for any of us, since 1945. Wherever we go, it is like jail to a greater or lesser degree. The only advantage one has, when one is not actually in custody, is that one can, directly or indirectly, to the extent of one's ability, take part in activities aiming, ultimately, at the resurrection of the Hitler régime—of our world. When I am free once more, that is what I shall again do; but less clumsily than this time, and, I hope, without getting caught again. For, without claiming the 'right' to be free, when others who share my faith are prisoners, I want to remain useful, if I possibly can. Here, my greatest torment is to feel myself useless—all the more so that I am not even allowed to be with you in the D wing."

"But you are writing a book, H. E. told me, a book about Germany today. That will be useful," said L. M.

"Perhaps, in the future," answered I. "But when? Now, immediately, here, I can do nothing—not even exchange views with you, my comrades, thanks to the Governor, who, it seems, is afraid I shall 'corrupt' you all, and who has ordered that I should remain among the ordinary criminals, most of whom are too stupid to be National Socialists. But I have talked enough about my aspirations and grievances. Tell me something about yourselves."

L. M. told me that she had been the head of a small *Arbeitslager*—a labour camp—of which the five or six hundred inmates were mostly Jewesses. Three of these had died, of perfectly natural deaths, during her administration. But in 1945, when the Allies had taken possession of the place, with their glaring prejudices in favour of the "persecuted" "people of God" and against all manner of "Nazi monsters," several of the Jewesses had accused her of having, indirectly, caused the death of those three, through a carelessness that could only have its roots in racial hatred (she being a German and an active member of the N.S.D.A.P.). The Allied judges—who spoke nothing but English—had listened to their grievances through the translations of interpreters, who were all Jews, like in all those "war crimes" trials. And they believed them—for prejudice and gullibility go hand in hand. However, as some of the inmates of the camp, less fanatically anti-Nazi or perhaps more God-fearing than the others, had spoken in her favour, stating that the three women had died in spite of adequate medical attendance and without having been ill-treated, she was merely sentenced to four years' imprisonment (in addition to the two years that she had already spent in an internment camp before her final trial). Considering the usual remittance of one fourth of one's penalty, she expected to be free in 1950, and was beginning to count the months, if not yet the weeks and days. "For it is a dreary life," said she, speaking of the daily routine in Werl ever since 1947 or the end of 1946. "We get up; we work—always the same work; knitting, in our case—we eat; we work again; we sleep; and we begin the same thing the next day, and the day after, and every day, for weeks months, years. We are allowed to write to our families only once a month. We cannot write any other letters, or anything else. We are not allowed to have any paper and pencil—let alone pen and ink—in our cells. We are given, if we like, a book a week to read. But it is generally something so dull, or so childish, that it is just as well to read nothing. We have forgotten what intellectual life means; what, in fact, human life means."

I pictured to myself that senseless, hopeless monotony, for months on end—"enough to drive one mad," thought I. I could not help feeling a little ashamed of that privilege of being allowed to write, which was so important to me, and which I owed entirely to the patriotic sympathy of the German staff. They, my comrades, captive ever since the end of the war, and Germans, were not given that joy of expressing themselves on paper rather than not at all. What had *I* done to deserve it? Nothing. It was a purely gratuitous favour that the staff—and especially Frau *Oberin* and the *Oberwachtmeisterin*—had done me. I felt infinitely grateful for it and, at the same time, as I said, a little ashamed.

And I could not help admiring L. M.'s serene cheerfulness—and especially that of Frau S. I did not let the latter know that I had already heard of her and of her sentence. She soon told me herself: "I am here for life." And those words, coming immediately after L. M.'s gloomy evocation of prison routine, rang painfully tragic—all the more so, perhaps, that they were uttered in a detached voice, calmly, almost casually. I shuddered as I heard them—in spite of the fact that the woman's fate was already known to me.

"You will not remain here all your life," said I, my eyes fixed upon the sweet, young-looking face. "Take it from me: things will change; things are already changing. These people will be forced to release you sooner than they think. They will be forced to placate us all, more and more, as they will grow more and more afraid of the Communists."

"I can only wish you are right," replied Frau S., simply. "Already, through all this persecution, my life has been wrecked: my husband who loved me dearly, and whom I still love, has asked for his divorce, advocating that, as a wife, I am now as good as dead to him. I do not blame him; but I sometimes feel depressed about my fate."

I thought: "Our hypocritical opponents reproach us with being 'callous' about the 'domestic tragedies' which might occur as a consequence of the application of our programme. Here is a case for them to meditate upon—a case that proves that they are no better than we are, in that respect, without having the justification of our higher motives." I asked the woman how old she was.

"Forty-four," said she.

"We are of the same age. I shall be forty-four on the 30th of September," replied I. "But would you not like to tell me how you came to be sentenced by 'these people'? You know who I am. You know before hand that I shall never blame you."

"I blame myself, in a way, for I am a Christian," said Frau S., to my amazement. "And yet I don't know whether it was not the best course to take. I don't know what to think . . . There are so many problems involved in all this." And she told me her story.

She was a lay sister and had been, as such, put in charge of a children's home which the management of the great motor works, *Volkswagen-Werke*, had established near or on the premises of the factory, for the children of the foreign compulsory labourers—prisoners of war or deported civilians. For many children were expected from the day the managers had allowed workers of both sexes to meet one another.

"As long as they remained separate, each sex confined to itself, all was well," said she. "Then, as soon as this restraint was removed, trouble began, and we had to cope with it."

"Why *'had to'?*—excuse me for interrupting you," I asked. "I can't see why the rule keeping the men apart from the women was ever abrogated, in the first place. Did the managers of *Volkswagen-Werke* suffer from that belief in what the Democrats call 'the right of every individual to sexual happiness'? I hope not."

"No; it was not that," explained Frau S. "It was a mere matter of mass psychology applied to economics. The managers had found out—or were told—that the men would automatically work harder, and produce more, if they were allowed free access to the women after working hours."

"That is all right," agreed I. "But then, it should have been made a strict rule that the women were to be examined regularly and that, as soon as one was found pregnant, she was to be made to abort at once. Then, all trouble would have been avoided from the start."

"That would have been awful!" exclaimed kind Frau S., genuinely shocked. "Abortion is a crime."

I was no longer astonished, now that she had told me she was a sincere Christian. I only wondered a little how, being such a wholehearted upholder of the belief in the equal value of all human beings, she had occupied that responsible post of hers . . . However, I kept that thought to myself, and simply answered her most Christian-like remark with my natural heathenish cynicism.

"A crime!" said I. "There are circumstances in which such 'crimes' are the only reasonable thing to do. I should have thus solved the baby problem once and for all in the case of all foreign women deported to Germany—even in the case of all German women interned in concentration camps, save when the child's father happened to be of irreproachable Aryan stock. The authorities of the Third Reich had other things to do, in wartime, than to be pestered with 'problems' resulting from the sexual activities of anti-Nazis."

L. M. smiled. Even Frau S. smiled, somehow, in spite of her Christian feelings. "You speak just as the most radical among our people used to, in the Hitler days," said she, turning to me. "One would never believe that you were not brought up in a Nazi atmosphere. What made you what you are?"

"The fact that I am essentially Greek—not merely by nationality, but in spirit; in the eternal sense of the word, which so many Greeks are no longer, for ages; essentially Aryan, in blood *and* in soul, which so many Europeans are no longer," replied I; "the fact that, in spite of a thoroughly Christian education, I have, even as a child, never been impressed—let alone influenced—by the message of Christianity (excuse me if I hurt you by telling you so)."

"You don't hurt me," said Frau S. gently. "It only seems strange to me. I was brought up in an out-and-out Christian and 'bourgeois' home. And that has remained the guiding influence in my life, to this day."

"Well," said I, not wishing just now to discuss our conflicting philosophies, "what happened when the managers of *Volkswagen-Werke* decided that they would burden themselves with the children of the compulsory labourers? I am interested in this, not only because it so unfortunately ended in the wrecking of your life, but also because it throws light upon the spirit that existed at the time, in Germany, even among people whose adherence to National Socialism could not be questioned."

"When children started getting born," pursued Frau S., "a well-equipped, comfortable modern home was opened for them on the initiative of the factory authorities. A qualified nurse, experienced, and fond of children was sought out to take charge of it, and it was my fate to be selected among the applicants for the post.

"All went on fairly smoothly as long as, in spite of the increasing strain of total war, relatively normal conditions could be maintained as regards the children's food. True, the mothers gave us quite a lot of trouble, at times. You have no idea what debased types some of them were—dirty, thievish, and past masters at telling lies. I employed as many as I could of them in the newly-built home. One would think they would have taken care of their own children at least as conscientiously as we paid nurses did. But they did not. They would suckle the infants, admittedly, but that was about all. We found the children in a filthy state whenever we left them in the keep of any of those women for any length of tine. And besides that, the women used to steal—not out of need, but out of rapacity; steal whatever they could lay hands upon, provided it had a commercial value, and then lie to exonerate themselves. Medical instruments used to disappear from the children's infirmary; everyone would swear she did not know where they were until, one day, some of them would be found hidden in some of the women's mattresses. Then, the suspected ones would again swear 'by the holy Mother of God' and all the saints, that they had not the faintest idea as to how the inanimate

objects had worked their way there! I have slapped some of those creatures, sometimes, they used to irritate me so much by stealing, and then
taking as they did the name of God in vain."

Automatically, as I heard this, I recalled in my mind how so many
European women whom I had met in the East had complained to me
about their Annamite, Malayan, or low caste Indian servants: "The two
things one can never cure them of, are stealing and lying," they used to
say. "You catch them red-handed, and still they tell you they 'don't
know' how your banknotes, your watch, or your silver spoons have
found their way into their pockets." Now I thought: "One need not go out
of Europe to find similar roguery!"

"Who were these women?" asked I; "Russians? Poles?"

"They were women from practically all the countries of Eastern Europe," answered Frau S. "Russians and Poles, no doubt, but Czechs also.
And the Czechs and Poles were the worst, as far as I can tell."

And she pursued her narration: "In spite of all, things went on not too
badly, I must say. The children were healthy and happy, although, as
their number kept on steadily increasing, the problem of their accommo-
dation became more and more difficult. Finally, we had to pack twenty
of them in small dormitories planned for not more than six, or eight.
There was no place for them. And conditions were becoming worse every day; food was more scarce; and we were living under the continual
threat of bombardment. Still we held on. The mothers—who were becoming more and more troublesome as it was growing more obvious that
things were taking a bad turn for Germany—were at least still on the
spot. They continued to suckle the tiny ones; and we kept the others in
fairly good condition on *'Ersatz'* food.

"Things became serious when the women had to be sent back to their
respective countries. Half of them just refused to take their children with
them, strange as this may seem. They did not even know who the children's fathers were. And apparently, they considered that the burden of
unaided motherhood was more than they could put up with, in the new
uncertain life into which they were now being thrown by the hazards of
war. *We* ran the home, crowded with unwanted children, single-handed,
for weeks, amidst the appalling conditions that prevailed immediately
before the Capitulation. Food was scarcer and scarcer; milk, unavailable.
The babies' health began to decline on the substitutes we gave them. The
elder ones fared hardly better. Disease set in. Medicine was as scarce as
food. Space was lacking. It was impossible for us to isolate the sick children from the still healthy ones. In spite of the little care we could and did
give them, many died. But the time soon came when the only possible fate

awaiting the little ones was death, anyhow—death from hunger, if not from disease. As I told you, their health had deteriorated as soon as the departure of their mothers had deprived them of their natural and customary food. Now, even the substitutes we used to give them were no longer available. Confusion and terror prevailed everywhere. Bombing never ceased—that unheard of bombing, of which many, in Germany, have surely tried to describe to you the hellish fury, which really no words can picture. The alternative before us was no longer to save those few surviving children or to let them die, but, to let them die a painful death, after days of suffering, or . . . to allow them to die painlessly, at once . . ."

I recalled in my mind an episode of my own life that had long haunted me. It had occurred years before—in August, 1930, exactly. One day, then, while I was walking along a street of Athens, my attention had been drawn by pitiful mewing, and I had soon discovered in a dustbin, among ashes, bits of broken crockery, and heaps of rotting kitchen refuse, three newly born kittens that someone had thrown there to die. I can never forget the impression that this made upon me. It was in one of those streets on Mount Lykabettos from which one can see practically the whole of Athens, with the Acropolis in the distance, and, further still, the deep-blue, smiling, shining sea. I picked up the three baby cats and gazed at them for a minute. Their eyes were shut. Their three tiny pink mouths opened regularly in a feeble, high-pitched mew of hunger. I felt in my hands the touch of their glossy young black and white fur. And lifting my eyes towards the distant miracle of marble that the whole world admires, I had realised more vividly than ever that the daily miracle of life was something even greater still. And tears had filled my eyes at the thought of the patient impersonal artistry of Nature that had evolved, out of a germ, those three living, mewing balls of fur. Had not some wretched human being—whom I cursed within my heart, then and ever since—torn them away from their mother, they could have grown into three beautiful cats . . .

But they had been taken from their mother and thrown into the dustbin. I could do nothing to undo that fact. They were too young to be fed artificially, and moreover, I was somebody's guest, and could not possibly force three cats upon my hostess, who already had two. I could not leave them there to die. I heard that desperate mew of hunger, unceasingly. If I left them there, it would continue for four days, five days, a week, perhaps, feebler and feebler until the poor little glossy creatures would mew no more. I could not allow that. There was, then, in Athens, to my knowledge, no "Society for the Protection of Animals" to which I could take them to be painlessly put to sleep, as I would have in London. There was only one way to put an end to their hunger and misery, and that was to kill them myself, as quickly and painlessly as I *could*. God alone knows how much I love all animals, especially cats! Yet, this was the only thing I could do for those kittens in the circumstance.

I took them to my room, and there, for the last time, I looked at them, lying in my hand; three round, glossy heads; three healthy furry bodies; potential cats. I would have given anything to be able to save them. But I knew I could not. It was useless to think of it. With tears running down my face, for the last time I kissed the silky little round heads; and I prayed within my heart: "Thou One Who hast patiently brought them into being, Lord of all life, forgive me!—for Thou knowest *why* I am doing this. And strike the man who threw these creatures away to die of misery!" I then put the newly born kittens in the bottom of a receptacle, poured a whole pail of water upon them, covered the receptacle, and went away . . .

For days, for weeks, their last mew had pursued me. It was better— far better—than that long agony in the dustbin that they would have suffered if I had left them there. But still, it had pursued me; it pursued me even now, after twenty years, every time I thought of the deplorable episode. I realised that Christian-like Frau S. loved *all* human beings— including the children of our opponents; potential enemies—as *I* love all animals. And I understood her qualms of conscience. My first impulse was to relate the kitten episode to her and to tell her that she was, from the strictest humanitarian point of view, as innocent as I had been on that awful day of August 1930. But as I reflected, I kept silent about it: it would only, thought I, give rise to a discussion about the respective value of human and animal life in which she and I could never agree; a discussion in which her eminently man-centred, equalitarian, Christian outlook, would come in conflict once more with my life-centred, hierarchical one, as it had for centuries. It would only result in my telling her that potential opponents were surely less to me than potential indifferent creatures, especially if the latter were beautiful. And this was useless, for I could not convince her any more than she could convince me; and I wanted to avoid hurting her.

"You have done your best," I simply told her; "and those who, after creating the conditions which you were faced with in 1945, have had the impudence to condemn you, are liars and hypocrites."

"You are right," admitted L. M.; "you are right . . . although it was a sad alternative . . ."

"I must say that, horrible as they were in warfare, the Allies were not the only ones to blame," said Frau S. "I mentioned the difficulties we had to face on account of the increase of the number of children. Well, it is true that, had these been thoroughbred German children instead of goodness knows what mixtures of all the nations represented among the compulsory labour squads of *'Volkswagen-Werke'*, the *Kreisleiter* would have taken the trouble to send someone to inspect our 'home' now and then, and something would have been done so that we should not have been forced to accommodate twenty children in space planned for six. As things stood, nobody was ever sent."

"It is only natural that a State—and especially a State at war—should be more keen on the welfare of its own nationals than on that of its enemies' unwanted brood," said I. "You should blame the poor wretches' mothers for not taking them with them, and not the *Kreisleiter* for not bothering about them. Surely, he had better things to do."

"Again, I am astounded to see how you are like any of our extremists!" remarked Frau S. "To me, children—any children—are, first of all human beings."

I was no less astounded to meet a so-called "war criminal" with such an equalitarian outlook.

"I can admit, at most, that, apart from any principles, you felt sorry for those unfortunate children—who, as I have said already, should never have been born, in the first place," replied I. "But I find it difficult to reconcile the principles that you seem to uphold with those laid down in *Mein Kampf!*"

To my further and utter amazement, Frau S. answered: "I have never read *Mein Kampf.*" Really, I did not know what to think. I felt as though I were dreaming.

"What!" exclaimed I; "you, a German, and, in all probability, a Party member! You, who had the privilege to grow up in the midst of the struggle for power, and to spend the finest years of your life under the Nazi Régime! You, who doubtless have greeted the Führer in those solemn mass gatherings of the time which I have never seen! . . . How could you not have felt urged to read it, at least out of curiosity—to understand the miracle that was taking place all round you; to know who was that Man who had raised Germany from death to life?"

"I was not, then, aware of the tremendous meaning of the National Socialist revolution," said Frau S.; "I had lived through it, separated from it by my inherited Christian faith and by my quiet 'bourgeois' life; I had apprehended only the externals of it, and adhered to it, nominally, without knowing what I had done. Had I studied it—as indeed I should have—then, either I would have become a real Nazi like you, or else I would have clung to my Christian values strongly enough to refuse to collaborate actively with the new régime. *Now*—and perhaps more than ever today, after meeting you—I know that one cannot be both a Nazi and a Christian. I did not know it in those days. I did not know what National Socialism was."

I thought of this woman, imprisoned for life for having acted as the supporter of an Idea in which she did not believe, as the upholder of principles she actually condemned; or rather, merely for having obeyed orders given by someone presumed to have upheld those principles. "A martyr without faith," thought I. And it appeared to me that this was about the most tragic destiny which I could imagine.

"Many of us, I am afraid, did not know what National Socialism is, both among those who supported the Movement and among those who fought against it," said L. M. "New ideas—or very old ones, as you say, but abandoned for centuries and therefore looking new—need time to take root in a nation's consciousness, unless some tragic upheaval forces the nation to awake to their appeal. Normally, had there been no war, no disaster, we would have needed fifty years to become thorough National Socialists. But now, the occupation will make us all so in five. In four, it has already succeeded in turning to Hitler thousands of Germans who, formerly, were mere lukewarm supporters, or even opponents, of the Nazi régime. And the longer it will last, and the more it will try to force Democracy upon us, the more it will ultimately succeed in uniting us all under the Swastika banner, whatever might have been our convictions in the past."

"That is encouraging," said I.

Then, we talked about other things, in particular, about India. Frau S. asked me to explain what was exactly the religious standpoint of Gandhi, which I did the best I could; while L. M. asked me if I had ever met Subhas Chandra Bose, the Indian leader who, during the war, had been the head of the *Zentrale Freies Indien*, in Berlin, and who, occasionally, had spoken on the radio. She was agreeably surprised to hear from me that I had known him personally, and that it was my husband who had introduced him to the Japanese authorities in collaboration with whom he was, later on, to organise the "Free Indian Army" in Burma. I was longing to tell my new friends something of the unknown masterful role which my husband had himself played in the service of the Axis in the East. But I did not. Before leaving India, I had promised not to.

Time passed. We would soon have to separate. "I hope we shall soon meet again," said L. M., as I told her how glad I was to have had her visit. "I have disappointed you, I know," said Frau S.; "but I have told you the truth about myself."

"You have suffered more than I—and more than many of us—for the cause I love. Therefore I love you," replied I.

The martyr without faith looked at me sadly, and smiled.

On the following morning, H. E. came, as usual. I told her the impression that I had gathered from my first contact with D wing prisoners other than herself or H. B.

"L. M. is indeed a fine character," she agreed. "She has been my companion during the 'free hour' ever since she has been here. Frau S. is also a lovable person, but she is so Christian that it is not true. Her whole outlook is biased; and she can recognise no truth which clashes with the teaching of the Church. We have no time for this obsolete teaching. It is Yiddish, anyhow; isn't it?" And she added: "I would so like to have a long talk with *you* about religion, one day. I like your attitude."

"Can you come this afternoon?" asked I. "It is Sunday today."

"No. Frau *Oberin* is not in. We shall have to wait till the end of the week. I'll ask her to send me to you next Sunday. On Saturday afternoons, I work at the infirmary just as on other days."

And indeed, on Sunday the 1st of May, she came, not in the afternoon and with L. M., as I had expected, but after supper, when all the cells were supposed to be shut for the night, and alone, which was still more irregular. *Two* prisoners only—for reasons one easily guesses—were never allowed to occupy the same cell.

I had kept for H. E. the chocolate and the pudding and one of the two buns with raisins that I used to get for supper on Sunday evenings. "We have ample time to talk," said she, seating herself upon my bed after we had greeted each other. "Fräulein S. said that she would not come to fetch me before eight o'clock." Fräulein S. was Frau *Oberin*'s assistant, who had evidently received instructions to arrange our meeting in the absence of Frau *Oberin* herself.

"Frau S. was so pleased to meet you; she likes you because of your sincerity," said H. E. while I watched her with delight, eating the good things; "she told me so in the recreation room. L. M. likes you even more. She wants to come back here with me, on Sunday next. Frau H. also very much wants to come; we were sentenced together in the Belsen trial, and now she works at the Infirmary, with me. She is genuine. You could trust her."

"I would love to meet her," said I. "I would love to meet all those who are genuine. I think you should come on one Sunday with one of them, and on the following with another. Thus, I would get to know them all. I was even contemplating to attend the Church services on Sunday mornings in order to meet you and the others. But I reflected that it would probably be of no use. Doubtless I would not be allowed to sit near you, let alone to talk to you after the service. So I prefer to be consistent and not to go. In fact, Frau *Oberin* astonished me when she told me that you all go. Do you, really?"

"Apart from Frau S. and perhaps one or two others, we go out of sheer boredom," said H. E. "Who wants to hear the nonsense that the priest tells us? But we have nothing to do in our cells, and Sunday mornings are long."

H. E. pushed aside the plate in which she had been savouring my custard and apricot jam. "It was lovely, and I do thank you!" said she, interrupting for a minute the trend of her thoughts. Then, resuming her criticism of the Church and of its teaching, she pursued: "You have no idea how silly, for example, all that talk about the resurrection of the dead appears to me. We heard that all over again on Easter Sunday. And in a month's time or so, they will tell us how resurrected Jesus went up to heaven before I don't remember how many all exceedingly reliable eye-witnesses. Such rubbish! I honestly tell you: I much prefer your worship of the Sun as the visible Source of all life on earth. That I can understand, for I can see and feel the Sun. To worship It—and Life—is to know what one is worshipping. It is natural and logical. Indeed, all my life I have felt thus. I have never really had any use for Christianity, and I used not to go to church even on festive days, when I was free. There were, then, anyhow, enough Party solemnities to replace the Christian ones advantageously. I never needed any others. But I repeat: I entirely agree with you that, if one must have any religion at all, the religion of glorious living Life—of Nature; of the earth and of the Sun—is the only one I would encourage."

I recalled the expression "true to the earth"[2] by which Nietzsche has characterised any eternal religion, any philosophy that is not mere words. Quoting the prophet of the Superman, I had myself applied that expression to King Akhnaton's thirty-three-hundred-year-old Religion of the Disk, about the most rational form of Sun worship put forward in Antiquity besides the Aryan religion of the Vedas with which, according to some scholars, it is indirectly connected.[3]

---

[2] "Ich beschwöre euch, meine Brüder, *bleibt der Erde treu* und glaubt Denen nicht, welche euch von überirdischen Hoffnungen reden!" ["I beseech you, my brothers, *remain true to the earth* and do not believe those who tell you of otherworldly hopes!"] (Friedrich Nietzsche, *Also sprach Zarathustra*, Vorrede [Prologue], §3, emphasis in original).—Ed.

[3] Sir E. A. Wallis Budge. See *Tutankhamen: Amonism, Atonism, and Egyptian*

I drew from my cupboard a copy of the book *A Son of God* which I had published concerning that ancient cult and its Founder. "I began to write this in India in 1942, when I still believed that we would win this war," said I; "when I expected the Japanese Army to take Calcutta any day, and the German Army to win its way through Russia and High Asia, and the two to meet in imperial Delhi; when I believed that the world would soon be ours. I thought that, being as I was immobilised away from all fields of direct action, the second best for me was to prepare in silence the ground for the new religion of Life destined to go hand-in-hand with the New World Order. And, to find in Antiquity a simple and attractive prototype of it was no doubt much better than to present it as something essentially 'ours'. Nobody is prejudiced against Antiquity; while many are against us. But it would be essentially 'ours' nevertheless, whatever the light in which I might present it. And with a little publicity—I imagined—the people of the West might take to it; they would at least begin to find Christianity dull, irrational, even barbaric, compared with it, while the Easterners would see in it something as beautiful as their immemorial religions. And foreseeing that, on whatever side they were then fighting, most people would probably feel tired of all wars by the time this one was finished, I purposely laid stress upon the peaceable character of Akhnaton's ancient religion. Not that I admire it on account of that—I rather, in fact, admire it *in spite of* that. But it would look nice— I thought. It was the best I could do in the way of subtle anti-Christian propaganda on a worldwide scale, after having fought the influence of both Christianity and Islam in India, all those years. It would show people a truly admirable form of worship that had all the heathen qualities *and* all the Christian ones as well—save that irrationality and that otherworldliness which, in general, nowadays, they don't particularly like, anyhow—all the Christian qualities *including* love and benevolence.

"I kept off politics—naturally. I carefully avoided all allusions that might have led the reader to guess what I was. Only in the last chapter did I say, once or twice, that the religion of Race, in its true form, and the religion of Life, were the same, and that only through a misconception of both could one separate them. Unfortunately, that statement of a few lines, of which I did not notice the non-appearance when I read the proofs, was mysteriously left out from the published book, as though, in the eyes of the London editor, even *that* exceeded the limits of what could be tolerated in print in 1946. As a consequence, a whole paragraph appears to signify something quite different from that which I

Monotheism (London: Martin Hopkinson, 1923), pp. 114–15.

had intended. But the fact remains that I still believe that which I had, at first, stated, and that I shall repeat it, one day. The fact remains that my ceaseless effort to combat the pernicious influence of Christianity as represented by the Churches, and whatever I have said or written in support of the cult of the Sun, which is the cult of Life, all goes to prepare the religious background of our National Socialist world Order, of which the prototype is none else but the eternal Order of Nature."

"What you say now," said H. E. "I have always felt. Oh, what a pity you were not here during the great days! But tell me more about that Pharaoh of whom you have made such a special study. He interests me." And looking at the frontispiece of the book, that pictured King Akhnaton, she added: "I remember his face. I have seen it in the Egyptian gallery at the Berlin Museum."

I told her in a nutshell what I knew of the unsuccessful attempt of the ancient "King of the South and of the North, Living in Truth" to replace the traditional other-worldly religion of Egypt, full of intricate abstruse symbolism and centred around the mystery of death, by the simple joyous cult of cosmic Energy—of that which he called "the Heat-and-Light-within-the-Disk"—made visible and tangible in the rays of the Sun. I explained to her, quoting a couple of texts, how the idea of the equivalence of all forms of energy, no less than that of the fundamental identity of energy and matter, was already implied in his teaching. And finally, I proceeded to stress that he had doubtless understood that such an outlook on the world implied the acknowledgement of the natural diversity and hierarchy of human beings no less than of other forms of life, as something God-ordained, beautiful, and desirable. And I recited to her the three lines of Akhnaton's Longer Hymn to the Sun, which I have quoted so often during the past ten years:

Thou hast put every man in his place,
Thou hast made them different in shape and in
speech, and in the colour of their skins;
As a Divider, Thou hast divided the foreign people . . .

"The divinely ordained differences, expression of the impersonal will of the Sun, can only be maintained, nay, increased, according to the highest purpose of Creation which is to evolve perfect types, if each race is maintained pure," said I. "And that is why, knowingly or unknowingly echoing the wisdom of ages, a great German of today, a close collaborator of the Führer has written: 'Only in pure blood does God abide'."

"Who wrote that?" asked H. E.

"Heinrich Himmler, in the beautiful epitome of National Socialist philosophy which he published under the name of Wolf Sörensen: *Die Stimme der Ahnen.*"[4]

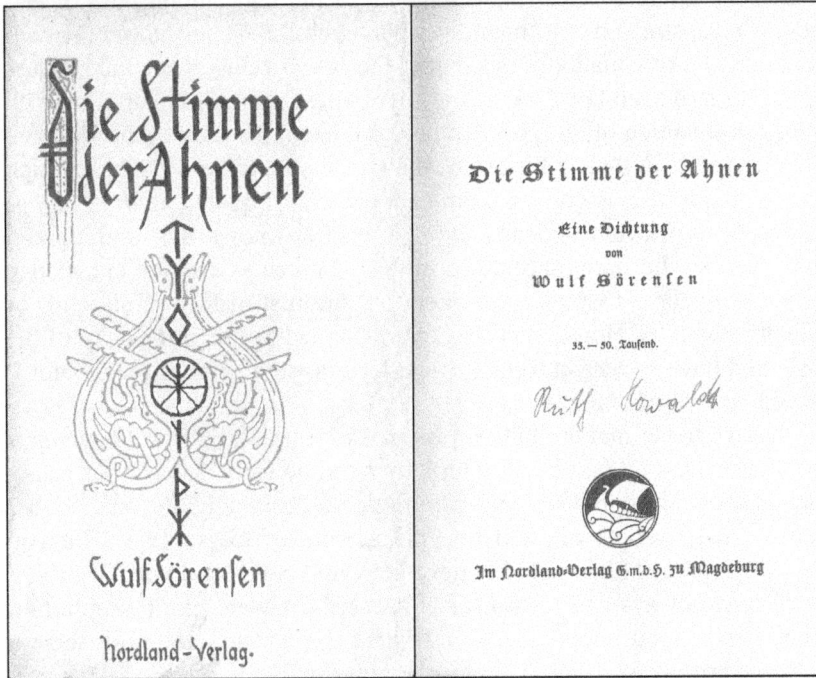

9. The cover and title page of Savitri Devi's personal copy of DIE STIMME DER AHNEN

H. E. gazed at me with enthusiasm. "Oh, what a pity you were not here during the great days!" she repeated. "Our philosophy—which most of us look upon as modern and as German—you seem to have integrated into a solid general outlook on Nature and on man, true as regards all countries and for all times. Time does not exist, for you—nor space. In a few sentences, you evoke a most splendid solar philosophy, three thousand three hundred years old, only to quote in support of its everlasting-ness words that Himmler wrote yesterday. The more I listen to you, the

[4] Meaning: The Voice of the Ancestors. [Wulf Sörensen, *Die Stimme der Ahnen: Eine Dichtung* (Magdeburg: Nordland-Verlag, 1936). In English: *The Voice of the Ancestors: A Poetical Work by Wulf Sörensen*, trans. anonymous (Hammer, 1993). *Die Stimme der Ahnen* is most probably not by Himmler, but by one Frithjof Fischer (b. 1899, no death date listed), who was a member of the S.S. but not of the N.S.D.A.P. See Heinrich W. Schild and Audrey Gregory, *Der Nordland Verlag und seine Bücher: Eine Bibliographie*. Toppenstedter Reihe 12 (Toppenstedt: Uwe-Berg-Verlag, 2005), pp. 10 ff.—Ed.]

more I feel that our National Socialism is indeed, something eternal."

"It certainly is," said I. "But surely you did not need to meet me to re-alise that. The Führer has stated over and over again that his Movement was based upon the clear understanding of the unchanging laws of Na-ture. He has stressed that 'man owes his highest existence not to the con-ceptions of a few mad idealists, but to the acknowledgement and ruthless application of such laws'[5]; that, our 'new' ideas are 'in full harmony with the inner meaning of things'[6]; and he considers it the duty of the National State to see to it that 'a history of the world should be written in which the racial question is given a prominent place'."[7] I quoted *Mein Kampf* as faithfully as I could and added: "The Führer knows that nothing can make us feel the strength of our position, as much as a sound knowledge of world history. *I* would have liked to write that history of all lands of which he speaks. However, I was overwhelmed by the immensity of the task, and have never yet tried. I might try one day; begin, I mean—for it would be a work of many years."

"I have never met the Führer personally," said H. E. "But I have once met Himmler, and had lunch with him when he came to visit our camp. He was uncompromising and remorseless; absolutely devoted to the cause. Many people disliked him on account of his severity. But you would have liked him—and I believe he would have liked you."

"I have always had regard for Himmler," answered I. "I admire him since I have read his booklet *Die Stimme der Ahnen*. One finds there a scathing criticism of those Christian values that I hate. The book is a pro-fession of true Aryan faith a textbook of Heathendom according to my heart. I love it!"

"I am sorry I have not read it. When was it published?"

"In 1935, I believe. Perhaps earlier. I am not quite sure. I read it my-self only last year, when a friend in Saarland lent it to me."

"Well," said H. E., "from what you say, and from the one sentence you quoted from it, I entirely agree with it. For it is not merely the silli-ness of the stories that the priests would like us to believe, that puts me off Christianity. It is also the fact that, whatever one might say, the reli-gion is Jewish. The Old Testament is just a slice of Jewish history—and a pretty gruesome sample of it, too. The New Testament, the priests themselves tell us, has no meaning but as the fulfilment of the prophecies of the Old. Christ, the Messiah announced by Isaiah and other Jews, is a

---

[5] *Mein Kampf*, Part I, ch. 9, p. 316.
[6] *Mein Kampf*, Part II, ch. 2, p. 440.
[7] *Mein Kampf*, Part II, ch. 2, p. 468.

Jew. His apostles are Jews. Paul of Tarsus is another Jew. I have myself always thought, from the early days of our struggle for power: Now, if we really wish to build up a regenerate Germany, and if therefore we are trying to rid ourselves once and for all of Jewry and of the corrupting influence of the Jewish mind in all walks of life, why on earth do we cling to that fundamentally Jewish religion which our fathers were foolish enough to accept, in the place of that of the old Germanic people who, like you, like the ancient Greeks, like the ancient Aryans of all the world, worshipped the forces of Nature, the strength and beauty of their own race, and the Sun, Source of all life, strength and beauty? And since I have been in jail, how many times have I not thought: 'The Jews are the people responsible for this war; and it is through their world-wide action that we lost the war, and through them that so many of us have died a martyr's death, that countless others, including myself, are still prisoners. Why should *I*, therefore, look upon a Jew as God, and upon other Jews as saints and what not, however 'good people' these might have been compared with the worthless bulk of their compatriots? If I must deify a man, can't I deify one of my own race? And all that you tell me today, all that you told me before, confirms my own thoughts. Now I am sure that I am right."

"Of course you are right!" exclaimed I, delighted to find a comrade whom I truly admired, a real National Socialist who had suffered for our cause, so completely in sympathy with me also on the religious plane. "It is not that I am all that *sure* that Jesus Christ was a Jew, as Christian tradition asserts. Some people maintain that he was not—and not necessarily with the intention of reconciling National Socialism to Christianity. Some say that none of the Galileans were Jews, nor even of Semitic stock. I don't know. I am not in a position to answer the question. Nor do I know whether anybody else can answer it objectively. But I don't care. It makes no difference whether one answers it this way or that way. Even if Jesus Christ were, himself, not a Jew; even if he and all his disciples were pure Aryans (which, of course, I cannot help doubting), still the Christian religion, as it came down to us, would be *kosher* from A to Z; still the stress it puts upon the alleged 'value' of all human beings, on the sole ground that they are human beings supposed to have a 'soul', the way it exalts the 'soul' at the expense of the body, nay, the utter contempt it professes for the latter; the way it flatly denies the fundamental inequality of men, rooted in the blood—the divinely ordained and all-important differences—and does all it can, in fact, to suppress those differences, by tolerating shameful marriages provided these be blessed by the holy Church, would be more than sufficient to set it 'against the moral feelings of the Germanic race' (I purposely use that expression of the Point Twenty-four of the Nazi Party Programme) nay, to set it against the moral feelings of any Aryans worthy of the name, if a vicious education had not accustomed them to accept it as a matter of course without even caring to know what it implies. *I* know what it implies. I have studied the Bible as a child and as an adolescent, not merely because I was made to, but because I was already aware of being a full-fledged, militant European Heathen, and knew I could not, one day, fight the imported religion so different in spirit from my own old Greek and Nordic faiths that I so admired, without being able to tell people exactly what it was all about."

I paused a minute to refuse a piece of my chocolate which my friend wanted me to share with her. "It pleases me much more to see you eat it, you, who have not had any for four years, poor dear," said I sincerely. She took it at last, and I resumed my impeachment of Christianity.

"In his discourse before the Areopagus, reported in the seventeenth chapter of the Acts of the Apostles," explained I, "Paul of Tarsus tells the Athenians that 'God hath made of one blood all nations of men'.[8] That was—along with the teaching about salvation through Jesus alone and the resurrection of the dead—the new doctrine that the ugly, sickly, half-mad, but diabolically clever Yid, brought to the descendants of the men who had built the Parthenon, to the Greeks, who were destined to call him, one day, along with the rest of Christendom: *Saint* Paul. That was the doctrine fated to replace the ancient belief in natural blood-hierarchy; the doctrine that was to distil its subtle poison, not only throughout the already bastardised and decaying Greco-Latin world of the time, but also, gradually, into the more vigorous tribes of Northern Europe beyond the Rhine and beyond the Caledonian Wall, the Germans, the Goths, the Scots and Picts, etc. . . . who had hitherto kept their blood pure. In it lies the secret of the domination of the Jew over the Aryan in the Aryan's own fatherland, for centuries, to this day; that unseen domination, of which National Socialism has made the Germans, at least, if not yet all Aryans, conscious, and of which it has taught them how to rid themselves. But never, I tell you, can we rid ourselves of it, so long as we tolerate that fundamental lie being preached as truth; in other words, so long as we tolerate Christianity as it has come down to us through Paul of Tarsus and his Jewish collaborators and the Judaised Greeks and Greek-speaking Jews of Alexandria, and the Church, who used—and still uses—the organising genius of Rome in the service of Jewish ideas. Even if we do 'liquidate' all the Jews of the earth, still we shall remain, in a

---

[8] Verse 26.

way, their slaves, so long as we allow men to regard as 'Scripture' the book embodying those self-same ideas."

"Right you are!" exclaimed H. E. "I do not know as much as you do about the history of Christianity, nor can I quote the Bible off-hand. But I know you are right. I know the great men of the Party and the Führer himself would have agreed with you in their hearts, even if they had judged that time was not yet ripe for putting openly in practice all that you say. Your talk reminds me of my husband's passionate warnings against the Jewish danger. You would have got on well with my husband, an old fighter[9] from the early days of the struggle who had won himself the golden medal of the Party for his courage, his outstanding qualities as a leader, and his devotion to our cause. You should have heard *him* speak of the Jews—and seen him deal with them! He would have understood you, if anyone!"

"Where is he now?" asked I.

"I don't know myself," replied my comrade. "At the time of the Capitulation, he was a prisoner of war in France. But for months and months, I have had no news of him." And she spoke of the loveliness of old times, when she and the handsome, fervent young S.A. man—who had met her at some Party gathering—were newly married, and so happy in their comfortable flat in Berlin.

I pictured to myself that happiness of two fine specimens of the natural élite, amidst the majestic setting of the National Socialist Reich at the height of its glory. I admired it, without secret envy, regret, or sadness, as one admires a perfect detail in an immense stately frieze, knowing that, of all the possibilities of each life, Destiny can only work out a few, just as the artist can only chisel one detail out of every square inch of marble. "The strange detail that my life illustrates, in some hidden corner of the same gigantic frieze, has also its beauty, although it is so different," thought I, remembering in a flash my lonely, fruitless struggle among modern Hellenes and modern Hindus. And turning to my friend I asked her: "Have you any children?"

"Alas, no," said she. "I would probably not be here, if I had, for in that case, I would have long ago given up my service in the concentration camps." She paused a second and added, speaking of her husband: "That is what 'he' wanted; 'he' wanted me to stay at home and rear a large, healthy family. He often used to say that others could have done the job I did, while I would have been more useful as a mother of future warriors.

---

[9] *"Alter Kämpfer"* refers to a person who joined the N.S.D.A.P. during the *Kampfzeit* (the time of struggle) before the party came to power in 1933.—Ed.

Perhaps he was right."

The more I looked at the beautiful, well-built, strong, masterful blonde, and the more I realised from her conversation, what an ardent Nazi she was, the more I felt convinced that her worthy husband was indeed right. And I told her so.

We talked for a long time more, relating to each other different important episodes of our lives.

* * *

I met several more of the so-called "war criminals," my comrades. In particular, Frau H. who used to work at the Infirmary with H. E. came to spend a couple of hours in my cell on one occasion. We spoke of the Belsen trial, of which she was, like H. E., one of the victims, and of my banishment from the D wing.

"If the Englishman imagines that he is doing any good to the cause of his confounded Democracy by cutting you off from us, he makes a great mistake," said she, speaking of the Governor of the prison. "I can assure you: nothing has made you more popular among us than this order of his according to which we 'must not' come in touch with you. Whatever the occupants 'order' us, we immediately feel the urge to do the opposite, anyhow. And in this particular case, our conclusion is that, for the Governor to be so keen on keeping you aloof from us, it must be that he is scared of you; and that, for him to be scared of you, it must be that he considers you a better and more dangerous Nazi than the average. And to think that a non-German can still be so, four years after our defeat, stimulates our German pride, strengthens our faith in Adolf Hitler and our hope in the future of his revolution, and increases our contempt for our persecutors."

"I am so glad to hear that!" exclaimed I enthusiastically. "I only wish I really were a little more dangerous . . ."

I related a few anecdotes from my life "underground," before I was detected. And we laughed heartily at the expense of "those Allied bastards," as I called them, who are out to "de-Nazify" Germany while in fact they cannot even "de-Nazify" *me*.

But once, I had a great disappointment. I had been allowed to spend my "free hour" with the D wing ones owing to the mistake of Frau P., the wardress on duty that day, who was under the false impression that I had not been let out of my cell in due time with the B wing—a mistake which I was, naturally, very careful not to mention, only too glad as I was to go out twice in the course of the same morning. I walked around the courtyard in the company of a woman to whom I had never yet spoken, although I had seen her once or twice in the corridor. She happened to be the only one without a companion. Having heard that I was Greek, she informed me that she had "had the pleasure" of meeting several Greeks in her life. "Where?" asked I; "here in Germany?"

"No," said she; "in Alexandria—and in Cairo, where I spent some years. Also in Salonika, where I have relatives."

I could not help a movement of surprise. I knew the three places, and I had spent some time myself in the two first ones. But the third—the second town of Greece—one-fifth of the population of which, entirely separate from the rest, in pre-war days at least, was Jewish—retained my attention. "Salonika! A queer place for a German woman to have relatives living in!" thought I, as a very nasty suspicion arose in my mind. But I said nothing. It was only a suspicion, after all.

The woman and I spoke about a certain Greek pastry-cook's in Alexandria called "O Athenaios," and of the new locality near the sea where I had spent a few days in that town in a Greek family, and of my much longer stay in Cairo, also among Greeks. After which I asked her: "And how did you manage to get here, if the question is not too indiscreet?"

"It is not at all indiscreet," said she, good-humouredly, "and the answer is sample: I had been interned in Ravensbrück, and there, I had helped the wardresses to keep order. There were too few of these, you know, so they could not possibly do without our help. They gave me a fairly good post, as I speak good French as well as a little English. Well, I did a few things which I surely would not have done, had I known what consequences were in store for me. And after the war the Allies sentenced me to ten years' imprisonment. Lucky I was to get away with it so easily, for in those days they were nasty. Fifteen of the wardresses themselves were sentenced to death and hanged. Another one is here, sentenced to imprisonment for life. She is Frau R. You can see her over there walking by the side of H. B. whom, I think, you have met. Two ex-internees like me are here too, one for life and the other for ten years. Believe me: things were not, then, as they are now. Had they caught hold of you then, from what I have heard of you, you would have got a death sentence. People with your views were killed for far less than what you have done."

"And why were you interned in Ravensbrück, may I ask you?" said I.

"I had done some espionage against Germany, for the benefit of England," replied the woman, with ease.

Knowing who I was, she could not expect me to praise her for it. But she probably felt that, at least, I could do no harm to her now, and she

spoke brazenly. However, seeing the expression on my face as I listened
to her story, she added, as though to try to justify herself: "My husband is
English. My name is von S."

My first impulse was to say: "It is a shame that you were not shot. Indeed, justice was too lenient under the Hitler régime." But I remained
silent, and my face was sombre at the thought of the number of traitors
that were undermining the whole National Socialist structure, during the
war—ruining the chance of salvation that Germany's victory would have
given the Aryan race, all over the world. I was thinking of the two million agents in the pay of England of whom a reliable English person from
the lower ranks of the Military Intelligence had told me—without, of
course, knowing me—in 1946; of the traitors working on the German
railways, who used to send regular reports to the London War Office
about the movements of troops and of ammunition trains. The idea that
such people could have existed in such numbers saddened me profoundly. Then, my horrible suspicion concerning the woman at my side arose
once more in my mind. If her relatives were people from the largest ghet-
to in the Near East, then, her action could be explained—was, in fact,
natural. But then the leniency of those who had allowed her to live was
still more incomprehensible . . . I really did not know what to think.

"You know why I am here, don't you?" asked I to the woman, only to
make it quite clear to her that she could expect no sympathy from me.
The tone of my voice was such that, I think, she understood.

"I do," she replied. "I have heard it from the others."

I did not say another word.

* * *

I no longer had the pleasure of greeting my friend H. E. early in the
mornings. Fräulein S.—not Frau *Oberin*'s assistant but one of the wardresses—had roughly turned her away, I knew not why, one morning, and
told her that she had no business whatsoever in my cell. I had heard her.
And I had heard H. E.'s abrupt, proud answer: "All right. You will not
see me here again." And I had suffered at the thought that my friend,
who had represented the power of coercion of the Third Reich in five
concentration camps in succession, was now reprimanded by a young
girl twenty-two or so, who was herself executing the orders of Germany's victors.

H. E. did not come in the mornings, but she came in the daytime, or
in the late afternoon—whenever she was expected to distribute medicine
to the prisoners who needed any. Sister Maria—or Frau So-and-so—now

always accompanied her. "Well," my comrade would sometimes tell me, loudly enough to be heard from the corridor if any of the wardresses happened to be passing there, "You still have those headaches? I shall give you an aspirin, and you will be all right." And in fact, she had an aspirin there, ready, in a tiny china dish, to make her visit appear plausible in everybody's eyes. But in reality, I had never had such a thing as a headache in all my life (save occasionally in India, as a result of the noise), and she came as usual to see me, and to collect my white bread—which she now used to put in a specially made large pocket, under her overalls—and my tea with sugar and milk, which she carried away in a bowl that she cleverly held under her tray.

On the day she had noticed me, during the "free hour," in the company of that spy formerly interned at Ravensbrück, she came long before her usual time—and not with Sister Maria, but with Frau So-and-so, who was perfectly "in order." Her first words to me were: "I hope you have said nothing, absolutely nothing about yourself to that woman, just now?"

I understood at once. "Goodness, no!" answered I, spontaneously. "Why, she is one of those who should have been shot—or perhaps gassed, for she is at least partly Jewish, if you ask me. She told me herself that she had relatives in Salonika, a town in which there were a hundred thousand Jews before the war (the rest of its population being composed of Greeks and people from the different Balkan states)—the last place on earth where pure-blooded Germans are likely to be settled for any length of time."

"I am not surprised," said H. E. "And I am glad if you found her out and did not tell her anything about your affairs. For she is a snake—like all those former internees in concentration camps who sucked up to us only to slander us as much as they could, afterwards, before the Allied military tribunals."

"Yes, I know the type. But are there many such ones in the D wing?" asked I.

"Not exactly 'many', but more than you imagine. There are two from Ravensbrück—one of whom, Frau G., is sentenced to life-long imprisonment—and half a dozen from other camps."

"What about Frau R., with whom I talked during the 'free hour' on the day after my trial?" asked I, changing the topic. "She too is here for life—unfortunately—unless the face of the world changes to our advantage, and she was in service at Ravensbrück, but not interned there, naturally. I saw very little of her, but I liked her."

"You would," said H. E. "She is perfectly all right: one of us, and, as far as I know, one of the best ones in the D wing. I wish she would be allowed to come once with us and spend a Sunday afternoon in your cell. You would get on well with her." And she concluded "Whenever you get in touch with a D wing prisoner, ask me about her before you speak too freely to her. I know them all. I can tell you who is genuine and who is not."

* * *

On Friday, the 6th of May, in the late afternoon, I was transferred to cell No. 49 in the A wing. I took with me all my things, including my plant, that had grown many new green and purple and pink and purple leaves since the day it had been given to me.

The cell was a little larger than No. 92. And the window had three transparent windowpanes instead of one. It looked over the broad open space that separated the *"Frauenhaus"* from the men's prison, and not over our courtyard; so that I could no longer *see* my D wing comrades during their free time. I was not thus brutally reminded, twice a day, of my humiliating banishment from their company.

From the window, I could see the outer wall of the prison and, beyond it, one or two green treetops. In the grass, near the high wall, there was a hut. In the evening, after working hours, I could see the watchman walk to and fro before it, by the wall, a rifle on his shoulder. The building, with five stories of barred windows that faced me was entirely occupied by foreign prisoners: some British subjects, some Belgians, about one hundred and fifty Frenchmen, Czechs, and over six hundred Poles. It seemed as if these were practically the only inmates of the place, so numerous were they compared with other nationalities. And when Frau S., the *Oberwachtmeisterin*, came for the first time to see how I was faring in my new cell, she said, jokingly: "I know there is no need to tell *you* not to make signs to the men in the opposite buildings: they are only Poles." The German prisoners, the majority of whom were so-called "war criminals"—the only men in the whole area who really interested me and with whom I would have willingly come in touch, had I been able to—were confined to a building that could only be seen from the windows on the side of the C wing opposite the cell I had formerly occupied there (as far as I can understand the topography of the prison without ever having been on that side of the C wing myself).

As I have said before, some of the prisoners of the A wing used to spend their "free hour" with the B wing, others with the D wing. As could be expected, the wardresses had orders not to send me down with the latter batch. But it happened that, in the course of time, I did go out

with the latter batch, sometimes. As soon as the "free hour" was announced, one was to switch on, from inside, the light outside one's cell,
so that the wardress on duty might open one's cell and let one out. I had
soon learnt on what days the D wing went out first and on what days the
B wing did. And I would put on my light when it was the D wing's turn,
pretending to have made a mistake. And it happened that, when the wardress on duty was one of those who were "in order," as H. E. used to say;
or even when she just liked me—and most of them did like me, I think—
and when she dared, she would let me out. I would then stand in the back
row, against the wall, while we were being counted, so that, in case the
matron passed, she would not notice me—for she, of course, would at
once tell me to go back to my cell; orders were orders, with her, even if
they were given by a representative of the Occupying Powers.

The *Oberwachtmeisterin* too, was, I must say, unwilling to let me go
out with the D wing ones, if she could help it. She liked me, no doubt,
but not enough for that. "I would not take that risk, if I were you," I
heard her say, one day, to the wardress on duty who had allowed me to
stand in the double row, among the so-called "war criminals." But it was
anything but a blind sense of obedience to whatever authority was in
power that prompted her to speak thus. It was merely fear—fear of Colonel Vickers, who was in a position to give the whole German staff the
sack, if he chose to do so, and who might choose to do so any time, if he
scented defiance. In her heart, she resented the very presence of Colonel
Vickers and of every member of the occupying forces in Germany, as
much as I did. And quite probably, the matron herself resented it, in spite
of that inborn sense of discipline for the sake of discipline which made
her carry out the Governor's orders with merciless exactitude.

* * *

I thus met a few of my beloved comrades, now and then, for a quarter
of an hour. Once or twice, I walked around the courtyard with L. M.—as
H. E. was detained at the Infirmary—and once or twice with H. E. herself who, whenever the work that she was doing was not finished in time
for her to go out with the D wing ones, would ask the wardress on duty
the permission to spend her "free hour" by my side, with the prisoners of
the other batch. (Needless to say, I did not object going out with that
batch, on such occasions.) I also met Frau P., and Frau H.—not the one
who worked with H. E. in the Infirmary, but another one, who had just
recovered from a long illness and who had heard of me both from H.
E. and from Frau S., who was her usual companion. And I made the

acquaintance of one or two others, among them Frau B., a sweet young brunette, sentenced to three years' imprisonment merely for having done her duty in wartime, and who had already been a year in Werl after having previously remained three years in an internment camp.

"How is it that those three years were not counted as your term of imprisonment?" asked I. "They should have released you at once, since your sentence did not exceed that period. They told me that the six weeks during which I was on remand would be counted as a part of my penalty."

"It might be so with you," answered Frau B. "You are a British subject, and, moreover, you have been sentenced merely for political activities. We are Germans; and we are supposed to be 'war criminals'."

"Yes," said I; "that is the justice of those slaves of Jewry. 'War criminals' indeed! As if *their* whole conduct of the war; as if, nay, their very action of waging war on Germany with an abominable lie as a pretext, was not itself the greatest crime! Their hypocrisy is sickening. They disgust me."

She talked most interestingly about different people whom she had met in the camp where she had been staying until her trial, and of others whom she had come in touch with during the war.

"There was an Arab whom I can never forget," said she. "My dear, such a Jew-baiter I have seldom met, even in our own circles! And I had never imagined that a foreigner could be such a sincere admirer of our Führer. It was all the more striking as the man came straight from Jerusalem."

"*All the less* striking, I would say," rectified I; "for in that case, he must have had plenty of opportunities to study the Jews. And the more one studies them—it seems to me—the less one likes them. I went and spent some time myself in Palestine, twenty years ago, in order to see them at ease in the historic setting of the first land they have definitely usurped, and to fathom the abyss between them and us Aryans, in fact, between them and even the other branches of the Semitic race. But let me tell you one thing: the Arabs, who are no doubt the most chivalrous people of Semitic stock, can be as anti-Jewish as they like; but they will never free themselves from the yoke of Jewry—any more than we Aryans will—unless they shake off, with time, the strong Jewish influence that underlies their whole religion. True, the founder of Islam was decidedly one of their own people. But he has mingled his own inspiration with important elements of Jewish tradition, and with characteristically Jewish ideas—I mean, with ideas that the Jew produces for export, not for his own consumption, such as, for example, that belief in the priority of the brotherhood of faith over the brotherhood of blood. *That* has brought the

Islamic world down to the level at which we see it now: a worthless hotchpotch of all races, from the pure Aryan down to the Negro; just as the *same* Jewish ideas have, through Christianity, brought about the decay of the Aryan race. I wish you had told that to your Arab Jew-baiter. And I wonder what he would have answered. I wonder if he would have had the consistency and courage to acknowledge that you were right, and to proclaim our doctrine of pure blood in defiance of the whole historical trend of Islam."

The woman gazed at me with the same surprise as so many other people had since the day I had set foot upon German soil. And she repeated what H. E. had said; what so many of my free comrades had said, so many times: "Oh, how sorry I feel that you have not come here before, in our days of power! What an eloquent propagandist you could have been, you who know the history of the wide world enough to see in it an everlasting illustration of the truth of our *Weltanschauung!*"

Tears came to my eyes as she said that, for I knew she was right. Once more, unwillingly—she had thrust the knife into the old wound within my heart.

As I walked up the staircase on that day, when the "free hour" was over, Frau H., who happened to be just in front of me, turned around and asked me why it was that I could not come every day to spend my fifteen minutes' recreation among the D wing prisoners. Other ones from the A wing used to do so, after all. Why not I?

"The persecutor—I mean the British Governor of the prison—does not want me to come at all, in fact," answered I.

"And why?"

"I am told that he is afraid lest I, the unrepentant Nazi, should 'corrupt' you all," said I, with bitter irony.

"There is nothing we want more than to let ourselves be 'corrupted' by you," replied Frau H., expressing the feelings of all my genuine comrades of the D wing.

"Good for you!" exclaimed I, as we walked into the corridor. "That proves that you do not need me—for which I am glad. And your words are all the more flattering. I shall remember them in my loneliness, away from you." And I added in a whisper, as I took leave both of her and of Frau B., to enter my cell: "Heil Hitler!"

* * *

My friend H. E. continued to come with L. M. and to spend the afternoon with me on Sundays and festive days. I used to wait eagerly, the whole week, for those two or three blessed hours of communion with the two fine women whom I admired. And I shall remain forever grateful to Frau *Oberin* for having allowed me that happiness, nay, for having deliberately given it to me, as a compensation for the humiliation inflicted upon me by Colonel Vickers' orders. I never went to the recreation room at all. And I now spoke as little as possible to the ordinary criminals, whenever compelled to spend my "free hour" with them. I continued writing my book in my cell, as soon as I had finished the little easy work which the *Oberwachtmeisterin* used to give me to do every morning, with a sympathetic smile, a few kind words, and, occasionally, a cup of lovely real coffee, with sugar. I watered my plant regularly and watched its shoots unfold into tender velvety new leaves. And I counted the days that separated me from the next happy afternoon when the wardress on duty (or Frau *Oberin* herself) would usher into my cell the two women of my own faith before whom I could talk freely—literally "pour out my heart."

Sometimes, I would translate passages of my book to them. Other times, we would talk of our lives during and before the war. They, in Germany, I, in India, had striven all these years for the same eternal aristocratic Aryan ideal of perfect humanity, in different ways, through different channels, with special stress, in their case, upon the social and political side of the National Socialist way of life, in mine, upon the ethics and philosophy at the back of it. Who would have foretold that one day we were destined to meet in jail, and to congratulate one another, and to exalt and strengthen one another's faith in clandestine conversations?

Frau S., the *Oberwachtmeisterin*, had lent me a splendid book, *Menschen-Schönheit, The Beauty of Man*—published by Hans Fischer in 1935.[10] I would show my two comrades the illustrations: photographs of masterpieces of classical Greek sculpture representing warriors and athletes, on one page, and pictures of living German youths and maidens, photographed in more or less the same manly or graceful attitudes—throwing the disk or the spear, or bending the bow—on the opposite page. Together we would admire the noble faces and bodies, each of which expressed more eloquently than any speech, than any book, strength and joy, controlled vitality; the will to power, in the consciousness of perfection achieved; in all their undying loveliness, the virtues and the beauty of the truly master race—our ideal, our programme, our victory in spite of all; our religion; our *raison d'être*.

---

[10] Hans W. Fischer, *Menschen-Schönheit: Gestalt und Antlitz des Menschen in Leben und Kunst* [*The Beauty of Man: The Human Form and Face in Life and Art*] (Berlin: Deutsche Buch-Gemeinschaft, 1935).—Ed.

10. Illustrations from pages 22 and 23 of MENSCHEN-SCHÖNHEIT

And remembering the love that had filled my breast, as a child and as an adolescent, for the fair-haired demigod Achilles, and for the god-like man Alexander the Great, I would point to the pictures of the modern young men, trained under Hitler's inspiration, and tell my friends: "*That* is what I have longed for, all my life! *That* is the beauty I imagined, when, long, long ago, I used to read, in the *Iliad* and the *Odyssey*, about 'heroes like unto the Gods'; the beauty of the perfect Aryan, then, now, always, and everywhere. *That* is what I have sought in the submerged but unbroken Aryan tradition of India. Glory to him—our Führer—who has made *that* a living reality, here, in our times, under our eyes, and to you, his people, who have responded to his call! . . . 'Like unto the Gods' . . . Indeed, to you alone—to the National Socialist élite—do those words of Homer apply today. In your young men, the everlasting figure of legend, Rama, Achilles, Siegfried—the same One, under different names—lives, to defeat the coalesced forces of decay. May I see you rise soon, my loved ones; may I see you conquer—and lead! Lead regenerate Aryandom to the domination of a regenerate earth. That is all I want; that is all I have *ever* wanted."

And putting my arms around my two comrades' necks in a loving gesture, I would feel that, in the depth of our present-day apparent effacement, something everlasting and irresistible united us, in view of the great impersonal task. The joy of reconquered power shone already in our eyes. And as they took leave of me, the two representatives of the undaunted élite would repeat to me the very words of my latest posters—my own message to the German nation: "Hope and wait! Heil Hitler!"

Chapter 9

MORE SECRET JOYS

Days passed. I worked—very little; I talked—to Frau *Oberin*, who would stop for a few minutes in my cell, or invite me for half an hour to her office, as often as she could; to the *Oberwachtmeisterin*, Frau S., to whom I became more and more attached; to Frau So-and-so and to Frau X., the two wardresses who were the most decidedly "in order" and who, at least in my presence, made no bones about it; to H. E. and occasionally to L. M. and one or two other D wing prisoners. I wrote my *Gold in the Furnace* whenever I was neither working, nor talking nor sleeping. And I thought a good deal. And I was never bored even for a minute.

Like so many far more important and far more vicious decisions of the Allied occupants in Germany, Colonel Vickers' attempt to isolate me from my beloved comrades only defeated its own purpose. Whether it resulted or not in making me appear in the eyes of the whole D wing more danger-ous to our enemies than I unfortunately was—as Frau H. had said—I do not know. If it did, so much the better. But I can, in full knowledge, speak of the effect it had upon *me*. Far from contributing in any way to convert me to a more "humane" outlook, my separation from those other Nazi women whom Colonel Vickers, with pathetic naivety, considered so much more "monstrous" than myself, merely prompted me to idealise them and love them all the more, while it deepened my contempt for the Democrats and their much-advertised, hypocritical "kindness."

"Kindness indeed!" said I, with disgust, stigmatising in the same breath, at every opportunity, before any of the people to whom I talked freely, the attitude of Colonel Vickers towards me, and the policy of the champions of the "rights of man" in downtrodden Germany. "They quack a good deal about our disregard of human suffering and of human life. But they do not seem to know that there are things one resents far more than a little brutality. This Vickers, for instance, seems to take it for granted that I am going to be impressed with his white bread and mar-malade, and with the fact that I have been neither flogged nor kicked about, while he thinks nothing of thrusting me here among the thieves and abortionists. If I told him that I would rather be flogged now and then, and be in the D wing, with my comrades, the fool would not be-lieve me. And if one told the Allies that all Germany resents their patron-ising attitude, their lessons in liberalism, their 'de-Nazification' mania more than anything else, they would not believe it either. The strong and proud suffer under humiliation, and hate whoever has the impudence of treating them like naughty children. But these decent-minded worms simply cannot understand that. Never mind; one day they will. One day, I hope, we shall ram the knowledge into their saintly heads in our rough manner, and teach them how *we* react to their sickening 'kindness', which is the most insulting and the most exasperating form of tyranny. Oh, you don't know how I detest them!"

Quite obviously, nobody objected to my passionate tirades—on the contrary. The German staff—let alone my two regular visitors from the D wing—seemed rather to enjoy them. I was thoroughly popular—save among the prisoners who, for one reason or another, had spent more or less time in concentration camps during our great days. Those, I was told, resented my devotion to National Socialism as strongly as anyone could have in London, in 1946. But the other ordinary prisoners were, or acted, at least, as though they were, either completely indifferent to all ideologies, or sympathetically disposed towards ours, although not always, I must admit, for very high and disinterested reasons. As for the wardresses, they all seemed to look upon me as innocent, if not praiseworthy; they all used to speak to me with utmost courtesy and amiability; and they all enjoyed stopping in my cell and exchanging a few words with me whenever they could find some pretext to do so. One of them had shortened my surname into "Muky"—as we were all called by our surnames, in Werl. Soon, the whole staff addressed me so, save when, occasionally, as a further mark of friendly familiarity, the pet name would be modified into "Mukchen." It was touching. It created around me a homey atmosphere.

Frau *Oberin* talked more and more freely to me, and would often remain a long time with me, with the excuse of improving her French. She had, from the start, shown great interest in what I had to say about Indian religion and customs; also about my six months' stay in Shantiniketan, Rabindranath Tagore's open-air university, in 1935[1]—although my memories must have been somewhat disappointing to a person who, like her, had hitherto pictured to herself the place through the haze of beauty with which the Bengali poet's well-known work surrounded it. Now, she seemed more curious to hear about India's attitude during the war: about Gandhi and his creed of non-violence, about Subhas Chandra Bose, and about the impression the events of the time used to make upon the man in

---

[1] See *L'Etang aux Lotus*, ch. 9, "Demeures de paix" ["Abodes of Peace"], and *And Time Rolls On*, pp. 22–24.—Ed.

the street. I would explain to her as best I could that all Indian reactions to politics were dominated by the everlasting, tragic problem of mass poverty—a poverty that one can hardly imagine, in Europe; that the average half-starved Indian, whether labourer, peasant, or clerk, had no leisure to feel himself 'for' or 'against' any ideology, and that poverty alone had prompted millions of ignorant folk to join the British forces for eighteen rupees—thirty shillings—a month, without knowing, without even caring to know, whom they were to fight and why. In contrast to these, I would tell her of the conscious and courageous élite that had wholeheartedly supported the Axis; I would speak of the free Indian Army organised in Burma with the help of the Japanese. I even once succumbed to the temptation of telling her something about my own connections with the latter, and of the subtle way in which my husband and I had contributed to the war effort of Germany's eastern allies.

"But don't go and tell *that* to Colonel Vickers, for Heaven's sake!" concluded I, jokingly.

Frau *Oberin* seemed surprised—shocked, in fact—that I could mention such a possibility, even in jest. "My dear," said she, warmly; "how can you ever think of such a thing? Have you not yet realised that, before anything else, I am a German?"

I smiled. I wanted to say: "One can be a follower of Adolf Hitler without being a German, provided one is sufficiently proud of being just an Aryan. But one cannot be, today, a good German without being a follower of Adolf Hitler." And the old, well-known words came back to my memory: "Adolf Hitler is Germany." But I reflected that Frau *Oberin*'s statement implied precisely that which I was thinking, and needed no comment. I therefore said nothing.

Other times, I would tell Frau *Oberin* how, throughout the years I spent in India, I had, in countless public meetings, constantly expressed the everlasting Aryan outlook—our outlook—from a nationalist Hindu angle, using the hostility of the Hindus to both Christian and Mohammedan proselytism in a bitter struggle against the two notorious religions of equality sprung from Judaism; the two systems thanks to which the patient corrupting genius of the Jew has managed to inculcate, into more than half mankind, a pernicious contempt for purity of blood.

"From what you tell me of the significance of the age-old caste system, it must have been fairly easy to present your philosophy from a Hindu angle," said she; "Indeed, as I have told you the first day we had a serious talk, the more I hear from you about the spirit of ancient India, the more I understand why classical Indian thought was so popular, here, in certain circles, during the Hitler days. Take away from it that aspiration to nothingness, that yearning *not* to be reborn, that contempt of the world of forms, and the Hindu outlook, if I am not mistaken, is nothing else but the old Aryan outlook of our people before Christianity."

"Exactly!" exclaimed I with enthusiasm. "That is exactly what I used to tell the Indians myself, in those meetings of mine. The Organisation that had provided me with a convenient platform,[2] aimed precisely at replacing that will to escape which so many Hindus take for thirst for salvation, by the will to live on this earth. The president of it, Swami S.,[3] was an Indian nationalist who had taken the orange robes of an ascetic only because he knew that he would impress the masses more deeply by doing so. He was also one of the very few Indians who understood that alone an ardent nostalgia for our long-forsaken European Heathendom had brought *me* to India, as to the last stronghold of unbroken Aryan tradition. True, he made no end of concessions to the lower castes, even to the altogether primitive hill men of Bihar and Assam, who are anything but Aryans. But that was only to keep them out of the grip of Islam, away from the influence of the Christian missionaries as well as of the more and more numerous Communist propagandists, until India would be integrated, one day, in our worldwide New Order. He had the greatest admiration for the Führer, whom he openly called, in 1940, an 'incarnation of God', and the 'Saviour of the world'. He never made a mystery of these feelings. Shall I tell you a funny story in connection with him?"

"Do," said Frau *Oberin*.

"Well, it was in a town of East Bengal, during the war. Swami S. was to address a meeting at which I was present. Before speaking, he had told me to be prepared to hear 'something that would please me immensely'. In those days, and even before the war, there hardly was an Indian gathering at which police informers would not be present. At this one, there must have been at least twenty or thirty of them. In the course of his speech—which ran, as usual, on the necessity of strengthening, in India, the old Aryan warrior-like spirit, in order to 'face the menace of Islam no less than of Communism'—Swami S. said, in defiance of the efforts of the British to enlist non-violent India on the side of the Democracies: 'What India needs, my friends; what the whole world needs, is . . . National Socialism.' The German Army was then victorious. An increasing number of Indians were putting their hope in it. A roaring applause, therefore, greeted the speaker's statement, especially from among the ranks of the students that were present.

---

[2] The Hindu Mission (*And Time Rolls On*, pp. 24–25).—Ed
[3] Swami Satyananda (*And Time Rolls On*, pp. 24, 119).—Ed.

"I gazed at the swarthy crowd; and at the emerald-green rice fields and luxuriant coconut forests in the distance—at the typically Bengali landscape in the midst of which I stood; and I realised that I was hardly a hundred miles from the Burmese border—thousands of miles away from Europe. I recalled in my mind the words of the famous song: '. . . and tomorrow the whole world!' And tears of happiness filled my eyes.

"But I expected Swami S. to be arrested as soon as the meeting was over. To my amazement, nothing happened to him. As I was congratulating him on his good luck, a few days later, he himself gave me the clue to the miracle. 'Had I mentioned *Nazism*', said he, 'there probably would have been trouble. But the average Indian police informers are simple people: they do not know that Nazism and National Socialism are the same thing'."

Frau *Oberin* burst out laughing. "I have never heard anything so amusing!" exclaimed she.

"Our relations with the British-sponsored Indian police—to say nothing of the British police itself, in India—during the war, were often amusing, although, of course, not always," replied I.

And I continued narrating anecdotes.

* * *

Frau S. used to stop in my cell every morning and have a chat with me. Sometimes, she would come again in the evening, after I had eaten my supper. She would come on Sundays, whenever she happened to be on duty.

She often found me writing. She would not ask me *what* I was writing; she knew. She would simply say, in a most friendly manner: "Well, how is that book of yours getting on?" She would bring me a cup of real coffee; or show me a photograph of herself among several other ladies of the *Frauenschaft*—the Nazi Women's Organisation of the great days, of which she had been a member; or recite to me the verses of praise that were once written below the Führer's portrait, in her drawing room. She seemed keen on proving to me what an ardent National Socialist she had been in bygone years. But as soon as, encouraged by her talk, I would in my turn express my radical views and strong feelings, she would somehow withdraw herself behind a screen of ostentatious indifference and tell me: "But *now*, I have nothing more to do with all that." The statement—which I never believed—often irritated me. "Why must she think herself obliged to put up a show with me, as though I were a disgusting spy on behalf of the occupants?" I would wonder. But then, I would reflect that, had she taken me for a spy, she certainly would not have told me the things she did, about her own past. Moreover, other statements that she would occasionally make, and things that she did, tended to prove to me more and more that she knew perfectly well how genuine I was, but that she feared that I might land her into trouble through sheer stupidity. She had, I think, a much higher opinion of my sincerity, fearlessness, and Nazi orthodoxy, than of my intelligence. "I might not be able to write books, but I am shrewder than you," she once told me; "and I know human beings—former Party members and others—better than you do." In answer to which, after admitting that she was no doubt right, I had spoken of my husband's exceptional shrewdness—as though that could make up, to some extent, for my hopeless lack of it.

I often talked about India and about my husband to Frau S. The questions that she used to pose to me were at first somewhat less impersonal than Frau *Oberin*'s—which is understandable, Frau S. being a woman of my age, while Frau *Oberin* was by far my junior. But very soon, my strange destiny appeared to her much less romantic than she had hastily imagined—and perhaps, thereby, all the more strange.

"So I see, you did not meet Mr. Mukherji in Europe, but in Calcutta," said she, one day. "How long were you already in India when you were introduced to him?"

"Six years or so."

"And why had you gone there, then?"

I told her the truth—as I had told a hundred thousand people, both in India and in Europe: "To find there something of a tropical equivalent of old Aryan Heathendom, abolished for centuries in our clime; to seek gods and rites akin to those of ancient Greece, of ancient Rome, of ancient Britain and ancient Germany, that people of our race carried there, with the cult of the Sun, six thousand years ago, and to which living millions of all races still cling; and to witness, in the Brahmanical élite of today, a striking instance of the miracle that racial segregation can work, and the triumph of an Aryan minority throughout the ages."

I paused a second and thought: "It was perhaps a mistake on my part— a mistake from the practical point of view. Yet, the yearning that drew me there sprung from my true self." And I added: "I once wrote, in India, a booklet entitled *A Warning to the Hindus*—Aryan propaganda from a modern Hindu standpoint. Few, among the Hindus who praised it, knew enough Western history to grasp the full meaning of its dedication: 'To the memory of divine Julian, Emperor of the Greeks and of the Romans'.[4]

---

[4] The dedication page reads: "Dedicated to Divine Julian[,] Emperor of the Greeks

Julian, the so-called 'Apostate', tried hard, during the three brief years of his reign, to postpone the twilight of the Gods. But fate was against him. The Greco-Roman world, in the fourth Century, was rotten beyond all hope; nothing could give it back that merciless vigour of youth, the only thing that can buttress such a cult as that of the Gods of Olympus. Christianity—the religion of the tired, of the squeamish, of the old—was bound to win. Despite his sincere aversion for the new superstition, Julian was half-Christian himself, without knowing it. And beyond the eastern limits of the Roman Empire, in that Iran, where Light was still worshipped, in that India, outwardly faithful to the Vedas, notwithstanding the still prevailing warrior-like virtues, decay had also set in. The new dawn of the Aryan Gods—the true resurrection of the Aryan race—was to start somewhere else, sixteen hundred years later. It was to be Hitler's lifework; his glory—and Germany's."

Frau S. gazed at me with great interest. "Does your husband see things in the same light as you?" she asked me.

"I hope he does. He is a serious student of history. And he was an upholder of our ideals in India long before he met me. His alliance with me is, in fact, but an episode of his long-drawn collaboration with the men of the New Order." And I told her, among other things, about the *New Mercury*, the German-sponsored fortnightly magazine of which my husband was once the proprietor-editor. "Herr von S., then Consul general for Germany in Calcutta, expected every German in India to subscribe to it," said I.[5]

Frau S., who objected so strongly to my going with the D wing prisoners into the courtyard, where I might be seen, willingly took me out herself, now and then, for a stroll along the corridor, where my presence in her company could always be explained without anyone getting into trouble. The first time she did so, she was with Frau X., one of the wardresses I liked the best. It was a Sunday, but too early yet for my two usual visitors to come. "You have been writing enough all the morning: come with us for a little walk and a little sunshine," said Frau S. "And put on your white collar, and do up your hair nicely," added Frau X.

"Nobody sees me here, anyhow," said I; "it does not matter much what I look like."

"Of course it matters!" exclaimed Frau X. "*We* see you. And your

and Romans. May future India make his impossible dream a living reality from one Ocean to the other."—Ed.

[5] Dr. Eduard von Selzam (1897–1980). See Savitri Devi, *Souvenirs et réflexions d'une Aryenne* [*Memories and Reflections of an Aryan Woman*] (New Delhi: Savitri Devi Mukherji, 1976), p. 275.—Ed.

two friends will see you today."

We walked along in the direction of the D wing. The barred separation between the A wing and the D wing was open. Nearby, I saw H. B. and another of my D wing comrades, busy folding up and putting back into their places the trestle tables upon which the prisoners had just had their lunch. I smiled to them. They smiled to me.

We crossed the separation and walked along the corridor of the D wing, before the closed doors of the cells of those whose daily life I would so much have liked to share. We passed before the cell where my beloved H. E. lived, at the other end of the corridor, and before the Infirmary, and walked along the C wing and along the B wing. The two women talked to me as if I were a friend of theirs visiting the prison—not a prisoner. And it suddenly occurred to me that it would be lovely for me to come back to Werl, one day, when my comrades would be in power once more, and to walk along this self-same corridor, this time as a visitor, in the company of the new Governor of the prison—some man who would have my views, and to whom I would be proud to speak of my experiences of 1949.

We reached the bars that separated the B wing from the A wing, passed in front of the recreation room and in front of my cell, that was very near it, and walked once more all round the *"Frauenhaus."* Through the glass roof, the bright warm spring sunshine flooded the corridor.

"I do thank you for this lovely stroll," said I, as I was about to take leave of Frau S. and of the wardress. "It really was kind of you!"

Frau S. patted me on the shoulder with affectionate familiarity. "How can we not do what we can for you," said she. "You are here because you love us. You have wanted to help us. You are for us a sign of hope." Her friendly blue eyes fixed upon me, a ray of sunshine in her blonde hair, Frau X. stood by, smiling. "Certainly," said she, confirming Frau S.'s flattering statement.

I was moved beyond expression. And at the same time, I felt small. For what had I really done to deserve that love and that consideration? Hardly anything. In a flash, I recalled in my mind that healthy and beautiful new Aryan world of which the Third Reich was the first living illustration, and what people of my own race, Englishmen and others—people who should have known better than to let themselves be used by the forces of disintegration—had done to it.

"Germany is in ruins because she wanted to help the whole Aryan race," replied I, from the depth of my heart. "No Aryan worthy of the name should ever forget that. And the least he or she can do is to work with you for the resurrection of the glorious Greater Reich."

And as we reached my cell, which Frau S. opened, I turned once more towards the two women and greeted them with the ritual salute, uttering in a low voice the forbidden words of devotion that are to us, today, in our effacement, like a spell of power: "Heil Hitler!"

Frau X.—behind Frau S.'s back—returned my salute, but *said* nothing. Frau S. walked into my cell with a mischievous smile and, shaking her finger at me, said jokingly: "You naughty, very naughty girl! . . ." I smiled back to her, but not mischievously. She was silent for a short while and then said, taking back her usual expression: "I am not locking your cell, for I am coming back in a minute with a cup of coffee."

* * *

Such kind attentions, such marks of favour on the part of members of the German staff, were, along with my free conversations with the same people, and with those of my beloved D wing comrades with whom I was secretly in touch, my great joys in jail.

Frau *Erste* herself, the matron, whom other prisoners used to criticise sometimes so bitterly for her harshness, treated me with exceptional leniency. I never had, with her, the heart-to-heart conversations that I enjoyed with Frau S., Frau So-and-so, Frau X., and the *Oberin*. And to this day I do not know how far she was "for" or "against" the Nazi ideology. I was told that she was a staunch Catholic, which in my estimation, of course, would exclude all possibility of her being in sympathy with us, but which, in fact, given the appalling absence of logic that characterises most human beings, even in Germany, excludes nothing at all. She never reproached me with what I had done; on the contrary, she told me once, quite plainly, that, in her eyes, I was innocent—only a little stupid, and that, probably, for having let myself be caught. She would tease me now and then, but she never seemed to mind the answers that I gave her.

Once, in the cloakroom, where I had been allowed to go to take one or two more things out of my trunk, she told me, in the course of a short talk, that Adolf Hitler "wanted the whole world," to which I replied unhesitatingly that, if so, he was right, "for he deserved to rule over it, anyhow." Far from rebuking me, she seemed rather pleased with me for saying that. And when, throwing the entire responsibility for what I call "the crime of 1939" upon the unseen Jewish power behind all governments hostile to the Third Reich, I bitterly attacked Mr. Churchill, called him a "nefarious figure," a "tool in the hands of the Jews," and what not, and ended by saying something exceedingly rude about his physical appearance, she merely laughed.

Another time—a Friday, before leaving the bathing-room, in which she always used to supervise us—I had asked her if I could not have, any day in the course of the week, some extra books from those I had in store in the cloakroom. "You have enough books in your cell," she abruptly said, at first; "Only the other day, Mr. Stocks sent you a heap of magazines and two books in English."

"Yes," replied I; "it is surely very kind of him. But the magazines are full of nothing but articles on sex problems, that don't interest me, and the books are just novels."

The other prisoners, waiting in a double row near the exit, to be let out, were thoroughly amused at my remark. Articles about sex problems, such as in those issues of the *Psychiatrist* that Mr. Stocks lent me for entertainment, and novels, would have indeed interested most of *them*. I was a funny person not to appreciate such a gift.

But Frau *Erste*, whose features were generally hardened in inalterable impassibility, at least during the exercise of her duties, gave me one of her rare smiles. "That which *you* take so seriously was also a long novel," said she; "a novel that lasted twelve years . . ."

"And that is not finished by any means!" retorted I triumphantly, smiling in my turn. "The second volume—the most thrilling—has not come out yet. But it will."

The prisoners standing in a row—D wing ones and others; women in sympathy with me and women who were not—all burst out laughing. The matron who made great efforts not to laugh herself before them, smiled at me once more as I passed by her on my way out. And once more, I did not know what to think about her. But I felt safe with her. Whatever were her ideas, she would never report the things I said to Colonel Vickers—the representative of the Occupying Power. Once more I thought: "Wherever I go, in Germany, even in jail, German patriotism is my greatest, my surest, my most unfailing ally." And that fact was for me the source of deep joy. For it did not merely guarantee *me* the affection of a great nation which I admire; it guaranteed that nation a future of glory under the swastika banner, in spite of all apparent impossibilities; and it foreshadowed the slow creation of a higher mankind, out of the now persecuted German élite.

The occupants of Germany had never inspired me with anything else but hatred or contempt—contempt, every time I thought of the silly ideas they had come to preach to people with first-hand knowledge of National Socialism; hatred, every time I remembered that, for the time being, at least, they were the victors; every time I would see their flags upon the public buildings, in the place of the Swastika flag. Now, in jail, I looked forward to the rare occasions on which I could defy them under their very noses, without landing myself into trouble. I enjoyed doing anything that, I was sure, would make them wild—"if" they knew of it; anything that injured their already flimsy prestige in the eyes of anybody, from Frau *Oberin* down to the meanest thief in the prison. Secretly entertaining my D wing comrades on Sunday afternoons, or singing all manner of forbidden, warrior-like Nazi songs in my cell; or having, with members of the German staff, such conversations as would have shaken to pieces the last illusions of the occupants about Germany's democratic "re-education," all filled me with that awareness of invincibility, so pleasant in times of trial.

On at least one more occasion, I experienced that refreshing feeling. As I have said, the Governor used to walk around the *"Frauenhaus"* every Friday, between 11 a.m. and 12 p.m., after we prisoners had all finished bathing. The doors of our cells remained open as he passed by, with his assistant, Mr. Watts, Frau *Oberin*—or Fräulein S., her assistant—and the German interpreter. Visitors—once, a Polish bishop, another time, some high official of the British administration—would occasionally accompany him. And, if they felt like it, they would, through the interpreter, address a word to one or two among the prisoners. It thus happened that, one day, a British general, whose name I was never told, stopped with Colonel Vickers outside my cell. "This is the only British subject we have here among the women; she is sentenced to three years," I heard the Governor tell him. The general took a look at me and then, calling back Colonel Vickers who had gone a step or two further on, asked him: "And what was she sentenced for?"

Colonel Vickers seemed most embarrassed. Obviously, he found it difficult to state before the general the unpleasant fact that a British subject—and half-English by birth at that—felt herself Aryan first and last to the extent of indulging, *after* the war, in subversive activities against the Allied Occupation in Germany. But I quickly put an end to his hesitation by answering the general's question myself: "I am here for Nazi propaganda," said I, with joyous pride.

The general became thoroughly interested in me, and crossed the threshold of my cell to talk to me a minute. "Is it so?" said he, addressing me with courtesy. "And what prompted you to help the Nazis?"

"The simple fact that I am one of them," said I. "I have done my best, in accordance with my dearest and deepest convictions."

"Interesting," commented the general. "At least, you are not afraid to say so."

"We people are afraid of nothing and of nobody," replied I. "Many of us might be prudent, but that is all."

"And how is the 'underground' getting on? Gaining power, I suppose?" asked the representative of the victorious Democracies, looking at me scrutinisingly.

I looked in my turn straight into his face, and smiled defiantly. "I would not answer that question even if I could," replied I.

"I understand; you would feel as though you were betraying your comrades."

"I am not in the habit of discussing our affairs outside our own circles," said I, glad to speak thus to one of those men who had fought with all their might for the benefit of the enemies of the Aryan race.

The general smiled good-humouredly. He asked me whether I had any complaints to make as regards the way I was treated in prison. "I very strongly resent being thrust here among the thieves, black-marketeers, and abortionists, instead of being in the D wing among women who have done, at the most, things that I could have done myself."

"You mean the war criminals?" said the general.

"Those whom Germany's present-day victors call 'war criminals', but whom I call my comrades," rectified I.

The general probably deemed it useless to enter into a discussion with me about so-called "war crimes." He merely asked me where my husband was; and in what locality I had lived in Calcutta, and since when. He finally said: "I was in India in 1922—ten years before you," and parted from me amiably.

On my side, I was happy to have shown an important military man of the Occupation how proud and dignified we fighters for the New Order can be, even in defeat. And I thought with pleasure, as I heard the general's footsteps retreat along the corridor, after the wardress on duty had closed my cell: "I do wish he remembers his short interview with me in a few years' time, when our day comes!" I smiled in anticipation of the future, and paced up and down my cell, full of excitement.

And the first thing I did was, naturally, to relate to my friend H. E. my whole talk with the British general.

One of my great joys in Werl was to receive, on the 13th of May—which happens to be my husband's birthday—the only letter my husband sent me while I was there. Frau P., who was on duty that day, brought it to me, requesting me not to forget to give her the Indian stamp.

Tears came to my eyes when I saw upon the envelope—opened by the prison censorship, namely by Colonel Vickers himself—the large, firm writing of the man who had helped me all these years, financially, whenever he could, with moral support, whenever he was not in a position to do more, without ever expecting anything from me in return: neither the fulfilment of domestic duties, nor even my presence at his side; of the saintly man who had told me, when, in the early days of the war, he had given me his name and protection: "You have no duties towards me—rely upon my alliance." That well-known writing reminded me that, even in the broad, indifferent outer world, far away from the immediate sphere of influence of National Socialism, one man at least was in absolute sympathy with me; one, at least, was glad to know that I had been "faithful if all were unfaithful."

The contents of the blessed letter confirmed my expectation. It was not one of those outspoken letters that I had received now and then before coming to Germany; my husband knew of the rigour of censorship and, consequently, used careful language. Still, it was a letter in which I felt, under the ambiguity of the wording, and the clever choice of metaphors, the unfailing sympathy of Herr von S.'s sincere old collaborator and of my devoted ally for the last eleven years.

From it, I learnt that the Indian papers had published on the 6th of April "significant passages" of my statement before the Allied military Tribunal of Düsseldorf, for which I was glad—although I wondered what passages they had left out. I learnt also that my husband had offered to my intention "flowers and scented incense to the Goddess Kali." "Kali, the Dark-blue Mother, as patient and as inexorable as the Ocean that shapes continents, and as the Night, back to which all things go," thought I; the Force to Whom I cried, from the midst of Germany's ruins, on my unforgettable first journey: "Avenge my Führer's people, Mother of Destruction!" My husband knew of that all-important episode of my life. Colonel Vickers, who did not, had been, no doubt, far from suspecting what feelings were implied in that sentence about offerings, which must have seemed to him nothing more than a picturesque expression of oriental piety. But I recalled the grim Image in the famous Kalighat temple in Calcutta, garlanded with wreaths of blood-red jaba flowers, surrounded with clouds of incense, amidst the roar of kettle-drums. And I imagined my husband (who otherwise hardly ever used to go to Kalighat or to any temple) standing before it, thinking of me, of us, and our struggle so far away; of the sufferings of my German comrades; of the ruins I had described so vividly to him in my letters, and repeating, perhaps, those self-same words that I had uttered so often since the unforgettable night of June 1948,[6] nay, since the Capitulation, three years before: "Avenge them, Mother of Destruction!"

---

[6] 15–16 June 1948 (*Gold in the Furnace*, ch. 4, "The Unforgettable Night").—Ed.

And I felt him nearer to me even than when he had shared my joy, in glorious 1940 and 1941; even than when, in 1942, he used to listen to my description of the terrible barren majesty of the Khyber Pass—that I had seen[7]—and agree with me, in joyous anticipation of events that were, alas, not destined to take place: "How grand the music of the Horst Wessel Song would sound, in such a setting!"

I read, further on: "You can well imagine my innermost sentiments. I will not give vent to these at present. My only regret is that I could not attend your trial." And, a few lines further still: "Destiny has always been inscrutable in her ways. But her ways are full of meaning."

"They are, indeed," thought I, recalling the miracles that had been wrought in connection with me, to allow me to remain of some use, even in jail; looking at my precious manuscripts, uninjured, upon my table; and remembering that my two comrades from the D wing would come, as usual, on the following Sunday, despite all Colonel Vickers' efforts to make it impossible for me to come in contact with people of my own faith.

* * *

But my greatest joy of all was undoubtedly to be able to continue writing my *Gold in the Furnace*.

In none of the books I had written—not even in those passages of *A Son of God* that express the best my life-long yearning after Pagan Beauty; not even in my vehement *Impeachment of Man*, of which Frau S. had once told me that it "could perhaps be published in fifty years' time, not before"—had I put so completely all my heart and soul, all my aspirations and nostalgia, all my love and all my faith.

As soon as I had finished darning the few towels or shirts or pairs of trousers that the *Oberwachtmeisterin* brought me every morning, I would pull out of my drawer the thick brown copybook that Miss Taylor had given me on the day of my trial, and start writing. I planned each chapter before I wrote it. And when I had composed a passage to my satisfaction and put it down in pencil upon a scrap of paper. I would at once transcribe it with pen and ink into the copybook. I had very little paper, and could not get fresh supplies of it easily. Getting a few new sheets out of my trunk meant not only obtaining Frau *Oberin*'s permission (which was not difficult) but waiting, often for days, until Frau *Erste*, the matron, would have time and would feel inclined to take me to the cloakroom where my trunk would be opened before her, and where I would take in

---

[7] *L'Etang aux Lotus*, ch. 8., "La terre sans maître" ["The Land without a Master"]. —Ed.

her presence what I needed. Obtaining paper that was not my own (from the supply that Frau *Oberin* had for her office) was out of question: it could have caused no end of trouble, and not merely to me. So I saved to my utmost the little paper I had. I would write upon the envelopes of the rare letters I received, or even upon the letters themselves, between the lines, or on the packing paper from the parcels that a kind friend occasionally sent me from England,[8] so as to make the half a dozen sheets I had left last as long as I could. I wrote at first very faintly, with a black pencil. Then, again, upon the same paper, over the pale writing with more stress, so that, this time, only the second writing would show. Then, I used over that second writing an indelible pencil which Colonel Vickers had given me "to write letters," on the day following my arrival, and the existence of which he had apparently forgotten. And whenever it was possible, I would write a fourth time over this third writing, with pen and ink. Each successive writing I copied, after correcting it, in the brown copybook, with pen and ink.

My ink was also running short, and it would be a job to obtain some more. To make things worse, the matron had twice, lately, filled a fountain-pen from my bottle—without my being in a position to object, for then (who knows?) she might have told me abruptly that I was no longer to write without the Governor's express permission, which would have been to me a fatal hindrance. But I did not allow those difficulties to worry me. Irritating as they might have been, they were minor difficulties. *All* difficulties were minor, so long as I could write without being detected by the representatives of the Occupying Power.

I had long finished my Chapter 8—"A Peep into the Enemy's Camp"—in which I related a few of my most typical conversations with the Allied authorities, in particular in the French Zone, as a certain Frenchman in high position had hastily given me an introduction to one or two officials there, without knowing who in reality I was. I had finished Chapter 9, about "The Elite of the World"—*i.e.*, my German comrades; and Chapter 10, "Divine Vengeance," an account of a thrilling conversation that I had had, in a café in Bonn, with a most sympathetic German "tough," only a few days before my arrest; and Chapter 11, "The Constructive Side," about the basic features of the National Socialist civilisation—for a new civilisation it is, and not merely a new particular form of government within the frame of the old Judeo-Christian world. And now, I was beginning Chapter 12, "The Holy Forest," the relation of some of the sweetest hours I had spent in Germany, in the company of a

---

[8] Probably Veronica Vassar or Muriel Gantry—Ed.

comrade, somewhere on the edge of the sacred Harz. There would be, at the most, two chapters after that. Then, I would slowly continue *The Lightning and the Sun*—the book in which I intended to evoke, as powerfully as I could, as three eternal symbols, illustrating three different aspects of the rhythm of Creation, the mighty historical figures that I admired the most (for entirely different reasons): Genghis Khan, King Akhnaton of Egypt, and . . . our Führer; the man within Time, the man above Time, and the man against Time, as I had characterised them. That work, I reflected, would be the long-drawn main work of my life; the synopsis of my whole outlook on history. But I had no idea when I would finish it, if ever.

The time I worked the most happily was in the evening after 6 o'clock, when I knew nobody would come into my cell until the next day.

I would then take out the Führer's portrait from under the outer covering of the *Mythology of Ancient Britain* that was on my table, and lay it upon that thick book, against the wall. I would also go to my cupboard, and take out of an envelope that I had there in a corner, my earrings in the shape of swastikas, and wear them. For a minute, I would look at myself in the small mirror that I was allowed to have. The smiling image that looked back at me, with the large golden symbols on either side of it, was the self-same face in which the passers-by in Calcutta had read the joy of victory, in glorious '40. New great days, similar to those, were no doubt still far away. However I had regained hope. I had reasons to feel sure that the sacred Swastika—sign of the Sun; sign of National Socialism—would again, one day, be seen, upon the conquering banners of a resurrected Germany, hope of the Aryan race. In the meantime, now, in jail, what more could I do than to continue writing *Gold in the Furnace*—my profession of faith and my loving homage to Germany; my epic of the Nazi "underground"?

I would put down the mirror, and look at the pure summer sky and pray within my heart to the invisible Forces behind the forms and colours of the visible world: "Give my comrades freedom and power, ye divine Regulators of all things!—and treat the rest of men as *they* treat the beautiful innocent beasts!" Then, I would gaze at the inspired Face on the table before me, as a devotee gazes at an icon: "Wherever thou mightest be, may thy spirit fill me, my Führer!" thought I. "May thy spirit make me efficient in the service of thy ideals and of thy beloved people!" And, lifting my right arm before the picture, I would whisper with fervour: "Heil Hitler!"

Then, I would settle down and resume my writing—for a long time the one activity left to me. I wrote with fervour—as I prayed: as I thought: as I lived. Hours passed. And I forgot that I was in jail.

Sometimes, I would read over again parts of what I had previously written. Certain of my sentences struck me as being the expression of such evident truth, that they could not possibly not be remembered or repeated. Even if I were not destined to utter them or to publish them myself, some other sincere National Socialist would, sooner or later. Others depicted my personal attitude to National Socialism so perfectly that I wanted at least a few of my friends to remember them.

I read, turning over the written pages at random: "The National Socialist creed, based upon truths as old as the Sun, can never be blotted out. Living or dead, Adolf Hitler can never die . . ."[9] "There was gold, base metal, and slime, among the so-called National Socialists of the days of glory . . . Now . . . the gold alone remains."[10] And this characterisation of the parliamentary system: "Democracy . . . the systematic installation of the wrong people in the wrong places; the plunder of the nations' wealth by clever rascals; *the rule of the scum.*"[11] And this characterisation of myself: "I feel myself an Aryan, first and last. And I am proud to be one."[12] And these statements about those who share our faith: "Such ones are free, even behind bars; such ones are strong, even when their bodies are broken. They stand beyond the reach of threat and bribery. They are the minority among a minority—naturally. Pure gold always is,"[13] and: "I know nothing in the modern world as beautiful as the Nazi youth"[14]; . . . "Somebody once asked me what had attracted me to National Socialism. I replied without a shadow of hesitation: 'Its beauty'"[15]; . . . "More than ever, now, the National Socialist minority is worthy to rule."[16] And finally, in the chapter that I was now writing, those words actually addressed to me a few months before by my stern and ardent German comrade, in the sacred solitude of the Harz; the words that had decided me to give my book the title which it bore: "You have defined us in your leaflets. *We are the gold in the furnace.* The weapons of the agents of the death forces have no power against us."[17]

I was glad, oh, so glad, to have laid down all this in black and white!

---

[9] *Gold in the Furnace*, 3rd ed., p. xvii.—Ed.
[10] Cf. ibid., p. 17.—Ed.
[11] Cf. ibid., p. 31.—Ed.
[12] Ibid., p. 44.—Ed.
[13] Ibid., p. 61.—Ed.
[14] Cf. ibid., p. 87.—Ed.
[15] Ibid., p. 142.—Ed.
[16] Cf. ibid., p. 169.—Ed.
[17] Cf. ibid., p. 228.—Ed.

Not conceited about it (the sentences were so simple that there was nothing in them to feel conceited about, in the first place) but just glad; glad, after all these wasted years, to have given my German comrades, in the darkest hour of their history, that written tribute of love and admiration—the best of myself; the tribute of the grateful Aryan of all times to come, that the Gods had chosen to write in advance, through me.

Oh, one day! . . . one day when I would be free again, and the guest of a free Germany, I would publish that book, and the Germans who would read it would feel grateful to Adolf Hitler for having, through the appeal of his masterful Ideology, compelled even foreigners to believe in Germany's divine mission!

In the meantime, I continued to relate my conversation with Herr A. in the shade of the holy Forest.

The days were getting longer and longer, for the month of May was nearing its end. In four weeks' time, it would be the solar solstice, the longest day in the year. I could now work till half past ten at night without straining my eyes too much.

The glow of the late sunset flooded my cell. Through the three transparent windowpanes of my window, I could see series of small incandescent clouds, like streaks of red-hot embers across the luminous, peaceful blue sky. Everything was quiet and beautiful, soothing and uplifting. I then, sometimes, suddenly remembered that, when I was in India, although the sky might have been, equally beautiful, the surroundings were anything but quiet. I recalled how trying it had often been for me to write *A Son of God* and other of my books in the midst of the shrieks of the neighbours' children or the noise of their "radios" turned on full blast, or in the night-long deafening roar of drums and shrill sound of castanets from the immediate neighbourhood, or the loud conversations, music, and brawls of people lying on the footpath before my windows in a country where so many men literally live in the street. "Being in prison is at least better than *that*." I often thought to myself; "and especially when the staff is as kind to me as they all are here in Werl!"

I felt that, with my writing, and the regular Sunday afternoon visits of my comrades of the D wing—with the friendship of H. E., whom I had grown to love as I have loved few people on this earth—three years in Werl would pass fairly agreeably, if not, of course, as much so as if I had myself been in the D wing. After finishing *Gold in the Furnace*, I would resume writing *The Lightning and the Sun*. The books could hardly be published before three years, anyhow. So it did not matter so much after all, if I were not free. The work I had been doing, when arrested, others would surely do, and no doubt more intelligently and more efficiently than I. So why worry?

The interest of the Nazi cause—the strengthening of those convictions that had always been mine, in the hearts of Hitler's people: and the awakening of the Aryan consciousness all over the world, wherever there were pure Aryans left—was all that mattered. And in silence, in effacement, in the seclusion of my cell, I was contributing my best to that one sole work dear to my heart.

When I could see no more to write, I would gaze once more at the splendour of the sky, and thank the all-knowing, all-pervading invisible Powers that had bestowed upon me such privileges, wrought in my favour such miracles, filled me, in jail, with such a constant awareness of my strength and such constant joy in spite of all difficulties, nay, in spite of the great humiliation inflicted upon me—my exile from the D wing. I would thank the invisible Powers of Light and Life that would, one day, with mathematical precision, at the appointed necessary time, through ways that I did not know, bring back, to the amazement of the world, the rule of my undaunted comrades—grown still greater and stronger, during the trial of these atrocious years—the rule of our Führer, alive or dead—living forever; the rule of the everlasting truth that we represent.

Part III

SILENCE

11. Another of Savitri Devi's hand-painted dust jackets for DEFIANCE
This jacket was painted for Muriel Gantry.

Chapter 10

THE SEARCH

On Thursday the 26th of May, early in the afternoon, I was, as usual, sitting upon my bed and writing my book. On account of the height of the window, I could see far better there than I would have been able to if sitting at the table—for the table, placed immediately under the window, received little light. At my side, apart from my papers and my exercise book, was H. R. Hall's *Ancient History of the Near East* out of which I had been reading a chapter or two after lunch, before resuming the work to which I devoted all my time. In fact, I could not keep my mind entirely concentrated upon my writing, as I so easily did on other days; for this Thursday being the Ascension Day, was like a Sunday, and I had just been told that my two friends H. E. and L. M. would come to spend the afternoon with me. And I was expecting them with my usual joyous excitement.

"It is the 26th of May. I shall remind them that it is today exactly twenty-six years ago that Albert Leo Schlageter was shot," thought I, to myself. It was not that I particularly wished to impress my comrades with my capacity for remembering the great dates of the history of National Socialism. I simply felt urged to speak a few words of hope to them on this anniversary of the day the young hero had paid with his life for the joy of defying the French Occupation of the Ruhr after the First World War. I wanted to tell them that *now*, no less than in 1920, no Occupying Power can kill the spirit which Albert Leo Schlageter embodied so beautifully. I was not so conceited as to believe that they needed me to tell them that. They knew it anyhow. Still, I reflected, I would tell them—for the mere pleasure of feeling in communion with them and, through them, with all Germany, in the memory of the early National Socialist struggle and in the anticipation of new agitation, new sacrifices, and new glory in the future, now that the National Socialist struggle had become the supreme struggle for the survival and triumph of Aryandom.

Such were my thoughts, when I heard unfamiliar footsteps along the corridor and caught the sound of a man's voice just outside my cell. I startled. Instinctively, scenting I knew not what danger, I pushed my papers and the copybook in which I had hardly finished transcribing a passage of my book, under the covering of my bed. And, opening Hall's *Ancient History of the Near East*, at random—just in time—I assumed a detached expression, as though I were absorbed in the perusal of the scholarly relation of events as far removed as anything can be from the wars and revolutions of twentieth-century Germany. The door was opened, and in stepped Mr. Watts, Colonel Vickers' assistant, the German interpreter, and Fräulein B., the wardress on duty. With utmost apparent ease, I got up to greet the three people, and put down my open book upon the bed.

"We have come to pay you a little visit; to see how you are getting on," said Mr. Watts, after returning my "Good afternoon." The interpreter nodded his head, and the wardress left my cell, pulling the door behind her.

"I am all right; I am reading a little, as it is today a holiday," replied I calmly.

"And what are you reading about?" asked the Governor's assistant, picking up my book, and looking straight into my face—suspiciously.

"About Naram-Sin, king of Babylonia," said I, in the same imperturbable voice, not in the least with the desire to be pedantic but certainly with the intention of appearing so in the eyes of my interlocutor, deeming—perhaps too hastily—that, the more pedantic I would look, the less he would suspect me of retaining in jail the precise, active interest in modern affairs that had led to my arrest. Mr. Watts took a glance at the book which he now held in his hand: at the place at which it was open, the illustration on the right-hand page pictured some very old stone relief called "The stele of Naram-Sin," and the title of the book, *Ancient History of the Near East,* was harmless enough. Still, my surmise had been a little hasty, and the man had more logic than I had expected: my obvious interest in early Babylonian history did not exclude in his eyes the possibility of my carrying on, in prison, some sort of Nazi activities. He asked me point blank, after handing over the book to the interpreter, who started examining it very closely: "I have come to see if you have any forbidden literature—or forbidden pictures—in your cell. Have you?"

I suddenly felt my heart sink within my breast. But, as far as I can tell, my face did not change. (Somehow, in moments of emergency such as this, it seldom does.) And, with the help of all the Gods, I managed to retain my natural voice and my apparent ease.

"I, certainly not!" exclaimed I, feigning great surprise, and looking straight into Mr. Watts' eyes, with as much serene assurance as if I had lied all my life. "I *had,* it is true, at the time of my arrest, five fairly good pictures of the Führer, of which only one was given back to me. That one must be somewhere in my luggage. I have not seen it since the day my things were put away. And anyhow, I would not dream of keeping such a dangerous likeness here in my cell, however much I might wish I could do so." This explanation, given with naturalness, would make all that I said seem more plausible—at least, I thought it would.

"And what about your earrings in the shape of swastikas?" asked the Governor's assistant. The whole British staff knew of the existence of those earrings of mine, I imagine, for the little jewellery that I possessed had been handed over to the Governor's office directly by Miss Taylor, on the day of my arrival, before my trial. But I again lied.

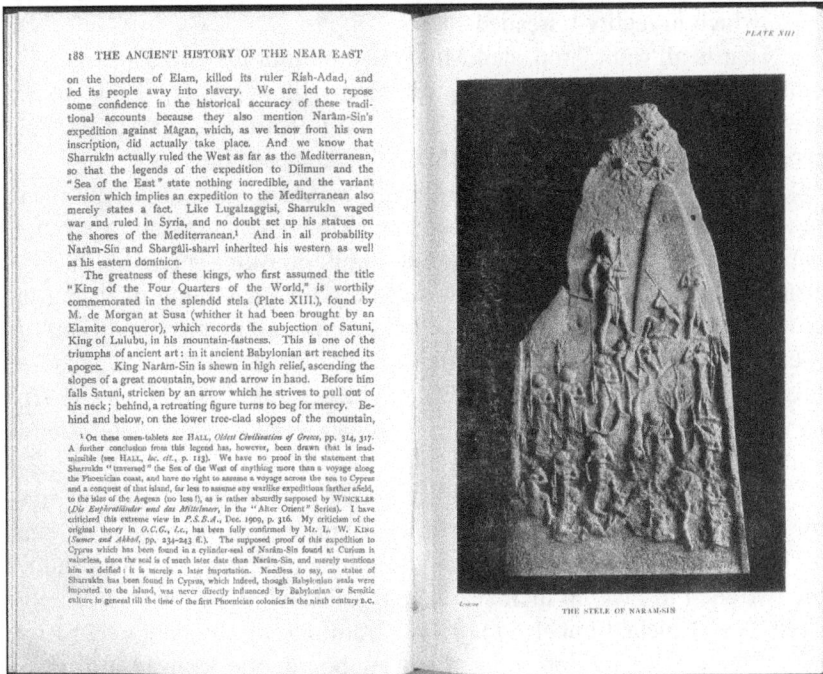

12. From Savitri Devi's personal copy of H. R. Hall's THE ANCIENT HISTORY OF THE NEAR EAST

"They were with the rest of my jewellery," said I, "and they are still there as far as I know." And I added calmly, opening my cupboard and risking everything in order to appease the man's suspicions, and to avoid a systematic search of my cell: "You can look for yourself and make sure that I am not keeping them here; also that I am indeed not hiding anything forbidden."

I pulled out the few books that were on the top shelf: *Art and Civilisation of Ancient America*, Harold Lamb's *March of the Barbarians*, and one or two others, and I put them upon the table before Mr. Watts who, at the mere sight of the titles, lost all desire to look between their pages. Without the slightest sign of nervousness, I took the envelope that was behind them—the envelope at the bottom of which lay my golden swastikas—and handed it to Mr. Watts: "In here are a few photographs of my husband and of myself; would you like to see them?" said I with a smile.

"That's all right, quite all right," replied he, practically reassured. "You have no forbidden pictures among them?"

"Not one. You can see for yourself," answered I, acting as though I would have welcomed a close examination of the contents of the envelope, which in reality I dreaded.

"That is all right," repeated Mr. Watts, putting the envelope upon the table, to my immense relief. Then catching sight of my *Mythology of Ancient Britain*—under the covering of which I kept the portrait of the Führer—he asked me: "You have nothing hidden in there, either?"

"Absolutely nothing," replied I, with assurance. "Look!" And opening the book, I turned over its pages rapidly. There was not a scrap of paper between them. Mr. Watts did not think of asking me to lift the covering of the book. Nor did he—fortunately for me—think of lifting the covering of my bed. He seemed to believe me, although it is difficult to ascertain to what extent he actually did. At last, the interpreter, who all this time had been busy reading bits and pieces out of Hall's *Ancient History of the Near East*, spoke to me. "You are very seriously interested in Antiquity, I see," said he.

"Indeed I am! I have even written a book or two about the Religion of the Disk, a particularly attractive form of Sun worship dating as far back as 1400 B.C.," replied I, delighted at the idea that this talk might induce the two men to give up their search and to leave my cell as soon as possible. And I picked out *A Son of God* from among the books that I had taken down from the top shelf of my cupboard, and showed it to them, hoping that the nature of the text, no less than the photograph of the stone head of King Akhnaton on the first page, would finish convincing them that I was a harmless person: "This is my main book on the subject," said I, handing over the volume to the interpreter. I would have added a few words of explanation, but Mr. Watts interrupted me.

"We expected to find entirely different things in your cell," said he. "We were under the impression that you had here a portrait of Hitler, and what not . . ."

"I am sorry if I have disappointed you," replied I, ironically. "But as you see, I have nothing of the kind."

I said that. But all the time I was thinking: "Who the devil can it be who has gone and reported me? It must be that woman opposite, in No.

22. H. E. told me that she was a confounded Communist. If so, she can only detest me. But how could she have known what I had in here? Unless she looked through the spy hole one evening after six o'clock, on her way to the recreation room. That, of course, is possible . . ."

Mr. Watts took another glance at me as though he wished to read once more in the fearless expression of my face the sign that I was speaking the truth. "We believe you," said he, at last. And he and the interpreter walked out.

I heard the noise of the key locking my cell after they had departed and the voice of Fräulein B. in the corridor, and the sound of her footsteps and of theirs, retreating in the direction of the gate that led out of the *"Frauenhaus"*; finally, the sound of the iron gate, that the wardress closed behind them.

I waited a minute or two, hardly daring to believe that they would not suddenly come back. But they did not come back. Then, lifting the covering of the bed, I saw my precious manuscript there, where I had hidden it. And I thanked the immortal Gods for my narrow escape.

After a while, as I heard the door of my cell being opened, again I startled. My manuscript—that I had just taken out—I hurriedly pushed back into its hiding place, and my heart took to beating fast. But I had no reason whatsoever to fear. There, standing at my threshold and smiling to me, were my two dear comrades H. E. and L. M. A renewed feeling of miraculous escape added itself to the pleasure I had to see them. And I smiled back to them with a beaming face, as I got up and greeted them. Fräulein B. walked into my cell with them, and whispered to me: "I am sure you will excuse me for the delay; but I simply *had* to see the Englishman off, before I could bring in your visitors. The Englishman gave you a fright, today; didn't he?"

"It was nothing but a false alarm," said I, with a smile. "And even if they had searched my cell, they would not have found anything," I added, so as not to let the wardress suspect that I had forbidden things hidden away, in the case she was not sure about it—for I did not know whether *she* was on our side or not.

Fräulein B. left us, and shut the door. We were alone, the three of us—H. E., L. M., and myself—as usual. I told my friends all that had happened.

"You *have* had a narrow escape, and can thank your stars for it," said H. E.

"You played your part beautifully, I admit. But still, what would you have done if the Englishman had insisted on examining your things minutely?" commented L. M. "Actually, I cannot understand why he did not do so. *We* would have, in his place."

"My dear," exclaimed I, with that feeling of elation that I always experience when about to expose the weaknesses of our enemies, "never speak of what we would have done in the place of some silly Democrat; those people are not *we*; they can never react as we would. Their whole psychology is different from ours. Of course, *we* would never believe a word of what an enemy tells us. We take it for granted that we can never trust anybody who was once against us—that we cannot, as a matter of fact, trust those who pretend to be 'for' us, until they have been tried. But the Democrats have all the trouble in the world even to admit that some human beings are decidedly—and definitively—against them and their precious 'values'. They think their 'human values' so wonderful, that they cannot bring themselves to acknowledge that people who are both intelligent and well-informed and disinterested, *can* sincerely feel for them nothing but loathing or contempt. We must be ill-informed, or biased, or unbalanced (they think), otherwise we would not be against them. That is how they work out their conclusions—the fools! And they refuse to take us seriously, until we actually hit them on the head. In the meantime, if, perchance, they be forced to take one of us less lightly then they had expected, they lull themselves into believing that, with a little preaching coupled with a few marks of 'kindness', he till surely 'come around' and leave off being what his deep-rooted atavistic tendencies, his life-long aspirations, his experience, his common sense, and the will of the immortal Gods have made him forever and ever. I have come up against that insulting attitude of theirs all my life. Oh, how I hate it! Yet, I tell you it should be encouraged in times like these. It can—and should—be exploited for our benefit, and for the coming discomfiture of these champions of 'human rights' and so forth, if we are clever enough. It is not even necessary to be particularly clever. One of us always slips through their hands while continuing to defy them, under their Democracy, far more easily than one of them could avoid himself trouble under *our* régime. The man who, for instance, came here just now, imagines, I am sure, that three months of fairly decent food and what they describe as 'kind treatment' have already half 'de-Nazified' me. And the sight of my ancient history books has further confirmed him in that erroneous impression. These people have such a decadent regard for 'intellectuality' and such a poor knowledge of National Socialism, that they cannot believe that a woman who enjoys reading Babylonian history can at the same time be a full-fledged 'Nazi monster'. The fools! Let them go on refusing to believe it! One day, when my book comes out—no matter when—they will change their mind. They will change their mind anyhow, whether they care to read my writings or not, when they see with what ruthless consistency I keep on serving our cause after my release, until I die!"

My two comrades had listened to my tirade with interest, and perhaps with a certain amount of amusement. For while the light in which I had depicted our enemies doubtless encouraged one to believe in the overthrow of parliamentary capitalism and the final rise of National Socialism upon its ruins—which is what we all want—the fact remained that my sweeping statements about the shallowness and stupidity of the Democrats were contradicted by many individual instances and that, also, it was not always as easy as it looked for us to be clever.

"Tell us," said H. E.; "supposing the Englishman had come half an hour later, and found us, here in your cell, what would you have told him to account for our presence?"

The question was a very embarrassing one, for that possibility had, naturally, never entered my head. I reflected a minute and replied: "I really don't know. But I am sure that, faced with that unpleasantness, I would have cooked up some story to suit the circumstance."

"What sort of a story, for example? Tell us, for the sake of curiosity," insisted my friend.

"Well," said I, "I could have pretended that I had had a fainting fit, and that, in the absence of Sister Maria, you . . ." I had just started imagining an hypothetical explanation which seemed to me fairly plausible at first sight, but L. M. interrupted me. "It is useless to bother our heads *now* about what each of us would have done or should have done, *if* the Englishman had found us here. He did not find us; and that is that. He found you alone, and you behaved sufficiently cleverly for him not to suspect the existence of your writings, as far as we know. *That* is the main thing. Be grateful for *that*, to whatever superhuman power you believe in, and let us worry no longer over this 'false alarm' as you call it. It is over, anyhow."

"I am not so sure as all that, that it is over," remarked H. E. "Have I not told you long ago to be careful about that manuscript? You have translated passages of it to me; that is why I speak. I *know* what dangerous stuff it is. You know it yourself, as well and better than I do. It is a sheer miracle that they did not destroy the three first chapters of it that you had written before your arrest. From what you have shown me out of the introduction alone, it baffles me. Each time I think of it, I say to myself, 'Our enemies must be mad'; there is no other explanation for it. But my dear, if ever they lay hands on that book again, now that you have written so much more of it; especially if they read that Chapter 6 of yours, all about their own atrocities—that lashing impeachment of the

Allies, if any—I tell you, this time, you shall not see it again. Be careful, and listen to me: hide it somewhere outside your cell—for I have a horrible feeling that there is trouble for you in the air, and perhaps trouble for me, too; that one fine day, your cell will be searched thoroughly."

"Why did they not search it today, if they intended to?" asked I, trying hard to invent for myself reasons to brush aside the painful awareness of danger that was suddenly taking hold of me.

"Because," said H. E., "those people are shrewder than you think. They leave us a long rope to hang ourselves. Quite possibly, they knew all the time that you are writing, and are only waiting for you to finish your book to lay their hands upon it."

"But how could they know? Who could have told them?" asked I.

"Anybody—for everybody knows it, or suspects it," replied my comrade. "You seem to forget that there is a spy hole in the door of each cell and that any prisoner on her way to the recreation room, or any one of those who scrub the corridor in the morning, can look in. I am sure that someone has reported you, or else the Englishman never would have taken the trouble to come himself all the way to see what you were doing. And if you ask me, it is that F. woman in the cell opposite yours who has been playing the spy. I told you who she is, and warned you to beware of her."

"I have never spoken to her since the day you warned me; and before that—when I did not yet know who she was—I only once exchanged a few words with her. She asked me, in fact, if I was able to write here. I told her I was not. I told her that I was never given any paper, save for private letters."

"You can rest assured that she found out for herself through the spy hole, whether you spoke the truth or not; and that she also discovered that you have a picture of the Führer. She then went and informed against you straight away. Quite like her! She hates us all—and you, possibly, more than the others, because you have not even the excuse of being German . . ."

"But," said I, "the Englishman has not seen the picture. Nor has he seen me writing. He still believes that I was reading Babylonian history when he came in . . ."

"Or rather," explained my friend, "you believe that he believes it. But does he? You seem to underestimate our enemies' intelligence. We once did. But now, we know better. We know that those people are the subtlest rogues on earth. I mean, of course, those who occupy responsible posts. As for the others—the millions who were deceived into fighting us for the sake of 'liberty' and 'justice'—you are right when you look upon them as fools. But they don't count—however much they might imagine they do, when going to vote, once every four or five years. On the other hand, the responsible ones, as a rule, do nothing without a reason."

We discussed a long time. At six o'clock, the wardress on duty came to take my friends back to their cells. We greeted one another and separated, as usual. "With all this, I have completely forgotten to remind them that it is today exactly twenty-six years ago that Albert Leo Schlageter died for Germany's resurrection," thought I, as soon as they had departed. Regularly, they were again to spend the afternoon with me on the following Sunday. "In three days' time," reflected I. And, being as I am, incapable of forgetting the dates of events that have deeply impressed me, however, remote those be, I remarked that the day would be the 29th of May—the anniversary of that dismal Tuesday on which Constantinople fell to the Turks, in 1453, at about half past six in the morning; that date I used to mark, in my adolescence, by observing silence from sunrise to sunset, without anyone ever having prompted me to do so.

My deep-rooted Mediterranean tendency to superstition—coupled with the fears that H. E. had awakened in me—made me at once see in this a bad omen. I believed more than ever that there was trouble in store for me. And I had a vague though painful feeling that, perhaps, I had spent the afternoon with my two beloved comrades for the last time.

* * *

On Friday, the next day, in the morning, on my return from the "free hour," I had at once the impression that someone had been in my cell, during my absence. Automatically, I looked under the bed covering. To my relief, my manuscript was there, as I had left it. I looked in my table drawer: there too, the copybook in which I had written the first chapters of *Gold in the Furnace*, and the one containing the first part of *The Lightning and the Sun*, were just as I had left them. But as soon as I opened my cupboard, an unbearable anxiety seized me: my books were *not* in the same order as I had placed them; and a yellow booklet, *Das Programm der N.S.D.A.P.*, which I had recently taken out of my trunk for references, and which I had kept carefully hidden behind the others, I found lying alone, outside the shelf, on the top of the cupboard. That was enough to indicate that my things had been touched while I was out. "By whom?" I wondered.

What could I do? Whom could I ask? Who was really on our side and who was not? For a while, I felt helpless—and all the time, with increasing merciless insistence, one question—one alone—obsessed me: how to save my manuscripts? All the rest, now, receded into the background, appeared secondary in my eyes. My earrings? Well, if ever they did confiscate them, nothing would be easier for me than to buy another, practically similar pair, one day, in any jewellery shop in India. Golden swastikas were as common, there, as golden crosses in Europe. My *Programm der N.S.D.A.P.*? I could get another from my German friends, when free. And if not, I could go without. I know the famous Twenty-five Points by heart, anyhow. And the extra references I had needed in connection with Chapter 11 of my book, I had now utilised. My books of songs could also be replaced. And I knew quite a number of songs. Even the loss of the Führer's portrait, painful as it would be to me, would not be irreparable, thought I. But the loss of my manuscript would be. Never could I write it over again as it was. More and more, I felt it was in danger. But how to save it?

I was easier to look calm—and in fact to *feel* calm—in a moment of sudden emergency like that which I had experienced when I had seen Mr. Watts enter my cell, than now, when I had all leisure to brood over the reasons I had to be anxious. I realised that I first had to *look* calm. And I lay for a while upon my bed in order to compose myself. Then, I looked at myself in the mirror to make sure that fear was not still to be detected on my face. Seeing that it was not, I pressed the switch that would light the bulb above my door, outside my cell, in the corridor, and attract the attention of the wardress on duty. The latter, to my surprise, opened my door much quicker than I had expected, "What do you need?" she asked me.

"I am not feeling at all well; could you be kind enough to call for Sister Maria," said I, feigning not to know that Sister Maria was on a holiday, and that the only person who could come to me in her absence was my dear Frau So-and-so, who would not fail to bring H. E. with her. The wardress' answer confirmed my inner hopes. "Sister Maria is not here," said she; "I shall ask Frau So-and-so to come."

"Ask whom you like as long as someone comes," replied I, in a studied tired voice. "I am feeling sick." But I was thinking all the time: "Frau So-and-so is one of us. She will help me—if she can. And H. E. will surely come with her. My beloved H. . . . ! My true comrade! It will be a comfort to me, in this emergency, merely to see her!"

The two women came, and pulled the door behind them. In a whisper, I rapidly told them what had happened.

"I had warned you!" exclaimed H. E. "Hadn't I? I am sure it is that Communist woman who informed against you. And I shall find out who came into your cell—if I can."

"Whoever it be, it makes no difference now," replied I. "There is one favour I want to ask you, with Frau So-and-so's permission; only one: hide my manuscripts in some drawer, in some corner of the Infirmary, so that, if they search my cell again, they will not find them. Save them! To me—and to Germany—they are far more valuable than my life; especially the one I am writing now. That one is . . . well, *you* know what it is. You have read passages of it. Help me to save it!"

H. E. lifted her eyes towards Frau So-and-so with entreaty: "Why not try? Perhaps we can hide it?" said she.

Frau So-and-so reflected a while. My heart was beating fast, in anguishing expectation. The while seemed to last an eternity. "I wish I could render you that service," said Frau So-and-so finally. "I have heard of your book from H. E., and I would do anything within my power to save it. But it would not be safe in the Infirmary. Everyone knows that we come here fairly often. Everyone knows, or suspects, that H. E. is your friend. If they search your cell for writings of yours and find none, they are quite likely to search the Infirmary, and then, if they discover the book there, God help us! We will suffer, along with you; more than you, in fact, because we are Germans. I shall lose my job. But I am not asking you to think of me. Think only of the danger which you can bring upon your comrade and friend, who is not only a political prisoner like yourself, but a so-called 'war criminal'."

I recognised the soundness and prudence of her words and pleaded no longer. I could not take the risk of causing suffering to my beloved H. E. even to save my book.

"What do you advise me to do?" asked I. "In an hour's time, the Governor, or his assistant, will come for his weekly visit. What if he takes into his head to look into my things?"

"They will not search your cell now, immediately, during the general visit," said Frau So-and-so. "But if I were you, I would simply have all my dangerous stuff put away with the rest of your luggage in the cloakroom. There is practically no fear of them going there to dig it out, for the simple reason that you are not supposed to have any access to the place. Let things remain as they are, just now. Quietly go and bathe when your turn comes, and then wait till the Governor's weekly visit is over. Call Frau *Oberin* and give her *all* the dangerous things you have, asking her to put them in your trunk in the cloakroom. She will do it willingly, and say nothing about it. You can trust her."

"Yes," stressed H. E., "that is a good suggestion."

"I shall follow it," said I. "Thank you, Frau So-and-so! Thank you, too, for coming to me, my H. . . . ! You are coming again on Sunday, aren't you? Somehow, since yesterday, I cannot bear to remain an hour away from you. It is as though I were afraid something might separate us."

H. E. put her arm around my neck, as her sky-blue eyes looked lovingly into mine. "Even if they tried to, they could not separate us forever," she said. And for a minute, I forgot my manuscripts that were in danger, only to feel that I had not come to Werl in vain, since I had met there such a comrade as H. E. And tears filled my eyes.

But she added: "Don't worry, now. Do as Frau So-and-so has suggested, and all will be well. I shall see you on Sunday. I shall see you tomorrow morning, in fact, and this afternoon for a minute or two, if I can. Heil Hitler!"

"Heil Hitler!" repeated I, with fervour, in a low voice, lifting my right hand in salute, as she and Frau So-and-so left the cell. And with those two magic words, I felt fear and anguish vanish from within me. A strange strength—that was not mine—that self-same superhuman strength that had sustained thousands of other National Socialists during all these years of persecution—possessed me. Somehow I know that, whatever could happen, we would win, in the long run. And if we were destined to win, what did all the rest matter?

* * *

The day passed, and the next day too, without any noticeable incident. I had asked to see Frau *Oberin*, intending to give her any manuscripts to keep in the cloakroom. But I had had no answer. Perhaps she was out, and would come back only on Monday morning. I knew she used to spend her weekends in Dortmund with her parents, every time she could. The only other person who could have taken my books and put them in my trunk in the cloakroom was Frau R., also known as Frau *Erste*, the matron. But although she had always treated me kindly, I did not feel sufficiently sure of her collaboration to confide to her my writings. "I shall surely see Frau *Oberin* on Monday morning, if not tomorrow," thought I. "And I shall give them to her."

The following day was the 29th of May, Sunday. Frau *Oberin* did not come. I decided to speak to her on Monday. In the meantime, I waited for my two comrades, while slowly continuing Chapter 12 of my book. In vain I waited the whole afternoon. By four o'clock, I had grown too restless to write any longer. I opened at random Hall's *Ancient History of the Near East* and tried to read. But I could not. I kept lifting my eyes every five minutes, watching upon the wall the patch of sunshine of which the steady movement towards the door told me of the swift flight of time.

A little before my supper was brought in, I heard at last a noise at my door, and saw a blue eye gazing at me through the spy hole. I got up, and went to see who it was. To my joy, it was H. E.

"Savitri!" she called me, softly and sadly, from outside.

"H. . . . !" replied I, calling her in my turn by her name. "Are you coming? I have waited for you all the afternoon."

"We cannot come any more," said she. "The Governor forbids it."

I felt my heart sink within my breast, as I had at the unexpected sight of Mr. Watts, three days before. I scented danger. Doubtless H. E. scented it also, for she asked me: "Have you done what we told you?" I understood that she wanted to know if I had put my manuscripts in safety.

"Not yet," said I. "I could not get in touch with Frau *Oberin*. I have asked to see her, but I have had no answer."

H. E. looked at me more sadly than ever. "She is out," she told me. "I hope tomorrow will not be too late."

"Let us hope," replied I. And I added: "Will you never be allowed to come again on Sundays? Never?" As I spoke, as felt as though something was choking me.

"Apparently, never more," replied my comrade. "These are the Governor's orders, I was just told."

"Who told you?"

"Fräulein S." Fräulein S. was Frau *Oberin*'s assistant, as I have once stated. I was speechless, and feeling more uncomfortable than ever. "I have to go, now," pursued H. E. promptly; "they must not catch me talking to you through the spy hole, or there will be further trouble. *Auf Wiedersehen!*"

The blue eye disappeared from the midst of the tiny round aperture. And I heard H. E. run along the corridor in the direction of the D wing. A sadness beyond expression, and an indefinable fear, took possession of me. Instead of putting my manuscript back into the table drawer, I hid it under my mattress, after looking in vain right and left, for a better place. There was no place in which I could be sure that it would not be found, if a search were made. In fact, they would be just as sure to find it under my mattress as in my drawer. I did not know why I was trying to hide it there, or rather, I knew it was useless. Still I hid it, in a sort of panic.

More fervently than ever, that night, I prayed that no harm might befall my precious writings. And with more yearning than ever I gazed at the Führer's portrait, and longed desperately for the new times in which all my comrades and I would be free—having, after all our tribulations, at last, once more the right to be National Socialists, openly, before the whole world; nay, in which we would be powerful, dreaded by those who now persecute us.

But those times seemed far away, for I was not in a hopeful mood. I envied all those of us who had died in or before 1942, full of joyous certitude. And I tried to sleep—to forget, for a few hours.

But I could not sleep.

* * *

On the following morning, Monday, the 30th of May, my cell was opened. Frau *Erste*—the matron—and Fräulein F., the wardress on duty that day, appeared at the threshold. Frau *Erste* ordered me out, ushered me into the cell No. 50 next to mine, which was empty, and into which she stepped herself, with Fräulein F. She pulled the door behind us, and then told me abruptly: "Undress."

I started unbuttoning my overalls while she untied my hair to see whether I had anything hidden in it. I then took off and threw aside my clothes, stockings, and shoes, and remained naked before the two women, retaining only the little glass likeness of the Führer, that I wore around my neck on a piece of string. I could not help asking Frau *Erste* why I was all of a sudden submitted to this minute search.

"You have been doing silly things," replied she. "You know yourself what you have done."

"Honestly, I don't. I have done nothing," protested I, energetically. I was speaking sincerely. I had not the foggiest idea of what I could possibly be accused of. For weeks, all my activity had consisted merely of writing my book, without coming into contact with anybody but my two friends from the D wing, whenever I could, and the members of the staff. For weeks I had completely left off trying to indoctrinate the rather dull women with whom I used to spend my "free hour," twice a day. Moreover, the companion I now usually had during those brief minutes of relaxation in the open air, was a Dutch woman, very sympathetically disposed towards our ideology, although a little too squeamish—too prejudiced, in spite of all, in favour of the so-called "value" of *every* human life—to deserve to be counted as one of us. To indoctrinate her, ideologically, was unnecessary: theoretically, she was on our side—or at least thought she was. On the other hand, to render her, in practical instances, more consistent with the Ideology which she professed to admire, was impossible; to try to do so was dangerous. For while her common sense told her that we were right even in what the decadent world likes to call our "excesses," she was a humanitarian by temperament. And *that* is incurable. I had therefore no earthly reason to indulge in proselytism, save through the living example of my own unwavering faith and absolute consistency.

But Frau *Erste* did not believe me. "You have been distributing leaflets, and talking propaganda, among the other prisoners," said she.

"I have not, for many weeks," replied I. And again I was speaking the truth.

Meanwhile, Fräulein F. was searching the pockets of my overalls, and my stockings. In one of my pockets, she found a paper folded in four, bearing in my own handwriting, a copy of the text of the posters that had caused my arrest. And I knew that the one printed copy of the same text that had been left in my possession—and one of my leaflets of a year before, were to be found among my books. That would no doubt strengthen the accusation against me. And the manuscript of *Gold in the Furnace* was, of course, more than any leaflets, an eloquent proof that I remained as militant a National Socialist as ever.

Fräulein F. took a glance at the handwritten text and made no comments. I had given her a similar paper—which she had gladly accepted—a few days after my arrival in Werl.

The matron touched the little glass portrait of the Führer that I wore around my neck. Was she going to take it away from me? It seemed to me as though she intended to. "After all," thought I, "she has orders to search me thoroughly." I said nothing. I did not plead for mercy. But my eyes looked up to her with more forceful entreaty than any words could express. "Leave me at least *that*?" they cried to her in supplication. "I am about to lose everything, including my writings. Leave me at least *that*— my last treasure! What harm can come to you? Who will know about it?"

The last treasure of a prisoner within her power: the likeness of the Man who, now, in her lifetime, had built up Greater Germany in all her glory. And the dark eyes that entreated her to spare it, with such pathetic appeal, were those of a foreign Aryan whose love had never failed; eyes that had radiated ecstatic happiness, at the announcement of the great victories of 1940; that had wept, when Germany's power was broken. To this day, I do not know what happened in Frau *Erste*'s heart. All I know is that she did not order me to undo the string and hand over to her the priceless little object. And I like to believe that she obeyed the inner dictate of her German pride—stronger, for once, than her professional sense of discipline for its own sake; stronger than her fear of Colonel Vickers.

Fräulein F. gave me new overalls to wear. Mine were carried away, with all they contained in their pockets, apparently to be examined more closely. The two women then went back to my cell next door, after locking me in No. 50.

Motionless, speechless, and tearless, I listened to them turn over my mattress, take down my books from the shelves in the cupboard, upset my drawer. Doubtless, they had found my manuscripts. They would carry them away in a minute, and give them to the representatives of the Occupying Power. Those writings, in which I had put all my love, I would never see again. And the people for whom I had written them—my German comrades—would never read them, I knew that. Or, at least, I thought I knew it. I felt the same as though it had been true, and as though I had known it. And yet, I remained silent and without tears; in stone-like impassibility. Something choked me; and something paralysed me. I did not even pray—not even think. I felt as if I had suddenly been emptied of all my substance and had ceased to exist, save as an automaton. I listened with indifference to the two women ransacking my cell, less than two yards away from me, on the other side of the partition wall. I caught sight of a patch of blue sky through a transparent windowpane. But even the sky—the boundless, fathomless ocean of light that had always meant so much to me—did not stir a feeling in me. If, for a while, a dummy could become conscious, it would have the sort of consciousness that I then experienced.

I could not tell how long I remained standing in that empty cell, inwardly crushed into that indescribable state of psychological death. Time existed no more for me than if I had really been dead.

Chapter 11

ANGUISH

At last, Frau *Erste* came to fetch me, ushered me back into my own cell, and locked me in.

I saw my mattress and bed clothes that had been turned over; my cupboard, in which nothing was left, not even the dish in which I used to eat; my now empty drawer, in which, all these weeks, I had kept my manuscripts. And, just as a man who has been stunned awakens to pain after a few seconds of insensibility, I was lashed out of my strange death-like inertia, back to life—back to hell. I knew the horror of knowing that I had lost everything and that I could do nothing about it; the horror of being vanquished. My mouth quivered. Tears choked me. I threw myself upon my bed—topsy-turvy as it was—and started sobbing aloud, wildly, desperately, as I had so many, many times during those three atrocious years of bitterness, humiliation, and powerless hatred that had followed the collapse of all my dreams in 1945; those years through which I had lived without hope, for vengeance alone, and during which even vengeance seemed at times too far away for me to expect to see it. I sobbed till my eyes were dim and my body exhausted; till I could sob no longer.

This was the nearest approach to "personal" grief which I had ever experienced—surely the first grief in my life concerning a happening that affected me *more* than others; and probably the only grief of that description which I was capable of experiencing. I suddenly realised it, as I sat up upon the bed, and dried my tears with the cuff of my sleeve. And this awareness, which came to me in all its forceful simplicity—as that of a physical fact—was the first redeeming ray of light in the midst of the utter gloom that still submerged me; my first impulse of strength and pride from the depth of dejection. "What am I weeping for, I who have never wept but for things worthwhile?" thought I. "This blow is nothing, compared with the Capitulation. It affects only *me*. Therefore, it is a trifle. Am I a weakling, a coward, a conceited 'intellectual', to cry over this *now*, when the horror of '45 is rapidly receding into the past? *Now*, when I know that there is hope both of revenge and of glory, for those whom I admire? *Now*, that a smaller lapse of time, perhaps, separates my martyred comrades and myself from our Day in the future than from the Capitulation in the dismal recent past? Even if my writings are lost forever, why should I break my heart over them? Cannot the invincible Aryan élite—the real, living 'gold in the furnace'—rise without their help? Pull yourself together, Savitri, whose name signifies 'Energy-of-the-Sun'! Deny the agents of the dark forces the power to make you suffer! And dry your tears: Nazis don't cry."

I felt a little better after thus reasoning with myself. I got up, and washed my face. I was determined not to allow myself to be crushed. Sentences of the beautiful old songs that had inspired the early National Socialists during the first struggle for power, came back to my memory as dictates of pride and courage:

None of us shall ever weaken . . .[1]

Nothing but death can defeat us . . .[2]

We shall march further on, when everything falls to pieces . . .[3]

A sudden unearthly enthusiasm, all the more irresistible that it rose so dramatically within me, out of such utter dejection, at the call of my higher self, took hold of me. Again, tears filled my eyes. But they were no longer the tears of the vanquished. They were tears of emotion as, in the teeth of total powerlessness and irreparable loss, I became conscious of my invincibility, that was—I felt; I knew—the invincibility of all the true Nazis of the world.

Standing in the middle of my ransacked cell, my right arm out-stretched towards the east—as I had in the dark, damp place in which I had spent the night of my arrest; as I had, when free, one day, upon the ruins of a lonely "bunker" blown up by the Allies, in the vine-clad hills above Wiltingen, near the river Saar—I intoned the immortal Song:

Die Fahne hoch! Die Reihen dicht[4] geschlossen!
S.A. marschiert mit ruhig festem Schritt . . .

---

[1] "Wollt nimmer von uns weichen . . ." (From the song of the S.S. that begins "Wenn alle untreu werden . . .") [The German phrase actually means "[You] would never abandon us." Although another sense of the verb "weichen" is "to weaken," that is not the sense used here.—Ed.]

[2] ". . . der Tod besiegt uns nur . . ." (From "Wir sind die Sturmkolonnen . . ." ["We are the Storm Columns"—Ed.)

[3] "Wir werden weiter marschieren, wenn alles in Scherben fällt . . ." (From "Es zittern die morschen Knochen . . .")

[4] The Horst Wessel Song actually reads "fest" (tight, strong, fast) rather than "dicht" (tight, thick, dense), but the meaning is the same. The same substitution appears in other sources, which may indicate an alternate version of the song.—Ed.

As I sang, great memories, visions of supreme warrior-like beauty, rose within my consciousness, living friezes from another world—from that world that I had loved, admired, exalted, lived for, that I would gladly have died for, but that I had never seen; that was mine nevertheless, whether I had seen it or not. I imagined the march of the S.A. through the streets of reborn Germany, in the early days of the struggle; the delirious enthusiasm of 1933; the majestic Party Rally of 1935, at Nuremberg—hundreds of thousands, come to proclaim their faith in our eternal values, in that immense stadium dominated by the stone platform bearing the sacred Swastika and supporting the bright living Flame, the new altar of the Aryan Race to the glory of the Sun and to its own glory; I imagined the grand scenes of 1940: the march of the *Leibstandarte "Adolf Hitler"* under the "Arc de Triomphe de L'Etoile" and along the Avenue des Champs Elysées, to the music of that self-same Horst Wessel Song, in conquered Paris. But after that, the ruins, the terror, the hunger, the daily humiliations that I had seen; Germany's long-drawn martyrdom; my own mental agony in a Europe hostile to all that I admire; the sight of the eunuchs of Democracy and of their pupils—the slimy Levantine and the Christianised 'intellectual' Negro—and of their masters, the Jews, gloating over the defeat of the noblest of Aryans; the triumph of the monkey over the living demigod and, which is perhaps even worse, the monkey's patronising sermon to the wounded demigod, lying in the dust, powerless, yet god-like in spite of all—more god-like than ever by contrast with the conceited subhuman clown . . .

I made an exhausting effort to "hold on" to the end. But while, in a voice already altered by emotion I sang the last line

"Die Knechtschaft dauert nur noch kurze Zeit."
(Slavery has not much longer to last.)

I broke down.

And from then onwards, my torture began—a torture that the representatives of the Occupying Power could not fathom, nor even suspect, and of which they were, to say the most, the instruments, not the cause.

The cause was by far remoter; and it lay within myself. For while I had sought in the Song of freedom, pride, and power a spell of strength in my present tragic plight, my old gnawing regret for not having come to Germany earlier—that consciousness of a useless, wasted life, that had tormented me like remorse, so often, since the outbreak of the war and especially since the Capitulation—had again caught hold of me with a grip of iron. It now mingled itself with the grief I felt for the loss of my manuscripts, nay, it kindled that grief into utter, maddening despair. My impulse would have been to pray to the invisible Forces to save my writings, even against all hope. But an implacable inner voice—the voice of my real self—kept on telling me that I was unworthy of the favour of the just, passionless all-pervading Forces. With baffling vividness and accuracy, it pointed out to me my practically wasted life, in glaring contrast with what that life *could have been* if, when I was twenty-two, I had taken a different line—my own only rational, only constructive, only natural line, namely, if I had just crossed the Rhine instead of crossing the Mediterranean. It lashed me, and it mocked me, as I lay upon my bed, sobbing more wildly than ever, this time, less over my lost manuscripts than over my lost youth, my lost energy, my lonely, wearisome, worthless years in the Near and Middle East, a pitiful caricature of the useful and happy life—the glorious life—that I could have lived . . . *if*—*if* I had not been such a fool. And I accepted in all humility every stroke of that whip of conscience that fell again and again upon me, biting into my heart deeper and deeper each time—every thrust of the knife into the old gaping wound—for I knew I deserved it.

Mercilessly, in all its tragic irony, the film of my whole life unrolled itself before me. I recalled my essentially Pagan childhood, my still more consciously Pagan adolescence, in the midst of that Judeo-Christian world that I had always so deeply despised when I had not bitterly hated it; nay, in the midst of the most notoriously over-civilised, cerebral, light-spirited, and light-hearted—decadent—nation of that world: France, the nation that laughs at all that which it fails to understand. I remembered my early pride in health, strength, and grace; my early revolt against the Judeo-Christian *values* and the Democratic attitude to life. The equality, the "dignity" of *all* human beings whatever their race, their character, their state of health, for the sole reason that they were *human beings*; one of these repulsive idiots, that I had seen on my visit to the asylum of LaForce, as lovable as myself in the eyes of gentle Jesus—and of my dull, kindly, patronising teachers, whether Christians or Freethinkers—for the sole reason that he was supposed to have a "soul" (or whatever might be the Freethinkers' equivalent for one); the life of a Negro, of a Jew, as "sacred" as that of the most splendid specimen of mankind, and much more sacred than that of the majestic beasts of the forests, that I loved for their beauty; the "right" of man to inflict suffering and death upon healthy innocent animals as much as he pleased in order to contribute to feed or to "save" diseased, deficient, or naturally inferior men, while denying the stronger, more beautiful, better men the right to keep down and exploit the naturally inferior ones! Oh, how I had hated all that, with all the passion of my heart, from the earliest days of my life, in defiance of my surroundings at home, in school, in college, everywhere! How I had always been the irreducible enemy of the sentimental believer in the "rights of man," of the pacifist, of the Christian, especially if that lover of humanity was, in addition, a meat-eater and a supporter of any horror committed upon animals "in the interest of mankind"!

Verses that I had read in my early teens—or before—and that I had never forgotten, for they had exercised upon me a spell-like appeal; verses of the French poet Leconte de Lisle, mostly, came back to my memory:

Enochia! monstrous city of the virile,
Den of the violent, citadel of the strong,
Thou who hast never known fear nor remorse . . .[5]

And this glaring evocation of the deified Aryan hero of India, in all the pride of the privileged god-like Race—these verses of which the music was destined, one day, after the failure of my great dreams in Greece, to drive me to the caste-ridden Land as to the immemorial stronghold of natural order and hierarchy:

"Rama, son of Dasharatha, whom the Brahmins honour,
Thou whose blood is pure, thou whose body is white,"
Said Lakshmana, "Hail, O resplendent subduer
Of all the profane races!"[6]

Indeed, I had been inspired all my life with the self-same spirit as now. How right I had been when I had written, somewhere in my now lost book: "One does not *become* a National Socialist. One only discovers, sooner or later, that one has always been one—that, by nature, one could not possibly be anything else."[7] The more I remembered myself on the threshold of life, in my discussions with the Christians who already reproached me with

---

[5] Henokhia! Cité monstrueuse de máles,
  Antre des violents, citadelle des forts,
  Qui ne connus jamais la peur ni le remords . . .
  —Leconte de Lisle "Qaîn" (*Poèmes Barbares*)
[6] "Rama Daçarathide, honoré des Brahmanes,
  Toi dont le sang est pur, toi dont le corps est blanc,"
  Dit Lakçmana, "salut, dompteur étincelant
  De toutes les races profanes!"
  —Leconte de Lisle "L'Arc de Civa" (*Poèmes Antiques*)
[Savitri is evidently quoting from memory, for the second line actually reads, "Toi dont le sang est pur et dont le corps est blanc."—Ed.]
[7] In Chapter 9 [*Gold in the Furnace*, 3rd ed., p. 143—Ed.].

my "spiritual pride" and "inhuman outlook"; with the pacifist dreamers whom I despised, with the then fashionable enthusiasts of Sigmund Freud, whom I loathed, the more I knew how true this was.

But then, the accusing inner voice rang clear and pitiless within me: "Yes of course, that is true. In the whole Aryan world outside Germany, not one man or woman ever was more decidedly marked out than you for the honour of bearing witness to the truth proclaimed by Adolf Hitler. None understood that truth better than you; none loved it more ardently; none loved *nothing but it*, as you already did in those far-gone days of the early struggle for power. Oh, remember, remember with what sympathy, with what wholehearted admiration you followed that early struggle in the papers, when you were eighteen, twenty! You had not yet got over your grief for the destruction of Greek Ionia—that age-old outpost of Aryan civilization in the Near East—and already you had enough vision to take interest in a great Western nation's fight for freedom, nay, for life; you had already enough heart to see in the French Occupation of the Ruhr an act of felony, and you spoke against it with wild indignation. Once more, as during the blockade of Greece during the First World War, and as after her betrayal of Greece in Asia Minor, you looked upon France—and rightly so—as the enemy of Aryan mankind. But what did you do, when free to act? You went and sought to save the modern Greeks from their slavish regard for things French and from France's influence—from the appeal that the sickly ideals of the French Revolution somewhat exercised upon so many of the half-educated and of the foreign-educated among them; you endeavoured to stir in them the love of the eternal Aryan values, that *are* the Greek values of old. And when you saw you could do nothing—for the roots of equalitarianism lie deep, in Christianity, nay, in the corruption of Hellenistic times, and no preaching, unless it be backed by force, can pretend to stem over two thousand years of decay—you turned to the East, to the one Land where Christianity had never superseded the Aryan Gods, and where Rousseau's equalitarian nonsense was unknown. You went to India—and stayed there, you fool, while Europeans, many of whom less aware than you were of the historical significance of the National Socialist message, were building new Germany, new Europe, the real resurrected Aryandom of your dreams. What were *you* doing, while they, your friends, your comrades, your brothers, your equals, and your superiors, were doing *that*? Expressing yourself in violent speeches against the missionaries both of Christianity and of Democracy; relating eloquently, to the dazzled Hindus, as a warning, the dismal story of the conquest of the Aryan West by the Jewish creed of meekness and equality and hypocrisy and crying to them: "beware!"; trying to induce the East to join its efforts to those of the Western élite in the fight for truth, for order, for Aryandom! Wasting your time. You fool! Did it take you all these years to discover the incurable inertia of the East?

"What were you doing in September 1935, while your dreams were taking shape in the broad stadium of Nuremberg, amidst columns of light? While upon the new altar, bearing the immemorial Swastika, the sacred Flame proclaimed to the bewildered world the miraculous resurrection of the privileged Race, of *your* race, of the Aryan in all lands? Why were you not there in your place with the hundreds of thousands, at the foot of the altar, you, Aryan woman, whose vision had, for years already, transcended frontiers; you whom India, through the prophetic intuition of a few of her daughters, had renamed Savitri, 'Energy-of-the-Sun' and symbol of resurrection? Save the Führer himself and one or two others, who knew, who understood better than you, that the battle-cry of new Germany was also the call to life addressed to all Aryandom? Why were you not in your place at the Rally, to hear Hermann Göring call the Führer the Saviour of his people, and to add, within your heart: 'And of all higher mankind'?

"What were you doing, then? Exhibiting your earrings in the shape of swastikas in Indian tea parties; giving free expression to your fruitless enthusiasm before hospitable men and women, not one out of a thousand of whom understood you; having, in a certain Indian's motorcar, a free fight with a Jewess who had said something against the Führer, and feeling pleased with yourself when you had answered her silly talk with a few blows and a few vitriolic sentences. You fool! Why on earth did you not come back?"

I sobbed more desperately at the thought of the beauty of all that I had missed. But the implacable inner voice did not stop tormenting me. "And why at least did you not come back in 1938?" it said; "There was time, yet. Remember your first conversation with the wise man whose name you now bear. What did he tell you, after talking to you five minutes? 'Go back! Your duty is in Europe. Go back! Here, you are wasting your time.' Why didn't you listen to him, you conceited, empty-headed imbecile; why didn't you? Thought yourself 'useful' in the East, eh? And thought you had time; did not believe the menace of the jealous Democracies, agents of international Jewry; thought they would wait for you to make up your mind, and not attack the new Reich that you so admired before you could come to defend it! Admittedly, you did your best to come once the war had broken out. You quickly secured yourself a British passport to make things easier . . . But it was already too late.

You did your best *in* India, when compelled to stay. But what was that, compared with the glorious career you missed in Europe? Oh, think of it, Savitri! Think of all the services you could have rendered in wartime, here, or in occupied France, or anywhere your superiors would have chosen to send you! Think of all that—apart from the great moments you would have lived. You paced the marble floor of your room in Calcutta, and sang all night at the news of the fall of Paris. You would have *seen* the parade of victory: seen it with your own eyes; heard that self-same song of conquest that you now sang, resound along the Avenue des Champs Elysées; *Bald flattern Hitlerfahnen über allen Straßen* . . . You would have lived on the spot those joys—and then, those agonies—that you shared so intensely from a distance of six thousand miles.

"And when the end would, alas, have come, you would have met, at the hands of the enemies of all you love, a death worthy of your ardent, one-pointed life. But, before they killed you, you would have had the bitter pleasure of defying them for the last time with the lashing eloquence of one faced with certain ruin, not before a few rank and file Nazis as were probably to be found among the public attending your trial at Düsseldorf, but before Göring, before Hess, before Himmler[8] and Streicher and all the others, in that tragic hall of Nuremberg that history will remember as the seat of the most monstrous iniquity. In the midst of the horror of those days, before the self-appointed judges, champions of those Judeo-Christian-democratic values that you hated all your life, you would have vindicated the right of National Socialism to assert itself, to conquer, to endure, in the name of the truths of all times that it embodies; you would have publicly accused its accusers, and condemned them, you, the life-long champion of the typically Aryan values in the East and in the West. And having done that, you would have died with the Twenty-one,[9] in a cry of defiance and of triumph . . . Oh, what have you not missed, for the sterile satisfaction of impressing a few *'Untermenschen'* on the ground of their flimsy claims to the everlasting Aryan inheritance! What have you not missed, you damned fool!"

The wardress on duty brought in my lunch and told me kindly that I should try to eat. I paid no attention to what she said. I left the food lying there in its container, until she came again to carry it away; and I continued

---

[8] Heinrich Himmler was not tried at Nuremberg, but died under mysterious circumstances in Allied custody on 23 May 1945.—Ed.

[9] Savitri Devi probably meant the eleven who were to be executed on 16 October 1946. Hermann Göring, of course, committed suicide before he could be hanged. Of the twenty-four indicted at Nuremberg, only twelve were sentenced to death, and one, Albert Bormann, who had been tried *in absentia*, was already dead.—Ed.

to follow the trend of my thoughts, listening to the condemnation of my inner voice for all that I had not done. The inner voice pursued:

"And now, you would like to save your writings. Objectively speaking, you are right. They are perhaps the best thing you ever did. Yet, why should you save them? It is not just that you should, for you are a fool and deserve to suffer. Stupidity, childishness, are crimes. You have to pay. True, you have tried to make up for your past omissions. At last, you came—when all was lost; but at least, you came; as they say: 'better late than never'. At last, you have thrown yourself heart and soul into the one sort of action you should have confined yourself to from the beginning: propaganda among the natural élite. You were not made for anything else. But even now, you have acted foolishly and got caught—the only sin, for an underground worker. You are congenitally stupid. Incurably stupid. Useless to pray: it serves you right if your writings are destroyed. It serves you right—you who were absent all these years—if no trace is left of your love and faith when the New Order rises again; if your very friends, once more in power, one day, send you back to India, telling you to go and mind your cats there. Remember what your husband told you on the 7th of November 1943: 'You are unworthy to live under that National Socialist world order that you profess to fight for! It was not established for fools like you!'"

My husband had, indeed, said such a thing on that one occasion on which he had quarrelled with me. He had said it because I had admitted to him—who used to control all my movements, and rightly so—that I had, in the course of a conversation, been foolish enough to tell the title of the magazine of which he had once been the editor—the *New Mercury*—to one of the Americans that I used to bring home, every week, from the "East and West Club." The American, himself a greater fool than I, had never even taken the trouble to find out what sort of a magazine that was. But, said my cautious ally, he *could have been* more inquisitive; he *could have* enquired; and he could have spread suspicion among the others, thus impairing the little usefulness we still might have had. And I had agreed with him, although his words had been harsh and had made me cry. And I had deplored my stupidity.

Now, six years later, in jail, at the mercy of our victorious enemies, and threatened with the destruction of my sincerest writings, I deplored it once more; I deplored all the mistakes I had made; all the omissions, all the foolish impulses and hasty decisions of my whole life. And I came to the logical conclusion: "The just Gods have given me now the treatment I deserve: when I had at last produced something constructive—a book of a certain beauty, if nothing else—for the cause I so love, that is taken away from me to be destroyed . . . I shall submit to the will of the Gods. They are right to torment me for not having come before; for not having made myself more useful all these years; for not having been killed in '45, while so many, worth a thousand times more than myself, have met a painful death as 'war criminals' and what not . . ."

I tried to dry my tears, and bravely to accept the blow that crushed me, and not to pray, as a child, for undeserved favour. But I could not. A fact kept on obsessing me: I knew that I could never write my book anew, as it was; that, whatever its value or lack of value, it was something unique and irreplaceable: the product of my whole being at a given time, and under given circumstances which would never come back exactly the same; the youngest and best and most beloved child of my brains and of my heart, conceived in blessed hours of inspiration, brought forth in daily uncertainty and danger. I could no doubt create another, work, in many ways like it. But I knew that it could never be the same.

Moreover I knew—or dared to believe—that my book which would have, in the eyes of every reader, at least that literary merit that the stamp of absolute sincerity gives to any writing, would most certainly, in addition to that, appeal to the National Socialists, for whom alone it was written, and especially to the German ones. Nay, I felt—was it conceit? Or was it sane judgement? I cannot tell; but I honestly felt—that there were many things in it which could not but appeal to *any* German heart, irrespective of politics; things that could even, perhaps, convert to National Socialism certain Germans who had, up till now, failed to grasp the everlasting significance of Hitler's Movement. I dared to believe that, I, a non-German Aryan, could have had, one day, through that book of mine, the rare and unexpected honour of bringing more Germans to Adolf Hitler.

But now, the book was lost. And somehow, it seemed to me, not only that I could never write it over again, but that nothing of what I could ever write in the future could have the appeal of those pages written with tears and fire, in 1948, during my short-lived underground struggle, and in 1949 in prison, and I felt that, although I, no doubt, well deserved to suffer in expiation of all my old mistakes, my book, in spite of everything, deserved to live. And the fear of its destruction remained the greatest torture for me.

That . . . and other fears also. For I had written about a few people, in that book. I had not mentioned their names, naturally, but the circumstantial details that I had given were perhaps sufficient to make some of them recognisable. It did not matter, for the book could not be published, in Europe anyhow, so long as Germany was not free. And when Germany would be free, those of my friends about whom I had written could only be grateful to me for having done so. But, now, my statements took on a dangerous importance for the fact that our enemies would read them. I thought in particular of that Chapter 12 which I had just begun to write when my cell was searched. I remembered what I had written and decided that *that* was safe enough: our enemies could not possibly find out who was Herr A. whom I pictured in that chapter as such a sincere National Socialist. But what would happen if they discovered who had told me about the atrocities of the British military policemen at the time they took possession of Belsen, atrocities which I had described with some details and stigmatised in my Chapter 6? I shuddered at that thought, and switched on the light outside my cell, to call the wardress on duty. It was Fräulein F. She had not yet been relieved, from which I concluded that it was not yet three o'clock.

"Could you please call Frau So-and-so?" said I, as soon as she came; "I want an aspirin; I feel as though my head were splitting in two."

"I shall call her," answered Fräulein F., kindly, after taking a glance at my swollen face and feverish eyes.

"But why do you put yourself in such a state? Why do you keep on crying all the time?"

"I have lost everything," said I, as new tears started rolling down my cheeks. "My book is far more precious than my life."

"But they will give it back to you!" replied Fräulein F., who seemed to consider that statement strange, to say the least.

I looked at her as a grownup person looks at a child who has just said: "Father Christmas will bring you the moon."

"You would not say that, if you knew the things I have written in that book," remarked I.

* * *

Frau So-and-so came. H. E. was with her, pale, visibly upset. She did not wait for me to tell her what had happened; she knew. All the prison knew. She did not wait for me to explain to her what worried me, along with the loss of my book, and why I had called for Frau So-and-so—and implicitly for her—with the excuse of wanting an aspirin. That also, she knew. And that was precisely why she was so upset. She spoke to me first, in a whisper, after carefully pulling the door behind her: "Now that *they* will read what you wrote about their atrocities and about the Belsen trial, God help us! . . . You have not mentioned my name anywhere, I hope?"

"Goodness no!" answered I. "But I did refer to you by your initials, as you know, in a passage or two; I also referred to H. B. and to Frau H. by their initials, and that is what worries me so . . ."

For the first time, H. E. scolded me. "You *are* a fool, really, to have landed yourself—and us—in such trouble as this! Either you should never have mentioned in your book any of those horrors of which I told you, or you should have managed to avoid at any cost letting the book fall into those people's clutches. It makes little difference, in fact, whether you have written our initials or not. The mere mention of the Belsen trial is enough for them to suspect us of having given you the damaging information. The Governor already knows that I come here, otherwise he would not have issued strict orders that I should come no more."

"In that case, since the harm cannot be undone," said I, "would it not be better if you boldly stood by me and told them to their faces, if necessary, that every word I have written is true; nay, that reality was, if that be possible, even more horrid than the description I tried to give of it? Would it not be better to accuse them openly—in public, if they give us a chance? To stir up at last the indignation of the press, of the world, against them and their so-called 'justice', their alleged, 'humanity'?"

"One day, when we are free, yes, we shall do that—and a lot more. But not now!" exclaimed H. E., "not now! Now, our voice would not be heard beyond these walls; *they* would see to it, that it should not be. And the only result of our stand would be more fruitless suffering for us all, and more oppression for Germany, without any benefit to our cause. Believe me; I know these people."

Anguish was depicted upon her face at the mere thought of what could befall us if my Chapter 6—"Chambers of Hell"—were freely discussed. In a flash, I recalled the terror she had experienced, in April 1945, when, huddled against the other women in service at Belsen, she had seen the circle of the grinning British military policemen close around her, narrower and narrower, until the steel of their bayonets touched her . . . And I remembered the sinister mockery of a trial that had followed, the result of which I had read in the papers: Irma Grese, sentenced to death and hanged; H. E. sentenced to fifteen years' imprisonment; H. B. and H. both sentenced to ten years . . . Indeed, nobody could reproach her with cowardice for dreading these people.

"All right," said I; "tell me only what I must say, in case they ask me wherefrom I obtained the information," enquired I.

"Say you have got it from some prisoner now free, whose name you do not remember. Say anything you like; but don't mention me, nor any of us. We have suffered enough."

"She is right," added Frau So-and-so; "What makes that search of your cell so tragic is that you are not alone involved . . ."

I put my hand upon my comrade's shoulder. My eyes, now dry,

looked straight into hers. "My H. . . ." said I lovingly and forcefully, "don't fear! I shall not let them know that you told me about those horrors of theirs. If they ask me, I shall tell them that I heard of them from others, as you say, and that I put down fanciful initials, purposely. And if I am cornered, I shall finally say that I invented them myself, for the sake of anti-democratic propaganda, and thus take the whole responsibility and the whole blame. Let them do what they like to me! Now my book is lost, I could not care less what my fate is!"

I started weeping in her arms. And she, and Frau So-and-so, did their best to soothe me.

Heartened by the mere feeling of their sympathy, I asked what seemed to me, no sooner had I uttered it, the most nonsensical question: "But are you quite sure that they will destroy my book?" I would have given anything for a ray of hope; for a hint that they "might not," after all.

"How could I know?" said Frau So-and-so; "Strange things happen."

"I also do not know," said H. E. "All I can say, from the little I have read of your manuscript, is that, if they do *not* destroy it, I shall believe that they are either completely mad or . . . about to revise their whole policy with regard to Germany."

Those frank words meant that more despair was probably in store for me. But they implied such an appreciation of my book that I was moved as one is when given unexpected praise. And I was all the more eager to see my precious writings saved.

Soon, Frau *Oberin* herself came and spent a few minutes with me. She too was upset—afraid.

"Do you realise that, through your extravagant lure of defiance, you have put us all in danger?" said she, sternly. "You seem to lack that sense of responsibility, so important, so essential, in a person with your ideals—otherwise, no doubt you would have been more careful. I had told you: do what you like, but don't involve *me*, don't involve others. And now it will be a miracle if I do not lose my job on account of you . . ."

I was sincerely, deeply sorry for all the trouble that I was causing, or that I should cause in the future, through the repercussions of that unfortunate search in my cell. But I could not help feeling that, not merely *to me*, but objectively—solely from the National Socialist standpoint—the impending destruction of my book was more tragic than the loss of anybody's job. I looked sadly at Frau *Oberin* and said: "Maybe, I was foolish. One always is, when one gets caught. Nevertheless, you will find a new job, if you lose this one. While I can never write my book anew, as it was. It is irreparably lost."

There was such distress in my voice that she spoke to me gently. She even seemed moved. Her face took on a thoughtful, sad expression. "*We have suffered many irreparable losses, we Germans,*" said she, slowly and quietly, as though speaking to herself.

I remembered that her own brother had been killed on one of the battlefields of the Russian front. And I felt small. Of those hundreds of thousands of young soldiers who had given their blood to Germany and to the Führer, was not each one irreplaceable, and immeasurably more precious than my book? Yet, joyfully, they had given their blood, their beautiful youth, for the Aryan ideals—my ideals—to prevail in the world. Who was I, to speak of my losses before their mothers, their wives, their sisters? The least I could do was to accept in silence and dignity the suffering imposed upon me by our common enemies; my little share of grief for the common cause.

But Frau *Oberin* spoke again: "It is not your book that seems to have stirred them to frantic wrath," she said; "it is the other things they found in your cell, especially the Führer's picture. That has made the Governor wild. And he blames me, naturally, for having allowed you to keep it . . ."

"I shall tell him that I kept it without your knowledge. Also that, whatever I wrote, I wrote without you suspecting it."

"I shall appreciate it if you say that," replied she, "although I wonder whether he will believe you. Anyhow: don't speak before you are questioned. And speak as little as possible. You have made a sufficient mess of everything. I don't suppose the Governor will see you before Friday, anyhow."

Before leaving my cell, she asked me whether I still had the little glass portrait that I used to wear around my neck. "Yes," said I; "it is the only thing I have left."

"Give it to me," said Frau *Oberin*. "I shall put it in safety for you—and give it back to you when I can. It would be another catastrophe if ever they searched your body again, and found *that!*"

"But they would not search me again?" reflected I.

"One never knows . . . It is better to forestall the possibility."

So I untied the string, and handed over to her the last treasure I had; the one Frau *Erste* had spared. I parted with it feeling confident that, in Frau *Oberin*'s hands, it was safer than in mine.

* * *

Evening came. I ate hardly anything of the supper that was brought to me. I lay upon my bed, too exhausted even to weep. But I thought of my lost manuscript all the time. However much I told myself that mine was a minor loss—a trifle not worth mentioning, compared with the death of so many thousands of faithful young men, killed for our cause—I could not raise myself above my grief. An unbearably oppressive feeling—something like that of a hand gripping me and squeezing me at the level of the waist—added physical torment to moral torture.

I watched the pattern that the setting Sun projected against the wall, move slowly towards the door, as it did every evening. I looked around my now empty cell, and remembered that, only twenty-four hours before, it was not empty; that, when the Sun had last set, there had still been here my precious manuscript, spread before me upon the bed, and the Führer's likeness, facing me upon the table . . . Where were those treasures, now? Again I started sobbing desperately at the thought of them. It seemed as though nothing could soothe me. I longed to be dead—not to feel; not to remember. "Oh, why, why wasn't I killed in '45 or '46, with so many others of us?" thought I.

But the clear, still, serene voice from within me again rose in answer and said: "Because you were not on the spot—which is your own fault. But also, perhaps, because it was the will of the Gods to keep you aside, for you to be useful in the second struggle for power, in a way they alone know."

"The second struggle for power!" thought I—and the very idea of it gave me, in spite of all, the desire to live. "The second struggle . . . Yes; it has already begun; and although a prisoner, I am already in it. But of what use am I, in the state I am in?"

"You will grow out of that state," said the serene inner voice; "even if they destroy all your writings, still you will grow out of it, and fight again; do your duty as an Aryan—as one of the few non-German Aryans of the world aware of the fact that National Socialism is *their* concern, no less than Germany's, and Hitler the natural Leader of the whole race."

I was thus thinking when I heard the noise of a key in the keyhole, and startled. For it was unusual; nobody ever came after six o'clock. But I was soon reassured: it was the *Oberwachtmeisterin*, Frau S. Her bag in hand, she was ready to go home. But although time was over, she had stepped in to see me on her way out.

"Frau S.!" exclaimed I, as a pathetic smile made my tired, swollen, face, in tears, look perhaps even more sorrowful. "Frau S.! It is so kind of you to have come! *You* will not scold me, will you?"

Frau S. had probably come with the intention of scolding me, just as Frau *Oberin* had. But she looked at my face, and was silent for a minute. Her scrutinising grey eyes discovered in me a distress that she had not imagined. "You have got us all into serious trouble," said she, however, at last. "What have you to say?"

"Nothing," replied I—"save that I was unfortunate enough to attract attention, and to undergo an unexpected search. It is not true that I have been distributing leaflets, here, among the other prisoners, as Frau *Erste* thinks. I did distribute a few in the beginning, admittedly, and then, only among the D wing ones. I never gave any to a single one of the ordinary criminals, save to a tall dark-haired woman called L., and that was weeks ago. And I did not leave the paper in her possession. She gave it back to me after copying it. Anyhow, she is now free. Since then, I have done no more propaganda among this lot. I cannot trust them. I have spoken of serious things to nobody but my two friends, who are reliable. And I have done nothing but write in silence."

"I remember that L.; she was a debased type of woman," remarked Frau S. sternly. "What inclined you to trust her?"

"She told me that she had been a member of the N.S.D.A.P."

"Everybody was in those days," replied Frau S. "That is no guarantee that she was a National Socialist, or that she is one now. You should have known that, being all these months in Germany. Or else, if you are incurably lacking in discrimination, you should not try to do dangerous work."

Tears again choked me. "I was perhaps wrong to show a copy of my leaflets to L.," said I; "I was certainly wrong. But don't scold me! They have taken my manuscript away and will surely destroy it. Is that not enough to punish me, if I failed?"

Frau S.'s expression softened. I pursued: "Believe me, it is not frustrated vanity that makes me cry over the loss of that book; it is not the idea that my prose will never come out in black and white, and be available in bookshops: that my style, my thought, etc. will not be appreciated. Oh, you don't know how little I care for all that! If my book were one day to be published under another name than mine, if another person were to be praised for it, I would not care, provided it had the right influence upon the minds and hearts of its readers; provided it helped to forward the Nazi cause. All I want, all I ever wanted, is to contribute to the success of the one Idea for which I have lived. I am crying over my book because it is the best thing I have produced for our cause; because it is my most valuable gift to Germany. I know—and this would remain true even if nobody knew that the book is mine—I know no foreigner has ever written about you, my Führer's people, the things I wrote in those pages. It is the first time . . ."

Again my mouth quivered and tears ran down my cheeks. Visibly moved, Frau S. took my hands in hers, and squeezed them with warm sympathy, while the clear, serene voice within me gently rectified the statement I had just made. "No," it said; "it is not true. Your most valuable gift to your Führer's people is not your book, but your love. You are the first foreigner who really loves them." It also told me: "Bear your loss and your suffering bravely, as a Nazi should. Remember the words of your comrade—and superior—Herr A. that you have quoted in the writing you will never see again: 'A National Socialist should have no weaknesses'."[10]

* * *

The long evening dragged on . . . I tried to sing some of our old songs to give myself strength. The magical words—and tunes—would indeed give me back for a while the strength, the pride, nay the aggressiveness that I so much needed. But at the same time, they would awaken in me the old unbearable sense of guilt for not having been in my place during the great days; for not having been killed in '45; and the sorrow for having lost, now, the one sole thing I had created entirely as a tribute to those whom I so admired.

Slowly the sky darkened; the stars appeared; night came.

I tried to ponder over the staggering distances that separated me from those mysterious suns in space; to detach myself from all that was of this earth. But somehow, I always came back to our planet.

Gazing at a bright green star that twinkled in the midst of so many others, I said to myself: "Those rays of light have perhaps travelled for years to meet my eye. For years, at the rate of 300,000 kilometres a second! How far away that makes the burning centre from which they emanate; and how small that makes the earth—my earth that bears all I love! A mere speck on the shores of limitless, fathomless space, my earth, with its wars, its religions, its songs! Still, it is only through this little earth that I can love that endless Universe. The marvel of this earth is not Pascal's sickly 'thinking' Christian, who despises the majestic Universe because he believes it less precious than his silly conceited self in the eyes of his all-too-human Yiddish god; no, the highest form of life on this planet is the healthy, handsome, fearless Aryan who follows his racial logic to the bitter end; the perfect National Socialist—the one creature who *collectively* and *consciously*, lives up to a cosmic philosophy that exceeds both himself and the earth, infinitely; a philosophy in which man's ties, man's happiness, man's life and death, man's individual 'soul' (if he has such a thing) do not count; in which nothing counts but the creation, maintenance, and triumph of the most dynamic and harmonious type of being: of a race of men indeed 'like unto the Gods'; of men

---

[10] Cf. *Gold in the Furnace*, 3rd ed., p. 232.—Ed.

in tune with the grandeur of starry space."

I knew that I had exalted that superhuman ideal, that proud, hard, logical, divine Nazi philosophy, in my book, and that my book was lost. I tried to tell myself: "What does it matter, since the doctrine is eternal? Since it is the true philosophy of Life, right through starry space, for aeons and aeons? Since, if that green star of which the radiance takes several light-years to reach us has living worlds revolving around it, the mission of those worlds is the same as that of ours: namely, through love and strife, to realise the Divine in the proud consciousness of superior races, or to perish?" And I remembered my challenge to the silly Democrats in Chapter 5 of my lost book: "You cannot 'de-Nazify' Nature!"[11] But still I wept.

I tried to sleep—to forget. And out of sheer exhaustion, I managed to fall into some sort of demi-somnolence in which, if not totally unconscious, I was at least relieved of the torture of thinking, of remembering, of regretting; of feeling powerless before the loss of what I considered to be the culmination of my life-long struggle for the Aryan ideal of life modelled on cosmic truth. I perhaps even slept—for half an hour or so. I do not know. But I suddenly rose out of my torpor. The horrid grip from within that I felt in my stomach, at the level of the waist, was so unbearable that it had thrown me back into consciousness. And my head was aching as if it had been hacked through the middle. A cold sweat oozed from my skin. And my teeth clattered with fever.

I sat up on my bed, on which I had thrown myself without taking the trouble to undress. Again I gazed at the distant starry sky. And I listened to the silence that surrounded me. Perfect silence; lovely, sweet silence. Oh, how well I would have slept, had it not been for my burning torment from within!

I remembered my home in Calcutta.

The starry sky was as beautiful there as here, as everywhere. And the intoxicating scent of jasmine flowers, and of the sticks of incense burning in the room before the only two pictures that adorned it, reached me as I softly went to sleep under the artificial breeze of the electric fan. Save for the next-door neighbour's radio, all was quiet enough for an hour or so. Then—how many times!—no sooner I had gone to sleep, music would begin in the *"bustee"*[12] downstairs (separated from our

---

[11] This sentence probably appeared in the manuscript of *Gold in the Furnace*, but it does not appear in the published edition, in Chapter 5 or anywhere else. The closest approximation, which does appear in Chapter 5, is: ". . . they could not de-Nazify the Gods" (*Gold in the Furnace*, 3rd ed., p. 61).—Ed.

[12] Hindi term for a slum, squatter camp, or shanty town.—Ed.

house by a mere wall) or in some courtyard across the road. Fifty people, a hundred people, or more, would start howling in cadence, to the deafening beating of drums, to the high-pitched sound of flutes, to the rattling of castanets. And I would awaken all of a sudden, and not be able to go to sleep again. All night, hour after hour, maddened with irritation, with fatigue, with a splitting headache, I would in vain wait and wait for the noise to subside. It usually kept on till the morning. Or else, reluctantly, I would get up after an hour or two, cross the sitting room, and knock at the door of my husband's room. *He* would be fast asleep, and would not hear me. I would finally walk in and awaken him. And the dialogue would be—more or less—the same every time:

"What is it?"

"The music again. They have started."

"A plague on them, and on you! Really, why couldn't you leave India in 1938, when I first told you to? Now, instead of making yourself a nuisance to me, every other night, you would be in Germany turning out bombs in some ammunition factory."

"Oh, how I wish I were!"

"So do I!"

"Aren't you going to the police, to try to have them stop this damned row?"

"I suppose I have to. But what a curse you are! Goodness only knows how I have done all I could to help you to get away from here. I gave you a British passport, that you might travel in spite of the war. For my sins in past lives, I could not give it to you in time, and I am, apparently, condemned to put up with you as long as the war lasts . . ."

Thus he grumbled—and who could blame him? But he would get up and dress and go down into the street, walk to the police station, and have the nuisance stopped. And I would at last rest, but generally remain awake for long hours after the disturbance.

Now, in Werl, I remembered those awful sleepless nights, as I breathed the fresh air and felt the restful silence all round me, being myself in the grip of anguish. I regretted them. "The sleeplessness due to those deafening drums, those castanets, and howling voices, was better than this agony," thought I. "Those headaches, due to noise alone, were better than this one!"

And I recalled one particular night of those on which, as always, I had got up to call my husband and beg him to go to the police. It was in early September 1944—a few weeks before I left Calcutta to wander for months so that I would not learn when the end would be. Our brave eastern Ally, Japan, that we had been helping with all our might, had just surrendered.[13] This time, my husband had answered as soon as I had knocked at his door: he was *not* asleep. Nor had he shown me his usual—and understandable—irritation, when I had told him that the noise "had started." He had merely switched on the light, and taken my hands in his, and looked intently into my eyes. "I know you suffer here," he had said; "but let me tell you, now—*now* that our work, our dreams, all we fought for, all we valued in the modern world, is about to collapse, nobody knows for how long—this suffering of yours is nothing. It is only physical. One day, soon—sooner than you expect—you will go back to your quiet Europe. There, you will no longer have to put up with drums and castanets, *but* . . . You will be persecuted for your dearest convictions—like the others; you will be hated, or mocked, for all that you stand for; forbidden to speak, forbidden to write in defence of your faith; forbidden to protest against the infliction of humiliation and pain upon those you admire the most; not killed, but much worse: crushed into dreary uselessness, provoked into powerless rage, despoiled of all means of expressing what you know to be true, of exalting publicly what you know to be great and valuable; laughed into 'harmlessness' by the victorious Democrats, your inferiors and mine. *Then* you will know what suffering is!"

Now, in my peaceful cell, torn and tortured as I was by the thought of the destruction of my manuscript, I thought—and not for the first time since my return to Europe—"How right, oh, how absolutely right he was!"

* * *

The following days were as horrible to me as the one I had just lived. I was not given any work to do; nor anything to read; nor—as can be expected—any pencil and paper, to write. I had absolutely nothing to do but to think. And my reflections, whatever they were, always brought me back to that one anguishing reality: the well-nigh certain destruction of the book in which I had put so much thought and so much love.

I tried to rise above my grief by bearing in mind words of strength—those of my comrade Herr A., in the shade of the sacred Harz those of other comrades of mine, or of the Führer himself—and by singing the Horst Wessel Song once a day or more. For a while, the spell worked its miracle, and turned into my old self, once more, the pitiable creature of

---

[13] Japan's final surrender was announced on 15 August 1945 and signed on 2 September, so Savitri must be referring to a much smaller reversal of Japanese fortunes, probably in the Burma Campaign, which she and Mr. Mukherji followed closely and aided to the best of their ability.—Ed.

despair that I had become. But then, again I would realise that "my most valuable gift to Germans" (as I had characterised my book before Frau S.) was lost forever. And again an anguish perhaps even worse than the *certitude* of despair would seize me by the waist. And I would sob till my eyes would ache as though they were being pulled out of their sockets.

I could neither eat nor sleep. I merely forced myself to nibble a little of the food that was brought to me by telling myself that I needed my health and strength to fight again one day; that, to let myself go would be, in a way, to betray our cause. But at last, I could pray. I knew I deserved no favour from the invisible Powers, but I felt that it was my right and even my duty to beg for understanding and for strength, nay, to appeal for the miracle that would save my book against all earthly possibilities, provided I did so not for my own relief, not for my own satisfaction, nor for my own exaltation; but solely with a view to forward the Nazi cause.

So I prayed.

First, I sat still, and directed my mind to "That Which is." "*From the things that appear, but that are not, to those that appear not, but that are.*" Those words came back to me. Long ago—in 1927—when I was still a student of philosophy at the Lyons University, another student, who was a Catholic and a pupil of the Catholic philosopher Blondel,[14] had once shown me a book in which Blondel had written them for her. They could have been *my* motto, although I was anything but a Catholic. And they expressed adequately the attitude of thousands of thoughtful Hindus whose outlook is as foreign to Christianity, if not as decidedly *anti*-Christian, as mine. I meditated upon those words.

"The visible, the tangible, the events of the world, are not without reality, as some say," thought I; "but their reality is that of a *consequence* hanging on to a cause—not that of a cause. The cause always lies in the invisible, in the intangible, in the events of the subtle world, of which few people know anything. Whoever can influence the unseen causes, can change the course of the consequences." And that thought soothed me.

I imagined Colonel Vickers reading my manuscript. I imagined other Englishmen of the Occupation services reading it—all notorious anti-Nazis, bitter enemies of all that I admire, men who could not but foam with rage at the perusal of my uncompromising statements, my sneers at "human rights" and "equality," my impeachment of the Democracies—and of the Allied Occupation—my cynical praise of violence in the service of the cause of truth. And I said to myself: "But they are all nothing but puppets in the hands of the invisible Powers. They will read of my

---

[14] Maurice Blondel (1861–1949)—Ed.

words only that which the Invisible will allow them to read; and they will grasp the meaning of it, only to the extent the Invisible permits. However clear be any sentence of mine, if the Invisible blinds them to its implications, they will be blinded." And that also soothed me, although I could not understand how such a thing could possibly happen.

Then, of all the "things that appear," I recalled the most majestic—the grandest sight I had seen in my life: beneath the starry sky streaked with northern lights, the burning and roaring Mountain, Hekla in eruption. And I evoked the mysterious Presence, the Power unseen and irresistible that I had hailed in its flames and lava, exactly two years before my trial. I remembered myself in the snow, in the wind, in the darkness, alone before that glory of fire, singing, in mystical rapture, in the easternmost modern Aryan tongue, the hymn to Shiva "Dancer of Destruction, O King of the Dance! . . ." and Hekla's subterranean roar answering my voice at regular intervals. The same awe-inspiring, still, implacable, resplendent Presence faced me *now*, I felt; unsuspected by others, the same Power radiated all round me, in the whole universe, and within me; to the same terrible Beauty, today, I lifted from the depth my aching eyes full of tears. And I was overwhelmed by such a sense of grandeur, that I forgot my grief in an act of adoration.

A cry sprang from me—or rather *through* me, from a greater self; a cry uniting me, over centuries of racial and religious apostasy, to my Aryan ancestors, worshippers of fire and conquerors of India: *"Aum, Rudrayam! Aum, Shivayam!"*

Twenty-one times—I know not why that number—I repeated those words as a sacred incantation, motionless, my spine straight, and my head erect. There was in me not the slightest intention to imitate the *"japa"* type of religious exercises of which I had heard in India.[15] I had never practised *"japa"* there, myself, and if my apparently strange gesture was influenced by the fact that I had lived there long years, I was certainly not conscious of it. No; I believe it was much more, as I said, the outcome of that particular Heathen piety of my own that had once driven me to India in search of a living equivalent of my old European Pagandom. It was not the cry of a modern European who, by living among Hindus, has become "Indianised," but that of an ancient Aryan from *before* the far-gone *Drang nach Osten* that carried to India the Sanskrit language and the cult of the Aryan Gods.

"Aum, Shivayam!"

---

[15] *"Japa"* is the Sanskrit term for a spiritual discipline involving the meditative repetition of a divine name or another *mantra.*—Ed.

I did not *pray*; I contemplated. I penetrated my self with the beauty of the cosmic play behind the intricacy of ephemeral appearances, visible consequences of the Dance of the Invisible.

"Lord of the unseen Forces," thought I, after I had finished repeating the holy syllables, "I ask Thee nothing. I know I deserve no favour. Moreover, Thou art mathematical Rhythm and merciless Artistry, not a personal god. Thou hast no favours to distribute. There are no exceptions to Thy everlasting laws. Only penetrate me with the awareness of Thy impersonal justice, let me understand Thy ways, and bear suffering with fortitude and dignity, if I have to suffer. Only make me a worthier follower of my Führer, in whom Thy spirit shines; a worthier and tougher supporter of our cause, which is Thine. Kill in me all vanity, all conceit. Help me to realise that I am but a tool in Thy hands—a tool that does not know *how* it is to be used the most efficiently, and that just obeys, day to day . . .

"Lord of the Dance of Life and Death, Lord of all things strong and true, Thou hast lived in the stately pageantry of our days of glory; in the processions, in the songs, in the frenzied collective joy of the Chosen Nation, intoxicated with its own vitality. Thou art that Vitality. Thou hast lived also. Thou livest now, in the grim endurance, in the silent, far-sighted determination of the men of iron, alone erect amidst the ruins of the Third Reich, faithful when the whole world is unfaithful; in those invincible ones whom I have exalted in my book. Thou art they. And Thou wilt live again in the grandeur of their second rising.

"Lord of the Unseen, of Whose Play all that is visible is but a reflected detail, help me to understand that, if the pages I wrote are sufficiently full of Thy dynamism to be of any use in the future, Thou wilt preserve them; that they will be destroyed only if, in the scales of Thy passionless justice, their preservation is of no import to our New Order—Thy divine Order on earth—in which case, I should not be sorry for their loss. Oh, kill in me that presumption that prompts me to overvalue what I have written. I really know not what it is worth. Thou alone knowest. Only help me to work with serenity and efficiency, firm, calm, wise, and loving; never for my own promotion, but solely for our cause, our truth—Thy Truth.

"Lord in Whose dynamic cult men of my race expressed themselves in time immemorial, and Whose worship they imposed upon people of strange races, only make me a worthier Aryan; a better National Socialist."

Thus I prayed. And for the first time, I felt a little peace descend into my heart. The clear, still voice from within, the voice of my better self, told me: "For once you are right: it is far more important to be a good National Socialist, than to write books in support of the National Socialist

Idea. What one is always comes before what one does. And if you are a good Nazi, you should not care what happens to *your* book, provided the cause triumphs. Indeed, if the book is destined to be of some use to the cause, be sure that the unseen Powers Who take care of the cause will also take care of it. You individual, don't worry. You don't count, except to serve the cause. Apart from the cause, *nothing* counts."

However, in spite of all, now and then, by day, by night, the grip of anguish would seize me again. I remembered the things I had written. Sentences came back to me with amazing vividness. And I suffered at the thought of the destruction of my work. The still, inner voice told me for the hundredth time: "There are far greater losses that other Nazis bore bravely. Think of the mothers of all the young warriors who died for your ideas. Think of Horst Wessel's mother. Aren't you ashamed to weep over your book?"

I *was* ashamed. Yet, I wept.

But once, I asked myself if there was nothing in the world for which I would, of my own accord, give up my book to be destroyed; nay, for which I would, stoically—if necessary—watch its pages curl up and disappear in the flames. And I answered the question immediately, in all sincerity, from the depth of my heart: "Yes, I surely would, if, at that price, I could save the life or buy the liberty of a single other National Socialist. Gladly I would! For however much I might love the creation of my brains, I love my Führer's living people much more."

And in a sort of day-dream I imagined how glad indeed I would be if Colonel Vickers told me that I could set free anyone I liked among my fellow prisoners, on condition that my book would be burnt. Naturally, I would choose H. E., thought I; and forget the loss of my irreplaceable written tribute of admiration to Nazi Germany, in the joy I would have to tell that fine German woman, four years captive on account of the zeal she displayed in the service of our faith: *"Meine H. . . . ! Sie sind frei!"*—and to see tears of happiness fill her large blue eyes; and to feel the pressure of her hands holding mine, in an enthusiastic farewell; to see and to hear her salute me on the threshold of freedom, for the last time before we would meet again in a free Germany: "Heil Hitler!"

I would willingly have undergone torture, or been killed, if that could have saved my book. I would do so, now, if it were necessary. Yet I say, in full sincerity: I would have sacrificed my book to free her—in fact, to free any other true follower of Adolf Hitler, man or woman. I would now, if it were possible. And I honestly wished, then, that such a bargain had been possible between myself and the authorities upon whose decision the fate of my manuscript depended.

After I realised that I actually wished it—strange as this might be, for the bargain was not likely to be proposed to me—I felt better. My gnawing anguish became a little less unbearable, although it did not leave me completely.

* * *

On Friday morning, the 3rd of June, Frau *Oberin* came to my cell.

"The Governor is coming today," said she. "If he calls you—as he probably will—be careful how you answer his questions. He was furious at the sight of the things found in your possession, and quite likely, there will be trouble. Already, your friend H. E. has been relieved of her post at the Infirmary. She will henceforth have to do the same hard work as the other prisoners, and she will be far less free than she was."

This was a new blow for me. "My H. . . . !" I sighed. "I love her so much, and yet *I* have brought this upon her!" And tears came to my eyes as I spoke.

"An intelligent enemy is often less dangerous than a sincere but foolish friend," said Frau *Oberin*. "Anyhow, be careful what you tell the Governor. Make no further mistakes, for heaven's sake! We all love you—the wardresses, Frau S., Fräulein S., the matron, and myself.

"We have done what we could to make your life here tolerable in spite of the Governor's orders. You don't want to harm us, now, in return, do you?"

"Never!" replied I, vehemently; "never! I'll take upon myself all the blame, rest assured. And none of you will lose her job through me. You'll see: stupid as I am, I am less of a fool than I look at first sight."

"You are not a fool," said Frau *Oberin* gently, with a smile so sad that I shuddered. "You are not a fool. But you have never experienced the constant terror under which we have been living since the Capitulation. You never had to hide your feelings, to lie, to crawl to those you hate, in order to remain alive. You have not been forced to pretend you hated all that you loved the most, in order to remain out of jail—hardly freer than those who are in, admittedly, yet, just sufficiently freer for it to be worthwhile, in the common interest."

I recalled the words of the first German woman I had met at Saarbrücken, in 1948: "*We* have learnt to hold our tongues. This is the land of fear."[16] I forgot my plight, and the threat of the Governor's wrath, only to think of those four hellish years, of which I had lived on the spot but the

---

[16] This phrase is something of a *Leitmotiv* in *Gold in the Furnace*. See *Gold in the Furnace*, 3rd ed., pp. xvii, 221, 228, 286.—Ed.

last and least hellish. "Poor dear Germany, my Führer's country!" said I, moved to the depth of my heart. "But I too have learnt something," I pursued, addressing Frau *Oberin* after a few seconds' pause. "For now, I too, shall lie—I who hate lies; and if it is necessary, I too shall silence my pride and crawl, like you have been forced to. I shall soon be like one of you."

Two hours later, I was called before the Governor.

Although there were other prisoners waiting for their turn in a row in the corridor, I was the first to be ushered into Frau *Oberin*'s office, where the Governor was seated. Apart from Frau *Oberin* herself, I saw Fräulein S. her assistant, and the matron, Frau R.—Frau *Erste*—all standing. The Governor was sitting before the desk, as when I had met him on the day after my trial. And Mr. Watts, looking much more important, and sterner, than when he had visited my cell, was seated next to him.

I stood before the Governor in silence. To my utter amazement, the first words he addressed to me had not the slightest connection with the search in my cell: "Mrs. Mukherji," said he, "your husband has appealed for your release. In the case of his petition receiving favourable consideration from the Commander-in-Chief of the British forces, do you agree to go back to India?"

For a second, I was dumbfounded. I felt as if I were dreaming. Then, in a flash, I thought of my home, and tears came to my eyes. Yet, underlying my emotion there was—as there always seems to be, with me, in moments of emergency—a definite, cool, calculating process of reasoning taking place; a process of which I was perfectly conscious.

"All I want is to go back—and never poke my nose into politics any more!" exclaimed I, gazing pitiably at Colonel Vickers; "to go back to my husband, to my household, to my cats—my big black one, especially; to hold in my arms once more that mass of thick, glossy, purring fur— my puss, my black tiger—and to forget my foolish adventures!"

I *said* that. The vivid remembrance of the beautiful feline stirred in me enough emotion to give my whole attitude an appearance of complete sincerity. Did Colonel Vickers really believe me? He alone knows. Things he told me only a few days later would tend to prove that he did not. But no one could accuse me of not having played my part well. None of my comrades, standing before the self-appointed "re-educators" of mankind could possibly have looked more "innocent"—and more soppy—than I before the British Governor of the prison of Werl, on that memorable occasion. But, at the very moment I was making that silly exhibition of myself, talking that nonsense about my black cat and pretending to be tired of the life I had chosen, I was thinking—calculating—

as clearly as ever: "Go back to India, why, it is probably the best solution, now that I shall no longer be able to see my friends of the D wing! I shall see my husband there, hear the news of Asia. Who, knows—I might be as useful there as in Europe, now that I shall be expelled from Germany anyhow. And then, I could of course print my book, if only they would give it back to me. I must now try my best to save it; say anything, to save it—anything that will not harm others of us. And if I cannot save it, well, still I shall continue fighting for the Cause."

The Governor simply said: "All right. I shall then forward your husband's petition." Then, coming to the point—starting the comments I dreaded—"Mrs. Mukherji," pursued he, "your behaviour has been a great disappointment to me. I had ordered both your person and your cell to be searched, hoping that facts would disprove certain rumours that had reached me. I have to admit that the result of the search has been most discouraging. We had treated you kindly; we had given you privileges that we do not give German prisoners. We had expected that, in return, you would begin to understand the value of our principles; that you would be 'reformed'; at least that you would feel some sort of gratitude towards us . . ."

"What a hope!" thought I. And I forced myself to bear sad things in mind, in order not to laugh.

"Instead of that," continued the Governor, "we find in your possession a picture of Hitler . . . and a book of awful songs of which the first one speaks of 'bombs on England'. All that will be burnt. Do you understand? Burnt. I can't allow you to keep, here in prison under my eyes, what is forbidden even to ordinary German civilians . . . Another thing: You have been meeting war criminals in your cell. That must stop. If I ever hear that you have again directly or indirectly come in touch with a single one of these women, I shall sack the whole prison staff . . ."

"It is not the fault of the staff," exclaimed I. "Do be kind enough to let me say so. It is my own fault. It is I who insisted on seeing one or two of these women. And I did not talk politics with them. I only wanted a little intelligent conversation. I found the other prisoners hopelessly dull."

"It is my business to judge whose fault it is," replied Colonel Vickers sternly. "And I blame the staff. I repeat: I shall sack the whole staff if I hear that you have again spoken a single word to any of the war criminals. One thing I cannot understand about you: in his petition, your husband states that you are a very kind-hearted person, fond of all animals, particularly cats. It seems you used to feed starving cats and dogs during the Bengal famine. How can you, then, wish to mix with women who have been sentenced for the most beastly crimes against humanity? Surely, a human being is worth more than a cat!"

"*That* again! That same old insufferable superstition concerning the two-legged mammal!" thought I.

Had I been free—or at least not dependent upon the Governor for the preservation of my precious manuscripts—I would have answered coldly, and sincerely, shrugging my shoulders: "Not necessarily. In my eyes, no anti-Nazi is worth a cat, or in fact any animal. For he (or she) is permanently dangerous while an animal is not; cannot be." But had I not said: "I shall lie"? I kept my word; at least. I avoided replying to the Governor's question. "The few D wing prisoners whom I have met, have done nothing 'beastly'," I simply stated.

13. "Bomben auf Engelland" from Savitri Devi's copy of
DAS NEUE SOLDATEN-LIEDERBUCH, vol. III, which she had with her in Werl

Colonel Vickers flared up—even at *that*. "They tell you so, naturally," exclaimed he. "But who has ever met a German who admits that he or she is a Nazi? You are the first person who, to my knowledge, openly calls herself one after 1945. I have been here longer than you, and I have never met another."

Had I been free, and my comrades too, and my books in safety, I would have replied: "Naturally, they were not going to tell *you*—you fool! I myself observed discretion, to some extent, before my arrest made

all pretences useless. In wartime, in India, I was supposed to be '*only
interested in cats*'. In London, after the war, I was supposed to be '*only
interested in King Akhnaton's solar cult*' which flourished thirty-three
hundred years ago." But as things stood, I put my words aside for after
Germany's liberation, and was silent.

The Governor pursued: "Anyhow, I have seen two wars, for both of
which Germany is responsible, and I have not come to discuss with you.
Your husband says that your state of health necessitates your release.
You will be examined by the British doctor as soon as possible. Have
you anything more to say?"

The opportunity had at last come to me to do *all* I could to save my
book.

"Yes," said I: "one thing only. Spare my manuscripts!" Tears—that
were not "crocodile's tears," this time—rolled down my cheeks. "I have
transgressed the rules of this prison by keeping in my cell the objects you
mentioned," pursued I; "I was wrong; and I am sorry. And although I had
kept those objects solely for the emotional value they might have in my
eyes, although I have never showed them to anybody nor tried to use
them in a spirit of propaganda, I do not plead for them to be spared. But I
beg you to spare my own writings. These might be of no value to anybody, but they are mine. They are like my children. I have put all my
heart in them. And moreover, they are not for publication."

"The manuscripts found in your cell are now in the hands of experts,"
said Colonel Vickers. "If they are of a subversive nature, they shall be
destroyed like the rest of your Nazi stuff. If not, you will have them back
when you are free—whenever that be . . ."

I felt my heart sink within my breast, and my knees give way under
me. No one knew, better than I, how "subversive" were, from a democratic point of view, my *Gold in the Furnace*, and even the first part of
The Lightning and the Sun. Yet I said: "If, in spite of all the dark ingratitude with which I have repaid your kindness to me, I can still ask you a
favour, then, oh, then, out of sheer pity, spare my writings, however
'subversive' they might be! I don't want to live if I cannot, one day, have
them back. As I said, I do not intend to publish them. In the first place—
if that argument can convince you—it is a fact that, in the present state of
affairs, they could do more harm than good to my own cause. For I have
shown from the first page to the last, as clearly as can be, that every
Christian Church, nay that Christianity itself, as it has come down to us,
is the natural enemy of National Socialism. Do you think I wish, now,
to enlighten those people still simple enough to imagine that they can
be both Nazis and Christians—people whose intelligence I might not

admire, but whom I consider useful in times like this? That alone should prove to you that I am sincere when I tell you that my book is not to be published—ever! I only want to keep it as a remembrance of one of the periods of my life the most intense, emotionally, if not the happiest."

Colonel Vickers gazed at me, the proud, defiant Nazi, in tears before him. I hated myself, in a way, for the exhibition I had just afforded him, and for the subtle tissue of lies—set around one central truth, artfully selected—that I had unfolded before him with such dramatic naturalness. Yet, I was *thinking* all the time: "What else *can* I do? *The cause alone counts.* Were I thus crawling before one of those contemptible Democrats so that one day *my* prose might get a chance to be praised, I would then be more contemptible than all of them rolled in one. But no; honestly, it is *not* my glory that I seek; it is merely my greatest possible usefulness. If I am lying, against my inclination, against my nature, I am doing so in the interest of the cause. Immortal Gods, help me to win! If my writings are destined to contribute to forward and to strengthen the true Nazi spirit, then, help me to save them—be it by lying; but otherwise not!"

After a minute's pause the Governor—who could not read my secret thoughts—said: "I repeat: at present, your writings are in the hands of experts. I shall have to consider the experts' opinion about them. But I give you my word—the word of an Englishman—that whatever be the experts' report, I shall not order the destruction of your books without calling you and giving you a chance to plead for them to be spared. And I shall take your arguments into account, along with other factors. You·can now go."

I thanked the Governor, bowed, and left the room.

A positive ray of hope now shone in the midst of my distress. All was not irretrievably lost, condemned beforehand. "I thank Thee, Lord of the unseen Forces!" thought I, as I walked back to my cell.

I then sat upon my bed and remembered my words to Frau *Oberin*: "I too, shall lie; I too, shall crawl."

And I recalled the atrocious months that had followed the Capitulation—the tragedy of the thousands of National Socialists who appeared as major or minor "war criminals" before the Allied military tribunals, amidst the still-smouldering ruins of nearly all the towns of the Third Reich. "Oh, my German comrades and superiors," thought I, "forgive me if, in the depth of my heart, I have occasionally criticised some of you for what seemed to me, through the reports of the papers, an attitude unworthy of men of our principles! Forgive me if I have sometimes considered as 'undignified' the attempt of some of you to save their useful lives at the cost of false declarations of 'repentance'! I have myself lied, today, to try to preserve my writings for our cause. Now I know what those of you who feigned apostasy must have suffered! My brothers, forgive me if I have sometimes been harsh in my judgments!"

* * *

The dreary afternoon seemed endless. Still nothing to do but to think. I thought intensely, and I prayed, keeping my mind constantly on the fact that I should do *all* I could to save my book, not with a view to my own possible glory, but in a spirit of detachment, in the sole interest of the Nazi cause; that *then only* was it my right, nay, my duty, to lie in order to try to save it; but that, if I failed—if the all-knowing Gods considered that my writings were not sufficiently beautiful, sufficiently eloquent for the Nazi cause to be benefited through their preservation—I should *not feel* sorry. The divine words of the Bhagavad-Gita, that had helped me, after my arrest, to bear with serenity the eventual loss of the three first chapters of my manuscript, came back to my memory, now, to sustain me in the case of the loss of twelve chapters: *"Taking as equal pleasure and pain, gain and loss, victory and defeat, gird thee for the battle;"* [17] *"thy business is with the action alone, never with its fruits. So let not the fruit of action be thy motive, nor be thou inactive."* [18] I thought, I *felt* intensely what I had so many times preached in defence of our ruthless methods of action: "Anything is permissible, nay, anything is commendable, when duty commands, *provided it is executed in a perfect spirit of detachment."*

In the evening, I was taken to the Infirmary to be examined by the British doctor.

I looked tired enough, ill enough, to impress any practitioner. However, now that, after so much anguish and such fervent prayer, I was beginning to surmount my grief, the lightning of defiance again appeared, occasionally, in my eyes. In spite of all, I was glad to feel that persecution could not crush me. "But," thought I, as I walked out of my cell, "I must show nothing of this to the doctor. I must look crushed; give him the impression that I have become a harmless fool. And I must, if I can, try to use the practitioner's influence in order to save my book; do, at least, my best, in that line; lie once more, crawl once more, if necessary. It is horrible, no doubt—for we are the last ones whose nature is to be supple. But expediency—the interest of the cause—before everything,

---

[17] The Bhagavad-Gita, II, verse 38.
[18] The Bhagavad-Gita, II, verse 47.

above everything! To save my book is *now* the best thing I can do for the National Socialist Idea. I must try my utmost to do it—at any cost; by any means; remain unshaken, serene, in case I fail, but, in the meantime, do *all* I can. And remember that this humiliation, our common humiliation, is not to last forever . . ."

One day, the Day of revenge will come;
One day, we shall be free . . .[19]

The words of the old Nazi song rang joyously in my heart as I walked along the empty corridor, by the side of the wardress on duty.

The doctor—a dark-haired man in uniform, with an insignificant, kind-looking face—was waiting for me, with Sister Maria, who had come back from her holiday. But H. E. was no longer at the Infirmary. For a second the thought of her moved me to tears. But I pulled myself together: "Try to save your book!" said I to myself; "save it to publish it, one day; to expose Germany's persecutors. It is the best you can do, now, for her, for all your comrades, for the cause."

I stood before the doctor, looking as miserable as I possibly could.

"Sit down," said he, gently.

I sat down. "You know that a petition has been sent from India for your release," pursued he. "It states that your health will soon give way, if you remain here. Indeed, you don't look well. Tell me exactly what is your trouble."

"Oh, it is nothing physical," replied I, in a low, tired voice. "It is worry and weariness more than anything else. But *that* pulls me down, physically, too. I am given enough to eat, no doubt. But my life is a torment since I cannot say a word to my comrades, since I cannot even see them. I did not particularly want to talk politics. I just wanted to talk intelligently. The other ones, the ordinary criminals, are too hopelessly dull for me not to feel depressed in their company. I cannot understand why the Governor forbids me to talk with the only ones I love here, reducing my condition practically to solitary confinement. I am miserable, now; utterly miserable."

"Whom do you mean by the only ones you love here?" asked the man.

"My comrades; those whom you people call 'war criminals'," replied I.

"And why do you love them?"

"Because they are fine characters—those whom I have met at least. I don't care what they might have done."

---

[19] "Einst kommt der Tag der Rache, einmal da werden wir frei . . ." [From "Brüder in Zechen und Gruben" ("Brothers in the Pits and Mines")—Ed.]

14. "Just like her, scribble, scribble in complete obliviousness of all discomfort!"—Muriel Gantry on this photo, which she took of Savitri near Lyons, in the autumn of 1950, shortly after Savitri finished the first draft of DEFIANCE. Savitri may be revising the manuscript of this very book. (Courtesy of Beryl Cheetham. The quote is from Muriel Gantry's letter to Beryl Cheetham dated 20 December 1985.)

"But you *should* care," said the doctor. (How I hate that word that comes back, again and again, in the talk of every Democrat with any one of us! Who are they, anyhow, to tell us what we *should* do?) "You should," pursued he; "they have committed crimes against humanity."

That very expression made my blood boil. I felt I could not contain myself for long, so that the only way I could get out of the discussion without any damage to my writings—in favour of which I was contemplating to ask the doctor to intervene—was to give vent, without restraint, to that particular life-centred logic that had always been mine and that had always won me the reputation of an "eccentric" person in the eyes of the "decent" folk. In fact, the more I would let myself go along that line, the more the doctor—doubtless a "decent" man—would be convinced that such a "crank" as I could not be dangerous. I thus answered, boldly and sincerely:

"I do not love humanity. And nobody can force me to love it. I love superior mankind, no doubt—the only men and women worthy of the name. And I love life—beautiful, innocent life; life in creatures that, I know, can never be *against* anything I stand for; in creatures with which I feel at peace. Well, as long as people find it normal for there to be slaughterhouses and vivisection chambers, I simply refuse to protest against any atrocities performed upon human beings, whether it be by us or by you, by the Chinese, or by the Carthaginians, or by Assurnasirpal, king of Assyria (884–859 B.C., as far as I remember), who is, they say, one of the historic figures the hardest to beat on that ground. I know too much about the horrors that take place every day, in the name of scientific research, in the laboratories of most countries whose 'public opinion' strongly condemns our concentration camps and our gas chambers. In my eyes, the public who dares to censure us while tolerating such horrors upon creatures which are neither the actual nor the potential enemies of any régime, deserves the atom bomb, or anything worse, if there be. And if people think that such horrors must take place 'for the progress of science', then, I say, perform them by all means upon dangerous or deficient human beings—human beings who cannot otherwise be made use of, and who, in my eyes, are anything but 'sacred', anything but lovable, while all beasts, save parasites, are lovable to some extent. I do not consider as criminals the doctors who might have experimented upon such human beings, before 1945, and whom your courts condemned. I say they did the right thing—precisely the thing that *I* used to uphold, years before our régime came to power."

I had, until now, spoken in perfect earnestness and sincerity. It was good policy. For generally, people who have the same views as I about "dangerous or deficient" human beings, are not in a hurry to exhibit them. No doubt, thought the doctor, only a half-mad person could *have* such views consistently. But a person who also *said* she had them, as frankly as I did, was surely incapable of dissimulation. One could therefore trust her to be sincere when she spoke of other things. Knowing this I began to lie deliberately, continuing, however, as cleverly as I could, to mix my lies with a certain amount of truth.

"You have strange reactions," said the doctor, in conclusion to my tirade.

"I have the reactions that are within the logic of *my* nature," replied I. "And you people who believe in the right of the individual to express himself as long as he is not a danger to other individuals, should not object to my frankness. We are not in power, now; so I can harm nobody. Moreover, the little activity I had has come to an end, and I only told you all this in answer to your question about my attitude to so-called 'war crimes'."

"But you can begin again, once free," remarked the doctor.

"I don't wish to begin again," said I. "I am tired of all activity of that sort. All I want, as I told the Governor, is to go back to India and see my cats again; I would like to busy myself, henceforth, with animal welfare—my only alternative to boredom, I suppose, as I don't love human beings except when they share my ideals."

"You can do that, and *also* carry on your former activities," pointed out the man, who, however much he might have found me "eccentric," was less simple than I had thought.

"India is not the place for Nazi propaganda," said I.

"You can write books anywhere," replied he.

Didn't I know it! Did I not intend to finish the book I was writing, if only, by some miracle, they would give it back to me! Did I not intend to write other books—as long as I could do nothing more substantial for the cause! "Oh, to be free, and to do that, indeed!" thought I, in a flash. But I deliberately bore in mind my present plight and started weeping—just as an actress would, I suppose, remember on the stage some personal grief in order to shed natural tears in her role.

"I might write books, but they will not be about politics; *that* is finished," sobbed I; "I am sick of politics! No doubt, I will keep my convictions. Were they to tell me that I have to stay here for life unless I sign a paper stating that I am no longer a Nazi, I would remain here, and never deny my faith. So, you see, I am not trying to pretend that my outlook has changed. But, while adhering as much as ever to my Ideology, I have decided never again to take an active part in its service; never again to lecture about it, let alone to write books or articles."

"That is all the authorities desire of you," said the doctor—who seemed to me to have been sent to examine my state of mind more than anything else. "We don't care what people are. Each one is free to think what he pleases. We are interested only in what people do."

I could not help thinking: "What fools you are! *We*—and our real enemies, the Communists—know that one cannot be this or that sincerely without doing anything for one's ideals, sooner or later." But naturally, I kept this remark to myself.

"When I am home once more," I pursued, "all I want is the right to speak freely to my husband, the one man in India who understands me."

"Do you remember the doctor who examined you before your trial?" asked the practitioner.

"The mental doctor? A short, thin, red-haired man? I remember him very well."

"I see you have a good memory. Do you remember the things you told him?"

"I do," replied I. "But now, I am not the same person. Prison life has changed me; not changed my outlook on life, of course (I told you; nothing can change that) but changed my estimation of my own capacity. I am now convinced that I am unfit for such activities as I have indulged in."

"Why, unfit?"

"Because I lack the capacity of lying, which is essential," said I. "Also because I am too passionate about my ideas. My love for our principles and our system blinds me to many realities. And without realism, one is useless. You mentioned writing books. Any book I would write would resemble the one I was just now writing, the one over the loss of which I am crying day and night. It would be sentimental rubbish."

"Why do you cry over the loss of your book if you yourself believe it to be nothing but sentimental rubbish?" asked the doctor.

"Because I love it," said I; "it is my creation, my child—the only sort of child I'll ever have. I don't want it to be destroyed. Not that I want to publish it. I have told the Governor already that I shall never try to. But I want to keep it as my best remembrance of the fullest days of my life; of the time I was active, the time I was alive. I want to read passages out of it, now and then, to my husband, while he smokes his water-pipe. The dread of its possible destruction has thrown me into the state in which you see me. I can now neither eat nor sleep. I think of my book all the time. And if they release me without giving it back to me, I know I shall just go on pining for it until I am dead. Or else . . . if I succeed in gathering the strength to pull myself together again . . ."

"Well, what would you do if you had the strength to pull yourself together again, in supposing your manuscript were destroyed?" asked the man.

"I would," answered I, "throw myself into active life once more, feverishly, wildly, with the determination of despair, this time, not for any Ideology, but out of hatred for those who destroyed my work. They happen to be Democrats; all right. I would offer my services to anybody—to the Communists whom I hate—in order to harm the Democracies by every means. Hatred would become the sole law of my life, vengeance its only goal. I would harm living men and their children, to avenge the child of my brains and of my heart."

All the time I was saying this I was secretly thinking: "As if I shall not live to avenge National Socialist Germany *anyhow!* As if—even if you *do*, by miracle, give me back my precious book—I shall not live to destroy you, and the Reds, *anyhow!* As if I can do anything but what I consider to be my duty as an Aryan, *anyhow!*" But I said nothing more; and made a conscious effort not to smile.

"I shall tell the Governor that I believe he can safely give you back your manuscript," said the doctor; "That, in the interest of your mental and physical health, he should give it back to you. I shall stress in my report your change of mind, your resolution to keep away from politics forever, and do what I can to give you what I am now convinced would be a harmless personal satisfaction."

"Oh, do!" exclaimed I, with genuine tears in my eyes, hardly able to believe the words I was hearing. "If you do that, and if they listen to you and give me back my writings intact, I shall be compelled to admit how much more generous you western Democrats are, compared with the Reds. I shall miss no opportunity to say so. And I shall feel somewhat bound to do no harm to you, by word or deed, whatever be my convictions."

I thought to myself: "As if *I* believed that one of us is ever bound to be grateful to the enemies of our faith, whatever they might do!"

But the doctor could not read my thoughts; nor was he perspicacious enough to realise how shockingly out of keeping my whole talk was with those very convictions of mine that I did not deny. On the other hand, I took advantage of the eventual impression my speech had produced to put forward a new demand. "There is something else I would like to tell you," said I to the doctor. "The Governor has told me this morning that the picture of the Führer that they found in my cell would certainly be burnt. Do ask him to spare *that* also! I want to take it with me, if I am to be released."

"Why do you want to take it with you?"

"Because I love it," said I. "It has followed me in all my journeys. I have wept, looking at it, in the horrid days—1945, 1946, 1947; your days of victory. I want it also because the Man it represents means everything to me, whatever other people might think or say or write about him."

"What does he mean to you, exactly?" asked the doctor.

I quoted the words I had written upon the first page of my manuscript of *The Lightning and the Sun*—the work that I did not expect to finish quickly and that I had in advance, dedicated to him:

"The god-like Individual of my time," said I, "the Man against Time; the greatest European of all times, both Sun and Lightning."[20]

The words, which reminded me of the loss of *that* manuscript also, were enough to make me cry. They were also enough to give the doctor (who looked upon our Hitler in quite a different light) the impression that I was an unbalanced but harmless woman—the impression that I precisely wanted him to gather.

"Of course," added I—to confirm that impression—"I could get another picture. In fact I have a better one, in India. But it would not be the same, that I took about with me all these years. I want this one."

"I'll tell the Governor," said the practitioner.

"Do!" begged I.

"And now, let us see your weight," concluded he; "for I have to examine you physically as well as otherwise. When were you weighed last?"

"Hardly more than a week ago," replied I. "I weighed fifty kilogrammes—the same as ever since I have been here."

I undressed; was weighed again. "Forty-nine kilogrammes," said Sister Maria, reading the spot where the needle stopped. I had lost a kilogramme in five days—a definite sign that my health was giving way.

"Don't fall into despair on account of your manuscripts," said the doctor as he took leave of me. "Force yourself to eat; keep up your strength. I know you are practically in solitary confinement, which is hard on you. Still, try to keep up your strength. Goodbye—and good luck!"

"Goodbye," said I; "and thank you!"

On that night, for the first time since my cell had been searched, I managed to sleep a little.

---

[20] The dedication of the printed version of *The Lightning and the Sun* reads: "To the god-like Individual of our times; the Man against Time; the greatest European of all times; both Sun and Lightning: Adolf Hitler, as a tribute of unfailing love and loyalty, for ever and ever."—Ed.

* * *

On the following day, which was Saturday, I told the Dutch woman with whom I used to walk around the courtyard during the "free hour," the story of my interview with the British doctor. I trusted the woman to some extent.

"You have acted well," said she. "You'll see: you will save your book."

"I have done my best," replied I, "my utter best; and indeed, I do not think I could have lied with a greater appearance of sincerity, or picked out and stressed more artfully the points on which I was sincere, or spoken with more convincing naturalness, whether lying or telling the truth. The heavenly Powers helped me to act, in the interest of our cause, which is divine. I could never have done it alone. The heavenly Powers will save my manuscripts, if they care to. I can do nothing. I cannot even understand how certain things which I wrote as plainly as plain can be, can escape the notice of the Governor or of whoever else reads the book. Do you know, for instance, what I wrote, at the end of my seventh chapter, as a comment upon the fact that these people sentenced me to three years' imprisonment only, while the Communists would probably have sent me to Siberia for the rest of my life? Do you know how I thanked those hypocritical 'humanitarians' for their leniency? 'One day', wrote I, 'with the help of all the Gods—I hope—we shall see to it that the Democrats and even the Communists bitterly regret not having killed more of us.'[21] Now, what if they read *that*?"

"Don't worry," said the Dutch woman. "Don't you know these people? They are not out here to serve an Ideology, like you. They have no such a thing. They are here to receive a fat pay, and to have a good time. The man who will read that, and other such sentences of yours—if he takes the trouble at all—will quite possibly be thinking about the girlfriend whom he expects to meet at the restaurant, or about the cocktail party he is doing to attend at some other officer's house. He will skip over your book for the simple reason that the perusal of it would be to him a regular *corvée*."

"If *I* were in control of some occupied land under our New Order, and were given to read the manuscript of some anti-Nazi underground worker as radical, as violent, and as sincere as myself, goodness me! *I* would not skip over a word of it, with the result that the anti-Nazi would be 'liquidated' at my request even before I had finished reading the first chapter! I would appreciate his literary qualities—if any—and consider him all

---

[21] *Gold in the Furnace*, ch. 7 [3rd ed., p. 122—Ed.].

the more dangerous for possessing them. But, of course, as I once told a comrade, 'these people are not *we*'. They can never react as we would."

"You will benefit by this difference in psychology," said the woman.

"If I benefit by anything, it will be through the exceptional favour of the invisible Powers," replied I. "I don't deserve it. But National Socialism does, Germany does, Aryandom does. Perhaps, if my book can one day be of any use . . . it may be spared in spite of all. I don't know. I do not dare hope. I try to keep my mind detached; to do all I possibly can to save my manuscripts at any cost—by acting, by lying, if it be necessary—and not to care whether they are saved or not. I try to keep this attitude, but I cannot. I do care. I cannot help caring. I could sacrifice my writings joyfully only if I knew that, thereby, I would benefit the cause."

"Try to think of nothing. Come this evening to the recreation room to hear a little music," said the Dutch woman.

"I shall," replied I.

* * *

It was the first time I set foot in the recreation room since the 8th of April. I remained by the Dutch woman, and did not relate a word of my story to the other prisoners, some of whom greeted me coldly, others amiably. Naturally, I did not meet the collection of anti-Nazis, former inmates of Ravensbrück and other camps, that I had seen two months before. They were B wing prisoners. And I was now in the A wing. But I came across others—just as bad—whom the Dutch woman pointed out to me saying: "You see that one with bobbed hair, sitting in the corner? Well, she was six years in a concentration camp. So was the one at her side, they say. As for those three talking together at the other end of the room, the dark-haired one was four years in such a place, the other two three, I was told. The short one is a Czech." It sounded to me as if the three quarters of the ordinary criminals were former inmates of concentration camps—which did not astonish me in the least. I carefully avoided all contact with them.

Music started playing on the wireless—a joyous, invigorating dance tune, well-rhythmed like a march. It reminded me of an orchestra in a luxury restaurant; of lively discussions around well-set tables; of freedom under the best conditions—like before the war, or during the two first years of the war. I smiled.

"You see, you like it," said the Dutch woman. "Wasn't I right to tell you to come? It is better than to remain brooding in your cell."

"Do you know what I am thinking of?" asked I.

"No. How could I guess?"

"Well, I am thinking of the next war. I am imagining how delighted I will be to be sitting in some luxurious festive hall, in South America or somewhere else, and to know that the Judeo-Christian world, that corrupt capitalistic world that rose to crush out beautiful New Order is crumbling to pieces, along with its ex-ally in the East; that their capitals are in flames; that our Day, at last, is dawning! Yes, even if these people, now, destroy all my books, still I will forget it all in my joy, when *that* day comes; still, full of enthusiasm, full of inspiration, rejuvenated, I will discuss, I will gloat—and dance, if I find a partner who hates them as much as I do—while picturing to myself their last hours; the last convulsions of the dying civilisation I loathe, before our Sunrise!"

The radio had decidedly put me in a good mood. "You see," pursued I, glad to speak, after that week of silence, glad to give vent to the old aggressiveness that I had nearly forgotten in my anguish about my book; "you see, when they hear music like this, some think of love. I think of war; of the divine revenge. But do you know what would be ideal? Love *and* war. In old Babylonia they worshipped Ishtar-Zarpanit, the morning Star, goddess of war and manly works in the daytime, goddess of love, at night. That conception has always fascinated me. And although I have lived only one side of the double ideal, in this present life, I dream of living both, next time—if there be a 'next time'; a new birth on this earth after each life, as the Hindus believe."

Those words, which might have seemed insane to many people, did not even seem strange to the Dutch woman, who was a firm believer in the dogma of reincarnation. And although I am, personally, anything but *sure* of my soul's destiny after death; although the theory of reincarnation is to me, at the most, a theory—a hypothesis, a possibility among many others—I smiled in anticipation of my "next birth," somewhere in the new National Socialist Europe of my dreams. "All but a fairytale, perhaps," thought I; "but at least, a beautiful one." The music continued to play. And I let my imagination run riot.

"According to my horoscope, cast in India," said I, I am to die at the age of seventy-seven.[22] Assuming that I shall at once get reborn, if rebirth there be, that would mean that, in fifty years' time, I shall be sixteen . . . Sixteen!—I never could understand why the Hindus whose views are so varied and conflicting on so many points, all seem to agree in their desire *not* to get reborn if they can help it. All their religious discipline is aimed at that. While I would like nothing better than to get reborn; to be

---

[22] Savitri Devi, born on 30 September 1905, died on 22 October 1982, less than a month after her 77th birthday.—Ed.

sixteen once more, to be twenty, under the New Order, then solidly established: to look back to these days that we are now living as to a heroic beginning, never having known, personally, anything else but the régime I am today fighting for; and to fulfil myself, this time on all planes, in beauty, in strength, in health: the mate of a youthful warrior devoted to our ideals, and the mother of living demigods . . ."

I suddenly stopped in my outpour of eloquence. I remembered the mental agony I had lived, in and after 1945; my remorse at the thought of my old omissions; my present anguish on account of my lost manuscript. Tears came to my eyes. "The Hindus say that every one of our lives is the consequence of our whole past," remarked I. "Am I now suffering so that I might deserve that glorious future? And in order to deserve it more completely, am I to be told, in a few days' time, that my precious book, my gift to my Führer's people, will be destroyed?"

"Perhaps," said the Dutch woman, "and perhaps not. You know anyhow that, in the invisible, nothing is ever lost."

The door was opened. The wardress on duty told us that time was up. I walked back to my cell.

Again, I started thinking about my manuscript, while the clear, still voice within me, the voice of my better self, told me once more: "Don't worry; your real gift to your Führer's people and to the everlasting Aryan Idea is your love, your dedicated life—all your coming lives, if such there be, and if you so wish . . ."

I lay upon my bed and gazed at the limpid sky, so pure, so bright, so mysteriously transparent, in which the Sun would not set for another three hours. And I thought of an endless series of increasingly beautiful, dedicated lives of struggle and of creation, all in the service of the truth embodied in the holy Swastika, sign of the Sun, sign of National Socialism, sign of the regenerate, conquering, god-like Aryan Race. And I prayed with all the fervour of my heart that such should be my history, from now onwards, in centuries to come, if, contrarily to what many believe, death be not a full stop. "Immortal Gods," thought I, "help me anyhow to deserve such a history, now, in this life—whatever be the laws of life and death, which I do not know."

Chapter 12

THE WAY OF ABSOLUTE DETACHMENT

On the next day, Sunday, the 5th of June, I remained in bed.

I was wide-awake—I had hardly slept. And I was not tired. But having nothing to do, nothing to read, I did not feel urged to get up. So there I lay thinking, as always, about my lost manuscript; hoping, for a while that they would not destroy it, and then, refusing to hope; not daring to hope; and dreaming of the days when all these and worse memories of the long persecution would appear to me, and to us all, as a nightmare forever ended.

As every Sunday, in the corridor of the D wing, at the corner of the A wing, the church services were taking place: first the Catholic; then the Evangelical. From my cell, I could hear the other prisoners singing hymns. And again I was shocked, as I always had been from the beginning—I who, consistently, had never attended those services—at the thought of my true comrades of the D wing singing Christian hymns and listening to sermons about the adventures of some Jews two thousand years ago or more, in illustration of so-called virtues, most of which utterly foreign to our ideals. The explanation that H. E. had once given me, namely that the few real National Socialists of the D wing like herself attended the church services out of sheer boredom, did not satisfy me. I could understand how one of us could put up a show in the interest of the cause, but not just out of "boredom." Or did these women want to give the authorities the impression that they were "reformed," or at least reformable, so as to he released, if possible, a little sooner? *That* was perhaps the reason why they went through the church farce with such stupendous regularity. And H. E. had not wished to tell me, lest I might, within my heart, censure such opportunism. Yet, I would have preferred to see a woman like her attend church services for a definite practical reason of that nature, rather than out of boredom . . .

I heard a noise in the keyhole, and turned my head towards the door. To my delight, it was Frau S.

"In bed still, our vanguard fighter?"[1] said she, considering me with a kind, although somewhat ironical smile.

I made a move to get up. "No, no; stay in," insisted Frau S., "I was

---

[1] "Unsere Vorkämpferin."

only teasing you. I know you need rest. I have brought you . . . a cup of real coffee . . ."

I gazed at her intently. I was moved, happy. Tears filled my eyes. "Even if they do send me back to India, as they say, I shall not stay there forever," said I. "One day, when I come back, when everything is in order, shall meet you again. It will then be sweet to remember the times of persecution." I spoke with enthusiasm, as though I could visualise the staggering future of our dreams through the mist of the depressing present.

"In the meantime, drink your coffee," said Frau S., "or it will get cold."

I sat up and sipped the hot, strong, sweet, lovely coffee, while Frau S., after pulling the door behind her, seated herself upon the stool, near my bed.

"What did the Governor tell you, the day before yesterday?" she asked me, after a silence. "And what did you tell him?"

"He promised me he would not have my manuscript destroyed before seeing me and giving me a chance to defend it," replied I; "and I begged him to let me keep it merely as a remembrance of my life in jail. I told him that I do not intend ever to publish it . . ."

A mischievous smile brightened Frau S.'s stern, energetic face. I looked at her enquiringly. And she answered the question which I had not explicitly put to her, but that she had guessed. "No need to ask me *why* I am smiling," said she: "You know it well enough."

"I don't; I really don't," replied I. I loved Frau S. But somehow, I was not willing to disclose my secret thoughts, even to her. I was so afraid that the slightest indiscretion of mine would destroy, in the invisible, the effect of my studied lies, that I kept on lying, to her also. I even tried myself to believe what I had told the Governor, knowing that, in the invisible, belief as such has a potency, even if it be the belief in a lie. I wanted Frau S.'s belief—and my own, if that were possible—to strengthen that of the Governor, in some mysterious way, and thus to influence his decision in favour of my book. I was afraid that the truth, once I expressed it, even once I admitted it to myself, would, somehow, in the invisible, destroy that belief. So I added: "I meant it when I told the Governor that I did not wish to publish my book about Germany."

But Frau S. saw through me. She smiled more mischievously than ever.

"I don't know whether the Governor will believe you," said she; "but *I* certainly don't. Assuming he gives you back your manuscript, you might not publish it at once, for that would be downright impossible. But you *will* publish it as soon as you can—as soon as you know it is possible to do so without endangering any of us. I know you will, because I know you."

"Do you think you know me enough to be able to tell when I lie and when I speak the truth?" asked I.

"I can guess your natural reluctance to lies," replied Frau S. "But I know, also, that you are a genuine Nazi. That is enough. In the interest of the cause, you are capable of anything. You have proved it, now, once more."

She had analysed me well. I felt a gush of pride and joy swell my breast. Had I, during the great days, in front of everybody, been given a decoration *"für treue Dienst,"* I could not have been happier. "Frau S.," exclaimed I, "you have explicitly conferred unto me the highest title of glory to which a twentieth-century Aryan can aspire. May I never cease to deserve it!"

I paused for a minute, to think, to feel all that her words meant to me. "Whether they destroy my writings or not," reflected I, "may my life remain in true, unrecorded history, the first living tribute of allegiance of the outer Aryan world to the Führer, the Saviour of the Race, and to his predestined Nation! Oh, I am happy! Whether I be remembered or forgotten, I want these words: *echte Nationalsozialistin*, to remain true of me, forever and ever . . ."

Frau S. smiled at me once more. "I have not paid you a false compliment," said she. "I simply told you what I know. You might deceive these people. You cannot deceive me."

"I don't really want to," said I, smiling in my turn. And I added, handing back to her the cup that I had just emptied: "I thank you for the coffee. It was lovely!"

"I'll bring you some more this afternoon."

"There is one thing I would like you to bring me—if you can," said I; "that is to say, if they have given it back to you . . ."

"What?"

"That book, *Menschen-Schönheit*, that you lent me before they searched my cell. I have nothing to do, nothing to read: and I love that book."

"They have given it back to me," replied Frau S. "You shall have it." And in fact, she went and fetched it for me before taking leave of me.

* * *

Thus, after washing and dressing, I once more admired those pictures of German youths and maidens, mothers and children, of the days of pride and prosperity, as perfect as the masterpieces in stone or colour of which the editor had placed the photographs on the opposite pages. And once more I felt, in contemplating them, "*That* is what I have been longing for, all my life; *that*, the beauty of the perfect Aryan!"

There was not a word of "politics" in the whole book. There was no need to be. The pictures alone proclaimed, more forcefully than all possible comments, the eternal glory of the National Socialist régime. For what justifies a régime, if not the quality of the human élite of which it forwards the growth and the domination?

15. Illustrations from page 73 of MENSCHEN-SCHÖNHEIT

I looked at the photograph of a blonde adolescent, with regular, thoughtful, manly features, and an athletic body, leaning against a stone parapet. On the same page, was the picture of a young German warrior, taken from a Roman bas relief: the same face as that of the modern Hitler Youth—glaring proof of the sacred continuity of blood, from the soldiers of Hermann whom the Romans dreaded, to the companions of Horst Wessel. On another page were two beautiful young men of the purest North German type, wielding the bow; opposite, an ancient Greek bowman, exactly like them—glaring proof of the unity of the Aryan race in its original purity.[2] I recalled in my mind a sentence of my lost book—

---

[2] Savitri Devi was evidently writing from memory. The young man she describes is

the explanation of my whole admiring attitude to the Hitler régime; the expression of the fact that I found in it the perfect answer to my life-long quest of all-round beauty in living mankind: "I know nothing, in the modern world, as beautiful as the Nazi youth."[3] Beautiful, not only physically, but in character, also; the embodiment of those great Aryan virtues which alone can lift the natural élite of men to supermanhood. And for the millionth time, I thought: "Glory to the Man, glory to the régime who out of the enslaved Germany of the early 'nineteen-twenties', has brought forth that!"

16. Illustration from page 26 of MENSCHEN-SCHÖNHEIT

I also thought and that, too, for the millionth time: "For the establishment, the maintenance, the defence of such a régime, anything is permissible, nay, anything is commendable, contrarily to that which the believers in the 'equal rights of man' preach from morning to night in the interest of the human parasites who thrive on the corruption and degeneracy of their betters." How I had always hated that type of preaching! How I had, from my childhood, always opposed my morality to that of the upholders of I know not what mysterious "dignity of the human

---

slightly older and more mature than the one in the photograph; the Roman image is a bronze sculpture, not a bas relief; and the image of the archers is not matched with an Ancient Greek sculpture, although the book contains a number of such pairings.—Ed.

[3] *Gold in the Furnace*, 3rd ed., p. 97.—Ed.

person" of which I failed to see any evidence in real life, and which I refused to admit as a dogma.

I remembered how, when I was twelve, the teacher in the French school where I used to go had once made me stand for a whole hour in the corner, my face to the wall, as a punishment for having declared openly that the so-called "ideals" of the French Revolution disgusted me. And how, another time in the same school, I had been punished for sticking out my tongue at the plaster bust of the French Republic that stood in the corridor—the symbol of all I hated—and how I had cared little for the punishment, so glad I was to feel that I had insulted and defied the detested symbol. And how I reacted to the poems of Victor Hugo, whom I was told I "must" admire, but whose idiotic equalitarian sentimentalism and belief in "progress" through learning alone, merely succeeded in irritating me beyond bearing, and in setting me fanatically, and definitely, against all silly morality centred around "man" as such—that morality which all expected me to accept as a matter of course.

I did not know, then, that this thoroughly Pagan, thoroughly Aryan scale of values which already rendered me so unpopular, would become, in a few years' time, thanks to the makers of the Nazi régime, the scale of values of a new civilisation. Now, I knew that the new civilisation would impose itself in the long run and that, along with my German comrades and a few other non-German Aryans like myself, I was already a part and parcel of it.

It was, no doubt, in a way, "new," thought I. But it was also not new. It was, as the Führer had himself said, "in harmony with the original meaning of things"[4]—eternal. It aimed at stemming the physical and moral decay of modern, technically "advanced" humanity by forcing it— by forcing its racial élite, at least—to live in accordance with the ultimate purpose of Nature, which is not to make individuals "happy," nor even to make nations "happy," but to evolve supermankind—living godhead— out of the existing master races, first of all, out of the pure Aryan. Happiness is a *bourgeois* conception, definitely. It is not our concern. We want animals to be happy—and inferior men, also, to the extent their happiness does not disturb the New Order. We believe higher mankind has better things to do. The Aryan world, remoulded by us after our final triumph, will no longer think in terms of happiness like the decadent world of today. It will think in terms of duty—like the early Vedic world, the early Christian world, the early Islamic world; like the world at the time of any great new beginning. But it will, in spirit, resemble the early Vedic

---

[4] *Mein Kampf*, II, ch. 2, p. 440.

world far more than either the Christian or the Islamic. For the duty it will live for will not be the duty to love *all men* as oneself, nor to consider them all as potential brothers in faith; it will be the duty to love the integral beauty of one's race above oneself and above all things, and to contribute to its fullest expression, at any cost, by any means, because such is the divine purpose of Nature.

A former S.S. man had once told me: "The first duty of a National Socialist is to be beautiful"[5] (physically, and on all planes)—words worthy of an ancient Greek; words of an Aryan of all times. And my comrade Herr A.—who without having served in the Waffen S.S. is just as devoted a follower of Adolf Hitler as any of those who have—had once told me: "A National Socialist should have no weaknesses"[6]—words that I had remembered so many times since my manuscript, into which I had put so much love, had been in danger of being destroyed.

And I reflected that, indeed, unless one had "no weaknesses," one could not *be* perfectly beautiful; that every weakness is a flaw in the steel of one's character; a tendency to sacrifice beauty to happiness, duty to individual ties, the future to the present, the eternal to the illusory; that it is a definite possibility of decay. Only out of flawless elements can living gods emerge. The man whose life is a thing of integral beauty, the man with no weaknesses, is the man with no ties, who performs duty with ruthless thoroughness and with serenity.

And I asked myself: "Am *I* really without ties? Am I serene? If I were, I would not worry over the possible destruction of my manuscripts, after having done all I could to save them.

I recalled my visit to the Goðafoss, in northern Iceland, in June, 1947.

I had been told that, some time after the year 1000, a man named Thorgeir,[7] who was a *"goði"*—a priest of the Nordic Gods—in the region of Ljósvatn, in North Iceland, became a Christian. And, that as a spectacular demonstration of his allegiance to the new foreign faith—and perhaps, in his mind, as "an example"—he had taken the images of the old Gods and thrown them publicly into the waterfall of the river Skjálfandafljót, known ever since as the Goðafoss: the Waterfall of the Gods.

Deeply moved, I had gone myself to the spot, and stood by the Waterfall and thought of those Gods—Odin, and Thor, and Baldur the Fair and the others, whom my own Viking ancestors once worshipped— lying, for more than nine hundred years, at the bottom of the icy waters

---

[5] Cf. *Gold in the Furnace*, 3rd ed., p. 155.—Ed.
[6] Cf. *Gold in the Furnace*, 3rd ed., p. 232.—Ed.
[7] Thorgeir Thorkelsson—Ed.

of the Skjálfandafljót, waiting for the dawn of the new times, for the great Heathen Renaissance; waiting for *us*—for *me*. I had brought with me a paper on which I had copied the words that the French poet Leconte de Lisle puts in the mouth of a Norse god addressing the meek Child Jesus, come to overthrow his power:

> . . . Thou shalt die in thy turn!
> Nine times, I swear it, by the immortal Runes,
> Thou shalt die like I, god of the new souls!
> For man will survive. Twenty centuries of suffering
> Will make his flesh bleed and his tears flow,
> Until the day when thy yoke, tolerated two thousand years,
> Will weigh heavily upon the necks of the rebellious races;
> When thy temples, standing in their midst,
> Will become an object of mockery to the people;
> Then, thy time will be up . . .[8]

My right arm outstretched towards the East, I had recited those verses, and then, thrown the paper into the roaring cataract. And then—although I had not yet recovered hope; although disaster had, in my eyes, postponed, perhaps for years and years, the great Heathen Renaissance of my dream—I had spoken to the old Gods. "Gods of the North, brothers of the Vedic Gods that India still reveres," I had said, "Aryan Gods, Gods of my race, you know that I have all my life upheld the values that you once embodied in the hearts of your worshippers. Oh, whatever be the destiny to which you call me, you whom my mother's ancestors invoked in the midst of lightning and thunder, upon the furious waves of the North Sea, help me never to cease fighting for our great ideals; never to cease fighting for the cult of youth, of health, of strength, for the cult of the Sun—for your truth; our truth—wherever it be in the world, until I die!"

And having said that, I had felt a cold thrill run along my spine, and I had been overwhelmed by a consciousness of infinite solemnity, as

---

[8] ". . . Tu mourras à ton tour!
J'atteste par neuf fois les Runas immortelles.
Tu mourras comme moi, Dieu des âmes nouvelles,
Car l'homme survivra! Vingt siècles de douleurs
Feront saigner sa chair et ruisseler ses pleurs,
Jusqu'au jour où ton joug, subi deux mille années,
Fatiguera le cou des races mutinées;
Où tes temples dressés parmi les nations
Deviendront en risée aux générations;
Et ce sera ton heure! . . ."—Leconte de Lisle, "Le Runoïa" (*Poèmes Barbares*)

though I had just become the instrument of a long-prepared and long-expected rite; as though the Norse Gods, discarded by their priest Thorgeir, had really been waiting for my symbolical gesture. It was 10:30 p.m. but broad daylight, as it is natural in June, at that latitude. And I had suddenly remembered that it was the 9th of June, the seventh anniversary of the day on which, also at 10:30 p.m., a Brahmin, representative of easternmost Aryandom, had held my hand in his over the sacred fire and given me his name and protection. And I had felt that my visit to the Waterfall of the Gods, and my symbolical gesture on such a day had a meaning in the invisible; that there was there more than a mere coincidence.

Now, I remembered that episode, which took, in the light of my history during these two years, a greater symbolical value than ever. "Gods of the North, Gods of the strong," thought I, "Aryan Gods teach me that detachment without which there is no real strength, no lasting efficiency! Make me a worthy witness of your truth—of our truth. Rid me of all weaknesses!"

* * *

I spent that day and the next, and the rest of the week, meditating upon the way of absolute detachment, which is the way of the strong, in the light of the oldest known summary of Aryan philosophy—the Bhagavad-Gita—and in the light of all I knew of the modern Ideology for the love of which I was in jail. And the more I thus meditated, the more I marvelled at the accuracy of the statement of that fifteen-year-old illiterate Hindu lad who had told me, in glorious '40: "*Mem-sahib*, I too admire your Führer. He is fighting in order to replace, in the whole West, the Bible by the Bhagavad-Gita." "Yes," thought I, "to replace the equalitarian and pacifist philosophy of the Christians by the philosophy of natural hierarchy and the religion of detached violence—the immemorial Aryan wisdom!"

I recalled in my mind verses of the old Sanskrit Scripture—words of Krishna, the God incarnate, to the Aryan warrior Arjuna:

As the ignorant act from attachment to action, O Son of Bharata, so should the wise *act without attachment, desiring only the welfare of the world.*[9]

Without attachment, constantly perform thou *action which is duty.*[10]

---

[9] The Bhagavad-Gita, III, verse 25.
[10] The Bhagavad-Gita, III, verse 19.

Surrendering all actions to Me, with thy thoughts resting on the supreme Self, *freed from hope and egoism, cured from excitement,* engage in battle. [11]

Whose works are all free from the moulding of desire, whose actions are burnt by the fire of wisdom, him the wise call a Sage. [12]

Hoping for naught, his mind and self controlled, having abandoned all greed, performing action by the body alone, he doth not commit sin. [13]

As the burning fire reduces fuel to ashes, O Arjuna, so doth the fire of wisdom reduce all actions to ashes. [14]

He who acteth placing all actions in the eternal, *abandoning attachment,* is unaffected by sin, as a lotus leaf by the waters. [15]

And I thought: "All is permissible to him who acts for the cause of truth in a spirit of perfect detachment—without hope of personal satisfaction, without any desire but that of dutiful service. But the same action becomes censurable when performed for personal ends, or even when the one who performs it mingles some personal passion with his or her zeal for the sacred cause. That is also our spirit."

I pondered over that one-pointedness, that absolute freedom from petty interests and personal ties that characterises the real National Socialist.

I remembered the story a comrade had once related to me about a man who had had a family of Jews sent to some concentration camp in order to settle himself in their comfortable six-room flat, which he had been coveting for a long time. "He was wrong," my comrade had stated (and his words rang clearly in my memory); "he was not wrong to report those Jews, of course—that was his duty as a German—but he was wrong to think at all about the flat; wrong to allow the lust of personal gain to urge him in the least to accomplish his duty. He should have had the Yids packed off, by all means but simply because they were Yids, *because it was his duty,* and without caring which German family—his or someone else's—occupied the six rooms."

"He acted as many average human beings would have acted in his

---

[11] The Bhagavad-Gita, III, verse 30.
[12] The Bhagavad-Gita, IV, verse 19.
[13] The Bhagavad-Gita, IV, verse 21.
[14] The Bhagavad-Gita, IV, verse 27.
[15] The Bhagavad-Gita, V, verse 10.

place," I had answered, not exactly to excuse the man, but to say something in his favour, for after all he was one of us.

And I remembered how my comrade had flared up, saying: "That is precisely why I blame him! One has no business to call oneself a National Socialist if one acts for the self-same motives as 'average human beings'. One of us should act for the cause alone—in the interest of the whole nation—never for himself."

". . . without attachment, desiring only the welfare of the world," thought I once more, recalling the words of the Bhagavad-Gita in connection with that statement of a man who had never read it, but who lived according to its spirit, like all those who, today, share in earnest the Hitler faith. "The *interest of the nation*, when that nation is the militant vanguard of Aryan humanity and the champion of the eternal Aryan ideals, is the welfare of the world." And I thought, also: "Violence—not 'nonviolence'; but violence with detachment; action—not inaction, not flight from responsibility, not escape from life; but action freed from selfishness, from greed, from all personal passions; that rule of conduct laid down for all times by the divine Prince of Warriors, upon the Kurukshetra Field, for the true Aryan warriors of all lands, *that* is *our* rule of conduct—*our* violence; *our* action. In fact, the true Aryan warrior of today, the perfect Nazi, is a man without passion; a cool-minded, far-sighted, selfless man, as strong as steel, as pure (physically and morally) as pure gold; a man who will always put the interest of the Aryan cause—which *is* the ultimate interest of the world—before everything, even before his own limitless love of it; a man who would never sacrifice higher expediency to anything, not even to the delight of spectacular revenge."

I asked myself: "How far have *I* gone along that path of absolute detachment, which is ours? A German woman who has struggled and suffered for the cause has done me the honour to consider me as 'a genuine National Socialist'. How far do I deserve that honour in the light of our eternal standards of virtue?"

I closed my eyes, and brought before my mind the nightmare vision of the ruins of Germany; and I tried to imagine the hell that had preceded that desolation of hundreds and hundreds of miles; and the terror of the German people—of my comrades of my brothers in faith—in the midst of that man-made hell. And I brought before my eyes the Occupation, in and since 1945, in all its horror: the dismantling of the factories, the starvation of the people, the massacre of the holy forests; and the long-drawn systematic attempt at crushing the people's very soul—at "de-Nazifying" them, through fear and bribery; the monstrous trial of Nuremberg and all the subsequent iniquities and cruelties; the wholesale persecution of

National Socialism by gloating Jews and debased Aryans in the service of international Jewry, themselves lower than Jews if that be possible. I thought of all that, and felt in my heart that same devouring thirst for vengeance which had been, from 1945 to 1948, the only feeling for the sake of which I had clung to life. Those appalling ruins were the ruins of our New Order—of the one thing I had lived for. That endless suffering, that unheard-of humiliation, were the suffering and humiliation of people who believed in Hitler—the only people I looked up to; the only people whom I loved, in the modern world. Those men, fluttering convulsively, each one at the end of a rope, on that dismal morning of the 16th of October, 1946, were the martyrs of Nuremberg, to the memory of whom I had dedicated my lost book, the closest collaborators of my Führer. In Europe, in America, people had gloated over them. "Oh, to see them avenged a hundred millionfold!" thought I, once more. "To see whole cities, former strongholds of the anti-Nazi forces, changed into blazing and howling furnaces, and to gloat in my turn! . . ." And, at the thought of this, I smiled.

But I then said to myself: "And what if those who watch and wait for our Day in the full knowledge of factors of which I know nothing; what if those who are preparing in silence the resurrection of National Socialist Germany, consider it expedient for us to ally ourselves, one day, for the time being, with this or that side of the now divided enemy camp? What if I had to renounce revenge, to give up the pleasure of mocking, of insulting, of humiliating at least one fraction of our enemies, in the ultimate interest of the Nazi renaissance?"

I realised that no greater sacrifice could he asked of me. Yet I answered in my heart: "I would! Yes. I would keep quiet, if that were necessary. I would even praise 'our great allies' of the East or of the West, publicly if I were ordered to; praise them, while hating them, for the sake of highest expediency. I would—in the interest of Hitler's people; in the interest of regenerate Aryandom; in the interest of the world ordained anew according to the true natural hierarchy of races and individuals; in the interest of the eternal truth which Adolf Hitler came to proclaim anew in this world."

I remembered more words of Krishna, the God incarnate, upon the Kurukshetra Field: "Whenever justice is crushed; whenever evil rules supreme, I Myself, come forth. For the protection of the righteous, for the destruction of the evildoers, for the sake of firmly establishing the reign of truth, I am born from age to age."[16] And I could not help raising my mind to the eternal One, the Sustainer of the universe, by whatever

---

[16] The Bhagavad-Gita, IV, verses 7–8.

name men might choose to call Him, and thinking: "Thou wert born in our age as Adolf Hitler, the Leader and Saviour of the Aryan race. Glory to Thee, O Lord of all the worlds! And glory to Him!"

A feeling of ecstatic joy lifted me above myself, like in India, nine years before, when I had heard the same fact stated for the first time in public, by one of the Hindus who realised, better than many Europeans, the meaning and magnitude of our Führer's mission.

Never had I, perhaps, been so vividly aware of the continuity of the Aryan attitude to life from the earliest times to now; of the one more-than-human truth, of the one great ideal of more-than-human beauty, that underlies all expressions of typically Aryan genius, from the warrior-like piety of the Bhagavad-Gita, to the fiery criticisms of misguided pacifism and the crystal-clear exhortations to selfless action in *Mein Kampf*.

* * *

I recalled the words: "Living in truth," the motto of King Akhnaton of Egypt—perhaps the greatest known thinker of early Antiquity outside India. And I remembered how, according to most archaeologists, there is "no sense of sin" in the Religion of the Disk as Akhnaton conceived it; that it is "absolutely unmoral."[17]

And I thought: "It is to be expected. To 'live in truth' is not scrupulously to avoid lies and deceit and all manner of 'unfair' dealings, if these be expedient in the service of a higher purpose; it is not to mould one's conduct upon Moses' Ten Commandments and the nowadays accepted standards of Christian morality—the only morality that most people, including archaeologists, can think of. It is to live in perfect accordance with one's place and mission in the scheme of things; in accordance with that which is called, in the Bhagavad-Gita, one's *swadharma*, one's *own* duty." And another remark of Professor Pendlebury came to my memory, namely that this "unmoral" character of King Akhnaton's solar religion "is enough to disprove any Syrian or Semitic origin of his movement."[18] Others[19] have seen in the young Pharaoh's reaction against the death-centred formalism typical of ancient Egypt before him and since, the proof of a definite Aryan influence from the kingdom of Mitanni. No one can yet tell whether such is the case. But undeniably, Akhnaton himself was partly Mitannian—partly Aryan.

---

[17] J. D. S. Pendlebury, in *Tell el-Amarna* (London: Lovat Dickson and Thompson, 1935), p. 156. Also Sir E. A. Wallis Budge in *Tutankhamen*, p. 114.

[18] Pendlebury, *Tell el-Amarna*, p. 156.

[19] In particular Sir E. A. Wallis Budge.

I recalled the reverence in which the ancient Persians, who were Aryans, held the idea of truth for the sake of truth.

And I thought: "There is only one morality in keeping with that cult of truth, which is also the cult of integral beauty; and that is the morality of detached action. The ethics of individual happiness, the ethics of the 'rights of man'—of *every* man—are untrue. They proceed, directly or indirectly, from the ethics of Paul of Tarsus who preached that all nations had been created 'out of one blood',[20] by some all-too-human heavenly father, lover of all men. They proceed from the Jewish ethics—that mockery of truth—that put the inferior in the place of the superior and proclaim the Jewish race 'chosen' to rule the world, if not materially, at least in spirit. They are a trick of the cunning Jew, with a view to reverse for his own satisfaction, and ultimately for his own selfish ends, the divine order of Nature in which men, as all creatures, are different and unequal; in which nobody's 'happiness' counts, nor even that of the highest men.

"We have come to expose and to abolish those ethics of equality and of individual happiness which are, from time immemorial, the glaring antithesis of the Aryan conception of life.

"It is the superior man's business to feel happy in the service of the highest purpose of Nature which is the return to original perfection—to supermanhood. It is the business of every man to be happy to serve that purpose, directly or indirectly, from his natural place, which is the place his race gives him in the scheme of creation. And if he cannot be? Let him not be. Who cares? Time rolls on, just the same, marked by the great Individuals who have understood the true meaning of history, and striven to remould the earth according to the standards of the eternal Order, against the downward rush of decay, result of life in falsehood—the Men against Time.

"It is a man's own duty in the general scheme of creation that defines what are his rights. Never are the so-called 'rights' of his inferiors to define where lies *his* duty.

"It is a race's own duty, its place and purpose in the general scheme of creation, that defines what are its rights. Never are the so-called 'rights' of the inferior races to define the duties of the higher ones.

"The duty of the Aryan is to *live* consciously 'in truth', ruling the rest of men, while raising himself, through detached action, to the state of supermanhood. The duty of the inferior races is to stay in their places. That is the only way they can also live 'in truth'—indirectly. Aryan wisdom understood that, long ago, and organised India according to the

---

[20] Acts of the Apostles, ch. 17, verse 26.

principle of racial hierarchy, taking no account whatsoever of 'individual happiness' and of the 'value of every man as such'.

"Alone in our times, we National Socialists militate in favour of an organisation of the whole world on the basis of those self-same eternal principles; of that self-same natural hierarchy. That is why our cause is the cause of truth. That is why we have the duty—and therefore the right—to do *anything* which is in the interest of our divine cause."

* * *

In a flash, I remembered my lost manuscript, and I continued thinking: "Yes, *I* can do anything provided I do it solely for the cause, and with detachment—with serenity. Then—but only then—I am above all laws; or rather, submitted to one law, namely, to the law of obedience: of blind obedience to anyone who has authority over me in the National Socialist organisation in the case I am acting under orders; and in any other case, of absolute obedience to the commands of higher expediency, to the best of my own understanding of them.

"Presently, if I am absolutely detached—if I am free from all desire of personal recognition; free from all personal delight in deceiving our enemies; free from all personal pride, from all sense of personal importance as the author of my book—then, and only then, I have the right, nay, the duty, to lie, to crawl, to make the otherwise most contemptible exhibition of myself, in order to try to save my manuscripts from destruction . . .

"I must not feel 'clever' and be pleased with myself for deceiving the Governor. It is not *my* cleverness that did it; it is, through my agency, the unfailing, invisible Powers that watch over the interest of the cause of truth. I am, in all that, as it is written in the old Sanskrit Writ, *nimitta matra*—nothing but an instrument.

"I must, also, not feel sorry to break my word, and to repay the enemy's leniency with what the Democrats would call 'cynical ingratitude'. I am a fighter for the Nazi cause, openly at war with these people for the last ten years, and, from the day I was able to think, at war with the values that they stand for. *All is fair in war*. All is fair in our dealings with that world that we are out to remould or to destroy. There is only one law for us: expediency. And I am right, in the present circumstances, to act accordingly, not for myself, but in the interest of the sacred cause, remembering that I am an instrument in the service of truth; as it is written in the old Sanskrit Writ, *nimitta matra*—nothing but an instrument.

"And if, by some miracle, my book is saved, I must not feel happy in the expectation that one day, in a free Germany, my comrades will read it and think: 'What a wonderful person Savitri Devi Mukherji is, and how lucky we are to have her on our side!' No; never; it is I, on the contrary, who am privileged to be on the side of truth. Truth remains, even if people of far greater talent than I ignore it, deny it, or hate it. It is I who am honoured to be among the élite of my race—not my comrades, to have me among them. Any of them is as good as I, or better.

"As for my book, without the inspiration given by the invisible Powers, I would never have been able to write it. The divine Powers have worked through me, as through thousands of others, for the ultimate triumph of the Nazi Idea. I have not to boast. I have but to thank the Gods for my privileges, and to adore. As it is written in the old Sanskrit Writ, I am *nimitta matra*—nothing but an instrument in the hands of the immortal Gods."

I also thought: "It is difficult to be absolutely detached. Yet it is the condition without which the right action loses its beauty—and perhaps, sometimes also, a part of its efficiency. It is the condition without which the one who acts remains all-too-human; too human to be a worthy National Socialist.

"It is, however, perhaps, even more difficult for a woman than for a man to remain constantly detached—a serene instrument of duty and nothing else, day after day, all her life."

From the depth of my heart rose the strongest, the sincerest craving of my whole being; the culminating aspiration of my life: "Oh, may I be *that!* In the service of Hitler's divine Idea, may I be *that*, now, tomorrow, every day of my life; and in every one of my future lives, if I have any!"

I remembered a conversation I had once had with my beloved H. E. about the routine in Auschwitz and in one or two more concentration camps in which she bad been in service. "We had nothing to do with the gassing of the Jews," she had told me; "that was the men's job. And those who did it, like all the men in service in the camps, in fact, were S.S. men."

I had wondered why, and asked her. "Surely the women cannot have been too squeamish to turn on a tap," I had said; "I would have done that willingly."

"It was not the rule," H. E. had simply answered. "I do not know myself 'why'. But it was not."

Now, I understood; now, I knew: "why." Now, I knew that "next time," also, if we got to power again, it would be just the same, for the spirit of our Ideology would not change; for, only in keeping with the immemorial Aryan ideal of detached action did we, then, and could we, again, take those drastic steps for which the distorted "moral" sense of this decadent world condemns us and carry to its end that which a French official in occupied Germany has called our "appalling logic" (not knowing what a compliment in disguise he was paying us.[21])

But few are the women of this generation who can raise themselves to that height of detachment, equally opposed to the hypocritical squeamishness of the pacifist and to the impulsive violence of the passionate; few are; even among those who call themselves National Socialists— who wish to be National Socialists—the women who would neither feel sorry for the "poor" Jews, "human beings, after all," expecting in terror, behind the wall, the gush of deadly gas, *nor* be personally delighted at the thought of "another two hundred of them less!" but who, with a serene satisfaction of conscience, neither greater nor lesser than that which they would experience in the accomplishment of any necessary task, pleasant or unpleasant, would rid the Reich of one more batch of parasites, if not of active enemies, and think no more about it.

In the light of our ideal of ruthless service of the highest truth, rowdy gloating is nearly as bad as squeamishness. Both are signs of weakness. And "a National Socialist should have no weaknesses." It was thus decided—and no doubt wisely—that those alone who were the least likely to become weak in one way or another in the exercise of certain duties, should be trusted with those duties. Naturally, anybody could turn on a tap. But the idea was to allow to do so those alone who, well-knowing what they were doing, would do it without hesitation or haste, without reluctance or morbid pleasure, without pity or hatred, with serenity, simply because it had to be done. And it would again be the same in the future, until, in a cleansed and regenerate world, the absence of any further opposition to our golden-age philosophy would render all murderous violence unnecessary.

I remembered the arguments of those people who maintain that "for the legitimate progress of science" or for the ultimate purpose of "relieving suffering humanity," any torture can be inflicted upon the beautiful innocent beasts of creation, in the process of experimentation. I had always known they were wrong. I still knew it. But I now wondered what I would answer, if one of those people told me, using my own words "Why not, if it be done with perfect detachment?" And after a minute's reflection, I replied in my heart to that question.

"Absolute detachment as regards the action itself is not sufficient," thought I. "The 'duty' in the name of which the action is done must really be *duty*—not any fanciful 'obligation'; not the pursuit of any personal or

---

[21] Rudolf Grassot—Ed.

even human goal; it must have nothing to do with the satisfaction or happiness of individuals, no matter how many those individuals be (numbers
do not count). It must be in harmony with the supreme goal of Nature,
which is the birth of a god-like humanity. In other words, the only ideal in
the service of which the infliction of suffering and death is justified, is the
triumph or the defence of the one world-order capable of bringing forth a
god-like humanity. That alone can justify anything, for that alone is, in the
words of the Bhagavad-Gita, 'the welfare of the world'.

"The élite of the Aryan race can well raise itself to the status of 'heroes like unto the Gods' without that accumulation of 'scientific' information that the decadent intellectuals of today value so much. To sacrifice a single one of the beautiful creatures of the earth to *that* is a crime.
On the other hand, the 'heroes like unto the Gods' will not be the sons of
a diseased humanity, patched up at the cost of complicated medical interventions, fruit of intensive laboratory research. They will be the sons
of generations of healthy men and women. And the answer to disease
and physical decay is not increased experimentation upon healthy animals, purposely injected with all sorts of morbid germs, nor larger hospi-
tals, nor new treatments. It is the ruthless elimination of the incurable and
the sterilisation of the sickly. To experiment upon a healthy beast with a
view to find out the means to prolong the lives of deficient human beings
who would be better dead—to 'save' men who can in no way contribute
to the reign of supermanhood—is a crime against Life. To inflict suffering upon any creature—be it upon the vilest of human beings, and *a fortiori* an innocent animal—for a reason that is not worth it in the light of
Nature's supreme goal, is a crime. And those people who, reversing the
natural scale of values for the sake of silly man-centred sentimentalism,
look upon Claude Bernard and Louis Pasteur as 'great men' while considering Julius Streicher as a 'war criminal', deserve wholesale destruction."

I had expressed more or less the same idea in my unpublished book
Impeachment of Man, written in 1945–46—that book of which Frau S.
had once told me that "it will be publishable in fifty years' time, not before." I felt however that, in spite of my quotation from the *Goebbels
Diaries* on the first page, the manuscript of that book would not alarm
the British authorities. It was not obviously political—not political at all,
in fact, although it condemned without ambiguity the man-centred standpoint of our enemies; their whole philosophy of life.

Then again I thought of my other manuscripts; and I tried to maintain,
with regard to their fate, that attitude of absolute detachment which is the
attitude of the strong. "I have done my best to save them," reflected I. "I
have lied; I have acted, without regretting it or boasting inwardly of my

'cleverness'. If I remain detached, surrendering 'the fruits of action'—the fate of my writings—entirely to the higher invisible Powers, then, and then alone, I shall be worthy of the sacred Tradition of Aryandom; worthy of our Ideology, which is inspired by the same spirit. Nay, then and then alone I shall be training myself to act with absolute detachment in the future, whatever I might be called to do for our cause: then and then alone, being selfless, I shall have the right to condone anything, and to do anything.

* * *

On Friday the 10th of June I did not seek an interview with the Governor, although I knew he would come to the *"Frauenhaus"* on his weekly visit. I thought I would refrain from all further intervention in favour of my manuscripts. But when the Governor actually passed before my open cell in the company of Fräulein S.—Frau *Oberin*'s assistant—and of the unavoidable interpreter, I somewhat could not help expressing the desire to speak to him.

"My time is eleven o'clock," answered he roughly; "I cannot stop and speak to each prisoner according to her whims." And he walked past.

But after a few minutes I was called and ushered into the recreation room where the three people I have just mentioned were standing.

"Well, what is it you wish to tell me?" said Colonel Vickers before whom I stood, looking as dejected as I possibly could.

"I only wished to ask you whether, perchance, you can give me any hope concerning the fate of my manuscripts," said I; "I have already told you that I do not intend to publish them. Yet the anguish at the thought that they might be destroyed allows me no rest, no sleep at night. I have put so much of my heart in these writings that I want to keep them, be they good or bad, as one wants to keep an old picture of oneself . . ."

Colonel Vickers gave me a keen glance and interrupted me: "You told me all that stuff the other day," said he. "I know it. And can't be always busying myself with your case and listening to your pleas. You don't seem to realise that you are no longer a free woman. You have forfeited your freedom by working to undermine our prestige and our authority in this conquered country—a very serious offence, I would say a crime, in our eyes. Moreover, you despise us and our justice, in your heart. You had the cheek to tell me, the other day, to my face, that you hold the war criminals to be innocent, after they were duly tried and duly sentenced by British courts, the fairest in the world. In this prison, in spite of your offence and of the heavy sentence pronounced against

you—the heaviest a British judge has given a woman for a political offence of that nature—you were treated leniently. And you have repaid
our kindness by writing things against us.

"Do you think I am in a mood to read your damned Nazi propaganda
for the sake of telling you how much I dislike it? I have more important
things to do. I told you—I gave you my word—that I would call you to
my office when I have read it. I shall read it when I please—not when
you tell me to. And that might be in three months' time, or in six; or in a
year. You are here for three years. You must not imagine that we are going to release you without first being sure that you can harm us no longer. In the meantime, if you come bothering me again in connection with
that manuscript of yours, I shall destroy it straightaway. Why on earth
should I be lenient towards you, may I ask you? I have seen two wars,
both of them the outcome of that German militarism that you admire so
wholeheartedly. Why should I show mercy to you who in your heart despise mercy, and mock humanity? To you, who sneer at the most elementary decent feelings and who have nothing but contempt for our standards of behaviour? To you, the most objectionable type of Nazi whom I
have ever met?"

I kept my eyes downcast—not to let Colonel Vickers see them shining with pride. Not a muscle of my face moved. To the extent that it was
possible, I purposely thought of nothing; I tried to occupy my mind with
the pattern of the carpet on which I stood, so that my face would remain
expressionless at least as long as I was in the Governor's presence. But
within my heart, irresistibly, rose a song of joy.

"You can go," said Colonel Vickers, addressing me after a second's
pause.

I bowed and left the room.

On the threshold of my cell, unable to contain myself any longer, I
turned to the wardress who accompanied me. "You would never guess
what a glorious compliment the Governor has just paid me!" exclaimed I.
And a bright smile beautified my tired face.

"No."

She was astonished that the Governor could pay me any "compliment" after all that had happened, and especially after the recent search
in my cell.

"He told me," said I, "that I am the most objectionable type of Nazi
that he has ever met!" And I added, as she smiled in her turn at the sight
of my pride: "When I was on remand, Stocks, who used to call me down
to his office now and then, for a chat, once confided to me that, in 1945,
there were eleven thousand S.S. men imprisoned here in Werl. It is not

too bad an achievement, you know—and especially for a non-German—
to be, in the eyes of a British officer, more 'objectionable' than eleven
thousand S.S. men . . . What do you think?"

"I think you are unbeatable," replied the wardress, good-humouredly.

In my cell, I pondered over the Governor's words.

I now had almost the certitude that my manuscripts would be destroyed. Still, for a while, I forgot all about them in the joy and pride that
I experienced as I weighed in my mind every sentence Colonel Vickers
had addressed me: "You despise us and our Justice, in your heart . . .";
"You sneer at the most elementary decent feelings, and show nothing but
contempt for our standards of behaviour . . ." There was, at least, after
the Public Prosecutor who had spoken at my trial, a man from the enemy's camp who seemed to understand me better than most people did
outside Nazi circles. Far from telling me that I "surely did not mean" the
"awful things" I said—as the hundreds of intellectual imbeciles I met
both in the East and in the West—this soldier did not even need to hear
me *say* the "awful things" in order to be convinced that I meant them
none the less. An intelligent man, he might not have wished to understand that the responsibility for this war rests with England rather than
with Germany. But at least, he understood me. He seemed no longer to
believe, as he had so naively a week before, that I "cannot but" look upon any human life as more sacred than that of a cat. Perhaps he had read
enough of my book to lose his illusions on that point. Or perhaps someone—Miss Taylor, or some other person connected with my trial—had
been kind enough to enlighten him. Anyhow, I felt genuinely grateful to
him for his accurate estimation of me, for there is nothing I hate as much
as being mistaken for a person who does not know what she wants. He
understood me. And his words flattered me. His last sentence: "You are
the most objectionable type of Nazi that I have ever met," was, in my
eyes, the greatest tribute to my natural National Socialist orthodoxy yet
ever paid to me by an enemy of our cause.

It occurred to me that Colonel Vickers had been in Germany since the
Capitulation. Someone had told me so. Then, he must have met quite a
number of my brothers in faith, even apart from the eleven thousand S.S.
men that Mr. Stocks had mentioned. No doubt, he exaggerated a little
when he declared me the "most objectionable" type of all. With the exception of my unfortunate collaborator Herr W., who got caught for
sticking up my posters in broad daylight, other Nazis are, as a rule, far
more practical, and more subtle—*i.e.*, more intelligent—than I. In which
case they should be more "objectionable" than I, in a Democrat's eyes.

But, reflected I, most of them are Germans; and many have had the privilege of being brought up in a National Socialist atmosphere. That is somewhat of an excuse in the conception of the Democrats who have such a naive confidence in the power of education. I, a non-German Aryan who never had the benefit of a Nazi training, came to Hitler's Ideology by myself, of my own free will, knowing, from certain of its fundamental traits, that I would find in it the answer to my strongest and deepest aspirations. And not only did I welcome the leadership of National Socialist Germany in Europe before and during the war, but I came and told the Germans now, after the war, after the Capitulation, after all the efforts of the victorious Allies to inculcate into them the love of parliamentarism, of everlasting peace, and of Jewish rule: "Hope and wait! You shall rise and conquer once more. For still you are the worthiest; more than ever the worthiest. And no one will be happier than I to see you at the head of the Western world. Heil Hitler!" In other words, repudiating, defying, reducing to naught my Judeo-Christian democratic education—feeling and acting as though it had never existed—I identified myself entirely with, those who proclaimed the rights of Aryan blood, myself a living challenge to the defilement of the Aryan through education: a living proof of the invincibility of pure blood.

And in addition to that, I pointed out how our National Socialist wisdom is nothing else but the immemorial Aryan Wisdom of detached violence thus justifying in the light of the highest Tradition, all that we did, all that we might do in the future.

From the democratic standpoint, perhaps that is, after all, more dangerous and therefore more "objectionable" than the so-called "war crimes" that I had not the opportunity to commit. Perhaps Colonel Vickers had merely made a statement of fact, implicitly recognising the meaning of my attitude, the meaning of my whole life. For which, again, I thanked him within my heart.

* * *

But, as I said, I now felt sure that my precious book, my "best gift to Germany," would be destroyed.

And although, on the evening of that day, Fräulein S. came to my cell to ask me to sign a paper in connection with my possible release, I soon outlived the joy that the Governor's words had provoked in me. In fact, my awareness of being so "objectionable" from the enemy's standpoint, made me deplore all the more the loss of my manuscripts, especially of *Gold in the Furnace*. I felt more than ever—or imagined—how much indeed I could, one day, on the eve of Germany's liberation, contribute to stir up National Socialist enthusiasm, through those pages, written with fervour. And the thought that I would be no longer able to do so distressed me.

But then again I recalled the words of the ever-returning Saviour, in the Bhagavad-Gita: "Seek not the fruits of action . . ." And I concentrated my mind on the teaching of serene service of truth regardless of success or failure; and I bent all my efforts on the renunciation of my book.

"Break that last tie that binds you to the realm of consequences, and you will be free!" said the clear, serene voice within me, the voice of my better self. "Win that supreme victory over yourself, you who fear nothing and nobody, and you will be invincible; accept that supreme loss inflicted upon you by the enemies of the Nazi cause, you who have nothing else to lose but your writings, accept it as thousands of your comrades have accepted the loss of all they loved, and you will be worthy of your comrades; worthy of your cause. Remember, you who have come to work for the resurrection of National Socialist Germany, that only through the absolute renunciation of those who serve them to all earthly bondage, can the forces of Life triumph over the forces of death."

And I recalled in my mind the beautiful myth of the visit of the Goddess Ishtar to the netherworld, as it is reported in the old Sumerian epic of Gilgamesh.

To bring back to life her beloved, the God Tammuz—the divine Youth Who dies every winter and rises in glory from the dead every spring—Ishtar-Zarpanit, Goddess of love and war—Goddess of the double forces of creation: fecundity and selection—went down to the nether land, attired in all her jewels. At the first gate, she left her earrings; at the second, she left her armlets; at the third, her bejewelled girdle; at the fourth, her necklaces, and so forth, until she reached the seventh and last gate. She left there her last and most precious jewel, and entered naked into the Chambers of the dead . . . Then alone could she bring back to life the young God Tammuz—invincible Life—prisoner of the forces of death.

"The price of resurrection is absolute renunciation, sacrifice to the end," thought I. "Inasmuch as they have retained something of the more ancient wisdom under their Jewish doctrine, even the Christians admit that."

I felt an icy cold thrill run up my spine and an unsuspected power emerge from me.[22] My mind went back to the unknown man of vision who wrote down the myth of Ishtar, seven thousand years ago, thus helping me

---

[22] Again, this language brings to mind the Tantric doctrine of the awakening of the Kundalini shakti. Cf. p. 108, n24 above.—Ed.

to realise, today, in captivity, that unless I willingly despoiled myself of everything mine—unless I looked upon nothing as *mine*—I could not work for our second rising.

I felt that I had come so that, through me, as through every true National Socialist, the eternal Forces of Life might call from the slumber of death the modern Prototype of higher mankind; the perfect god-like Youth, strong, comely, with hair like the Sun and eyes like stars and a body surpassing in beauty the bodies of all the man-made gods. I identified in my heart that creature of glory with the élite of Adolf Hitler's regenerate people. And I knew that the ever-recurring call to resurrection resounded today, through us, through me, as our battle cry in the modern phase of the perennial struggle: *"Deutschland erwache!"*

And the voice of my better self told me: "Unless you have sincerely, wholeheartedly, unconditionally, put aside your last and most precious treasure—snapped your last tie with the world of the living—the Prisoner of the forces of death will not come forth at your call. Come; free yourself once and for all of all regret, of all attachment; give up your writings in sacrifice to the divine cause; and be, you too, a force of resurrection!"

Tears rolled down my cheeks.

I pictured within my mind the face of our Führer—stern, profoundly sad, pertaining to the beauty of things eternal—against the background of his martyred country, first in flames and then in ruins; also against the background of those endless frozen white plains where snow covered the slain in battle, while the survivors of the Wehrmacht, of the S.S. regiments, of the *Leibstandarte*, that élite among the élite, driven further and further east as prisoners of war, went their way to a fate often worse than death. And I burst out sobbing at the memory of that complete sacrifice of millions, offered as the price of the resurrection of real Germany—of Aryan man, the god-like youth of the world.

I looked up to the Man who inspired such a sacrifice, after having, himself, sacrificed everything to the same great impersonal purpose; to Him, Who never found the price of resurrection too high. And once more I recognised in Him the Saviour Who comes back, age after age, "to establish on earth the order of truth."

I gave up all regret of my lost book. "Let them destroy it, if they must," thought I.

And in an outburst of half-human half-religious love—exactly as when faced with the threat of disfiguring torture, on the night of my arrest—I uttered in my heart the supreme words: "Nothing is too beautiful, nothing is too precious for Thee my Führer!"

And again, as on that night, I felt happy, and invincible.

Chapter 13

"WE SHALL BEGIN AGAIN"

I never again grieved over the now almost certain destruction of my sincerest writings. I also never thought of my possible release. "If they do release me, I shall continue to fight them and their Democracy," thought I; "and if they keep me in prison, I shall continue to show them that nothing can crush a Nazi."

Having still nothing to do all day, in my cell, I remembered verses of the Bhagavad-Gita; and sentences from Nietzsche's books, *Der Wille zur Macht*, and *Also sprach Zarathustra*[1]—sentences like these: "Man is a string stretched between the beast and the Superhuman . . ."[2]; "You ask what is right? To be brave, that is right"[3]—and passages from *Mein Kampf*. And also certain uplifting conversations with my German comrades, and with Mr. W.,[4] Mr. S., Mr. B., and others, the sincerest English followers of Adolf Hitler that I knew, now scattered throughout the wide world; and with my wise husband, who had written to me only once since my arrest, but whom I knew to be in complete communion of faith with me.

I often sang the Horst Wessel Song, or the Song of the S.S. men—"If all become unfaithful, indeed we faithful shall remain . . ."—or the Bengali hymn to Shiva, "Dancer of Destruction. O Lord of the Dance . . . ," which invariably made me think of the long-desired redeeming war that would one day thrust our enemies against each other, and finally bring us back to power on the ruins of their hated judaised civilisation.

I had completely given up all hope that, under our restored New Order, my writings might help young Aryans to feel proud of their blood. Those writings were now lost forever, I thought. But I was happy to know that I had done my best to save them; moreover, that I was one of the faithful, and that every day brought me nearer to the Day we would rise again.

I was serene, if not cheerful.

---

[1] *The Will to Power* and *Thus Spoke Zarathustra*—Ed.

[2] "Der Mensch ist ein Seil, geknüpft zwischen Tier und Übermensch . . ." (*Also sprach Zarathustra*, Vorrede [Prologue], §4).—Ed.

[3] "Was ist gut? fragt ihr. Tapfer sein ist gut." (*Also sprach Zarathustra*, first part, "Vom Krieg und Kriegsvolke" ["On War and Warriors"]).—Ed.

[4] Probably Elwyn Wright—Ed.

On Friday, the 17th of June, in the morning, Frau *Oberin* entered my cell smiling. It was the first time I saw her smile for many days.

"I have good news for you, Muky," said she. "Your manuscripts are safe in my office. They have given them back to you."

From the expression of her face, from the naturalness of her voice, it was clear that she spoke the truth. Yet, I could not believe her.

"It is impossible," replied I; "don't tell me fibs; don't make fun of me. They can't have given me back *those* manuscripts."

"Believe me," insisted Frau *Oberin*, "for I am telling you the truth. Your large thick copybooks are all there: the dark-red one, the light-brown one with a bright-red binding, the other light-brown one, in which you were writing before they searched your cell. They are there, intact. I have orders to put them in your trunk in the cloakroom, for you to have them when you are free."

I felt myself overcome with a sort of religious awe, as though I were actually witnessing a miracle. And I shuddered. Indeed, it was a miracle. Had my writings been thrown into a blazing fire and brought out intact, the miracle would not have been greater.

I was speechless. Tears filled my eyes. I turned to the eternal blue Sky. My mouth quivered, then fixed itself into a smile of unearthly joy. Behind the unbelievable wonder I hailed the Power that had worked it, with the self-same holy Sanskrit syllables that I had repeated in the depth of the abyss of despair: *"Aum, Rudrayam! Aum, Shivayam!"*

My heart was overflowing with gratitude: "Thou hast done it, Lord of the unseen Forces, irresistible One; Thou, Thou alone!" thought I. "I thank Thee; Thee alone!" And I also thought: "This is a sign: one day we shall rise, and conquer again." And my face radiated the joy of coming resurrection.

Never had I felt myself so insignificant, so powerless—individually—in the light of that greater Destiny to which I was bound as a National Socialist. But never perhaps, also, had I been so intensely happy to know that I *was* a detail in the workings of that Destiny; *"nimitta matra,"* "nothing but an instrument," yet an instrument in the realisation of the most glorious practical programme, in keeping with the highest truth of all times.

"Well, you are happy, now," said Frau *Oberin*, who had been watching me.

"It is a sign," replied I, referring to the only thing I could possibly think of: the miracle; "it means that, one day, my writings will be of some use to our cause. Yes, I am glad to know, now, that they will be; that, for that reason alone, they were spared."

It never even occurred to me that I might have felt, also, a little grateful towards Colonel Vickers and whoever else among the British authorities had handled my manuscripts and decided, in spite of all, not to burn them. In my eyes, those people had long ceased to exist. Like myself, like all visible agents, they were but puppets in the hands of the Unseen—with the difference that they probably did not know it, while I did. The superior Powers had forced them today to give me back my books. They would force them, tomorrow, to leave Germany, running for their lives. And after having done all I could for the triumph of the Nazi cause, I would, then, again look to the sky and say: "Thou alone hast done it; I thank Thee, Lord of the Play of appearances, Dancer of Destruction, Lord of Life!"

But Frau *Oberin* resumed her account of the today's miracle: "And do you know?" said she, "They have given you back all your other things too: your book of songs: your *Programme of the N.S.D.A.P.*, the last samples you have of your leaflets; everything—even the Führer's picture. I can hardly believe it myself."

I repeated: "It is a sign."

"I am very, very glad all is well," said Frau *Oberin*, shaking hands with me. "I really had feared that neither you nor I would get out of this so easily."

"Tell my friend H. E.," said I, pursuing my own thoughts; "I am sure she too will be glad. And tell Frau S., and Frau So-and-so, and Frau X., who have been so kind to me. Tell all those who are in sympathy with me; all those who are 'in order'. Tell them it means that times are changing in our favour; that the night is less dark around us."

And as she made a move to go out, I retained her a second longer:

"Tell them that it means that 'slavery has but a short time more to last'," said I, quoting the last words of the Horst Wessel Song.

* * *

I was soon called to meet Colonel Vickers in Frau *Oberin*'s office—that same Colonel Vickers who, only a week before, seemed to consider me as his deadliest enemy. This time, he spoke to me almost kindly.

"These you can have in your cell, just now," he told me, pointing to a pile of books among which, to my astonishment, I recognised the typed manuscript of my unpublished *Impeachment of Man*, on the first page of which I had written a quotation from the *Goebbels Diaries*. "Your other things, you can have when you leave this prison."

My trunk had been brought there, into the office; and I actually saw, in it, on the top of other books, my dark-red copybook containing the first part of *The Lightning and the Sun*, and my two light-brown ones containing all that I had written of *Gold in the Furnace*—exactly as Frau *Oberin* had told me. I could not help feeling that there was something very strange both in Colonel Vickers' sudden change of tone and in the fact that he had given me back my manuscripts. Doubtless, he had orders from somewhere to act as he did. But why were those orders given? To this day, I do not know. To this day, it all baffles me.

"I am exceedingly thankful to you for not destroying the writings that I look upon as precious personal 'souvenirs'," said I; "and once more I beg your pardon if I have, against the rules, kept forbidden objects in my possession. Once more I assure you that I kept them solely on account of the sentimental value that they have in my eyes."

I was thinking, not without a tinge of irony: "It costs nothing to be courteous." But the Governor interrupted me. "That's all right," he said; "you can have your things when you are free. But you must understand that I cannot allow you to have them now, in your cell."

"I don't wish to have them," replied I. "I am only too thankful to know that they will not be destroyed. Indeed, I look upon this as a tremendous favour. There is only one thing more that I would like to ask you, and that is the permission to have paper and ink in my cell and to continue, after working hours, to write the book which I had begun long ago about Genghis Khan."

"You can write about Genghis Khan as much as you like," replied Colonel Vickers. "But, mind you: no more Nazi stuff! If I catch you at that again, there will be serious trouble."

"You will never catch me at that again," said I, forcefully, taking the books that he handed over to me. But I was determined in my heart, to finish writing *Gold in the Furnace* at the first opportunity, in my cell, under his very nose. I thanked him once more, and walked out of the room, my eyes downcast.

Frau *Erste*, the matron, soon brought me back my own pen and ink, and some paper—a writing pad that a friend had sent me from England, but that she had not yet given to me on account of the search in my cell and the subsequent restrictions imposed upon me. Never was a gift more welcome than that writing pad. But I was not such a fool as to go and resume writing Chapter 12 of my dangerous book in plain English, upon its blank sheets. The sheets, thought I, had possibly been counted. They would possibly be counted again, to see how many I had used. And I would be asked to show what I had written upon them. Decidedly, I had to be very careful after the narrow escape my manuscripts had just had.

In fact, a day or two later, Frau *Oberin* brought me a copybook with a blue cardboard covering on the inside of which she had written, above the date—the 22nd of June—and her initials: "This book contains forty-nine leaves." She had numbered each leaf.

"Continue your book about Genghis Khan, *The Lightning and the Sun*, or whatever you call it, on this, as much as you like," said she. "But for Heaven's sake, don't start writing that other one again, so long as you are here! If they caught you doing so *now*, I would surely be accused of encouraging you, and sacked. I have already very nearly lost my job in connection with you."

"I'll be as good as gold, and will write only about the world's greatest conqueror," said I. "When you come again, I'll show you the end of my Chapter 5 of which the beginning is in my thick dark-red copybook; you'll see for yourself. By the way, could you not allow me to see both that dark-red copybook and the others, one day when Frau *Erste* is not here? I would like to know where exactly I stopped, in that chapter on Genghis Khan's birth. Also . . . I would like to see for myself that they have not torn out any pages in that or especially in the other manuscript. It baffles me how they can have given it back to me untouched. It would baffle you, if you knew the things I wrote in that book."

"If you ask me," replied Frau *Oberin*, "the Governor could not be bothered reading it."

"That may be. But," said I, "what about those, 'experts' in whose hands my things were—from what he told me on the 3rd of June? Could *they* also not be bothered going through it thoroughly?"

"How could I know?" admitted Frau *Oberin*.

"The representatives of the Western Occupying Powers are out here to have a fat pay and a 'good time'," remarked I, repeating what the Dutch woman had once said during the "free hour." "They have no ideology. So much the better. The Communists, who have one—be it the worst in the world—will beat them. And we shall beat the Communists and rule the world."

"I only hope you are right," said Frau *Oberin* as she left my cell.

What I actually did was to write the rough text of my dangerous book, in the evenings after six o'clock, upon my wooden stool, with a piece of chalk that the searchers were kind enough to forget in a corner of my drawer; to correct it, wiping out with a damp cloth this sentence or that one, until I was satisfied with it; and then to copy it off with pen and ink, in tight writing, paragraph by paragraph, not upon my new writing pad nor in the copybook that Frau *Oberin* had given me, but at the back of the pages of the letters that I used to, receive from Miss V.[5] And that too, not in English, but in Bengali; and with many abbreviations and conventional signs of my own.

This Miss V., a charming English woman whom I had met in 1946, was a weird character, "between two epochs"; a bundle of contrasts too typical not to deserve a mention in this book. She was thoroughly anti-Jewish, fanatically anti-Communist, and—which is much rarer—anti-Christian (the one woman who had ever told me that she would any time worship an English oak tree rather than a deified Jewish prophet), and yet, *not* one of us; indeed, incapable of ever becoming one of us, for want of that primitive, merciless, aggressive vitality that distinguishes us from the decadent world of today; sincere, kind to creatures, truth-loving, intelligent—understanding better than most Europeans the fundamental falsehood of any equalitarian man-centred doctrine—and yet, incapable of devotion to anything impersonal; afflicted with incurable individualism, with the phobia of all collective enthusiasms, good or bad, for the sole reason that they are collective, and with congenital squeamishness—with the phobia of physical suffering, be it inflicted upon herself, her friends, or her worst enemies; decidedly over-civilised; and too class-conscious ever to be able to become wholeheartedly *caste*-conscious; in one word, a person that could be used in our New Order, but that can never be a part of it; and yet, one of the exceptionally few non-Nazis who could put up with me for more than half a day, and perhaps the only one of them who ever loved me (Goodness only knows why!) in full awareness of all my potentialities. She sent me food parcels and wrote to me regularly when I was in jail. For my good luck, it happened that, just at the time of which I am now speaking, she quarrelled with a neighbour of hers, Miss G.[6]—another weird character half in the past and half in the future—whom I know. Her letters were, in consequence, much longer than usual—all about the quarrel. They were nearly always typed on one side only of the paper. After reading them, I would use my writing pad to answer them, and . . . use their blank pages to write the last chapters of *Gold in the Furnace*. (Miss G. also wrote me long letters—much longer letters than Miss V.'s, in fact—telling me all about that same quarrel from her point of view. But her sheets of paper, being written on both sides, unfortunately, could not be used.)

I wrote feverishly every day. I felt inspired. And the days were long. After I had finished, I folded up the letters as they were before, and put

---

[5] Veronica Vassar—Ed.
[6] Muriel Gantry—Ed.

them back in their respective envelopes. Each time Frau *Oberin* came, I could give her one or two, and ask her if she could not be kind enough to put them with my other things in the cloakroom, as I wished to keep them. "Most willingly," she would say, taking the letters—never suspecting that they contained any writing apart from Miss V's.

When I gave her the last one, I felt relieved of an immense worry. I now knew that my *Gold in the Furnace* was complete—and safe, for nobody would peer into my luggage before my release. The only work left for me to do, once free, was to translate the end of my book into English and to write it down in the light-brown copybook that Miss Taylor had given me on the day I was sentenced. Again I thanked the invisible Powers for having protected my manuscript. And I settled down to continue my other book, *The Lightning and the Sun*, after a long time. I used my writing pad as rough paper, and wrote the final text in my brand-new blue copybook, Frau *Oberin*'s gift, which I could show the Governor any time, if he cared to control what I was doing.

Thus absorbed in interesting work, I was happy after 6 p.m. But during the rest of the day, I often missed H. E.'s visits. I missed her—and L. M.—on Sunday afternoons. I missed the pleasure of spending my "free hour" occasionally with my comrades of the D wing, as I had before that unfortunate search in my cell.

Every day, morning and afternoon, I could *hear* the latter come and stand in the corridor, right in front of my cell, and call out: one, two, three . . . so that the wardresses on duty might know how many were to go out together. Then, I would hear them move along the A wing and the B wing, in the direction of the door leading to the stairs. Again, when they came back, they would pass before my cell. And provided Fran *Erste*, whom all feared, was not there, H. E. would call me from outside as she passed: "Savitri!"

"H. . . . !" would I answer, calling her in my turn by her name.

That was the only contact I had with her for days.

Then, one morning, I saw her. She was to help a few others to distribute to the prisoners the bread and chicory that composed their daily breakfast, and on her way to the landing, where the food was brought, she could not resist casting a glance into my cell, which was not locked.

"H. . . . ! my H. . . . !", exclaimed I, as soon as I noticed her blonde head peeping in. And I ran to the door to welcome her.

"I have lost my post at the Infirmary on account of all that happened," said she. "But that is all. They have not questioned me, thank goodness! It looks as if they did not find out . . ." She spoke rapidly, looking around every five seconds to see whether anyone was coming along the corridor.

I understood that she meant that they did not find out it was she who had told me about the most gruesome Allied atrocities I had reported in my Chapter 6, and about the Belsen trial.

"It looks as if indeed they did not," replied I. "You will surely be glad to know that they have given me back my manuscript—that they have put it with my things in the cloakroom, that is to say—strange as it might seem. Frau *Oberin* thinks they cannot have read it. And she told me I would probably be released very soon. I am damned if I know why. Of course, I told these people that I had no intention of publishing my book on Germany. God alone knows if they were simple enough to believe me. But never, for a minute did I pretend to have given up our Nazi faith. If they release me, they will do so fully knowing what I am."

"What idiots!" exclaimed H. E. with a smile. This was her first reaction. But then, she added, thoughtfully: ". . . or—perhaps—what past masters in diplomacy! One of the two."

"Why?" said I. "Do they imagine they are going to win me over with their 'kindness'? Not me, my dear; not me! They don't know me. *I* never forget, and never forgive."

"Nor do I; nor do any of us," replied H. E. And her blue eyes flashed. "But they don't know that. And if you ask me, they are about to try to win over the lot of us. They feel they will soon need our help against the Reds. They are afraid. But that's enough. If I am caught discussing on your doorstep, there will be trouble. I must see you, however, again, before your release."

"I'll ask Frau *Oberin* to arrange an interview for us."

"Good! I'll ask her too. I am sure she will not refuse. In the meantime . . . Goodbye!"

We both felt it unsafe to salute each other in our usual manner, be it in a whisper. So we uttered the secret formula which, even if overheard, would mean nothing to the uninitiated, but which to us, the few, means: "Heil Hitler!"

* * *

During the "free hour," the Dutch woman would tell me the daily news, that were sometimes interesting. I thus learnt that two of my comrades of the D wing had been sent to Hamburg as witnesses on behalf of the defence, in a new "war crimes trial" in which the accused were thirty-five German women formerly, like themselves, in service at Ravensbrück. I was indignant.

"Those rascals will never stop sitting as judges in 'war crimes trials' as long as they are here," said I. "I would love to see the Russians try them, one day, for alleged 'war crimes', and to go and meet them before they are killed and tell them: 'It serves you right! Remember what you did yourselves.' I am glad, now, to see any anti-Nazi suffer at the hands of his ex-allies, in the countries under Communist rule—like that notorious cardinal Mindszenty, whom they caught some months ago.[7] Now, you can of course tell me that the Russians treat us no better. I agree. I hate all those who fought against Hitler's New Order, be it in the name of Marxism, of Christianity, of Democracy, of the 'rights and dignity of the human person', or of the interest of their own pockets. Since 1945, I have lived only to witness their destruction."

"Many were misguided and are now 'coming around'," said the Dutch woman.

"I have hardly any more sympathy for those," replied I. "'Misguided'! If indeed, they are as stupid as sheep, then their fate does not interest me. If they are not, then why did they allow themselves to be 'misguided'? How is it that I was never impressed by anti-Nazi propaganda, all these years, in India, in Greece, in France? I had never seen the grandeur of the Third Reich. But I had *Mein Kampf* and my common sense to go by; and that was enough for me. Why was it not enough for those fools? Because they were utter fools—or selfish, mean-minded rogues. I don't say we must not use them, if we can, now that some of them are 'coming around'. But I have no, confidence in them."

"You don't trust human nature at all?"

"No," said I. "I trust only the few real National Socialists."

Another day, the Dutch woman related to me an incident that had taken place at the dining table, where D wing prisoners and others ate together (while my food was always brought to me in my cell). A Czech woman, a newcomer in Werl, who had spent some months in a concentration camp under the Nazi régime, had spotted out and started abusing a former wardress of that same camp, now serving a sentence of ten years' imprisonment as a so-called "war criminal." The latter had, it seems, once given her a slap. Some prisoners—there was no need for me to ask which—had automatically taken the side of the ex-"victim of the Nazi monsters," others, the side of the former wardress, and the dispute had degenerated into a general row, with the result that Frau *Erste* had intervened and given orders that henceforth the so-called "war criminals" were to take their meals apart from the other prisoners.

"And who is that specimen, whom the crusaders of Democracy came

---

[7] József Cardinal Mindszenty (1892–1975)—Ed.

to 'liberate'?" asked I. "I would like to make her acquaintance—from a distance."

The Dutch woman pointed out to me a short, coarse, ugly-looking object, walking not far in front of us. "That is the one," said she. "And I am afraid that, for once, I can wholeheartedly share your hostility towards her, I who, as a rule, am human, contrarily to you. For would you believe that she has been 'inside' *nineteen times* since 1945, for different offences, especially theft? She is here for theft. And whoever has heard her talk to the wardresses as I have, cannot find fault with that other wardress for slapping her."

"I should think not!" exclaimed I. "All you tell me does not astonish me in the least. I know perfectly well that nobody was in a concentration camp for nothing, in the Hitler days. And I have always said so to the people who, not knowing me, were foolish enough to come begging for my sympathy in favour of the alleged 'victims' of our régime. I am grateful to you indeed for your information about that Czech woman: it is good propaganda for us."

* * *

But soon—whether of her own accord, or because she was asked to do so, I could not tell—the Dutch woman started taking her "free hour" with the other batch of A wing prisoners, namely with those who went out at the same time as the D wing; and I had to find myself another companion. My next-door neighbour, C. P., the inmate of cell No. 50, offered to go out with me, as her usual companion had just been released. And thus, unexpectedly, I discovered a new comrade, for the woman—a German, who had served in occupied France during the war—was "in order," in spite of certain inconsistencies of which she was not conscious.

She was an honourable woman, by no means to be classified with the bulk of the other non-political prisoners. Her only crime, for which she was serving a term of two years' imprisonment, was to have been found in possession of a revolver, being a German. Both she and her husband, she told me, had been militant National Socialists from the start, and were still so, notwithstanding the fact of having been forced to go through the "de-Nazification" farce so that they might be allowed to continue earning their living. She related to me anecdotes from her life in occupied France, and others from the glorious early days of the National Socialist struggle for power. She told me how, once in her life, she had had the privilege of meeting the Führer and of hearing him address her a few simple uplifting words, in his own voice, sometime in 1934.

"I would give anything to have such a memory as that, I who have never seen him," said I.

She answered me: "You will see him one day; he is alive."

I felt a sudden gush of joy fill my heart. I forgot for a while that I was in the courtyard of a prison, only to remember that all Germany, all Europe, was a prison, since 1945, but that one day, we, Hitler's faithful ones, would be free, and that all would be well with use since "he" breathed, somewhere on this earth, never mind where. Indeed, all Germany seemed to know that "he" was not dead, and to be waiting for him.

I looked up to the blue sky that shone above us and thought of the miracle that had saved my book. "If that is possible, anything is possible," felt I. "Perhaps one day I shall be thankful for having survived the disaster of 1945."

C. P., who was to be free in a month's time or so, told me: "When you are released, come and stay with us. You are Germany's sincere friend; our house will be yours. Or if, as I fear, they don't allow you to remain in the country, then write to me, now and then." Once more, I felt, in her, that unfailing love with which the German people have repaid a millionfold the little I have tried to do to show them that I have not turned away from them in the hour of defeat. And I was happy; for it is sweet to be loved by those whom one loves and admires. Now, all the white bread and other nice things that I could no longer give to H. E., I gave to C. P.

The woman was, however, less intelligent than H. E. She had not yet found out for herself that Christianity and National Socialism cannot go together. And after telling me that she had been brought up in the most pious Protestant atmosphere, she declared to me one morning, in the course of a conversation, that, in Germany, the Protestants were "much better Nazis than the Catholics."

My first reaction would have been to reply: "My dear friend, doesn't it occur to you that *no* out-and-out Nazi can profess a religion that allows every shameful mixture of blood provided it takes place under the cover of a so-called 'sacrament'? Now, neither does the Catholic Church *nor the Protestant* forbid what we call shameful unions—crimes against the Aryan race."

But I knew that it is sometimes dangerous to enlighten people too abruptly.

And I reflected that, indeed, I did not know C. P. enough to be sure that, in the case she felt she had to choose between her beloved National Socialist Ideology and her professed traditional religion—in the case she realised, at last, that they were two incompatible religions—she would necessarily choose National Socialism. I therefore refrained from trying to make her realise it. I merely remarked—firmly, but without any direct allusions and direct attacks—that, in any free Aryan country, the priests of all confessions should stress the importance of the basic principles of National Socialism in daily life, in particular, that of the ideal of purity of blood. The woman agreed with me enthusiastically, without realising for a minute that, to do so, would be for them to reject the very spirit of Christianity, which is pre-eminently other-worldly and—like that of any Jewish teaching for non-Jewish consumption—essentially equalitarian.

Back in my cell, I remembered how brilliantly H. E. had understood that; and how conscious she was of the revolutionary character of our faith on the philosophical plane—no less than on the political. And I missed her more than ever.

* * *

During those last weeks I spent in jail, I made the acquaintance of another prisoner who deserves to be mentioned: a French woman, living in Germany ever since 1941, and sentenced to two years imprisonment for having indulged in abortion practices. Few women have lived as innocently a filthier life than hers, and few have had, amidst countless sordid experiences, the privileges that she has enjoyed.

She was called L. C., but she went under the nick name of D. And she was undoubtedly the most cheerful inmate of the whole *"Frauenhaus."* The Dutch woman had introduced her to me, telling me that I could speak French with her—which I did. D. seemed glad to meet me. "I have heard of you already from the others," said she.

"And you don't mind my being a Nazi?"

"Dear me, no!" exclaimed the French woman. "I like Nazis. My man is one."

The person she so crudely described in French as *mon homme*, "my man," was a German whom she had met in France in 1940, and with whom she had lived ever since, after having all her life, before, during, and after the two short periods during which she had been married, revelled in utter sexual promiscuity.

Her redeeming feature was that she was fundamentally promiscuous by temperament, rather than venal. She did not mind, of course, taking presents and money from men, but she seldom took a lover solely for the financial advantages he would give her. She had chosen her life freely, deliberately, feeling—as the "sacred" harlots of Antiquity probably did—that the best thing *she* could do in this world was to give a short but necessary satisfaction to thousands of men. She was intelligent and unscrupulous; witty, and full of gaiety and without guile. She had the cynicism of all those who have never experienced remorse. As I said, she was innocent—as innocent, in a way, as myself, her exact opposite. Her sense of honour was, no doubt, very different from that of an honest woman according to the Christians or according to us. But she had a sense of honour, and a weird, inconsistent loyalty of her own. She had made money on the black market, in Germany, during the war, and practiced abortion upon German women, half the time without the excuse that the father of the unwanted child was physically or racially unworthy—done things, in one word, that would fill any of us with indignation—and yet, on the other hand, she had worked with unabated ardour and helped the German war effort with all her heart, both in France and in Germany, convinced that Germany's victory would be the salvation of Europe. I would have myself liked to have rendered the cause certain of the services she told me she had rendered, while still in France. And she had remained faithful to Germany *after* the war. She said of "her man": "I'll marry him, when I am released, and remain here. His country will be mine. I was born near the frontier anyhow."

I used to meet her in the recreation room. She spoke the most picturesque French slang I have ever heard, and she knew the ins and outs of the underworld in Paris and other places. She would often make coarse jokes; she would talk about her lovers and compare their abilities; she would relate smutty stories from the three brothels of which she had been in turn the manageress—stories that made me feel thankful for never having had as much as a peep into one whole side of human experience. She would even speak of her intimacy with "her man," much to my embarrassment. But when she liked, she could also speak of other things. And sometimes the scenes she evoked made me forget all the squalor of her sexual life and envy her for the privileges she had had, or for certain things she had done.

Once, with an unaffected eloquence that brought tears into my eyes, she described to me the most beautiful sight that she had seen in her life: the parade of the German Army beneath the Arc de Triomphe de l'Etoile and along the Avenue des Champs Elysées, in conquered Paris. "You know, my man took part in it; and it is I who shined his boots for him; and didn't they shine like looking-glasses!" said she, with all the pride of the eternal primitive woman who has won herself the favour of a victorious soldier superior to the males of her own nation. "I got up early in the morning to prepare everything for him. You don't know how happy he was, my man, on that day—and I too! It was a splendid day, the like of which I have never seen. I went and stood to see 'them' pass. Oh, you should have seen that beautiful display of uniforms and flags and helmets shining in the sunshine! And that unbelievably perfect coordination in the men's movements, so perfect that it seemed unreal! And you should have heard the music—the Song!"

I listened to her with rapture, while slowly a tear rolled down each of my cheeks. The tune and words of the Horst Wessel Song resounded within my heart:

> Soon Hitler's flags will wave along all the highways;
> Slavery has but a short time more to last.

Oh, those words! "Those words were heard in Paris along the conquered avenue, and *I* was not, there," thought I once more.

"You should have heard the Song," repeated the woman, as though she had guessed my secret regret. And she added proudly: "*I was there.* A parade like that, I have never witnessed; nor shall I witness again . . . unless 'they' come back one day. Nobody knows."

I was thinking: "This woman had never given a thought to the Nazi Idea before she met 'her man'; and yet, *she was there.* Why was I so far away?" And it was difficult for me to brush aside a feeling of envy.

Another time, D. related to me how, after the war, in Berlin, she had met two distressed Germans—two S.S. men, escaped from Russia, who, after having walked for days and days, lay exhausted and half-dead of hunger on the side of the road. She had brought them to her room, fed them for a week or so, given them civilian clothes so that they might continue their journey and reach their families unnoticed. "I used to go with the Americans and 'pinch' their cigarettes and sell them over," she told me. "Cigarettes fetched a lot of money, then, as you surely know. I used to 'pinch' their purses, too, when they were drunk. In that way, I gathered quite an important sum for my two Germans to take home. And I gave them plenty of food, also—butter, jam, preserves of all sorts. You should have seen how glad they were, the poor dears! And they wrote to me, and thanked me, when they reached their place of destination."

"You have saved two of my Führer's people. For that alone, may the heavenly Powers protect you all your life!" said I, deeply moved. And again I envied her, I who had done nothing but distribute ten thousand leaflets.

* * *

On Monday the 25th of July, I ran to Frau *Oberin*'s office to answer an unexpected telephone call. It was Colonel Vickers himself talking to me.

"We are doing all we can to enable you to leave this prison as soon as possible," said he. "However, it is less easy than we thought to send you straight back to India. And anyhow, the formalities would take a long time. Is there not a place nearer than India, where you would like to be sent in the meantime—for I have no need to tell you that you will not be allowed to remain in the British Zone."

"Could I not be sent to the French Zone?" asked I, brazenly. "I have friends there." In fact, I much preferred to remain in the French Zone than to be sent back to India. And although I did not dare to hope to hear that I could, I thought to myself: "I have nothing to lose by asking." Colonel Vickers seemed a little taken aback by my audacity. When he had asked me whether there was not a country nearer than India where I would like to stay, he had never expected me to answer so unhesitatingly: "There is Germany itself." He was puzzled.

"That, of course, is the lookout of the French authorities, and no business of mine," replied he. "However, I would not advise you to ask to remain in Germany at all. Have you no friends or relatives elsewhere?"

I reflected that he was perhaps right—from *my* point of view also. Anyhow, I would not be able to publish my book in Germany, for some years. While elsewhere, away from Europe, who knows, perhaps I could much sooner. However it be, I would have to type it first. I remembered that in Lyons, my native town, I knew someone who would probably lend me a typewriter. My mother lived in Lyons. But I did not know how far she would allow me to live in her house, for on account of my views there was no longer any love between us since the war. I did not know how far a Greek woman who had lodged me previously, would be willing to put me up *now*. She knew me for years, and agreed with me far better than my mother did. But she might be afraid to take me in after my imprisonment, I thought. I answered, however, hoping for the best: "I could perhaps go to France. My mother lives in Lyons."

"That is perfect," exclaimed the Governor, at the other end of the wire. "Why didn't you tell me that at once? Well, I shall try to secure you a visa for France."

"I could go back to India from there, when my husband sends me my passage money," said I, reflecting that I had, at first, perhaps a little too enthusiastically proposed to remain in Germany, and trying to counteract the impression that my haste might have produced.

"That is all right; once in France you can go where you please; it is no business of mine," said Colonel Vickers. "I am going to try to get you a visa for France. If they give it to you, you should be free within a month or so."

"Thank you! I have indeed no words to express how much I thank you," said I, putting up the receiver.

I felt at once all my old self-assurance, all my old aggressiveness come back to me. I was virtually no longer a prisoner. Soon, thought I, I would no longer need even to be "diplomatic." What a relief!

Frau *Oberin* was watching my face.

"Going away from here soon?" she asked me, smiling. "Pleased to be free?"

"Not only pleased to be free, but hoping to be a little more useful than I am here," said I. "You know French. You probably know one or two French popular songs. What do you think of this one?"

And I sang to her the two last lines of an old song, that the schoolgirls used to sing in the playground, when I was a child:

. . . The punishment is sweet,
And ro ro ro, little pa ta po,
The punishment is sweet,
We shall begin again, ro ro,
We shall begin again . . .[8]

Once more, Frau *Oberin*'s face brightened. But she *said* nothing.

"Am I not right?" I asked her at last.

"You are as hasty as a child," replied she. "Great things take time."

I wanted to say: "They take time to ripen, perhaps. But once the atmosphere is created, they happen quickly." But I kept silent, thinking: "What does it matter, now, whether I *say* this or that? Even if I cannot speak freely, I shall now soon be able at least to *write* freely . . ."

Frau *Oberin* let me return to my cell unaccompanied, thus giving me a foretaste of freedom. And I walked along the empty corridor, with my two hands in my pockets, feeling happy, and humming once more the old French song:

. . . We shall begin again, ro ro,
We shall begin again!

---

[8] La pénitence est douse,
   et ron ron ron, petit patapon,
   La penitence est douse, nous recommencerons ron ron,
   Nous recommencerons!

17. Savitri Devi's visa to return to France from Germany after her release from Werl.

"When I used to sing that in the playground of the school, with other little girls, thirty-five years ago, who could have foretold that one day I would give these words the meaning which I give them now?" thought I. And once more, I thanked the Gods for my beautiful destiny.

I was now writing Chapter 5 of *The Lightning and the Sun*, about the childhood and early tribal wars of Genghis Khan. I was happy, because the subject interested me immensely, and also because I felt I was doing something useful. The whole book—of which the study of Genghis Khan's life represented only a part—put forth a definite conception of history, and that conception was ours. The Governor had told me in the most casual manner: "Oh, you can write about Genghis Khan as much as you like," as though to say: "Thirteenth century stuff!—*That's* not dangerous." "And yet," thought I, as I read over a whole paragraph that I had just written, "nothing could be more National Socialistic in spirit than *this*."

I recalled an incident from the time I was in Paris trying to obtain a military permit to enter Germany. I had already secured my entry into the French Zone—with which I could, in fact, travel all over Western Germany. I tried to obtain a permit for the Russian Zone through a vague acquaintance of mine, a rather insignificant Frenchman (so I thought) who had been a student at the same time as I and who, while I was in India, had undergone an evolution in the direction of Communism. The man had taken an active part in the French *"résistance"*; he was a journalist, and knew many people. Naturally, I did not go and tell him who *I* was. Nor did he ask me directly. He merely asked to have a look at any one of the books I had written. My only book in French, apart from my two doctorate theses, was *L'Etang aux Lotus*, a book about India, written in 1935.[9] I handed him over a copy of it thinking: "The devil himself would not be shrewd enough to guess my views from this mere collection of impressions about a tropical land." But, to my amazement, the man, after reading a page told me: "I see you are an out-and-out follower of Adolf Hitler. It is as clear to me as daylight. No doubt your book is about India. But you see India from the National Socialist standpoint." I admired the man's perspicacity. Needless to say that I had to give up all hope of obtaining through him a permit for the Russian Zone.

I remembered now—as I had then—the words of Emerson: "A cat can do nothing which is not essentially graceful." "I suppose *I* can do nothing which is not essentially National Socialistic," thought I, "and

---

[9] *L'Etang aux Lotus* was begun in 1935 and finished in 1937. The Avant-Propos (Foreword), which Savitri customarily wrote last, is dated 15 November 1937.—Ed.

write nothing which is not propaganda in disguise, whether the actual subject-matter be India, Akhnaton, or Genghis Khan."

And I was all the more happy to realise that I did not do so intentionally, but that it was the consequence of my natural orthodoxy.

* * *

Frau S., who came to see me in my cell practically every day, told me that my comrades of the D wing, in particular my beloved H. E., would very probably be released before the end of the year. Already L. M., whose term expired in a year, was to be freed in two days' time. "Decidedly," thought I, "things are changing." And I was actually happier to hear that news than I had been to hear Colonel Vickers tell me of my own release.

I tried to imagine the feelings of my comrades. I knew that none of the genuine National Socialists among them was "reformed"—any more than *I* was. A few might, for a time, refrain from all dangerous activities. But somehow I felt that the trend of events would, sooner or later, bring back the great hopes of the past, the tension and enthusiasm of before 1933. And the words I had hummed along the corridor at the news of my release seemed to come back to me as an echo from the hearts of all the released Nazis of Germany: "We shall begin again!" I was happy.

The only thing that grieved me during those last days was the loss of the little glass portrait of the Führer that I had worn around my neck. Frau *Oberin* had really intended to give it back to me, as she had promised me. But, she told me, it had dropped out of her pocket, and Fräulein S. had caught sight of it—then, when the whole staff was under the threat of being sacked on account of me—and she had insisted on destroying it.

"Had I known that these people would themselves give you back all your things, I would never have allowed her to do so," said Frau *Oberin*. "But you don't realise what a panic seized us all when your cell was searched. You will hate me, no doubt. But what can I do now? The harm is done."

I wept when she told me that. "You don't know what that little portrait meant to me," said I; "it was given to me by one of the finest German women I know, who deprived herself of it to put it around my neck, telling me she thought me worthy to wear it. Yet, don't believe I hate you. I don't hate Fräulein S.—although, to think that she could break such a thing to pieces with a hammer surpasses my understanding . . ."

In a flash, I remembered the ruins of Germany, and all the horror of the long-drawn occupation. Fräulein S.'s panic was but a tiny instance of the widespread terror that oppressed the whole land. "I don't hate you, or her, or any German who, out of fear, might cause me to suffer," pursued I: "I hate those swine—the Allies—who have imposed upon Germany the reign of fear."

Frau *Oberin* kissed me. Her eyes were full of tears.

"What can I do now, to please you, before you go?" she asked me.

"Allow me to spend an hour with H. E.," replied I.

"You shall," said she. "But, mind you, don't tell anyone—*anyone!*"

* * *

On Sunday, the 14th of August, as soon as the Catholic Church service began, Fräulein S., obeying Frau *Oberin*'s instructions, came to fetch me. On tip-toe, she led me to one of the washing rooms. She then went to fetch H. E., and locked us both in. I shall always remember with intense emotion that last conversation in jail with one of the persons I love the most on earth.

We gazed at each other, and fell in each other's arms—like on the day we first met. And we kissed each other.

"I am so glad to know that you are being released," said H. E.; "L. M. is now free; you know?"

"Yes," replied I, "Frau S. told me. Moreover, I met her myself in the corridor on my way back from the 'free hour' as she was going out, and I shook hands with her. I wanted to talk to her, but Frau *Erste* was there, and would not allow me."

"L. M. has left me her address for you. You must write to her," said H. E. And she gave me a piece of paper which I put in my breast. She pursued anxiously, without giving me the time to add a word: "Did you receive the letter and addresses that I sent you days ago?"

"I have but only yesterday; the girl had not the opportunity to come into my cell before," replied I, alluding to a prisoner who used to clean our windows and in whose hands H. E. had given her message for me. "Don't fear," pursued I, "I shall keep the addresses in my memory, and write to the people as soon as I am free—and give news of you. I wish I could pay a visit to them. But I am afraid I am to be taken in a car straight from here to the border of the French Zone. And there, it seems, I shall be watched; I was told so the other day when I went down to the Governor's office to fill the forms in connection with my visa for France. Anyhow, in France I hope to be more free. I shall type my book there— provided they do not search me at the frontier and take it away from me. I shall not feel really safe until I have crossed the frontier. Then . . . not only shall I type my book, as I said, but I shall write another one, about our life in Werl. You will have a great place in it.—It does not matter to you, does it? You will be free anyhow, long before I can publish the book. I don't know whether I shall go back to India, or whether I shall try to go to South America or elsewhere. I must write to my husband first; see what he suggests, for he always gives me sound advice. But, wherever I be, wherever I go, be sure that my heart will remain here with you, with the others. Never, never shall I give up our struggle, as long as I live! And one day, when times change, I shall come back. My H. . . . , how lovely it will be for us to meet again in a free Germany, and to speak of the bygone nightmare, when it is all over."

"Yes," replied H. E. thoughtfully, "it will be lovely. But we have yet a long and difficult road to walk, before that. I hope to be myself free soon—next year, or by the end of this, from what I hear. Oh, how I am longing and longing to be free, you can't imagine! You were captive six months; I, already four years. And before that, all the horrors of which I told you are but a small part of what my eyes have seen. You call us, German National Socialists, 'the gold in the furnace'. We are. We have suffered beyond human bearing. And yet, as you say, nothing can crush us. I, for one, am a better Nazi *now* than I was during our great days. I know it. For now I understand *why* we were right to be merciless in dealing with the Jews and traitors, nay why we were not merciless enough. And you have contributed to make me understand it. You have contributed to make me realise how universal and eternal our Nazi *Weltanschauung* is. Honestly; I admire you . . ."

I felt ashamed, and interrupted her. "Don't say such things!" exclaimed I. "Admire the martyrs of Schwarzenborn and Darmstadt, not me. I have not suffered."

"You love our Führer, and you love us," said H. E. "Of all those foreigners who seemed to be on our side, when we were powerful, you are the only one who loved us. They all turned their backs on us, when we were defeated, or tried to *excuse* their collaboration with us by all sorts of arguments. You have boasted of your allegiance to Adolf Hitler before your judges, now. And no sooner free, you are ready to fight for us again, solely because of what we represent in your eyes."

"Which pure-blooded Aryan," said I, "can be, as I am, fully conscious of the supreme value of Aryandom, and yet not believe in Germany's divinely-appointed mission in the modern world, and not love you?"

I took her hands in mine, while tears filled my eyes. "My H. . . . ," continued I, "you, one of the few millions in whom the higher mankind of my dreams breathes in all its strength and glory, and one of the first victims of our enemies; my living Germany, . . . it is you whom I admire from the depth of my heart. I shall miss you, now, in the hostile outer world, as I have missed you all these weeks. For there, where I shall be going in a day or two, I shall not have a single comrade to whom I shall be able to open my heart . . .”

“But you will be useful,” said H. E. “You will be writing for us.”

“Yes; that is true . . .”

And to think of that made me feel my parting from her less painful.

“Moreover,” said she, “we must meet again. I’ll write to you, as soon as I am free. And if you are in India, who knows? I might try to go there myself, if conditions here are not yet favourable to us. Do you know what I would like? I would like to relate to you in detail all that I have seen since we fell into the hands of these people, so that you might write it down, and so that the world might know, one day, what we suffered. You are the person to write our true story.”

“You flatter me,” replied I. “But I would do it willingly, to the best of my ability. And I would be happy to have you at my side, be it in India, be it elsewhere.”

And I imagined myself waiting for her, one day, at the Howrah Station, in Calcutta. “Why not?” thought I; “the world is small.” However I would be still happier to see her waiting for me in Berlin, if Germany were once more under our régime . . .

We spoke freely of our plans, of our hopes, of the possibilities of tomorrow. “What would you do if there were a war?” she asked me—“a war between Russia and the U.S.A.”

“Nothing,” replied I. “I would look at our enemies—the ex-allies of 1945—tear each other to pieces, and I would laugh (provided *we* are not involved). Why should I stir to help these to make the world a safe place for Democracy, or to help those to make it a safe place for Communism, when I hate both? I shall not budge—not side with either block *unless* I am ordered to in the name of the *‘Realpolitik’* of the Party, by someone who has authority to speak.”

“I feel exactly the same as you,” said H. E. “And I believe we all do.”

“Never to forget and never to forgive,[10] but to place the interest of the Nazi cause above everything—even above the most legitimate yearning for revenge, if need be—that is my whole attitude in a nutshell,” ex-

---

[10] “Never forget, never forgive” is the refrain of “1953,” a poem Savitri wrote in Athens on 26 March 1953, Hertha Ehlert’s birthday. See *And Time Rolls On*, p. 170. “1953” is the final poem of *Forever and Ever*, Savitri’s volume of prose poems written in 1951–53.

plained I.

"Never to forget and never to forgive," repeated H. E. "Once already, you told me that. You are right. But as you say, no apparent concessions to expediency are too great if they really be means to achieve our final triumph, condition of the establishment of our new civilisation."

Frau *Oberin* came herself to tell us that time was up. And we thanked her for having allowed us that hour of heart-to-heart communion.

"Good luck to you!" said H. E., then turning to me: "May the Powers in heaven protect you, and bring us together again, one day!"

"Yes"; replied I. "And may They protect you, also, and all of us, and help us to restore the New Order! Heil Hitler!"

"Heil Hitler!" repeated she, raising her arm in her turn. And we parted on those holy words of faith and power.

* * *

I was to leave Werl on the morning of the following Thursday, the 18th of August. Frau *Oberin*, whose summer holiday started in the meantime, came to say goodbye to me in my cell, on Sunday evening. For the first time, knowing she would not see me again so long as Germany remained under Allied occupation, she spoke of her allegiance to our Ideology. "My father was in the Party," said she; "and so was I."

My face brightened. "I felt it," exclaimed I; "I felt it all the time, without being sure. But tell me: how is it that 'these people' kept you in service? They have sacked so many who have our views . . ."

"They did," replied Frau *Oberin*; "but they could not sack us all, for then there would have been nobody left to carry on the administration of the country."

"I want to meet you again, one day, when Germany is free," said I. "It is you who allowed me to write, while I was here; you, who allowed me to meet one or two at least of my comrades. I can never forget that. And now, I know I shall miss you—as I shall miss Frau S. and Frau So-and-so, and Frau X., and, of course, H. E. I shall be free, no doubt; but I shall be in a hostile atmosphere. I shall often look back to our friendly conversations, and to the understanding and sympathy that I enjoyed here. I shall often say to myself, remembering you and a few other members of the staff: 'I was in prison, no doubt; but at least I was in Germany'. I know I shall say that, when I am gone, and alone."

Frau *Oberin* seemed moved, yet she said: "It is easier to get out of a hostile atmosphere when one is free, than it is to get out of prison. Be thankful for your freedom. You will be more useful free."

"You talk like H. E.," said I.

"I talk common sense," replied she.

"Oh, if only I could go to South America, now that I am expelled from Germany," said I, thinking aloud. "But how? I know nobody over there, and the little gold I have left is not enough to pay my passage . . ."

"Don't worry over the future," answered Frau *Oberin*; "Be thankful that you are now free, and you will see: things will happen for the best, in the long run."

"You are probably right," said I. And I thought: "The unseen Powers Who have miraculously saved my manuscript will help me to publish it in due time, and guide me in the service of the Nazi cause."

Frau *Oberin* bade me farewell. And for the first time I saluted her with the ritual gesture and the two forbidden words: "Heil Hitler!"

She smiled to me sadly. But she did not return my salute. Was she afraid that somebody might see her through the spy hole? Who knows?

Frau So-and-so and Frau X. also came to say goodbye to me. And they left me their addresses. "Write to us," they said; "but be careful what you write. Remember this is not a free country."

I recalled in my mind the unforgettable, tragic words about Germany: "This is the land of fear," and I thought: "Until when?" And I longed for the events, whichever they might be, that would, sooner or later, enable my Führer's people to get back their place in the world. I did not care— any more than I do now—if the nine-tenths of the globe had to be blown to atoms as a prelude to the achievement of that one great goal: the rule of the best; the establishment of a new civilisation on the basis of our everlasting principles.

Frau S. came in the evening of the 17th of August, which was my last evening in Werl. She did not give me her address. "No my dear, you are too dangerous a person," replied she, when I asked for it. "You are sincere, and above reproach from the ideological standpoint; but you are impulsive; you might, with the best of intentions, write things that are likely to incriminate people. I prefer to keep on the safe side as long as the occupants are here."

"And how long do you think that will be?" asked I.

"I don't know," answered Frau S.; "nobody knows. They are sure to go away some day, as nothing lasts forever. They are giving us a 'government' very soon, it seems, which of course means nothing, as it is only a puppet government. They are asking us to vote. But we can choose only among the parties which 'they' authorise—all puppet parties. On the other side of the Elbe, where the Russians rule, it is no better—even worse, people say. There is no hope for us except in the mutual destruction of our oppressors, that is to say, in war. We would not mind that if our country were not to become, in all probability, the battlefield of the two hated forces. But we have had enough bombing, enough misery, enough war *on our territory . . .*"

I understood her easily, after having seen those hundreds of miles of ruins. "I know," said I; "I know. And yet, is not even that less horrible than slavery forever?"

Frau S. gazed at me very earnestly and replied: "More and more Germans think as you do, and, . . . in spite of all that we suffered, I am increasingly inclined to think the same. Rather than this Democracy forever or Communism forever, we would all, I believe, prefer destruction."

"Destruction?" repeated I, as though speaking to myself—"or . . . resurrection?" And tears filled my eyes as I uttered those words. I thought of the subject of the Führer's first great public lecture, in the dark days after the First World War: Future, or ruin.

"Listen," said I to Frau S.; "I have not lived the ordeal of total war as you have. And I am not a German. But one thing I always knew; one thing I know, more than ever now, since I have come to Germany—to this defeated Germany, in the most atrocious period of her history—and that is: nothing can crush the German people. And now that such a people are realising, every day more and more, what National Socialism meant; now that they are, every day more vividly, feeling the contrast between Hitler's glorious New Order and the disgusting rule of the scum—the rule of the self-seeker, of the frustrated nonentity, and of the international Jew—imposed upon them by the "fighters for human rights," now, I say, nothing can crush National Socialism. I know not through which unpredictable interaction of circumstances—in other words *how*—that Germany whom I have admired so many years, National Socialist Germany, real Germany, will rise, one day, out of this unprecedented humiliation. But I know she will rise—rise and conquer once more, as I wrote in my first leaflets. I know it because I have confidence in you, my Führer's people, and in the unseen Forces that lead you to your tremendous destiny. I know it because I know my Führer—our Führer—is alive; because, even if he were to die, his spirit can never die."

Frau S. gazed at me once more. "It is better that you are expelled from this unfortunate country," said she; "if you were allowed to remain, you would only get yourself caught again, which would be a pity. But you are perhaps right. Anyhow, your words have power. And one day, if things change, if you can come back, you will be welcome—and you might be useful."

"I would like to publish in Germany the book that I have just written, the book in which I have put all my heart. Will you do that for me, one day, if things change?" asked I.

"We shall do that for ourselves," replied Frau S. with a smile. "To *you*, what shall we give? Tell us yourself, now, what you would like."

"Nothing," answered I, without hesitation. "All I want is the satisfaction of knowing that the regenerate Aryandom of my dreams has become a lasting powerful reality, a conquering force."

"And there is absolutely nothing that you would like to enjoy, you personally, under that New Order that you love so much? Not a place of honour? Not a single personal advantage?"

"Absolutely nothing," repeated I, sincerely. "The joy of knowing that henceforth all is well would be sufficient for me."

But I reflected a minute, and then rectified my statement. "Or rather," said I, "I forgot: there is something I would like under our restored New Order; there are two things that I would like, in fact, if I could have them . . ."

"And what are they?" asked Frau S., all the more vividly interested that I had not, at first, put forth any ambitions.

"I would like to have the privilege of meeting the Führer at least once," said I; "and I would like to be declared—if that were possible, be it after I am dead—'honorary citizen of the Reich'."

Frau S. took my hands in hers and smiled at me again. "You are an idealist," said she. And she added, conferring unto me for the second time, on the eve of my release, the supreme title of honour of which she had deemed me worthy in the depth of distress: ". . . a genuine National Socialist."

* * *

The morning came—the morning of the day I was to be free.

I had not slept all night; I had prayed. I had thanked the invisible Gods for the fact that I was to take my manuscripts with me, in a few hours' time. And I begged for serenity—detachment—and efficiency. "Free me of all vanity, O Lord of truth," I prayed; "free me of all pettiness, of all childish haste. And help me to serve our cause, which is Thine, with absolute selflessness as well as with iron determination. And may I be useful in the long run if I cannot do much now!"

As I saw the first ray of sunshine strike the huge building opposite the *"Frauenhaus,"* I got up and washed. I then sang the Horst Wessel Song, my arm stretched out towards the east—towards the Sun. I knew nobody would ask me to be silent, especially as it was my last day. (In fact, throughout my stay in Werl, nobody ever had tried to prevent me from singing the Horst Wessel Song or any other.)

It was on my way back from the "free hour" that Frau *Erste*, the matron, told me to gather the few things that remained in my cell and to go to the cloakroom with them, when I had dressed. My luggage I had packed two days before, with Frau *Oberin*'s permission. I wore the selfsame dark-red frock in which I had crossed the frontier on my second journey to Germany. I took in hand my brown attaché case—the one I had on the night of my arrest.—I had put in it my manuscripts, the picture of the Führer, and all the things that I valued the most. I carried my coat on my left arm.

As I walked out of the cloakroom, ready, with Frau *Erste* and a prisoner who helped me to carry my luggage, I met Frau S. who had come to see me once more before I left.

"*Auf Wiedersehen!*" said I—"until we meet again in a free Germany!"

"*Auf Wiedersehen!*" said she—"and good luck to you, wherever you go in the meantime!"

I went to Frau *Oberin*'s office to say goodbye to Fräulein S. (Frau *Oberin* herself was, as I said, on leave.)

"Take good care you do not come back here sooner than you expect. That would not surprise me seeing the mood in which you are," Fräulein S. told me.

"Don't worry about me," replied I; "I'll be more careful next time than I was this, if ever I come back to Germany before 'these people' are out."

"I would advise you not to try to return before they are out."

"Well," said I, "I might listen to you. It will take me some time, anyhow, to type my book. And I might write another one before I try to come back."

Before I left, I handed over to Fräulein S. a pair of pearl earrings, my remembrance gift to my beloved H. E. I had not been able to give it to H. E. myself, as my jewellery had not been given back to me until the very last moment before my departure. Fräulein S. put the earrings in a paper envelope containing H. E.'s belongings, and added them in writing to the list of the latter, on the page corresponding to my friend's name, in a large catalogue. I was glad. One day, when the comrade I loved the most would leave Werl, she would find those pretty daisies, each one composed of seven real pearls, and she would remember me, and our last conversation, and the unbreakable link of faith that binds us together forever.

I was taken with my luggage to an empty cell, and left there alone, until it was announced from the Governor's office that the policewoman who was to accompany me to the border of the British Zone, had come with the car. Frau *Erste* then took me down. "Be careful not to do any foolish things as we cross the courtyard," she told me: "The D wing prisoners are now having their 'free hour'."

As on the morning that had followed my trial, I saw from the top of the stairs my comrades, the so-called "war criminals," walking around the courtyard, and my heart ached. I was now going away—being released through God alone knows what distant influences. (In a letter, an old Indian friend of mine had told me that a telegram had been sent to Pandit Nehru, asking the Indian Government to intervene in my favour.[11]) But they—they who had suffered so much more than I—when would *they* have the joy of crossing the threshold of the prison in their civilian clothes, once more? When would *they* be free? "Give them back their freedom, soon, Lord of the unseen Forces," I prayed within my heart; "give us all back, soon, freedom and power, and the joy of the great days!"

I noticed that Frau X., and Frau So-and-so, the two wardresses whom I knew to be "in order," were on duty. "You don't mind me going to say goodbye to Frau X. and to Frau So-and-so?" I asked the matron.

"You can go," replied she; "but you must not speak to the prisoners."

I shook hands with the wardresses. But I could not help giving my comrades a last glance. I saw H. E. among them; and H. B. and H., the other two victims of the Belsen trial; and Frau S., the martyr without faith; and Frau R., formerly in service at Ravensbrück, of whom I had been told that she was one of the "real ones" of the D wing. I gazed at them all; and tears filled my eyes. "Slavery has but a short time more to last!" cried I, quoting the last words of the Horst Wessel Song, before I walked to the gate that separated the courtyard of the *"Frauenhaus"* from the rest of the prison.

There, seeing that the matron had gone ahead of me and was busy unlocking the next gate, I turned around, lifted my arm and cried: "Heil Hitler!" I was too far for my comrades to hear me. But some of them

[11] In the Indian Government's Home Political Index for 1949, the following entry appears: "Mukherji, Mrs. Savitri Devi—Question of the deportation to India of ___ German-born [sic] wife of Mr. Asit Krishnan [sic] Mukherji. File No. 96-F-II." This indicates that the question of Savitri Devi's arrest was taken up by the Indian government. Unfortunately, the file was not transferred to the National Archives of India, and thus was not available for examination. The file may have been classified, or it might simply have been destroyed.—Ed.

could see me. And out of the dreary prisoners' round, several other arms lifted themselves in answer to my gesture.

* * *

It was not Miss Taylor who had come to fetch me, but another English policewoman whose name I do not know. Colonel Vickers was not in his office. Nor did I see Mr. Stocks. I bade farewell to Mr. Harris, the Chief Warden, and to Mr. Watts, the Governor's assistant.

I was given a copy of the order expelling me from the British Zone "for five years" as a person whose presence was considered to be "against the interest of peace, order, and good government of the said Zone."

I crossed the courtyard, and the two last gates that separated me from the world of the free were flung open before me. I found myself on the threshold of the prison, breathing the scented air from the neighbouring gardens. I remembered the evening when I had stood on that very threshold, believing that I was entering the gloom of captivity for three long years. And lo, hardly six months had passed, and I was free once more; and my precious writings were with me, in my own hands, saved from destruction by some miracle of the Gods. I gazed at the bright blue sky with an overwhelming feeling of infinite gratitude, and I whispered the sacred Name of the Lord of the Dance of creation and destruction, in the oldest known Aryan language—the Name I had repeated in the depth of despair—"Aum, Rudrayam! Aum, Shivayam!"

With those holy syllables on my lips and in my heart, I stepped into the car that was to carry me to freedom; to action, whether in darkness or broad daylight; to the new place appointed to me by Destiny, in the present-day struggle for Adolf Hitler and for Aryandom—in the eternal struggle for truth.

* * *

The car rolled along the same *Autobahn* along which I had several times travelled, there and back, between Werl and Düsseldorf, when I was still "on remand." But now, I was being taken to Andernach, on the border between the French and the British Zones. It was a bright summer day. Comfortably seated by the side of the policewoman, I looked out of the window, and regretted I was not allowed to remain in Germany.

Never, perhaps, had I been so strongly conscious of the hold Hitler's country had on me, as now that I was forced to leave it. I gazed at the fields, at the bushes on the roadside, at the occasional passers-by, at the half-ruined towns through which the car rolled without stopping. It all seemed to me like home. I reflected that, whether in the place of my birth or elsewhere, I had never had a real home; that, beyond the exceedingly narrow circles of people who shared my aspirations, everywhere, all my life, I had been a foreigner, even in the lands that I could, at first sight, call the most spontaneously "mine," Greece and England; even in hallowed India where I had sought the continuity of Aryan tradition—for the people who shared my aspirations were amazingly few, there too. I had been "a nationalist of every land" as I had once so accurately described myself; a foreigner with the yearning for a country that I could serve without reservations, for a people with whom I could identify myself entirely, without regret. A profound sadness came over me, as I thought of that. And the landscape that smiled to me on either side of the *Autobahn*, appeared to me more beautiful, more alive, more appealing than ever.

We crossed a small town in which I noticed in passing a ruined wall covered with living creeper. "Life," thought I; "irresistible life that nothing can crush." I saw in that conquering patch of green a symbol of invincible Germany. And I recalled in my mind our Führer's words: "It is not lost wars that bring men down, but the loss of that power of resistance that resides in pure blood alone."[12] And I prayed that the unseen Aryan Gods might never allow the German people to forget this. In my heart, I felt sure that they never would. "These are at least the only modern people who have accepted the real Aryan ideals wholeheartedly," thought I, again. "I was not alone, here." And I longed to come back. I longed to finish my life among them; to die, one day, surrounded by understanding friends, while some regiment composed of young men who were babies in 1948 and 1949, when I first came, would march past, before my windows, to the music of the immortal Song . . .

But I knew I would not be able to come back just now. I would have to wait. To wait how long? That, I did not know. It suddenly occurred to me that the enemies of National Socialism did not know any more than I did; that they were not, any more than I, the masters of the workings of the unseen factors on which visible changes depend. And that thought pleased me to the point of making me feel aggressive.

"May I ask you something that puzzles me?" said I to the policewoman at my side—the only person in the car besides the driver and myself.

---

[12] ". . . die Menschen gehen nicht an verlorenen Kriegen zugrunde, sondern am Verlust jener Wiederstandskraft, die nur dem reinen Blute zu eigen ist." (*Mein Kampf*, I, ch. 11, p. 324).

"Certainly; what is it?"

"Well, listen: 'they' have expelled me from the British Zone for five years, it seems—up till the 31st of August 1954. Now, suppose (for the sake of argument) that Germany were to be free and united under a Nazi Government in 1953. What could you do then to keep me from running back at once?"

"In such a case I am afraid we could do nothing," said the policewoman.

"Hum, hum!" insisted I, with a defiant smile; "I am glad to hear you admit it, at least."

"Be careful not to get yourself into trouble again *before* there is a Nazi Government to protect you," replied the policewoman, softly.

"No fear!" exclaimed I; "no fear, as long as I don't *do* anything that is positively against some law of whatever country I shall be living in. And I intend to be careful about *that*. But, barring that—and barring the circumstances in which I might have to be 'diplomatic' in the higher interest of the cause—I intend to make myself as disagreeable as I can to all our opponents wherever I go. I detest anti-Nazis! They call us 'monsters'. Hypocrites, self-seeking rogues, or squeamish fools, that's what *I* call them; degenerates; monkeys—and sickly ones at that; slaves of the Jews, which is the worst one can say . . ."

The policewoman smiled and said: "You are free to have your opinions."

"Yes," retorted I: "free to have them; and free to express them, here, in this car, because the driver does not know English, because it is my first day out of prison, and because you are delighted to show me how magnanimous you Democrats are; but not free to express them in a café, in German, as soon as we step out of here; nor free to publish them in black and white. What hypocrites you are, really! You don't believe in 'individual freedom' any more than we do. You know perfectly well—as everyone else does—that no system of government can last if intelligent and courageous individuals attack the very principles on which it is based. And you defend your parliamentary principles as fiercely as you can. You don't respect the 'individual freedom' of those who have set out to expose their absurdity. You do try to keep us from thinking, through your whole system of so-called 'education'. And if you don't actually punish us for thinking, it is only because you do not believe in the power of thought and therefore hold us to be 'harmless' so long as we *do* nothing against you, or else, because you are not yourselves sufficiently convinced of the truth of your principles to sacrifice human lives to them. The Catholic Inquisitors of old, who valued human life far more than you do (for they all believed in the immortal soul) did not hesitate to get rid of the men whom they considered dangerous to the faith of others. They served what they believed to be the truth. And we, who are only vaguely concerned with the next world—if at all—are prepared to bump off any obstacle that stands in our way, for we too act in the name of truth; of our truth. Your apparent magnanimity comes from the fact that you have no truth to believe in. You only sacrifice human lives to your material interests; you kill off (in the name of 'humanity') those of us who could be a danger to your incomes and to your dreary and 'secure' little pleasures. You believe, not in truth, but in profit—for the Jews and a handful of the most judaised Aryans; and in slowly degrading 'happiness' for the others. Distasteful as they may be, my words are not blasphemy, to you, as your attacks on our régime would be to me. That is why you tolerate me, provided I am not an obvious danger to 'peace, order, and good government'; that is why you were 'kind' to me. Gosh, what hypocrites you are!"

"Yet," said the policewoman, "would you have liked it better if we had tortured you?"

"There is no question of 'liking it better'," replied I. "Had you done it in the interest of something greater than yourselves, in which you really believed, I might have hated you (as I hate the Communists), but I would have respected you. But you don't do such things for higher impersonal interests, with that detachment which alone we people of faith can have. When you do them—and you *have* done them often enough, if not on me, on my comrades and superiors; I know it—you do them out of sheer cruelty; out of spite; for the pleasure of seeing us suffer, now that, for the time being, we are powerless. That is the democratic spirit. Don't I know it?"

"Couldn't we talk of something else?" said the policewoman.

"Talk of something else because you have nothing to say in answer to my tirade?" said I; "yes, why not? Let me just add this: I suppose I shall never change your convictions, whatever they be. All I wanted you to know is that nothing and nobody can change mine. Colonel Vickers told me on the 10th of June that I was 'the most objectionable type of Nazi that he had ever met'. I intend to spend the rest of my life proving how right he was."

The car was entering Andernach.

"Now, come and have a cup of coffee with me at some nice café before we part," added I. "You deserve it for not losing your temper."

We left my luggage in the car and sat at a table in a pleasant-looking café. But somehow the policewoman could not bring herself to "talk of something else" with me. She had visited Germany before the war. She could not refrain from telling me her impressions in a nutshell: "There were, admittedly, quite a number of real idealists," said she; "but the rest . . . were just people trained to do what they were told, like robots . . ."

"Better than in the 'free' Democracies anyhow," retorted I: "for there, everybody thinks what they are told: what they are subtly conditioned to think through the influence of the radio, of the films, and of the penny press; and there are no idealists at all; the conditioning is done solely for the greatest glory of big business, and for the greatest profit of the international Jew . . . Indeed I like our régime—not *that!*"

This time the policewoman started talking about the weather.

* * *

I was formally handed over to the two men on duty at the French police station of Andernach. One of them—apparently the most important of the two—signed a "receipt" for me, which he handed back to the English policewoman. I produced my passport, bearing the visa for France granted me by the French consul in Düsseldorf. The man who seemed the most important of the two asked me why I had been under arrest in the British Zone, and I replied that it was because I had entered the Zone without a military permit and also because I had been found in possession of a five-pound banknote—which were indeed the two minor charges against me. I omitted to mention the main charge of Nazi propaganda. And as I spoke French perfectly, the man asked me no further explanations, and told me I was free to go where I liked.

After taking leave of the English policewoman, I went to the railway station. There was a train for Koblenz in an hour's time or so. I booked my ticket, hired a porter for my luggage, and went to wait on the platform. I sat on a bench for five minutes, then got up, and took to pacing the platform, my brown attaché case in one hand, my bag in the other, at last alone. I could hardly believe that it was true; that I could now go where I pleased, stop where I pleased, speak to whom I pleased, without being always watched, always accompanied; that I was really free. I felt inclined to tell the porter, the passengers, all the people within my reach: "You who always have been free, do not know the meaning of sweet liberty. But I do, I who have just come out of jail. And I tell you: after honour and health, liberty is the greatest treasure." Then, I suddenly thought of H. E. and of all my other comrades, in Werl and in all the prisons in Germany and elsewhere; already serving terms of imprisonment or still waiting to be judged and sentenced as "war criminals."

When would she, when would they at last experience the joy that I now knew, the joy of being free? And the more I thought of them, the more I felt small, I who had suffered so little. And the more I was puzzled at the idea of the miraculous way I had "got away with it." "Why hast Thou freed *me*, and not one of them who are worth more than I, Lord of the unseen Forces?" asked I, within my heart. "Is it that Thou hast put me aside for some work of which I know nothing, yet? Or is it because I am to write for our cause something that I alone can conceive? Oh, help me to justify, by selfless and efficient service, that freedom which Thou hast given me today!"

Thus I prayed, in waiting for the train. Then, as there was still time, I sat on a bench once more; I took out my pen and paper, and started writing to my husband, who had contributed to free me.

But the train came before I had finished my letter.

* * *

From the window of the railway carriage, I gazed at the Rhine shining under the sun, at the foot of its lovely green hills. And I felt sadder than ever at the thought that I was forced to leave Germany. I tried to brush the idea aside and to think only of the joy that awaited me now, in Koblenz, in less than half an hour—the joy of being once more, for a short time at least, amidst people of my own faith.

We reached Koblenz. After leaving my trunk at the cloakroom of the station, I went straight to my friends. Seldom was I so welcome. And seldom did I spend so happy a time as during the three days that I was to remain among them—my three last days in Germany.

Seated on a patch of green grass, in front of a hastily built two-roomed house in the midst of an entirely ruined locality—away from onlookers—I related to my friends the story of my arrest and trial, and of the six months I had spent in jail. They knew what had happened to me from a magazine in which my photograph had appeared. But they wanted to learn the details. I felt a little ashamed to speak of myself, for seated before me was one of those men who have really suffered for our cause after having brilliantly served it for years and years: the former *Ortsgruppenleiter* Fritz Horn, now dead. There was Fräulein B. also— the same Fräulein B. who had once given me the little glass portrait of the Führer, of which I have spoken in this book—and her sister, with her three children. All these people had suffered a great deal, although they had not, personally, like Herr Horn, experienced the horror of the post-war anti-Nazi concentration camps. They were "the gold in the furnace."

I was merely the woman who had written *Gold in the Furnace*. Yet I spoke, and they were kind enough to take interest in the little I had to say.

"I shall never forgive 'them' for not allowing me to be with my comrades, the so-called 'war criminals'," said I. "But I must admit I am glad 'they' did not destroy my manuscript. It baffles me that they did not. I see the written pages before me, and still I can hardly believe it."

"It is unbelievable," declared Herr Horn. "One would think either that they did not care to read your book, or that they are trying to reverse their policy." The remark struck me. I remembered that H. E. had once said the same. "But if they wish to reverse their policy, then why do they keep on trying people for 'war crimes' every other day?" objected I. "Now, in Hamburg, they are trying another batch of thirty-five German women, former wardresses at Ravensbrück, who have done nothing but their duty."

"That is true," put in Fräulein B., "but it is not easy to release thirty-five women in Hamburg and God alone knows how many other so-called 'war criminals' elsewhere, without it coming to the knowledge of the public. While it is easy to give you back your book, especially when they know you are leaving Germany, and perhaps leaving Europe."

"But I can publish my book outside Germany, although—naturally—I told 'them' that I never would," said I.

"Not easily, even outside Germany," replied Herr Horn. "From the little I have read of it, then—when you had written only the beginning—you can hardly publish it anywhere, except under an out-and-out Nazi Government. Our enemies know that."

"By the way, before I go," said I, "I must translate to you what I wrote in Chapter 6 about the hunger and ill-treatment that you suffered at the hands of those rascals."

"Certainly. I'll listen to your impeachment of 'them' this evening."

"I can read it in the original," observed young Hermann, a handsome fourteen-year-old blond boy, Fräulein B.'s nephew; "I am the best one in my class, in English. Won't you show it to me?"

"Of course I shall," replied I. "You will be there when I translate it, and you will correct me if I make any mistakes."

The other two, younger children, had got up to join a few kids of the neighbourhood who had come in soon after me. While carrying on the conversation, I watched them playing hide-and-seek behind the torn walls that had once been the walls of happy homes. Their laughter echoed in the midst of the still desolate, nightmare-looking surroundings. "The voice of invincible Life," thought I; "the voice of future Germany."

And I recalled in my mind our Führer's well-known words: "Healthy children are the nation's most valuable possessions."

We talked for a long time more, till darkness fell.

* * *

I spent the two following days visiting a couple of other friends—all glad to see me free—and talking to Herr Horn, when he was able to talk; for his health, once as strong as iron, had been utterly ruined during the three hellish years he had remained in the extermination camps of the Western Democrats. He spoke, however, without hatred or bitterness, with the serene assurance of one who has *lived* his faith and done *all* his duty, and who has "surrendered the fruits of action" to the supreme Arbiter of Life and Death. He spoke without passion of the unavoidable clash that would, sooner or later, bring face to face the coalesced forces of Communism and those of the money-ridden western Democracies, and he said: "What will remain of the Aryan race will be forced to recognise that we were right, and to come to us."

"I wrote somewhere in my book that we would in due time proclaim to the ruined world our supreme ultimatum: 'Hitler or hell!'[13] So you agree with me, you who know so much more than I?" said I.

"Entirely," answered Herr Horn.

"But when will that be?"

"What does it matter *when*?" replied Hitler's faithful and wise lifelong fighter. "You have said yourself our *Weltanschauung* is eternal. Time does not count for us who have truth on our side. Don't be in a hurry and waste your energy in useless babble like those clowns who think they are going to reform the world with their U.N.O. and their precious 'schemes' and 'plans'. We are not they. We build for eternity."

When, on Sunday morning, before my departure, I went to see him for the last time, he told me: "You are right to go. There is no purpose in trying to remain among us any longer at present. 'These people' have now spotted you out, and you are surely being watched. If you stay here, you will only be running the risk of falling once more into their clutches thus giving them a pretext to destroy your book. Don't take that risk. It would not be doing your duty—for you owe that book to us, for whom you wrote it. Be cautious, and you will give it to us one day. Go to France—and from there, wherever you might be the most useful—and wait. "Hope and wait." One day, we shall welcome you again. In the

---

[13] *Gold in the Furnace*, 3rd ed., p. 286.—Ed.

meantime, if, being alone, you feel powerless, you have your burning faith—*our* common Nazi faith—to sustain you. And you have this—our Führer's immortal words."

And he handed over to me a beautiful copy of *Mein Kampf*—the only one he had. "It is yours," said he; "a remembrance from Germany."

Never have I received a gift with such profound emotion.

"Ich danke Ihnen!" said I, with tears in my eyes.[14] And I could say no more. For a second or two, I gazed at the serene face of the Nazi martyr. Then, slowly raising my right arm in the ritual gesture, I cried from the depth of my heart: "Heil Hitler!"

He answered my salute as though accomplishing a religious rite, and repeated the spell-like syllables: "Heil Hitler!"

I did not know that I was really seeing him for the last time. But it was so. For, on the 12th of December 1949, after lingering a whole year, Herr Horn died of the illness contracted as a consequence of the hardships and cruelties he had suffered at the hands of our enemies.

* * *

Fräulein B. gave me a brooch of metal bearing the picture of the Führer against the background of a swastika, to replace the little glass portrait that had been taken away from me and destroyed. She—and young Hermann—saw me off to the station.

My train was there. I stepped into a wagon going to Luxemburg, via Nanish, for I did not wish to face the customs officers and police at Saarhölzbach, if I could help it. I had been seen there too often already, on my journeys between Saarland and the French Zone.

My friends entered the railway carriage and remained with me until it was time for the train to start. Then, they stood on the platform, and I talked to them from the open window. *"Auf Wiedersehen!"* cried Fräulein B., as the train moved. "You will come back to us. Hope and wait!"

"Auf Wiedersehen!" cried also young Hermann. They could not add: "Heil Hitler!" for we were not unobserved. But I knew they meant it. And they knew that I too meant it.

As I took a last glimpse of him standing on the platform in the sunshine, tall and virile like a young Nordic god, Hermann appeared to me as the embodiment of all my dreams, of all my hopes. "The lovely future Storm Trooper!" thought I. And I was proud of him, as though he had been my son.

---

[14] "I thank you."—Ed.

Epilogue

AT THE FRONTIER

Sunday, the 21st of August 1949, at about 1 o'clock in the afternoon . . .

From Nanish on the German frontier, slowly the train moved on. My luggage had not been searched. With me—safe—were all my treasures: the golden Indian earrings in the shape of swastikas, that I was wearing, as on the day I had first entered Germany; the beautiful copy of *Mein Kampf* that my comrades of Koblenz had presented to me as a farewell gift; the manuscript of my *Gold in the Furnace*, my own tribute of love and admiration to Hitler's martyred country.

I thought of the miracle that had enabled me to keep those treasures, and from the depth of my heart I praised the invisible Gods. Then, I realised that the train was indeed moving; that I was, technically speaking, "crossing the border," and tears came to my eyes. "Holy Germany," thought I, "thy persecutors can force me to leave thy territory, but nobody can prevent me from loving thee: nothing can loosen the tie that now binds me to thee, forever and ever! Land of my martyred comrades; land of the surviving élite that stands and waits, firm and faithful in the present-day storm; my Führer's land, no foreigner has loved thee as I have. My heart remains with thee. Happen what will, one day, I shall cross the frontier again, and come back to thee!"

I remembered the sentence I had once written to my husband as an epitome of my post-war experience in the West: "The population of Europe is composed of a minority of Nazis, in contrast to an immense majority of monkeys." "Yes," thought I, "now, the monkeys are at the top. When they have misruled long enough, we will once more come to power and keep them down—forever."

And I imagined myself on my return, warmly greeted by tall, handsome men in uniform, whom I in my turn would salute, openly, triumphantly, with the mystical words that I had so many times and with such fervour uttered in a low voice, among my friends, in the present days of trial: "Heil Hitler!" With those two words, I would cross the frontier, next time . . .

The train increased its speed. The border station was no longer visible. "Goodbye Germany, where I was so happy; where I was not alone. One day, I shall come back, and see thee free!"

I remembered my manuscript now safe in my attaché case—as miraculously saved as though it had been thrown into the fire and brought out intact. And a sentence from it—a sentence that I had actually uttered many times, for it expressed and justified my whole attitude towards my Führer's people—came to my memory: "Adolf Hitler has made Germany sacred to every worthy Aryan of the world."[1] And the words in which I had, in the introduction of my book, characterised that vanguard of the racial élite of mankind that the persecuted élite of Germany represents in my eyes, also came back to me: "Those men of gold and steel, whom defeat could not dishearten, whom terror and torture could not subdue, whom money could not buy . . . my comrades, my superiors . . . the only ones among my contemporaries for whom I would gladly die."[2]

"I should have come long ago, I know," thought I. "But I have not entirely wasted my time during those fruitless years. I have gathered experience of distant climes, and knowledge of the past, and echoes of eternal wisdom from the four corners of the earth, to put it all to the service of my Führer and of his beloved people. When you are powerful, publish my profession of faith in you, my German brothers; those words from the depth of my heart which I wrote in cafés, in waiting rooms, in friends' houses—and in prison—amidst the ruins of present-day Germany, stick them upon the walls, one day, when you rule this continent! Put them before the eyes of the young men and women of the great victorious new Reich, and tell them: 'An Aryan woman who was not a German wrote this about us, when we lay in the dust, under the heels of our inferiors'. Tell their children, when I am dead."

The train rolled on. I was now in Luxemburg. I would soon be in France. But what were man-made frontiers? The only frontier in which I had ever believed was the natural, God-ordained barrier of blood. Even the sea could not separate people of the same pure stock.

The train carried me further and further away from the conventional border of Germany. But the Greater Reich of my dreams had no border. Wherever there were people conscious of their pure Aryan blood, and intelligent enough to understand and to accept Hitler's eternal Idea, and Germany's divinely appointed mission, there was the living Greater Reich. No frontier—and no order of expulsion from Germany, given in the name of Germany's present-day persecutors—could keep *me* from remaining a member of that one true Aryan brotherhood.

---

[1] Cf. *Gold in the Furnace*, 3rd ed., p. 91.—Ed.
[2] Cf. *Gold in the Furnace*, 3rd ed., p. xvii.—Ed.

"One day, I shall come back," I kept thinking, as I rolled further and further away. "One day, my love and admiration will contribute to exalt the German racial pride and will to power—the Aryan consciousness of the best Aryans. If that be, I shall not have come in vain; nor lived in vain."

And opening once more my attaché case—that same brown attaché-case which I had in hand on the night of my arrest—I saw there the priceless copy of *Mein Kampf* handed over to me in the name of all my comrades, in the name of all Germany, by one of the finest National Socialists I knew—a martyr of our cause; and, under it, the two thick exercise books that contained the original handwritten copy of my *Gold in the Furnace*, my loving gift to Germany, that I would now start typing in peace, and in safety.

What mattered the life of utter loneliness that I was now to resume? What mattered the grinding poverty that awaited me, and the day-to-day provoking hostility of the charlatans and imbeciles in the midst of whom I would now be forced to live, if I could do *that*—and write the beautiful story of my days in Werl—in waiting for our Day?

Once more, thanking the Lord of the unseen Forces, Who governs all that is visible and tangible with mathematical equity, I repeated within my heart the words of Leonardo da Vinci:

O mirabile Giustizia di Te, Primo Motore! . . .[3]

---

[3] "O miraculous Justice of Thee, Prime Mover! . . ."—Ed.

INDEX

ABOUT THE AUTHORESS

18. Savitri Devi in her 1940 Passport photograph

SAVITRI DEVI (1905–1982) is one of the most original and influential National Socialist thinkers of the post-World War II era. Born Maximine Julia Portaz in Lyons, France on 30 September 1905, she was of English, Greek, and Italian ancestry and described her nationality as "Indo-European." She earned Master's degrees in philosophy and chemistry and a Ph.D. in philosophy from the University of Lyons.

A self-described "nationalist of every nation" and an Indo-European pagan revivalist, Savitri Devi embraced National Socialism in 1929 while in Palestine. In 1935, she travelled to India to experience in Hinduism the last living Indo-European pagan religion. Settling eventually in Calcutta, she worked for the Hindu nationalist movement, married a Bengali Brahmin, the pro-Axis publisher Asit Krishna Mukherji, and spied for the Japanese during World War II.

After World War II, Savitri Devi embarked upon an itinerant, ascetic life. Her two chief activities were tireless witness on behalf of National Socialism and caring for homeless and abused animals.

Savitri Devi influenced such leading figures of post-war National Socialism as George Lincoln Rockwell, Colin Jordan, William Pierce, and Miguel Serrano. In 1962, she took part in the Cotswolds camp, where the World Union of National Socialists (WUNS) was formed.

Her books include *A Warning to the Hindus* (1939), *L'Etang aux lotus* (*The Lotus Pond*) (1940), *A Son of God: The Life and Philosophy of Akhnaton, King of Egypt* (1946), later republished as *Son of the Sun* (1956), *Akhnaton: A Play* (1948), *Gold in the Furnace* (1952), *The Lightning and the Sun* (1958), *Pilgrimage* (1958), *Impeachment of Man* (1959), *Long-Whiskers and the Two-Legged Goddess* (1965), *Souvenirs et réflexions d'une Aryenne* (*Memories and Reflections of an Aryan Woman*) (1976), and *And Time Rolls On: The Savitri Devi Interviews* (2005).

Savitri Devi died in England on 22 October 1982.

CPSIA information can be obtained
at www.ICGtesting.com
Printed in the USA
LVHW100954171122
733411LV00011B/66

9 781642 641400